Penguin Books

In Cold Blood

Truman Capote was born in New Orleans in 1925 and raised in various parts of the south, he and his family spending winters in New Orleans and summers in Alabama and New Georgia. By the age of fourteen he had already started writing short stories, some of which were published. After leaving school at fifteen he worked for the *New Yorker*, his first – and last – regular job. Following this Capote spent two years on a Louisiana farm where he wrote *Other Voices, Other Rooms* (1948). He lived, at one time or another, in Greece, Italy, Africa and the West Indies, and travelled in Russia and the Orient. Capote wrote many highly acclaimed books, including *A Tree of Night and Other Stories* (1949), *The Grass Harp* (1951), *Breakfast at Tiffany's* (1958), *In Cold Blood* (1965), which immediately became the centre of a storm of controversy on its publication, *Music for Chameleons* (1980) and *Answered Prayers* (1986), all of which are published by Penguin. Truman Capote died in August 1984.

Truman Capote

In Cold Blood

A True Account of a Multiple Murder
and Its Consequences

Penguin Books

PENGUIN BOOKS

Published by the Penguin Group
Penguin Books Ltd, 80 Strand, London WC2R 0RL, England
Penguin Putnam Inc., 375 Hudson Street, New York, New York 10014, USA
Penguin Books Australia Ltd, 250 Camberwell Road, Camberwell, Victoria 3124, Australia
Penguin Books Canada Ltd, 10 Alcorn Avenue, Toronto, Ontario, Canada M4V 3B2
Penguin Books India (P) Ltd, 11 Community Centre, Panchsheel Park, New Delhi – 110 017, India
Penguin Books (NZ) Ltd, Cnr Rosedale and Airborne Roads, Albany, Auckland, New Zealand
Penguin Books (South Africa) (Pty) Ltd, 24 Sturdee Avenue, Rosebank 2196, South Africa

Penguin Books Ltd, Registered Offices: 80 Strand, London WC2R 0RL, England

www.penguin.com

First published in the USA 1965
Published in Great Britain by Hamish Hamilton 1966
Published in Penguin Books 1966
16

Copyright © Truman Capote, 1965
All rights reserved

Printed in England by Clays Ltd, St Ives plc

Acknowledgements

ALL the material in this book not derived from my own observation is either taken from official records or is the result of interviews with the persons directly concerned, more often than not numerous interviews conducted over a considerable period of time. Because these 'collaborators' are identified within the text, it would be redundant to name them here; nevertheless, I want to express a formal gratitude, for without their patient cooperation my task would have been impossible. Also, I will not attempt to make a roll-call of all those Finney County citizens who, though their names do not appear in these pages, provided the author with a hospitality and friendship he can only reciprocate but never repay. However, I do wish to thank certain persons whose contributions to my work were very specific: Dr James McCain, President of Kansas State University; Mr Logan Sanford, and the staff of the Kansas Bureau of Investigation; Mr Charles McAtee, Director of the Kansas State Penal Institutions; Mr Clifford R. Hope, Jr, whose assistance in legal matters was invaluable; and finally, but really foremost, Mr William Shawn of *The New Yorker*, who encouraged me to undertake this project, and whose judgement stood me in good stead from first to last.

T.C.

Contents

Frères humains qui après nous vivez,
N'ayez les cuers contre nous endurcis,
Car, se pitié de nous povres avez,
Dieu en aura plus tost de vous mercis.

FRANÇOIS VILLON
Ballade des pendus

1

The Last to See Them Alive

THE village of Holcomb stands on the high wheat plains of western Kansas, a lonesome area that other Kansans call 'out there'. Some seventy miles east of the Colorado border, the countryside, with its hard blue skies and desert-clear air, has an atmosphere that is rather more Far West than Middle West. The local accent is barbed with a prairie twang, a ranch-hand nasalness, and the men, many of them, wear narrow frontier trousers, Stetsons, and high-heeled boots with pointed toes. The land is flat, and the views are awesomely extensive; horses, herds of cattle, a white cluster of grain elevators rising as gracefully as Greek temples are visible long before a traveller reaches them.

Holcomb, too, can be seen from great distances. Not that there is much to see – simply an aimless congregation of buildings divided in the centre by the main-line tracks of the Santa Fe Railroad, a haphazard hamlet bounded on the south by a brown stretch of the Arkansas (pronounced 'Ar-kan-sas') River, on the north by a highway, Route 50, and on the east and west by prairie lands and wheat fields. After rain, or when snowfalls thaw, the streets, unnamed, unshaded, unpaved, turn from the thickest dust into the direst mud. At one end of the town stands a stark old stucco structure, the roof of which supports an electric sign – DANCE – but the dancing has ceased and the advertisement has been dark for several years. Near by is another building with an irrelevant sign, this one in flaking gold on a dirty window – HOLCOMB BANK. The bank failed in 1933, and its former counting rooms have been converted into apartments. It is one of the town's two 'apartment houses', the second being a ramshackle mansion known, because a good part of the local school's faculty lives there, as the Teacherage. But the majority of Holcomb's homes are one-storey frame affairs, with front porches.

Down by the depot, the postmistress, a gaunt woman who wears a rawhide jacket and denims and cowboy boots, presides over a falling-apart post office. The depot itself, with its peeling sulphur-coloured paint, is equally melancholy; the Chief, the Super-Chief, the El Capitan go by every day, but these celebrated expresses never pause there. No passenger trains do – only an occasional freight. Up on the highway, there are two filling stations, one of which doubles as a meagrely supplied grocery store, while the other does extra duty as a café – Hartman's Café, where Mrs Hartman, the proprietress, dispenses sandwiches, coffee, soft drinks, and 3.2 beer. (Holcomb, like all the rest of Kansas, is 'dry'.)

And that, really, is all. Unless you include, as one must, the Holcomb School, a good-looking establishment, which reveals a circumstance that the appearance of the community otherwise camouflages: that the parents who send their children to this modern and ably staffed 'consolidated' school – the grades go from kindergarten through senior high, and a fleet of buses transport the students, of which there are usually around three hundred and sixty, from as far as sixteen miles away – are, in general, a prosperous people. Farm ranchers, most of them, they are outdoor folk of very varied stock – German, Irish, Norwegian, Mexican, Japanese. They raise cattle and sheep, grow wheat, milo, grass seed, and sugar beets. Farming is always a chancy business, but in western Kansas its practitioners consider themselves 'born gamblers', for they must contend with an extremely shallow precipitation (the annual average is eighteen inches) and anguishing irrigation problems. However, the last seven years have been years of droughtless beneficence. The farm ranchers in Finney County, of which Holcomb is a part, have done well; money has been made not from farming alone but also from the exploitation of plentiful natural-gas resources, and its acquisition is reflected in the new school, the comfortable interiors of the farm-houses, the steep and swollen grain elevators.

Until one morning in mid-November of 1959, few Americans – in fact, few Kansans – had ever heard of Holcomb. Like the waters of the river, like the motorists on the highway, and like the yellow trains streaking down the Santa Fe tracks, drama, in the shape of exceptional happenings, had never stopped there. The inhabitants of the village, numbering two hundred and seventy, were satisfied that this should be so, quite content to exist inside ordinary life – to work, to hunt, to watch television, to attend school socials, choir practice, meetings of the 4-H Club. But then, in the earliest hours of that morning in November, a Sunday morning, certain foreign sounds impinged on the normal nightly Holcomb noises – on the keening hysteria of coyotes, the dry scrape of scuttling tumbleweed, the racing, receding wail of locomotive whistles. At the time not a soul in sleeping Holcomb heard them – four shotgun blasts that, all told, ended six human lives. But afterwards the townspeople, theretofore sufficiently unfearful of each other to seldom trouble to lock their doors, found fantasy re-creating them over and again – those sombre explosions that stimulated fires of mistrust in the glare of which many old neighbours viewed each other strangely, and as strangers.

The master of River Valley Farm, Herbert William Clutter, was forty-eight years old, and as a result of a recent medical examination for an insurance policy, knew himself to be in first-rate condition. Though he wore rimless glasses and was of but average height, standing just under five feet ten, Mr Clutter cut a man's-man figure. His shoulders were broad, his hair had held its dark colour, his square-jawed, confident face retained a healthy-hued youthfulness, and his teeth, unstained and strong enough to shatter walnuts, were still intact. He weighed a hundred and fifty-four – the same as he had the day he graduated from Kansas State University, where he had majored in agriculture. He was not as rich as the richest man in Holcomb – Mr Taylor Jones, a neighbouring rancher. He was, however, the community's most widely known citizen, prominent both there and in Garden City, the close-by county seat, where he had headed the building committee for the newly completed First Methodist Church, an eight-hundred-thousand-dollar edifice. He was currently chairman of the Kansas Conference of

Farm Organizations, and his name was everywhere respectfully recognized among Midwestern agriculturists, as it was in certain Washington offices, where he had been a member of the Federal Farm Credit Board during the Eisenhower administration.

Always certain of what he wanted from the world, Mr Clutter had in large measure obtained it. On his left hand, on what remained of a finger once mangled by a piece of farm machinery, he wore a plain gold band, which was the symbol, a quarter-century old, of his marriage to the person he had wished to marry – the sister of a college classmate, a timid, pious, delicate girl named Bonnie Fox, who was three years younger than he. She had given him four children – a trio of daughters, then a son. The eldest daughter, Eveanna, married and the mother of a boy ten months old, lived in northern Illinois but visited Holcomb frequently. Indeed, she and her family were expected within the fortnight, for her parents planned a sizeable Thanksgiving reunion of the Clutter clan (which had its beginnings in Germany; the first immigrant Clutter – or Klotter, as the name was then spelled – arrived here in 1880); fifty-odd kinfolk had been asked, several of whom would be travelling from places as far away as Palatka, Florida. Nor did Beverly, the child next in age to Eveanna, any longer reside at River Valley Farm; she was in Kansas City, Kansas, studying to be a nurse. Beverly was engaged to a young biology student, of whom her father very much approved; invitations to the wedding, scheduled for Christmas Week, were already printed. Which left, still living at home, the boy Kenyon, who at fifteen was taller than Mr Clutter, and one sister, a year older – the town darling, Nancy.

In regard to his family, Mr Clutter had just one serious cause for disquiet – his wife's health. She was 'nervous', she suffered 'little spells' – such were the sheltering expressions used by those close to her. Not that the truth concerning 'poor Bonnie's afflictions' was in the least a secret; everyone knew she had been an on-and-off psychiatric patient the last half-dozen years. Yet even upon this shadowed terrain sunlight had very lately sparkled. The past Wednesday, returning from two weeks of treatment at the Wesley Medical Centre in Wichita, her customary place of retirement, Mrs Clutter had brought scarcely credible tidings to tell her husband; with joy she informed him that the source of her misery, so medical opinion had at last decreed, was not in her head but in her spine – it was *physical*, a matter of misplaced vertebrae. Of course, she must undergo an operation, and afterwards – well, she would be her 'old self' again. Was it possible – the tension, the withdrawals, the pillow-muted sobbing behind locked doors, all due to an out-of-order backbone? If so, then Mr Clutter could, when addressing his Thanksgiving table, recite a blessing of unmarred gratitude.

Ordinarily, Mr Clutter's mornings began at six-thirty; clanging milk pails and the whispery chatter of the boys who brought them, two sons of a hired man named Vic Irsik, usually roused him. But today he lingered, let Vic Irsik's sons come and leave, for the previous evening, a Friday the thirteenth, had been a tiring one, though in part exhilarating. Bonnie had resurrected her 'old self'; as if serving up a preview of the normality, the regained vigour, soon to be, she had rouged her lips, fussed with her hair, and, wearing a new dress, accompanied him to the Holcomb School, where they applauded a student production of *Tom Sawyer*, in which Nancy played Becky Thatcher. He had enjoyed it, seeing Bonnie out in public, nervous but nonetheless smiling, talking to people, and they both had been proud of Nancy; she had done so well, remembering all her lines, and looking, as he had said to her in the course of back-stage congratulations, 'Just beautiful, honey – a real Southern belle.' Whereupon Nancy had behaved like one; curtsying in her hoop-skirted costume, she had asked if she might drive into Garden City. The State Theatre was having a *special*, eleven-thirty, Friday-the-thirteenth 'Spook Show', and *all* her friends were going. In other circumstances Mr Clutter would have refused. His laws were laws, and one of them was: Nancy – and Kenyon, too – must be home by ten on week nights, by twelve on Saturdays. But weakened by the genial events of the evening, he had consented. And Nancy had not returned home until almost two. He had heard her come in, and had called to her, for though he was not a man ever really to raise his voice, he had some plain things to say to her, statements that concerned less the lateness of the hour than the youngster who had driven her home – a school basketball hero, Bobby Rupp.

Mr Clutter liked Bobby, and considered him, for a boy his age, which was seventeen, most dependable and gentlemanly; however, in the three years she had been permitted 'dates', Nancy, popular and pretty as she was, had never gone out with anyone else, and while Mr Clutter understood that it was the present national adolescent custom to form couples, to 'go steady' and wear 'engagement rings', he disapproved, particularly since he had not long ago, by accident, surprised his daughter and the Rupp boy kissing. He had then suggested that Nancy discontinue 'seeing so much of Bobby', advising her that a slow retreat now would hurt less than an abrupt severance later for, as he reminded her, it was a parting that must eventually take place. The Rupp family were Roman Catholics, the Clutters, Methodist – a fact that should in itself be sufficient to terminate whatever fancies she and this boy might have of some day marrying. Nancy had been reasonable – at any rate, she had not argued – and now, before saying good night, Mr Clutter secured from her a promise to begin a gradual breaking off with Bobby.

Still, the incident had lamentably put off his retiring time, which was ordinarily eleven o'clock. As a consequence, it was well after seven when he awakened on Saturday, 14 November, 1959. His wife always slept as late as possible. However, while Mr Clutter was shaving, showering, and outfitting himself in whipcord trousers, a cattleman's leather jacket, and soft stirrup boots, he had no fear of disturbing her; they did not share the same bedroom. For several years he had slept alone in the master bedroom, on the ground floor of the house – a two-storey, fourteen-room frame-and-brick structure. Though Mrs Clutter stored her clothes in the closets of this room, and kept her few cosmetics and her myriad medicines in the blue-tile-and-glass-brick bathroom adjoining it, she had taken for serious occupancy Eveanna's former bedroom, which, like Nancy's and Kenyon's rooms, was on the second floor.

The house – for the most part designed by Mr Clutter, who thereby proved himself a sensible and sedate, if not notably decorative architect – had been built in 1948 for forty thousand dollars. (The resale value was now sixty thousand dollars.) Situated at the end of a long, lane-like driveway shaded by rows of Chinese elms, the handsome white house, standing on an ample lawn of groomed Bermuda grass, impressed Holcomb; it was a place people pointed out. As for the interior, there were spongy displays of liver-coloured carpet intermittently abolishing the glare of varnished, resounding floors; an immense modernistic living-room couch covered in nubby fabric interwoven with glittery strands of silver metal; a breakfast alcove featuring a banquette upholstered in blue-and-white plastic. This sort of furnishing was what Mr and Mrs Clutter liked, as did the majority of their acquaintances, whose homes, by and large, were similarly furnished.

Other than a housekeeper who came in on weekdays, the Clutters employed no household help, so since his wife's illness and the departure of the elder daughters, Mr Clutter had of necessity learned to cook; either he or Nancy, but principally Nancy, prepared the family meals. Mr Clutter enjoyed the chore, and was excellent at it – no woman in Kansas baked a better loaf of salt-rising bread, and his celebrated coconut cookies were the first item to go at charity cake sales – but he was not a hearty eater; unlike his fellow-ranchers, he even preferred Spartan breakfasts. That morning an apple and a glass of milk were enough for him; because he touched neither coffee nor tea, he was accustomed to begin the day on a cold stomach. The truth was he opposed all stimulants, however gentle. He did not smoke, and of course he did not drink; indeed, he had never tasted spirits, and was inclined to avoid people who had – a circumstance that did not shrink his social circle as much as might be supposed, for the centre of that circle was supplied by the members of Garden City's First Methodist Church, a congregation totalling seventeen hundred, most of whom were as abstemious as Mr Clutter could desire. While he was careful to avoid making a nuisance of his views, to adopt outside his realm an externally uncensoring manner, he enforced them within his family and among the employees at River Valley Farm. 'Are you a drinking man?' was the first question he asked a job applicant, and even though the fellow gave a negative answer, he still must sign a work contract containing a clause that declared the agreement instantly void if the employee should be discovered 'harbouring alcohol'. A friend – an old pioneer rancher, Mr Lynn Russell – had once told him, 'You've got no mercy. I swear, Herb, if you caught a hired man drinking, out he'd go. And you wouldn't care if his family was starving.' It was perhaps the only criticism ever made of Mr Clutter as an employer. Otherwise, he was known for his equanimity, his charitableness, and the fact that he paid good wages and distributed frequent bonuses; the men who worked for him – and there were sometimes as many as eighteen – had small reason to complain.

After drinking the glass of milk and putting on a fleece-lined cap, Mr Clutter carried his apple with him when he went outdoors to examine the morning. It was ideal apple-eating weather; the whitest sunlight descended from the purest sky, and an easterly wind rustled, without ripping loose, the last of the leaves on the Chinese elms. Autumns reward western Kansas for the evils that the remaining seasons impose: winter's rough Colorado winds and hip-high, sheep-slaughtering snows; the slushes and the strange land fogs of spring; and summer, when even crows seek the puny shade, and the tawny infinitude of wheatstalks bristle, blaze. At last, after September, another weather arrives, an Indian summer that occasionally endures until Christmas. As Mr Clutter contemplated this superior specimen of the season, he was joined by a part-collie mongrel, and together they ambled off towards the livestock corral, which was adjacent to one of three barns on the premises.

One of these barns was a mammoth Quonset hut; it brimmed with grain – Westland sorghum – and one of them housed a dark, pungent hill of milo grain worth considerable money – a hundred thousand dollars. That figure alone rep-

resented an almost four-thousand-per cent advance over Mr
Clutter's entire income in 1934 – the year he married Bonnie
Fox and moved with her from their home town of Rozel,
Kansas, to Garden City, where he had found work as an
assistant to the Finney County agricultural agent. Typically,
it took him just seven months to be promoted; that is, to install himself in the head man's job. The years during which
he held the post – 1935 to 1939 – encompassed the dustiest,
the down-and-outest the region had known since white men
settled there, and young Herb Clutter, having, as he did, a
brain expertly racing with the newest in stream-lined agricultural practices, was quite qualified to serve as middle-man
between the government and the despondent farm ranchers;
these men could well use the optimism and the educated
instruction of a likeable young fellow who seemed to know
his business. All the same, he was not doing what he wanted
to do; the son of a farmer, he had from the beginning aimed
at operating a property of his own. Facing up to it, he resigned as county agent after four years and, on land leased
with borrowed money, created, in embryo, River Valley
Farm (a name justified by the Arkansas River's meandering presence but not, certainly, by any evidence of valley).
It was an endeavour that several Finney County conserva-
tives watched with show-us amusement – old-timers who had
been fond of baiting the youthful county agent on the subject of his university notions: 'That's fine, Herb. You always
know what's best to do on the other fellow's land. Plant this.
Terrace that. But you might say a sight different if the place
was your own.' They were mistaken; the upstart's experiments succeeded – partly because, in the beginning years, he
laboured eighteen hours a day. Setbacks occurred – twice the
wheat crop failed, and one winter he lost several hundred
head of sheep in a blizzard; but after a decade Mr Clutter's
domain consisted of over eight hundred acres owned outright and three thousand more worked on a rental basis –
and that, as his colleagues admitted, was 'a pretty good
spread'. Wheat, maize seed, certified grass seed – these were
the crops the farm's prosperity depended upon. Animals
were also important – sheep, and especially cattle. A herd of

several hundred Hereford bore the Clutter brand, though one would not have suspected it from the scant contents of the livestock corral, which was reserved for ailing steers, a few milking cows, Nancy's cats, and Babe, the family favourite – an old fat workhorse who never objected to lumbering about with three and four children astride her broad back.

Mr Clutter now fed Babe the core of his apple, calling good morning to a man raking debris inside the corral – Alfred Stoecklein, the sole resident employee. The Stoeckleins and their three children lived in a house not a hundred yards from the main house; except for them, the Clutters had no neighbours within half a mile. A long-faced man with long brown teeth, Stoecklein asked, 'Have you some particular work in mind today? Cause we got a sick-un. The baby. Me and Missis been up and down with her most of the night. I been thinking to carry her to doctor.' And Mr Clutter, expressing sympathy, said by all means to take the morning off, and if there was any way he or his wife could help, please let them know. Then, with the dog running ahead of him, he moved southward towards the fields, lion-coloured now, luminously golden with after-harvest stubble.

The river lay in this direction; near its bank stood a grove of fruit trees – peach, pear, cherry, and apple. Fifty years ago, according to native memory, it would have taken a lumberjack ten minutes to axe all the trees in western Kansas. Even today, only cottonwoods and Chinese elms – perennials with a cactus-like indifference to thirst – are commonly planted. However, as Mr. Clutter often remarked, 'an inch more of rain and this country would be paradise – Eden on earth.' The little collection of fruit-bearers growing by the river was his attempt to contrive, rain or no, a patch of the paradise, the green, apple-scented Eden, he envisioned. His wife once said, 'My husband cares more for those trees than he does for his children,' and everyone in Holcomb recalled the day a small disabled plane crashed into the peach trees: 'Herb was fit to be tied! Why, the propeller hadn't stopped turning before he'd slapped a lawsuit on the pilot.'

Passing through the orchard, Mr Clutter proceeded along

beside the river, which was shallow here and strewn with islands – midstream beaches of soft sand, to which, on Sundays gone by, hot-weather Sabbaths when Bonnie had still 'felt up to things', picnic baskets had been carted, family afternoons whiled away waiting for a twitch at the end of a fishline. Mr Clutter seldom encountered trespassers on his property; a mile and a half from the highway, and arrived at by obscure roads, it was not a place that strangers came upon by chance. Now, suddenly a whole party of them appeared, and Teddy, the dog, rushed forward roaring out a challenge. But it was odd about Teddy. Though he was a good sentry, alert, ever ready to raise Cain, his valour had one flaw: let him glimpse a gun, as he did now – for the intruders were armed – and his head dropped, his tail turned in. No one understood why, for no one knew his history, other than that he was a vagabond Kenyon had adopted years ago. The visitors proved to be five pheasant hunters from Oklahoma. The pheasant season in Kansas, a famed November event, lures hordes of sportsmen from adjoining states, and during the past week plaid-hatted regiments had paraded across the autumnal expanses, flushing and felling with rounds of buckshot great coppery flights of the grain-fattened birds. By custom, the hunters, if they are not invited guests, are supposed to pay the landowner a fee for letting them pursue their quarry on his premises, but when the Oklahomans offered to hire hunting rights, Mr Clutter was amused. 'I'm not as poor as I look. Go ahead, get all you can,' he said. Then, touching the brim of his cap, he headed for home and the day's work, unaware that it would be his last.

Like Mr Clutter, the young man breakfasting in a café called the Little Jewel never drank coffee. He preferred root beer. Three aspirin, cold root beer, and a chain of Pall Mall cigarettes – that was his notion of a proper 'chow-down'. Sipping and smoking, he studied a map spread on the counter before him – a Phillips 66 map of Mexico – but it was difficult to concentrate, for he was expecting a friend, and the friend was late. He looked out a window at the silent small-town street, a street he had never seen until yesterday. Still no sign of Dick. But he was sure to show up; after all, the purpose of their meeting was Dick's idea, his 'score'. And when it was settled – Mexico. The map was ragged, so thumbed that it had grown as supple as a piece of chamois. Around the corner, in his room at the hotel where he was staying, were hundreds more like it – worn maps of every state in the Union, every Canadian province, every South American country – for the young man was an incessant conceiver of voyages, not a few of which he had actually taken: to Alaska, to Hawaii and Japan, to Hong Kong. Now, thanks to a letter, an invitation to a 'score', here he was with all his worldly belongings: one cardboard suitcase, a guitar, and two big boxes of books and maps and songs, poems and old letters, weighing a quarter of a ton. (Dick's face when he saw those *boxes*! 'Christ, Perry. You carry that junk *every*where?' And Perry had said, '*What* junk? One of them books cost me thirty bucks.') Here he was in Little Olathe, Kansas. Kind of funny, if you thought about it; imagine being back in Kansas, when only four months ago he had sworn, first to the State Parole Board, then to himself, that he would never set foot within its boundaries again. Well, it wasn't for long.

Ink-circled names populated the map. COZUMEL, an island off the coast of Yucatán, where, so he had read in a men's magazine, you could 'shed your clothes, put on a relaxed grin, live like a Rajah, and have all the women you want for fifty dollars a month!' From the same article he had memorized other appealing statements: 'Cozumel is a hold-out against social, economic, and political pressure. No official pushes any private person around on *this* island', and 'Every year flights of parrots come over from the mainland to lay their eggs.' ACAPULCO connoted deep-sea fishing, casinos, anxious rich women; and SIERRA MADRE meant gold, meant *Treasure of the Sierra Madre*, a movie he had seen eight times. (It was Bogart's best picture, but the old guy who played the prospector, the one who reminded Perry of his father, was terrific, too. Walter Huston. Yes, and what he had told Dick was true: He *did* know the ins and outs of hunting gold, having been taught them by his father, who was a professional prospector. So why shouldn't they, the two

of them, buy a pair of pack horses and try their luck in
the Sierra Madre? But Dick, the practical Dick, had said,
'Whoa, honey, whoa. I seen that show. Ends up everybody
nuts. On account of fever and blood-suckers, mean conditions all around. Then, when they got the gold – remember,
a big wind came along and blew it all away?') Perry folded
the map. He paid for the root beer and stood up. Sitting, he
had seemed a more than normal-sized man, a powerful man,
with the shoulders, the arms, the thick, crouching torso of a
weight-lifter – weight-lifting was, in fact, his hobby. But
some sections of him were not in proportion to others. His
tiny feet, encased in short black boots with steel buckles,
would have neatly fitted into a delicate lady's dancing slippers; when he stood up, he was no taller than a twelve-year-
old child, and suddenly looked, strutting on stunted legs that
seemed grotesquely inadequate to the grown-up bulk they
supported, not like a well-built truck driver but like a retired
jockey, overblown and muscle-bound.

Outside the drugstore, Perry stationed himself in the sun.
It was a quarter to nine, and Dick was a half hour late; however, if Dick had not hammered home the every-minute importance of the next twenty-four hours, he would not have
noticed it. Time rarely weighed upon him, for he had many
methods of passing it – among them, mirror gazing. Dick
had once observed, 'Every time you see a mirror you go into
a trance, like. Like you was looking at some gorgeous piece
of butt. I mean, my God, don't you ever get tired?' Far from
it; his own face enthralled him. Each angle of it induced a
different impression. It was a changeling's face, and mirror-
guided experiments had taught him how to ring the changes,
how to look now ominous, now impish, now soulful; a tilt of
the head, a twist of the lips, and the corrupt gipsy became the
gentle romantic. His mother had been a full-blooded Cherokee; it was from her that he had inherited his colouring – the
iodine skin, the dark, moist eyes, the black hair, which he
kept brilliantined and was plentiful enough to provide him
with sideburns and a slippery spray of bangs. His mother's
donation was apparent; that of his father, a freckled, ginger-
haired Irishman, was less so. It was as though the Indian

blood had routed every trace of the Celtic strain. Still, pink
lips and a perky nose confirmed its presence, as did a quality
of roguish animation, of uppity Irish egotism, which often
activated the Cherokee mask and took control completely
when he played the guitar and sang. Singing, and the
thought of doing so in front of an audience, was another mes-
meric way of whittling hours. He always used the same mental scenery – a night club in Las Vegas, which happened to
be his home town. It was an elegant room filled with celebri-
ties excitedly focused on the sensational new star rendering
his famous, backed-by-violins version of 'I'll Be Seeing You'
and encoring with his latest self-composed ballad:

> Every April flights of parrots
> Fly overhead, red and green,
> Green and tangerine.
> I see them fly, I hear them high,
> Singing parrots bringing April spring . . .

(Dick, on first hearing this song, had commented, 'Parrots
don't sing. Talk, maybe. Holler. But they sure as hell don't
sing.' Of course, Dick was very literal-minded, *very* – he had
no understanding of music, poetry – and yet when you got
right down to it, Dick's literalness, his pragmatic approach
to every subject, was the primary reason Perry had been attracted to him, for it made Dick seem, compared to himself,
so authentically tough, invulnerable, 'totally masculine'.)

Nevertheless, pleasant as this Las Vegas reverie was, it
paled beside another of his visions. Since childhood, for more
than half his thirty-one years, he had been sending off for
literature ('FORTUNES IN DIVING! Train at Home in Your
Spare Time. Make Big Money Fast in Skin and Lung Diving.
FREE BOOKLETS . . .'), answering advertisements ('SUNKEN
TREASURE! Fifty Genuine Maps! Amazing Offer . . .') that
stoked a longing to realize an adventure his imagination
swiftly and over and over enabled him to experience: the
dream of drifting downward through strange waters, of
plunging towards a green sea-dusk, sliding past the scaly,
savage-eyed protectors of a ship's hulk that loomed ahead, a
Spanish galleon – a drowned cargo of diamonds and pearls,
heaping caskets of gold.

A car honked. At last – Dick.

'Good grief, Kenyon! I *hear* you.'

As usual, the devil was in Kenyon. His shouts kept coming up the stairs: 'Nancy! Telephone!'

Barefoot, pyjama-clad, Nancy scampered down the stairs. There were two telephones in the house – one in the room her father used as an office, another in the kitchen. She picked up the kitchen extension: 'Hello? Oh, yes, good morning, Mrs. Katz.'

And Mrs Clarence Katz, the wife of a farmer who lived on the highway, said, 'I *told* your daddy not to wake you up. I said Nancy must be *tired* after all that wonderful acting she did last night. You were lovely, dear. Those white ribbons in your hair? And that part when you thought Tom Sawyer was dead – you had real tears in your eyes. Good as anything on TV. But your daddy said it was time you got up; well, it *is* going on for nine. Now, what I wanted, dear – my little girl, my little Jolene, she's just dying to bake a cherry-pie, and seeing how you're a champion cherry-pie maker, always winning prizes, I wondered could I bring her over there this morning and you show her?'

Normally, Nancy would willingly have taught Jolene to prepare an entire turkey dinner; she felt it her duty to be available when younger girls came to her wanting help with their cooking, their sewing, or their music lessons – or, as often happened, to confide. Where she found the time, and still managed to 'practically run that big house' and be a straight-A student, the president of her class, a leader in the 4-H programme and the Young Methodists League, a skilled rider, an excellent musician (piano, clarinet), an annual winner at the county fair (pastry, preserves, needlework, flower arrangement) – how a girl not yet seventeen could haul such a wagon-load, and do so without 'brag', with, rather, merely a radiant jauntiness, was an enigma the community pondered, and solved by saying, 'She's got *character*. Gets it from her old man.' Certainly her strongest trait, the talent that gave support to all the others, derived from her father: a fine-honed sense of organization. Each moment was assigned; she knew precisely, at any hour, what she would be doing, how long it would require. And that was the trouble with today: she had overscheduled it. She had committed herself to helping another neighbour's child, Roxie Lee Smith, with a trumpet solo that Roxie Lee planned to play at a school concert; had promised to run three complicated errands for her mother; and had arranged to attend a 4-H meeting in Garden City with her father. And then there was lunch to make and, after lunch, work to be done on the bridesmaids' dresses for Beverly's wedding, which she had designed and was sewing herself. As matters stood, there was no room for Jolene's cherry-pie lesson. Unless something could be cancelled.

'Mrs Katz? Will you hold the line a moment, please?' She walked the length of the house to her father's office. The office, which had an outside entrance for ordinary visitors, was separated from the parlour by a sliding door; though Mr Clutter occasionally shared the office with Gerald Van Vleet, a young man who assisted him with the management of the farm, it was fundamentally his retreat – an orderly sanctuary, panelled in walnut veneer, where, surrounded by weather barometers, rain charts, a pair of binoculars, he sat like a captain in his cabin, a navigator piloting River Valley's sometimes risky passage through the seasons.

'Never mind,' he said, responding to Nancy's problem. 'Skip 4-H. I'll take Kenyon instead.'

And so, lifting the office phone, Nancy told Mrs Katz yes, fine, bring Jolene right on over. But she hung up with a frown. 'It's so peculiar,' she said as she looked around the room and saw in it her father helping Kenyon add a column of figures, and, at his desk by the window, Mr Van Vleet, who had a kind of brooding, rugged good looks that led her to call him Heathcliff behind his back. 'But I keep smelling cigarette smoke.'

'On your breath?' inquired Kenyon.

'No, funny one. Yours.'

That quieted him, for Kenyon, as he knew she knew, did once in a while sneak a puff – but, then, so did Nancy.

Mr Clutter clapped his hands. 'That's all. This is an office.'

Now, upstairs, she changed into faded Levis and a green sweater, and fastened round her wrist her third-most-valued belonging, a gold watch; her closest cat friend, Evinrude, ranked above it, and surmounting even Evinrude was Bobby's signet ring, the cumbersome proof of her 'going-steady' status, which she wore (*when* she wore it; the least flare-up and off it came) on a thumb, for even with the use of adhesive tape its man-size girth could not be made to fit a more suitable finger. Nancy was a pretty girl, lean and boyishly agile, and the prettiest things about her were her short-bobbed, shining chestnut hair (brushed a hundred strokes each morning, the same number at night) and her soap-polished complexion, still faintly freckled and rose-brown from last summer's sun. But it was her eyes, wide apart, darkly translucent, like ale held to the light, that made her immediately likeable, that at once announced her lack of suspicion, her considered and yet so easily triggered kindliness.

'Nancy!' Kenyon called. 'Susan on the phone.'

Susan Kidwell, her confidante. Again she answered in the kitchen.

'Tell,' said Susan, who invariably launched a telephone session with this command. 'And, to begin, tell why you were flirting with Jerry Roth.' Like Bobby, Jerry Roth was a school basketball star.

'Last night? Good grief, I wasn't flirting. You mean because we were holding hands? He just came backstage during the show. And I was so nervous. So he held my hand. To give me courage.'

'Very sweet. Then what?'

'Bobby took me to the spook movie. And *we* held hands.'

'Was it scary? Not Bobby. The movie.'

'He didn't think so; he just laughed. But you know me. Boo! – and I fall off the seat.'

'What are you eating?'

'Nothing.'

'I know – your fingernails,' said Susan, guessing correctly. Much as Nancy tried, she could not break the habit of nibbling her nails, and, whenever she was troubled, chewing them right to the quick. 'Tell. Something wrong?'

'No.'

'Nancy. *C'est moi* . . .' Susan was studying French.

'Well – Daddy. He's been in an awful mood the last three weeks. Awful. At least, around me. And when I got home last night he started *that* again.'

'*That*' needed no amplification; it was a subject that the two friends had discussed completely, and upon which they agreed. Susan, summarizing the problem from Nancy's viewpoint, had once said, 'You love Bobby now, and you need him. But deep down even Bobby knows there isn't any future in it. Later on, when we go off to Manhattan, everything will seem a new world.' Kansas State University is in Manhattan, and the two girls planned to enroll there as art students, and to room together. 'Everything will change, whether you want it to or not. But you can't change it now, living here in Holcomb, seeing Bobby every day, sitting in the same classes – and there's no *reason* to. Because you and Bobby are a very happy thing. And it will be something happy to think back about – if you're left alone. Can't you make your father understand that?' No, she could not. 'Because,' as she explained it to Susan, 'whenever I start to *say* something, he looks at me as though I must not love him. Or as though I loved him *less*. And suddenly I'm tongue-tied; I just want to be his daughter and do as he wishes.' To this Susan had no reply; it embodied emotions, a relationship, beyond her experience. She lived alone with her mother, who taught music at the Holcomb School, and she did not remember her own father very clearly, for years ago, in their native California, Mr Kidwell had one day left home and not come back.

'And, anyway,' Nancy continued now, 'I'm not sure it's *me*. That's making him grouchy. Something else – he's really worried about something.'

'Your mother?'

No other friend of Nancy's would have presumed to make such a suggestion. Susan, however, was privileged. When she had first appeared in Holcomb, a melancholy, imaginative child, willowy and wan and sensitive, then eight, a year younger than Nancy, the Clutters had so ardently adopted her that the fatherless little girl from California soon came to seem a member of the family. For seven years the two friends had been inseparable, each, by virtue of the rarity of similar and equal sensibilities, irreplaceable to the other. But then, this past September, Susan had transferred from the local school to the vaster, supposedly superior one in Garden City. It was the usual procedure from Holcomb students who intended going on to college, but Mr Clutter, a die-hard community booster, considered such defections an affront to community spirit; the Holcomb School was good enough for his children, and there they would remain. Thus, the girls were no longer always together, and Nancy deeply felt the daytime absence of her friend, the one person with whom she need be neither brave nor reticent.

'Well. But we're all so happy about Mother – you heard the wonderful news.' Then Nancy said, 'Listen,' and hesitated, as if summoning nerve to make an outrageous remark. '*Why* do I keep smelling smoke? Honestly, I think I'm losing my mind. I get into the car, I walk into a room, and it's as though somebody had just been there, smoking a cigarette. It isn't Mother, it can't be Kenyon. Kenyon wouldn't dare . . .'

Nor, very likely, would any visitor to the Clutter home, which was pointedly devoid of ashtrays. Slowly, Susan grasped the implication, but it was ludicrous. Regardless of what his private anxieties might be, she could not believe that Mr Clutter was finding secret solace in tobacco. Before she could ask if this was really what Nancy meant, Nancy cut her off: 'Sorry, Susie. I've got to go. Mrs Katz is here.'

Dick was driving a black 1949 Chevrolet sedan. As Perry got in, he checked the back seat to see if his guitar was safely there; the previous night, after playing for a party of Dick's friends, he had forgotten and left it in the car. It was an old Gibson guitar, sandpapered and waxed to a honey-yellow finish. Another sort of instrument lay beside it – a twelve-gauge pump-action shotgun, brand-new, blue-barrelled, and with a sportsman's scene of pheasants in flight etched along the handle. A flashlight, a fishing knife, a pair of leather gloves, and a hunting vest fully stocked with shells contributed further atmosphere to this curious still life.

'You wearing that?' Perry asked, indicating the vest.

Dick rapped his knuckles against the windshield. 'Knock, knock. Excuse me, sir. We've been out hunting and lost our way. If we could use the phone . . .'

'Si, señor. Yo comprendo.'

'A cinch,' said Dick. 'I promise you, honey, we'll blast hair all over them walls.'

' "Those" walls,' said Perry. A dictionary buff, a devotee of obscure words, he had been intent on improving his companion's grammar and expanding his vocabulary ever since they had celled together at Kansas State Penitentiary. Far from resenting these lessons, the pupil, to please his tutor, once composed a sheaf of poems, and though the verses were very obscene, Perry, who thought them nevertheless hilarious, had had the manuscript leather-bound in a prison shop and its title, *Dirty Jokes,* stamped in gold.

Dick was wearing a blue jumper suit; lettering stitched across the back of it advertised BOB SANDS' BODY SHOP. He and Perry drove along the main street of Olathe until they arrived at the Bob Sands establishment, an auto-repair garage, where Dick had been employed since his release from the penitentiary in mid-August. A capable mechanic, he earned sixty dollars a week. He deserved no salary for the work he planned to do this morning, but Mr Sands, who left him in charge on Saturdays, would never know he had paid his hireling to overhaul his own car. With Perry assisting him, he went to work. They changed the oil, adjusted the clutch, recharged the battery, replaced a throw-out bearing, and put new tyres on the rear wheels – all necessary undertakings, for between today and tomorrow the aged Chevrolet was expected to perform punishing feats.

'Because the old man was around,' said Dick, answering Perry, who wanted to know why he had been late in meeting him at the Little Jewel. 'I didn't want him to see me taking the gun out of the house. Christ, then he would have knowed I wasn't telling the truth.'

' "Known." But what did you say? Finally?'

'Like we said. I said we'd be gone overnight – said we was going to visit your sister in Fort Scott. On account of she was holding money for you. Fifteen hundred dollars.' Perry had a sister, and had once had two, but the surviving one did not live in Fort Scott, a Kansas town eighty-five miles from Olathe; in fact, he was uncertain of her present address.

'And was he sore?'

'Why should he be sore?'

'Because he hates me,' said Perry, whose voice was both gentle and prim – a voice that, though soft, manufactured each word exactly, ejected it like a smoke ring issuing from a parson's mouth. 'So does your mother. I could see – the ineffable way they looked at me.'

Dick shrugged. 'Nothing to do with you. As such. It's just they don't like me seeing anybody from The Walls.' Twice married, twice divorced, now twenty-eight and the father of three boys, Dick had received his parole on the condition that he reside with his parents; the family, which included a younger brother, lived on a small farm near Olathe. 'Anybody wearing the fraternity pin,' he added, and touched a blue dot tattooed under his left eye – an insigne, a visible password, by which certain former prison inmates could identify him.

'I understand,' said Perry. 'I sympathize with that. They're good people. She's a real sweet person, your mother.'

Dick nodded; he thought so, too.

At noon they put down their tools, and Dick, racing the engine, listening to the consistent hum, was satisfied that a thorough job had been done.

Nancy and her protégée, Jolene Katz, were also satisfied with their morning's work; indeed, the latter, a thin thirteen-year-old, was agog with pride. For the longest while she stared at the blue-ribbon winner, the oven-hot cherries simmering under the crisp lattice crust, and then she was overcome, and hugging Nancy, asked, 'Honest, did I really make it myself?' Nancy laughed, returned the embrace, and assured her that she had – with a little help.

Jolene urged that they sample the pie at once – no nonsense about leaving it to cool. 'Please, let's both have a piece. And you, too,' she said to Mrs Clutter, who had come into the kitchen. Mrs Clutter smiled – attempted to; her head ached – and said thank you, but she hadn't the appetite. As for Nancy, she hadn't the time; Roxie Lee Smith, and Roxie Lee's trumpet solo, awaited her, and afterwards those errands for her mother, one of which concerned a bridal shower that some Garden City girls were organizing for Beverly, and another the Thanksgiving gala.

'You go, dear, I'll keep Jolene company until her mother comes for her,' Mrs Clutter said, and then, addressing the child with unconquerable timidity, added, 'If Jolene doesn't mind keeping *me* company.' As a girl she had won an elocution prize; maturity, it seemed, had reduced her voice to a single tone, that of apology, and her personality to a series of gestures blurred by the fear that she might give offence, in some way displease. 'I hope you understand,' she continued after her daughter's departure. 'I hope you won't think Nancy rude?'

'Goodness, no. I just love her to death. Well, everybody does. There isn't anybody like Nancy. Do you know what Mrs Stringer says?' said Jolene, naming her home-economics teacher. 'One day she told the class, "Nancy Clutter is always in a hurry, but she always has time. And that's one definition of a lady."'

'Yes,' replied Mrs Clutter. 'All my children are very efficient. They don't need me.'

Jolene had never before been alone with Nancy's 'strange' mother, but despite discussions she had heard, she felt much at ease, for Mrs Clutter, though unrelaxed herself, had a relaxing quality, as is generally true of defenceless persons who present no threat; even in Jolene, a very childlike child, Mrs Clutter's heart-shaped, missionary's face, her look of helpless, homespun ethereality aroused protective compassion. But to think that she was Nancy's mother! An aunt – that seemed possible; a visiting spinster aunt, slightly odd, but *nice*.

'No, they don't need me,' she repeated, pouring herself a cup of coffee. Though all the other members of the family observed her husband's boycott of this beverage, she drank two cups every morning and often as not ate nothing else the rest of the day. She weighed ninety-eight pounds; rings – a wedding band and one set with a diamond modest to the point of meekness – wobbled on one of her bony hands.

Jolene cut a piece of pie. 'Boy!' she said, wolfing it down. 'I'm going to make one of these every day seven days a week.'

'Well, you have all those little brothers, and boys can eat a lot of pie. Mr Clutter and Kenyon, I know they never get tired of them. But the cook does – Nancy just turns up her nose. It'll be the same with you. No, no – why do I say that?' Mrs Clutter, who wore rimless glasses, removed them and pressed her eyes. 'Forgive me, dear. I'm sure you'll never know what it is to be tired. I'm sure you'll always be happy . . .'

Jolene was silent. The note of panic in Mrs Clutter's voice had caused her to have a shift of feeling; Jolene was confused, and wished that her mother, who had promised to call back for her at eleven, would come.

Presently, more calmly, Mrs Clutter asked, 'Do you like miniature things? Tiny things?' and invited Jolene into the dining-room to inspect the shelves of a whatnot on which were arranged assorted Lilliputian gewgaws – scissors, thimbles, crystal flower baskets, toy figurines, forks and knives. 'I've had some of these since I was a child. Daddy and Mama – all of us – spent part of most years in California. By the ocean. And there was a shop that sold such precious little things. These cups.' A set of doll-house teacups, anchored to a diminutive tray, trembled in the palm of her hand. 'Daddy gave them to me; I had a lovely childhood.'

The only daughter of a prosperous wheat grower named Fox, the adored sister of three older brothers, she had not been spoiled but spared, led to suppose that life was a sequence of agreeable events – Kansas autumns, California summers, a round of teacup gifts. When she was eighteen, inflamed by a biography of Florence Nightingale, she enrolled as a student nurse at St Rose's Hospital in Great Bend, Kansas. She was not meant to be a nurse, and after two years she confessed it: a hospital's realities – scenes, odours – sickened her. Yet to this day she regretted not having completed the course and received her diploma – 'just to prove,'

as she had told a friend, 'that I once succeeded at something.'
Instead, she had met and married Herb, a college classmate of her oldest brother, Glenn; actually, since the two
families lived within twenty miles of each other, she had
long known him by sight, but the Clutters, plain farm
people, were not on visiting terms with the well-to-do and
cultivated Foxes. However, Herb was handsome, he was
pious, he was strong-willed, he wanted her – and she was in
love.

'Mr Clutter travels a great deal,' she said to Jolene. 'Oh,
he's always headed somewhere. Washington and Chicago
and Oklahoma and Kansas City – sometimes it seems like
he's never home. But wherever he goes, he remembers how
I dote on tiny things.' She unfolded a little paper fan. 'He
brought me this from San Francisco. It only cost a penny.
But isn't it pretty?'

The second year of the marriage, Eveanna was born,
and three years later, Beverly; after each confinement the
young mother had experienced an inexplicable despondency
– seizures of grief that sent her wandering from room to
room in a hand-wringing daze. Between the births of Beverly
and Nancy, three more years elapsed, and these were the
years of the Sunday picnics and of summer excursions to
Colorado, the years when she really ran her own home and
was the happy centre of it. But with Nancy and then with
Kenyon, the pattern of postnatal depression repeated itself,
and following the birth of her son, the mood of misery that
descended never altogether lifted; it lingered like a cloud
that might rain or might not. She knew 'good days', and
occasionally they accumulated into weeks, months, but even
on the best of the good days, those days when she was otherwise her 'old self', the affectionate and charming Bonnie her
friends cherished, she could not summon the social vitality
her husband's pyramiding activities required. He was a
'joiner', a 'born leader'; she was not, and stopped attempting
to be. And so, along paths bordered by tender regard, by
total fidelity, they began to go their semi-separate ways –
his a public route, a march of satisfying conquests, and hers
a private one that eventually wound through hospital corri-

dors. But she was not without hope. Trust in God sustained her, and from time to time secular sources supplemented her faith in His forthcoming mercy; she read of a miracle medicine, heard of a new therapy, or, as most recently, decided to believe that a 'pinched nerve' was to blame.

'Little things really belong to you,' she said, folding the fan. 'They don't have to be left behind. You can carry them in a shoebox.'

'Carry them where to?'

'Why, wherever you go. You might be gone for a long time.'

Some years earlier Mrs Clutter had travelled to Wichita for two weeks of treatment and remained two months. On the advice of a doctor, who had thought the experience would aid her to regain 'a sense of adequacy and usefulness', she had taken an apartment, then found a job – as a file clerk at the Y.W.C.A. Her husband, entirely sympathetic, had encouraged the adventure, but she had liked it too well, so much that it seemed to her unchristian, and the sense of guilt she in consequence developed ultimately outweighed the experiment's therapeutic value.

'Or you might never go home. And – it's important always to have with you something of your own. That's really yours.'

The doorbell rang. It was Jolene's mother.

Mrs Clutter said, 'Good-bye, dear,' and pressed into Jolene's hand the paper fan. 'It's only a penny thing – but it's pretty.'

Afterwards Mrs Clutter was alone in the house. Kenyon and Mr Clutter had gone to Garden City; Gerald Van Vleet had left for the day; and the housekeeper, the blessed Mrs Helm to whom she could confide anything, did not come to work on Saturdays. She might as well go back to bed – the bed she so rarely abandoned that poor Mrs Helm had to battle for the chance to change its linen twice a week.

There were four bedrooms on the second floor, and hers was the last at the end of a spacious hall, which was bare except for a baby crib that had been bought for the visits of her grandson. If cots were brought in and the hall was used

as a dormitory, Mrs Clutter estimated, the house could accommodate twenty guests during the Thanksgiving holidays; the others would have to lodge at motels or with neighbours. Among the Clutter kinfolk the Thanksgiving get-
together was an annual, turnabout to-do, and this year Herb
was the appointed host, so it had to be done, but coinciding,
as it did, with the preparations for Beverly's wedding, Mrs
Clutter despaired of surviving either project. Both involved
the necessity of making decisions – a process she had always
disliked, and had learned to dread, for when her husband
was off on one of his business journeys she was continually
expected, in his absence, to supply snap judgements concerning the affairs of the farm, and it was unendurable, a tor-
ment. What if she made a mistake? What if Herb should be
displeased? Better to lock the bedroom door and pretend not
to hear, or say, as she sometimes did, 'I can't. I don't know.
Please.'

The room she so seldom left was austere; had the bed been
made, a visitor might have thought it permanently unoccu-
pied. An oak bed, a walnut bureau, a bedside table – nothing
else except lamps, one curtained window, and a picture of
Jesus walking on the water. It was as though by keeping this
room impersonal, by not importing her intimate belongings
but leaving them mingled with those of her husband, she
lessened the offence of not sharing his quarters. The only
used drawer in the bureau contained a jar of Vick's Vaporub,
Kleenex, an electric heating pad, a number of white nightgowns, and white cotton socks. She always wore a pair
of these socks to bed, for she was always cold. And, for the
same reason, she habitually kept her windows closed. Summer before last, on a sweltering August Sunday, when she
was secluded here, a difficult incident had taken place. There
were guests that day, a party of friends who had been
invited to the farm to pick mulberries, and among them was
Wilma Kidwell, Susan's mother. Like most of the people who
were often entertained by the Clutters, Mrs Kidwell accepted the absence of the hostess without comment, and
assumed, as was the custom, that she was either 'indisposed'
or 'away in Wichita'. In any event, when the hour came to go

to the fruit orchard, Mrs Kidwell declined; a city-bred woman, easily fatigued, she wished to remain indoors. Later, while she was awaiting the return of the mulberry pickers, she heard the sound of weeping, heartbroken, heartbreaking. 'Bonnie?' she called, and ran up the stairs, ran down the hall to Bonnie's room. When she opened it, the heat gathered inside the room was like a sudden, awful hand over her mouth; she hurried to open a window. 'Don't!' Bonnie cried. 'I'm not hot. I'm cold. I'm freezing. Lord, Lord, Lord!' She flailed her arms. 'Please, Lord, don't let anybody see me this way.' Mrs Kidwell sat down on the bed; she wanted to hold Bonnie in her arms, and eventually Bonnie let herself be held. 'Wilma,' she said, 'I've been listening to you, Wilma. All of you. Laughing. Having a good time. I'm missing out on everything. The best years, the children – everything. A little while, and even Kenyon will be grown up – a man. And how will he remember me? As a kind of ghost, Wilma.'

Now, on this final day of her life, Mrs Clutter hung in the closet the calico housedress she had been wearing, and put on one of her trailing nightgowns and a fresh set of white socks. Then, before retiring, she exchanged her ordinary glasses for a pair of reading spectacles. Though she subscribed to several periodicals (the *Ladies' Home Journal*, *McCall's*, *Reader's Digest*, and *Together: Midmonth Magazine for Methodist Families*), none of these rested on the bedside table – only a Bible. A bookmark lay between its pages, a stiff piece of watered silk upon which an admonition had been embroidered: 'Take ye heed, watch and pray: for ye know not when the time is.'

The two young men had little in common, but they did not realize it, for they shared a number of surface traits. Both for example, were fastidious, very attentive to hygiene and the condition of their fingernails. After their grease-monkey morning, they spent the better part of an hour sprucing up in the lavatory of the garage. Dick stripped to his briefs was not quite the same as Dick fully clothed. In the latter state, he seemed a flimsy dingy-blond youth of medium height, fleshless and perhaps sunken-chested; disrobing revealed that he was nothing of the sort, but, rather, an athlete constructed on a welterweight scale. The tattooed face of a cat, blue and grinning, covered his right hand; on one shoulder a blue rose blossomed. More markings, self-designed and self-executed, ornamented his arms and torso: the head of a dragon with a human skull between its open jaws; bosomy nudes; a gremlin brandishing a pitchfork; the word PEACE accompanied by a cross radiating, in the form of crude strokes, rays of holy light; and two sentimental concoctions – one a bouquet of flowers dedicated to MOTHER-DAD, the other a heart that celebrated the romance of DICK and CAROL, the girl whom he had married when he was nineteen, and from whom he had separated six years later in order to 'do the right thing' by another young lady, the mother of his youngest child. ('I have three boys who I will definitely take care of,' he had written in applying for parole. 'My wife is remarried. I have been married twice, only I don't want anything to do with my second wife.')

But neither Dick's physique nor the inky gallery adorning it made as remarkable an impression as his face, which seemed composed of mismatching parts. It was as though his head had been halved like an apple, then put together a fraction off centre. Something of the kind had happened; the imperfectly aligned features were the outcome of a car collision in 1950 – an accident that left his long-jawed and narrow face tilted, the left side rather lower than the right, with the results that the lips were slightly aslant, the nose askew, and his eyes not only situated at uneven levels but of uneven size, the left eye being truly serpentine, with a venomous, sickly-blue squint that although it was involuntarily acquired, seemed nevertheless to warn of bitter sediment at the bottom of his nature. But Perry had told him, 'The eye doesn't matter. Because you have a wonderful smile. One of those smiles that really work.' It was true that the tightening action of a smile contracted his face into its correct proportions, and made it possible to discern a less unnerving personality – an American-style 'good kid' with an outgrown crew cut, sane enough but not too bright. (Actually, he was very intelligent. An I.Q. test taken in prison gave him a rating of 130; the average subject, in prison or out, scores between 90 and 110.)

Perry, too, had been maimed, and his injuries, received in a motor-cycle wreck, were severer than Dick's; he had spent half a year in a State of Washington hospital and another six months on crutches, and though the accident had occurred in 1952, his chunky, dwarfish legs, broken in five places and pitifully scarred, still pained him so severely that he had become an aspirin addict. While he had fewer tattoos than his companion, they were more elaborate – not the self-inflicted work of an amateur but epics of the art contrived by Honolulu and Yokohama masters. COOKIE, the name of a nurse who had been friendly to him when he was hospitalized, was tattooed in his right biceps. Blue-furred, orange-eyed, red-fanged, a tiger snarled upon his left biceps; a spitting snake, coiled around a dagger, slithered down his arm; and elsewhere skulls gleamed, a tombstone loomed, a chrysanthemum flourished.

'O.K., beauty. Put away the comb,' said Dick, dressed now and ready to go. Having discarded his work uniform, he wore grey khakis, a matching shirt, and, like Perry, ankle-high black boots. Perry, who could never find trousers to fit his truncated lower half, wore blue jeans rolled up at the bottom and a leather windbreaker. Scrubbed, combed, as tidy as two dudes setting off on a double date, they went out to the car.

The distance between Olathe, a suburb of Kansas City, and Holcomb, which might be called a suburb of Garden City, is approximately four hundred miles.

A town of eleven thousand, Garden City began assembling its founders soon after the Civil War. An itinerant buffalo hunter, Mr C. J. (Buffalo) Jones, had much to do with its subsequent expansion from a collection of huts and hitching posts into an opulent ranching centre with razzle-dazzle saloons, an opera house, and the plushiest hotel anywhere between Kansas City and Denver – in brief, a specimen of frontier fanciness that rivalled a more famous settlement fifty miles east of it, Dodge City. Along with Buffalo Jones, who lost his money and then his mind (the last years of his life were spent haranguing street groups against the wanton extermination of the beasts he himself had so profitably slaughtered), the glamours of the past are today entombed. Some souvenirs exist; a moderately colourful row of commercial buildings is known as the Buffalo Block, and the once splendid Windsor Hotel, with its still splendid high-ceilinged saloon and its atmosphere of spittoons and potted palms, endures amid the variety stores and supermarkets as a Main Street landmark – one comparatively unpatronized, for the Windsor's dark, huge chambers and echoing hallways, evocative as they are, cannot compete with the air-conditioned amenities offered at the trim little Hotel Warren, or with the Wheat Lands Motel's individual television sets and 'Heated Swimming Pool'.

Anyone who has made the coast-to-coast journey across America, whether by train or by car, has probably passed through Garden City, but it is reasonable to assume that few travellers remember the event. It seems just another fair-sized town in the middle – almost the exact middle – of the continental United States. Not that the inhabitants would tolerate such an opinion – perhaps rightly. Though they may overstate the case ('Look all over the world, and you won't find friendlier people or fresher air or sweeter drinking water,' and 'I could go to Denver at triple the salary, but I've got five kids, and I figure there's no better place to raise kids than right here. Swell schools with every kind of sport. We even have a junior college,' and 'I came out here to practise law. A temporary thing, I never planned to stay. But when the chance came to move, I thought, Why go? What the hell for? Maybe it's not New York – but who wants New York? Good neighbours, people who care about each other, that's what counts. And everything else a decent man needs – we've got that, too. Beautiful churches. A golf course'), the newcomer to Garden City, once he has adjusted to the nightly after-eight silence of Main Street, discovers much to support the defensive boastings of the citizenry: a well-run public library, a competent daily newspaper, green-lawned and shady squares here and there, placid residential streets where animals and children are safe to run free, a big, rambling park complete with a small menagerie ('See the Polar Bears!' 'See Pennie the Elephant!'), and a swimming pool that consumes several acres ('World's Largest FREE Swimpool!'). Such accessories, and the dust and the winds and the ever-calling train whistles, add up to a 'home town' that is probably remembered with nostalgia by those who have left it, and that, for those who have remained, provides a sense of roots and contentment.

Without exception, Garden Citians deny that the population of the town can be socially graded ('No, sir. Nothing like that here. All equal, regardless of wealth, colour, or creed. Everything the way it ought to be in a democracy; that's us'), but, of course, class distinctions are as clearly observed, and as clearly observable, as in any other human hive. A hundred miles west and one would be out of the 'Bible Belt', that gospel-haunted strip of American territory in which a man must, if only for business reasons, take his religion with the straightest of faces, but in Finney County one is still within the Bible Belt borders, and therefore a person's church affiliation is the most important factor influencing his class status. A combination of Baptists, Methodists, and Roman Catholics would account for eighty per cent of the county's devout, yet among the élite – the businessmen, bankers, lawyers, physicians, and more prominent ranchers who tenant the top drawer – Presbyterians and Episcopalians predominate. An occasional Methodist is welcomed, and once in a while a Democrat infiltrates, but on the whole the Establishment is composed of right-wing Republicans of the Presbyterian and Episcopalian faiths.

As an educated man successful in his profession, as an eminent Republican and church leader – even though of the Methodist church – Mr Clutter was entitled to rank among the local patricians, but just as he had never joined the Garden City Country Club, he had never sought to associate with the reigning coterie. Quite the contrary, for their pleasures were not his; he had no use for card games, golf, cocktails, or buffet suppers served at ten – or, indeed, for any pastime that he felt did not 'accomplish something'. Which is why,

instead of being part of a golfing foursome on this shining
Saturday, Mr Clutter was acting as chairman of a meeting of
the Finney County 4-H Club. (4-H stands for 'Head, Heart,
Hands, Health', and the club motto claims, 'We learn to do
by doing.' It is a national organization, with overseas
branches, whose purpose is to help those living in rural areas
– and the children particularly – develop practical abilities
and moral character. Nancy and Kenyon had been conscien-
tious members from the age of six.) Towards the end of the
meeting, Mr Clutter said, 'Now I have something to say concerning one of our adult members'. His eyes singled out a
chubby Japanese woman surrounded by four chubby Japanese children. 'You all know Mrs Hideo Ashida. Know how
the Ashidas moved out here from Colorado – started farming
out to Holcomb two years ago. A fine family, the kind of
people Holcomb's lucky to have. As anyone will tell you.
Anyone who has been sick and had Mrs Ashida walk nobody
can calculate how many miles to bring them some of the
wonderful soups she makes. Or the flowers she grows where
you wouldn't expect a flower could grow. And last year at the
county fair you will recall how much she contributed to the
success of the 4-H exhibits. So I want to suggest we honour
Mrs Ashida with an award at our Achievement Banquet
next Tuesday.'

Her children tugged at her, punched her; the oldest boy
shouted, 'Hey, Ma, that's you!' But Mrs Ashida was bashful;
she rubbed her eyes with her baby-plump hands and
laughed. She was the wife of a tenant farmer; the farm, an
especially wind-swept and lonesome one, was halfway between Garden City and Holcomb. After 4-H conferences,
Mr Clutter usually drove the Ashidas home, and he did so
today.

'Gosh, that was a jolt,' said Mrs Ashida as they rolled
along Route 50 in Mr Clutter's pickup truck. 'Seems like I'm
always thanking you, Herb. But thanks.' She had met him
on her second day in Finney County; it was the day before
Halloween, and he and Kenyon had come to call, bringing
a load of pumpkins and squash. All through that first hard
year, gifts had arrived, of produce that the Ashidas had not

yet planted – baskets of asparagus, lettuce. And Nancy often brought Babe by for the children to ride. 'You know, in most ways, this is the best place we've ever lived. Hideo says the same. We sure hate to think about leaving. Starting all over again.'

'Leaving?' protested Mr Clutter, and slowed the car.

'Well, Herb. The farm here, the people we're working for – Hideo thinks we could do better. Maybe in Nebraska. But nothing's settled. It's just talk so far.' Her hearty voice, always on the verge of laughter, made the melancholy news sound somehow cheerful, but seeing that she had saddened Mr Clutter, she turned to other matters. 'Herb, give me a man's opinion,' she said. 'Me and the kids, we've been saving up, we want to give Hideo something on the grand side for Christmas. What he needs is teeth. Now, if your wife was to give you three gold teeth, would that strike you as a wrong kind of present? I mean, asking a man to spend Christmas in the dentist's chair?'

'You beat all. Don't ever try to get away from here. We'll hogtie you,' said Mr Clutter. 'Yes, yes, by all means gold teeth. Was me, I'd be tickled.'

His reaction delighted Mrs Ashida, for she knew he would not approve her plan unless he meant it; he was a gentleman. She had never known him to 'act the Squire', or to take advantage or break a promise. She ventured to obtain a promise now. 'Look, Herb. At the banquet – no speeches, huh? Not for me. You, you're different. The way you can stand up and talk to hundreds of people. Thousands. And be so easy – convince anybody about whatever. Just nothing scares you,' she said, commenting upon a generally recognized quality of Mr Clutter's: a fearless self-assurance that set him apart, and while it created respect, also limited the affections of others a little. 'I can't imagine you afraid. No matter what happened, you'd talk your way out of it.'

By mid-afternoon the black Chevrolet had reached Emporia, Kansas – a large town, almost a city, and a safe place, so the occupants of the car had decided, to do a bit of shopping. They parked on a side street, then wandered about until a suitably crowded variety store presented itself.

The first purchase was a pair of rubber gloves; these were for Perry, who, unlike Dick, had neglected to bring old gloves of his own.

They moved on to a counter displaying women's hosiery. After a spell of indecisive quibbling, Perry said, 'I'm for it.'

Dick was not. 'What about my eye? They're all too light-coloured to hide that.'

'Miss,' said Perry, attracting a salegirl's attention. 'You got any black stockings?' When she told him no, he proposed that they try another store. 'Black's foolproof.'

But Dick had made up his mind: stockings of any shade were unnecessary, an encumbrance, a useless expense ('I've already invested enough money in this operation'), and, after all, anyone they encountered would not live to bear witness. '*No* witnesses,' he reminded Perry, for what seemed to Perry the millionth time. It rankled in him, the way Dick mouthed those two words, as though they solved every problem; it was stupid not to admit that there might be a witness they hadn't seen. 'The ineffable happens, things *do* take a turn,' he said. But Dick, smiling boastfully, boyishly, did not agree: 'Get the bubbles out of your blood. Nothing can go wrong.' No. Because the plan was Dick's, and from first footfall to final silence, flawlessly devised.

Next they were interested in rope. Perry studied the stock, tested it. Having once served in the Merchant Marine, he understood rope and was clever with knots. He chose a white nylon cord, as strong as wire and not much thicker. They discussed how many yards of it they required. The question irritated Dick, for it was part of a greater quandary, and he could not, despite the alleged perfection of his over-all design, be certain of the answer. Eventually, he said, 'Christ how the hell should I know?'

'You damn well better.'

Dick tried. 'There's him. Her. The kid and the girl. And maybe the other two. But it's Saturday. They might have guests. Let's count on eight, or even twelve. The only *sure* thing is every one of them has got to go.'

'Seems like a lot of it. To be so sure about.'

'Ain't that what I promised you, honey – plenty of hair on them-those walls?'

Perry shrugged. 'Then we'd better buy the whole roll.'

It was a hundred yards long – quite enough for twelve.

Kenyon had built the chest himself: a mahogany hope chest, lined with cedar, which he intended to give Beverly as a wedding present. Now, working on it in the so-called den in the basement, he applied a last coat of varnish. The furniture of the den, a cement-floored room that ran the length of the house, consisted almost entirely of examples of his carpentry (shelves, tables, stools, a ping-pong table) and Nancy's needlework (chintz slip covers that rejuvenated a decrepit couch, curtains, pillows bearing legends: HAPPY? and YOU DON'T HAVE TO BE CRAZY TO LIVE HERE BUT IT HELPS). Together, Kenyon and Nancy had made a paint-splattered attempt to deprive the basement room of its unremovable dourness, and neither was aware of failure. In fact, they both thought their den a triumph and a blessing – Nancy because it was a place where she could entertain 'the gang' without disturbing her mother, and Kenyon because here he could be alone, free to bang, saw, and mess with his 'inventions', the newest of which was an electric deep-dish frying-pan. Adjoining the den was a furnace room, which contained a tool-littered table piled with some of his other works-in-progress – an amplifying unit, an elderly wind-up Victrola that he was restoring to service.

Kenyon resembled neither of his parents physically; his crew-cut hair was hemp-coloured, and he was six feet tall and lanky, though hefty enough to have once rescued a pair of full-grown sheep by carrying them two miles through a blizzard – sturdy, strong, but cursed with a lanky boy's lack of muscular coordination. This defect, aggravated by an inability to function without glasses, prevented him from taking more than a token part in those team sports (basketball, baseball) that were the main occupation of most of the boys who might have been his friends. He had only one close friend – Bob Jones, the son of Taylor Jones, whose ranch was a mile west of the Clutter home. Out in rural Kansas, boys start driving cars very young; Kenyon was eleven when his father allowed him to buy, with money he had earned raising sheep, an old truck with a Model A engine – the Coyote Wagon, he and Bob called it. Not far from River Valley Farm there is a mysterious 'stretch of countryside known as the Sand Hills; it is like a beach without an ocean, and at night coyotes slink among the dunes, assembling in hordes to howl. On moonlit evenings the boys would descend upon them, set them running, and try to outrace them in the wagon; they seldom did, for the scrawniest coyote can hit fifty miles an hour, whereas the wagon's top speed was thirty-five, but it was a wild and beautiful kind of fun, the wagon skidding across the sand, and fleeing coyotes framed against the moon – as Bob said, it sure made your heart hurry.

Equally intoxicating, and more profitable, were the rabbit round-ups the two boys conducted: Kenyon was a good shot and his friend a better one, and between them they sometimes delivered half a hundred rabbits to the 'rabbit factory' – a Garden City processing plant that paid ten cents a head for the animals, which were then quick-frozen and shipped to mink growers. But what meant most to Kenyon – and Bob, too – was their week-end, overnight hunting hikes along the shores of the river: wandering, wrapping up in blankets, listening at sunrise for the noise of wings, moving towards the sound on tiptoe, and then, sweetest of all, swaggering homeward with a dozen duck dinners swinging from their belts. But lately things had changed between Kenyon and his friend. They had not quarrelled, there had been no overt falling-out, nothing had happened except that Bob, who was sixteen, had started 'going with a girl', which meant that Kenyon, a year younger and still very much the adolescent bachelor, could no longer count on his companionship. Bob told him, 'When you're my age, you'll feel different. I used to think the same as you: Women – so what? But then you get to talking to some woman, and it's mighty nice. You'll see.' Kenyon doubted it; he could not conceive of ever wanting to waste an hour on any girl that might be spent with guns, horses, tools, machinery, even a book. If Bob was unavailable, then he would rather be alone, for in temperament he was not in the least Mr Clutter's son but rather Bonnie's child, a sensitive and reticent boy. His contemporaries thought him 'standoffish', yet forgave him, saying, 'Oh, *Ken*yon. It's just that he lives in a world of his own.'

Leaving the varnish to dry, he went on to another chore – one that took him out of doors. He wanted to tidy up his mother's flower garden, a treasured patch of dishevelled foliage that grew beneath her bedroom window. When he got there, he found one of the hired men loosening earth with a spade – Paul Helm, the husband of the housekeeper.

'Seen that car?' Mr Helm asked.

Yes, Kenyon had seen a car in the driveway – a grey Buick, standing outside the entrance to his father's office.

'Thought you might know who it was.'

'Not unless it's Mr Johnson. Dad said he was expecting him.'

Mr Helm (the late Mr Helm; he died of a stroke the following March) was a sombre man in his late fifties whose withdrawn manner veiled a nature keenly curious and watchful; he liked to know what was going on. 'Which Johnson?'

'The insurance fellow.'

Mr Helm grunted. 'Your dad must be laying in a stack of it. That car's been here I'd say three hours.'

The chill of oncoming dusk shivered through the air, and though the sky was still deep blue, lengthening shadows emanated from the garden's tall chrysanthemum stalks; Nancy's cat frolicked among them, catching its paws in the twine with which Kenyon and the old man were now tying plants. Suddenly, Nancy herself came jogging across the fields aboard fat Babe – Babe, returning from her Saturday treat, a bathe in the river. Teddy, the dog, accompanied them, and all three were water-splashed and shining.

'You'll catch cold,' Mr Helm said.

Nancy laughed; she had never been ill – not once. Sliding off Babe, she sprawled on the grass at the edge of the garden and seized her cat, dangled him above her, and kissed his nose and whiskers.

Kenyon was disgusted. '*Kissing* animals on the mouth.'

'You used to kiss Skeeter,' she reminded him.

'Skeeter was a *horse*.' A beautiful horse, a strawberry stallion he had raised from a foal. How that Skeeter could take a fence! 'You use a horse too hard,' his father had cautioned him. 'One day you'll ride the life out of Skeeter.' And he had; while Skeeter was streaking down a road with his master astride him, his heart failed, and he stumbled and was dead. Now a year later, Kenyon still mourned him, even though his father, taking pity on him, had promised him the pick of the next spring's foals.

'Kenyon?' Nancy said. 'Do you think Tracy will be able to talk? By Thanksgiving?' Tracy, not yet a year old, was her nephew, the son of Eveanna, the sister to whom she felt particularly close (Beverly was Kenyon's favourite.) 'It would thrill me to pieces to hear him say "Aunt Nancy". Or "Uncle Kenyon". Wouldn't you like to hear him say that? I mean, don't you love being an uncle? Kenyon? Good grief, why can't you *ever* answer me?'

'Because you're silly,' he said, tossing her the head of a flower, a wilted dahlia, which she jammed into her hair.

Mr Helm picked up his spade. Crows cawed, sundown was near, but his home was not; the lane of Chinese elms had turned into a tunnel of darkening green, and he lived at the end of it, half a mile away. 'Evening,' he said, and started his journey. But once he looked back. 'And that,' he was to testify the next day, 'was the last I seen them. Nancy leading old Babe off to the barn. Like I said, nothing out of the ordinary.'

The black Chevrolet was again parked, this time in front of a Catholic hospital on the outskirts of Emporia. Under continued needling ('That's your trouble. You think there's only one right way – Dick's way'), Dick had surrendered. While Perry waited in the car, he had gone into the hospital to try and buy a pair of black stockings from a nun. This rather unorthodox method of obtaining them had been

Perry's inspiration; nuns, he had argued, were certain to have a supply. The notion presented one drawback, of course: nuns, and anything pertaining to them, were bad luck, and Perry was most respectful of his superstitions. (Some others were the number 15, red hair, white flowers, priests crossing a road, snakes appearing in a dream.) Still, it couldn't be helped. The compulsively superstitious person is also very often a serious believer in fate; that was the case with Perry. He was here, and embarked on the present errand, not because he wished to be but because fate had arranged the matter, he could *prove* it – though he had no intention of doing so, at least within Dick's hearing, for the proof would involve his confessing the true and secret motive behind his return to Kansas, a piece of parole violation he had decided upon for a reason quite unrelated to Dick's 'score' or Dick's summoning letter. The reason was that several weeks earlier he had learned that on Thursday, 12 November, another of his former cellmates was being released from Kansas State Penitentiary at Lansing, and 'more than anything in the world', he desired a reunion with this man, his 'real and only friend', the 'brilliant' Willie-Jay.

During the first of his three years in prison, Perry had observed Willie-Jay from a distance, with interest but with apprehension; if one wished to be thought a tough specimen, intimacy with Willie-Jay seemed unwise. He was the chaplain's clerk, a slender Irishman with prematurely grey hair and grey, melancholy eyes. His tenor voice was the glory of the prison's choir. Even Perry, though he was contemptuous of any exhibition of piety, felt 'upset' when he heard Willie-Jay sing 'The Lord's Prayer'; the hymn's grave language sung in so credulous a spirit moved him, made him wonder a little at the justice of his contempt. Eventually, prodded by a slightly alerted religious curiosity, he approached Willie-Jay, and the chaplain's clerk, at once responsive, thought he divined in the cripple-legged body builder with the misty gaze and the prim, smoky voice 'a poet, something rare and savable'. An ambition to 'bring this boy to God' engulfed him. His hopes of succeeding accelerated when one day Perry produced a pastel drawing

he had made – a large, in no way technically naïve, portrait
of Jesus. Lansing's Protestant chaplain, the Reverend James
Post, so valued it that he hung it in his office, where it hangs
still; a slick and pretty Saviour, with Willie-Jay's full lips and
grieving eyes. The picture was the climax of Perry's never
very earnest spiritual quest, and, ironically, the termination
of it; he adjudged his Jesus 'a piece of hypocrisy', an
attempt to 'fool and betray' Willie-Jay, for he was as uncon-
vinced of God as ever. Yet should he admit this and risk for-
feiting the one friend who had ever 'truly understood' him?
(Hod, Joe, Jesse, travellers straying through a world where
last names were seldom exchanged, these had been his
'buddies' – never anyone like Willie-Jay, who was in Perry's
opinion, 'way above average intellectually, perceptive as a
well-trained psychologist.' How was it possible that so gifted
a man had wound up in Lansing? That was what amazed
Perry. The answer, which he knew but rejected as 'an eva-
sion of the deeper, the human question', was plain to simpler
minds: the chaplain's clerk, then thirty-eight, was a thief, a
small-scale robber who over a period of twenty years had
served sentences in five different states.) Perry decided to
speak out: he was sorry, but it was not for him – heaven, hell,
saints, divine mercy – and if Willie-Jay's affection was
founded on the prospect of Perry's some day joining him at
the foot of the Cross, then he was deceived and their friendship false, a counterfeit, like the portrait.

As usual, Willie-Jay understood; disheartened but not dis-
enchanted, he had persisted in courting Perry's soul until the
day of its possessor's parole and departure, on the eve of
which he wrote Perry a farewell letter, whose last paragraph
ran: 'You are a man of extreme passion, a hungry man not
quite sure where his appetite lies, a deeply frustrated man
striving to project his individuality against a backdrop of
rigid conformity. You exist in a half-world suspended between two superstructures, one self-expression and the other
self-destruction. You are strong, but there is a flaw in your
strength, and unless you learn to control it the flaw will prove
stronger than your strength and defeat you. The flaw?
Explosive emotional reaction out of all proportion to the

occasion. Why? Why this unreasonable anger at the sight of others who are happy or content, this growing contempt for people and the desire to hurt them? All right, you think they're fools, you despise them because their morals, their happiness is the source of *your* frustration and resentment. But these are dreadful enemies you carry within yourself – in time destructive as bullets. Mercifully, a bullet kills its victim. This other bacteria, permitted to age, does not kill a man but leaves in its wake the hulk of a creature torn and twisted; there is still fire within his being but it is kept alive by casting upon it faggots of scorn and hate. He may successfully accumulate, but he does not accumulate success, for he is his own enemy and is kept from truly enjoying his achievements.'

Perry, flattered to be the subject of this sermon, had let Dick read it, and Dick, who took a dim view of Willie-Jay, had called the letter 'just more of Billy Grahamcracker's hooey', adding, ' "Faggots of scorn!" *He's* the faggot.' Of course, Perry had expected this reaction, and secretly he welcomed it, for his friendship with Dick, whom he had scarcely known until his final few months in Lansing, was an outgrowth of, and counterbalance to, the intensity of his admiration for the chaplain's clerk. Perhaps Dick *was* 'shallow', or even, as Willie-Jay claimed, 'a vicious blusterer'. All the same, Dick was full of fun, and he was shrewd, a realist, he 'cut through things', there were no clouds in his head or straw in his hair. Moreover, unlike Willie-Jay, he was not critical of Perry's exotic aspirations; he was willing to listen, catch fire, share with him those visions of 'guaranteed treasure' lurking in Mexican seas, Brazilian jungles.

After Perry's parole, four months elapsed, months of rattling around in a fifth-hand, hundred-dollar Ford, rolling from Reno to Las Vegas, from Bellingham, Washington, to Buhl, Idaho, and it was in Buhl, where he had found temporary work as a truck driver, that Dick's letter reached him: 'Friend P., Came out in August, and after you left I Met Someone, you do not know him, but he put me on to Something we could bring off Beautiful. A cinch, the Perfect

score . . .' Until then Perry had not imagined that he would
ever see Dick again. *Or* Willie-Jay. But they had both been
much in his thoughts, and especially the latter, who in
memory had grown ten feet tall, a grey-haired wise man
haunting the hallways of his mind. 'You pursue the negative,' Willie-Jay had informed him once, in one of his lec-
tures. 'You want not to give a damn, to exist without responsibility, without faith or friends or warmth.'

In the solitary, comfortless course of his recent driftings,
Perry had over and over again reviewed this indictment,
and had decided it was unjust. He *did* give a damn – but who
had ever given a damn about him? His father? Yes, up to a
point. A girl or two – but that was 'a long story'. No one else
except Willie-Jay himself. And only Willie-Jay had ever
recognized his worth, his potentialities, had acknowledged
that he was not just an undersized, overmuscled half-breed,
had seen him, for all the moralizing, as he saw himself – 'exceptional', 'rare', 'artistic'. In Willie-Jay his vanity had
found support, his sensibility shelter, and the four-month
exile from this high-carat appreciation had made it more
alluring than any dream of buried gold. So when he received
Dick's invitation, and realized that the date Dick proposed
for his coming to Kansas more or less coincided with the
time of Willie-Jay's release, he knew what he must do. He
drove to Las Vegas, sold his junk-heap car, packed his collection of maps, old letters, manuscripts, and books, and
bought a ticket for a Greyhound bus. The journey's aftermath was up to fate; if things didn't 'work out with Willie-
Jay' then he might 'consider Dick's proposition'. As it turned
out, the choice was between Dick and nothing, for when
Perry's bus reached Kansas City, on the evening of 12
November, Willie-Jay, whom he'd been unable to advise of
his coming, had already left town – left, in fact, only five
hours earlier, from the same terminal at which Perry
arrived. That much he had learned by telephoning the
Reverend Mr Post, who further discouraged him by declin-
ing to reveal his former clerk's exact destination. 'He's
headed East,' the chaplain said. 'To fine opportunities. A
decent job, and a home with some good people who are

willing to help him.' And Perry, hanging up, had felt 'dizzy with anger and disappointment'.

But what, he wondered when the anguish subsided, had he really expected from a reunion with Willie-Jay? Freedom had separated them; as free men, they had nothing in common, were opposites, who could never have formed a 'team' – certainly not one capable of embarking on the skin-diving south-of-the-border adventures he and Dick had plotted. Nevertheless, if he had not missed Willie-Jay, if they could have been together for even an hour, Perry was quite convinced – just 'knew' – that he would not now be loitering outside a hospital waiting for Dick to emerge with a pair of black stockings.

Dick returned empty-handed. 'No go,' he announced, with a furtive casualness that made Perry suspicious.

'Are you sure? Sure you even asked?'

'Sure I did.'

'I don't believe you. I think you went in there, hung around a couple of minutes, and came out.'

'O.K., sugar – whatever you say.' Dick started the car. After they had travelled in silence a while, Dick patted Perry on the knee. 'Aw, come on,' he said. 'It was a puky idea. What the hell would they have thought? Me barging in there like it was a goddam five-'n'-dime . . .'

Perry said, 'Maybe it's just as well. Nuns are a bad-luck bunch.'

The Garden City representative of New York Life Insurance smiled as he watched Mr Clutter uncap a Parker pen and open a cheque book. He was reminded of a local jest: 'Know what they say about you, Herb? Say, "Since haircuts went to a dollar-fifty, Herb writes the barber a cheque." '

'That's correct,' replied Mr Clutter. Like royalty, he was famous for never carrying cash. 'That's the way I do business. When those tax fellows come poking around, cancelled cheques are your best friend.'

With the cheque written but not yet signed, he swivelled back in his desk chair and seemed to ponder. The agent, a

stocky, somewhat bald, rather informal man named Bob
Johnson, hoped his client wasn't having last-minute doubts.
Herb was hard-headed, a slow man to make a deal; Johnson had worked over a year to clinch this sale. But, no, his
customer was merely experiencing what Johnson called
the Solemn Moment – a phenomenon familiar to insurance
salesmen. The mood of a man insuring his life is not unlike that of a man signing his will; thoughts of mortality
must occur.

'Yes, yes,' said Mr Clutter, as though conversing with himself. 'I've plenty to be grateful for – wonderful things in my
life.' Framed documents commemorating milestones in his
career gleamed against the walnut walls of his office: a college diploma, a map of River Valley Farm, agricultural
awards, an ornate certificate bearing the signatures of
Dwight D. Eisenhower and John Foster Dulles, which cited
his services to the Federal Farm Credit Board. 'The kids.
We've been lucky there. Shouldn't say it, but I'm real proud
of them. Take Kenyon. Right now he kind of leans towards
being an engineer, or a scientist, but you can't tell me my
boy's not a born rancher. God willing, he'll run this place
some day. You ever met Eveanna's husband? Don Jarchow?
Veterinarian. I can't tell you how much I think of that boy.
Vere, too. Vere English – the boy my girl Beverly had the
good sense to settle on. If anything ever happened to me,
I'm sure I could trust those fellows to take responsibility;
Bonnie by herself – Bonnie wouldn't be able to carry on an
operation like this . . .'

Johnson, a veteran at listening to ruminations of this sort,
knew it was time to intervene. 'Why, Herb,' he said. 'You're
a *young* man. Forty-eight. And from the looks of you, from
what the medical report tells us, we're likely to have you
around a couple of weeks more.'

Mr Clutter straightened, reached again for his pen. 'Tell
the *truth*, I feel pretty good. And pretty optimistic. I've got
an idea a man could make some real money around here
the next few years.' While outlining his schemes for future
financial betterment, he signed the cheque and pushed it
across his desk.

The time was ten past six, and the agent was anxious to go; his wife would be waiting supper. 'It's been a pleasure, Herb.'

'Same here, fellow.'

They shook hands. Then, with a merited sense of victory, Johnson picked up Mr Clutter's cheque and deposited it in his billfold. It was the first payment on a forty-thousand-dollar policy that in the event of death by accidental means, paid double indemnity.

> 'And He walks with me, and He talks with me,
>   And He tells me I am His own,
> And the joy we share as we tarry there,
>   None other has ever known . . .'

With the aid of his guitar, Perry had sung himself into a happier humour. He knew the lyrics of some two hundred hymns and ballads – a repertoire ranging from 'The Old Rugged Cross' to Cole Porter – and, in addition to the guitar, he could play the harmonica, the accordion, the banjo, and the xylophone. In one of his favourite theatrical fantasies, his stage name was Perry O'Parsons, a star who billed himself as 'The One-Man Symphony'.

Dick said, 'How about a cocktail?'

Personally, Perry didn't care what he drank, for he was not much of a drinker. Dick, however, was choosy, and in bars his usual choice was an Orange Blossom. From the car's glove compartment Perry fetched a pint bottle containing a ready-mixed compound of orange flavouring and vodka. They passed the bottle to and fro. Though dusk had established itself, Dick, doing a steady sixty miles an hour, was still driving without headlights, but then the road was straight, the country was as level as a lake, and other cars were seldom sighted. This was 'out there' – or getting near it.

'Christ!' said Perry, glaring at the landscape, flat and limitless under the sky's cold, lingering green – empty and lonesome except for the far-between flickerings of farmhouse lights. He hated it, as he hated the Texas plains, the Nevada desert; spaces horizontal and sparsely inhabited had always induced in him a depression accompanied by agoraphobic sensations. Seaports were his heart's delight – crowded, clanging, ship-clogged, sewage-scented cities, like Yokohama, where as an American Army private he'd spent a summer during the Korean War. 'Christ – and they told me to keep away from Kansas! Never set my pretty foot here again. As though they were barring me from heaven. And just look at it. Just feast your eyes.'

Dick handed him the bottle, the contents reduced by half. 'Save the rest,' Dick said. 'We may need it.'

'Remember, Dick? All that talk about getting a boat? I was thinking – we could buy a boat in Mexico. Something cheap but sturdy. We could go to Japan. Sail right across the Pacific. It's been done – thousands of people have done it. I'm not conning you, Dick – you'd go for Japan. Wonderful, gentle people, with manners like flowers. Really considerate –not just out for your dough. And the women. You've never met a real woman...'

'Yes, I have,' said Dick, who claimed still to be in love with his honey-blonde first wife though she had remarried.

'There are these baths. One place called the Dream Pool. You stretch out, and beautiful, knockout-type girls come and scrub you head to toe.'

'You told me.' Dick's tone was curt.

'So? Can't I repeat myself?'

'Later. Let's talk about it later. Hell, man, I've got plenty on my mind.'

Dick switched on the radio; Perry switched it off. Ignoring Dick's protest, he strummed his guitar:

> 'I came to the garden alone, while the dew was
>   still on the roses,
> And the voice I hear, falling on my ear,
> The Son of God discloses...'

A full moon was forming at the edge of the sky.

The following Monday, while giving evidence prior to taking a lie-detector test, young Bobby Rupp described his last visit to the Clutter home: 'There was a full moon, and I thought maybe, if Nancy wanted to, we might go for a drive – drive out to McKinney Lake. Or go to the movies in Garden City. But when I called her – it must have been about ten of seven – she said she'd have to ask her father. Then she came back, and said the answer was no – because we'd stayed out so late the night before. But said why didn't I come over and watch television. I've spent a lot of time at the Clutters' watching television. See, Nancy's the only girl I ever dated. I'd known her all my life; we'd gone to school together from the first grade. Always, as long as I can remember, she was pretty and popular – a *person*, even when she was a little kid. I mean, she just made everybody feel good about themselves. The first time I dated her was when we were in the eighth grade. Most of the boys in our class wanted to take her to the eighth-grade graduation dance, and I was surprised – I was pretty proud – when she said she would go with me. We were both twelve. My dad lent me the car, and I drove her to the dance. The more I saw her, the more I liked her; the whole family, too – there wasn't any other family like them, not around here, not that I know of. Mr Clutter may have been more strict about some things – religion, and so on – but he never tried to make you feel he was right and you were wrong.

'We live three miles west of the Clutter place. I used to walk it back and forth, but I always worked summers, and last year I'd saved enough to buy my own car, a '55 Ford. I drove over there, got there a little after seven. I didn't see anybody on the road or on the lane that leads up to the house, or anybody outside. Just old Teddy. He barked at me. The lights were on downstairs – in the living-room and in Mr Clutter's office. The second floor was dark, and I figured Mrs Clutter must be asleep – if she was home. You never knew whether she was or not, and I never asked. But I found out I was right, because later in the evening Kenyon wanted to practise his horn – he played baritone horn in the school band – and Nancy told him not to, because he would wake up Mrs Clutter. Anyway, when I got there they had finished supper and Nancy had cleaned up, put all the dishes in the dish-washer, and the three of them – the two kids and Mr Clutter – were in the living-room. So we sat around like any other night – Nancy and I on the couch, and Mr Clutter in his chair, that stuffed rocker. He wasn't watching the television so much as he was reading a book – a "Rover Boy", one of Kenyon's books. Once he went out to the kitchen and came back with two apples; he offered one to me, but I didn't want it, so he ate them both. He had very white teeth; he said apples were why. Nancy – Nancy was wearing socks and soft slippers, blue jeans, I think a green sweater; she was wearing a gold wristwatch and an I.D. bracelet I gave her last January for her sixteenth birthday – with her name on one side and mine on the other – and she had on a ring, some little silver thing she bought a summer ago, when she went to Colorado with the Kidwells. It wasn't my ring – *our* ring. See, a couple of weeks back she got sore at me and said she was going to take off our ring for a while. When your girl does that, it means you're on probation. I mean, sure we had fusses – everybody does, all the kids that go steady. What happened was I went to this friend's wedding, the reception, and drank a beer, one bottle of beer, and Nancy got to hear about it. Some tattle told her I was roaring drunk. Well, she was stone, wouldn't say hello for a week. But lately we'd been getting on good as ever, and I believe she was about ready to wear our ring again.

'O.K. The first show was called "The Man and the Challenge". Channel 11. About some fellows in the Arctic. Then we saw a Western, and after that a spy adventure – "Five Fingers". "Mike Hammer" came on at nine-thirty. Then the news. But Kenyon didn't like anything, mostly because we wouldn't let him pick the programmes. He criticized everything and Nancy kept telling him to hush up. They always quibbled, but actually they were very close – closer than most brothers and sisters. I guess partly it was because they'd been alone together so much, what with Mrs Clutter away and Mr Clutter gone to Washington, or wherever. I know Nancy loved Kenyon very specially, but I don't think even she, or anybody, exactly understood him. He seemed to be off somewhere. You never knew what he was thinking, never even knew if he was looking at you – on account of he was slightly cockeyed. Some people said he was a genius, and maybe it was true. He sure did read a lot. But, like I say, he was restless; he didn't want to watch the TV, he wanted to practise his horn, and when Nancy wouldn't let him, I remember Mr Clutter told him why didn't he go down to the basement, the recreation room, where nobody could hear him. But he didn't want to do that, either.

'The phone rang once. Twice? Gosh, I can't remember. Except that once the phone rang and Mr Clutter answered it in his office. The door was open – that sliding door between the living-room and the office – and I heard him say "Van", so I knew he was talking to his partner, Mr Van Vleet, and I heard him say that he had a headache but that it was getting better. And said he'd see Mr Van Vleet on Monday. When he came back – yes, the Mike Hammer was just over. Five minutes of news. Then the weather report. Mr Clutter always perked up when the weather report came on. It's all he ever really waited for. Like the only thing that interested me was the sports – which came on next. After the sports ended, that was ten-thirty, and I got up to go. Nancy walked me out. We talked a while, and made a date to go to the movies Sunday night – a picture all the girls were looking forward to, *Blue Denim*. Then she ran back to the house, and I drove away. It was as clear as day – the moon was so bright – and cold and kind of windy; a lot of tumbleweed blowing about. But that's all I saw. Only now when I think back, I think somebody must have been hiding there. Maybe down among the trees. Somebody just waiting for me to leave.'

The travellers stopped for dinner at a restaurant in Great Bend. Perry, down to his last fifteen dollars, was ready to settle for root beer and a sandwich, but Dick said no, they needed a solid 'tuck-in', and never mind the cost, the tab was his. They ordered two steaks medium rare, baked potatoes, French fries, fried onions, succotash, side dishes of macaroni and hominy, salad with Thousand Island dressing, cinnamon rolls, apple-pie and ice-cream, and coffee. To top it off, they visited a drugstore and selected cigars; in the same drugstore, they also bought two thick rolls of adhesive tape.

As the black Chevrolet regained the highway and hurried across a countryside imperceptibly ascending towards the colder, cracker-dry climate of the high wheat plains, Perry closed his eyes and dozed off into a food-dazed semi-slumber, from which he woke to hear a voice reading the eleven-o'clock news. He rolled down a window and bathed his face in the flood of frosty air. Dick told him they were in Finney County. 'We crossed the line ten miles back,' he said. The car was going very fast. Signs, their messages ignited by the car's headlights, flared up, flew by: 'See the Polar Bears', 'Burtis Motors', 'World's Largest FREE Swim-pool', 'Wheat Lands Motel', and, finally, a bit before street lamps began, 'Howdy, Stranger! Welcome to Garden City. A Friendly Place.'

They skirted the southern rim of the town. No one was abroad at this nearly midnight hour, and nothing was open except a string of desolately brilliant service stations. Dick turned into one – Hurd's Phillips 66. A youngster appeared, and asked, 'Fill her up?' Dick nodded, and Perry, getting out of the car, went inside the station, where he locked himself in the men's room. His legs pained him, as they often did; they hurt as though his old accident had happened five minutes before. He shook three aspirins out of a bottle, chewed them slowly (for he liked the taste), and then drank water from the basin tap. He sat down on the toilet, stretched out his legs and rubbed them, massaging the almost unbendable knees. Dick had said they were almost there – 'only seven miles more'. He unzipped a pocket of his windbreaker and brought out a paper sack; inside it were the recently purchased rubber gloves. They were glue-covered, sticky and thin, and as he inched them on, one tore – not a dangerous tear, just a split between the fingers, but it seemed to him an omen.

The doorknob turned, rattled. Dick said, 'Want some candy? They got a candy machine out here.'

'No.'

'You O.K.?'

'I'm fine.'

'Don't be all night.'

Dick dropped a dime in a vending machine, pulled the lever, and picked up a bag of jelly beans; munching, he wandered back to the car and lounged there watching the young attendant's efforts to rid the windshield of Kansas dust and the slime of battered insects. The attendant, whose name was James Spor, felt uneasy. Dick's eyes and sullen expression and Perry's strange, prolonged sojourn in the lavatory disturbed him. (The next day he reported to his employer, 'We had some tough customers in here last night', but he did not think, then or for the longest while, to connect the visitors with the tragedy in Holcomb.)

Dick said, 'Kind of slow around here.'

'Sure is,' James Spor said. 'You're the only body stopped here since two hours. Where you coming from?'

'Kansas City.'

'Here to hunt?'

'Just passing through. On our way to Arizona. We got jobs waiting there. Construction work. Any idea the mileage between here and Tucumcari, New Mexico?'

'Can't say I do. Three dollars six cents.' He accepted Dick's money, made change, and said, 'You'll excuse me, sir? I'm doing a job. Putting a bumper on a truck.'

Dick waited, ate some jelly beans, impatiently gunned the motor, sounded the horn. Was it possible that he had misjudged Perry's character? That Perry, of all people, was suffering a sudden case of 'blood bubbles'? A year ago, when they first encountered each other, he'd thought Perry 'a good guy', if a bit 'stuck on himself', 'sentimental', too much 'the dreamer'. He had liked him but not considered him especially worth cultivating until, one day, Perry described a murder, telling how, simply for 'the hell of it', he had killed a coloured man in Las Vegas – beaten him to death with a bicycle chain. The anecdote elevated Dick's opinion of Little Perry; he began to see more of him, and, like Willie-Jay, though for dissimilar reasons, gradually decided that Perry possessed unusual and valuable qualities. Several murderers, or men who boasted of murder or their willingness to commit it, circulated inside Lansing; but Dick became convinced that Perry was that rarity, 'a natural killer' – absolutely sane, but conscienceless, and capable of dealing, with or without motive, the coldest-blooded deathblows. It was Dick's theory that such a gift could, under his supervision, be profitably exploited. Having reached this conclusion, he had proceeded to woo Perry, flatter him – pretend, for example, that he believed all the buried-treasure stuff and shared his beachcomber yearnings and seaport longings, none of which appealed to Dick, who wanted 'a regular life', with a business of his own, a house, a horse to ride, a new car, and 'plenty of blonde chicken'. It was important, however, that Perry not suspect this – not until Perry, with his gift, had helped further Dick's ambitions. But perhaps it was Dick who had miscalculated, been duped; if so – if it developed that Perry was, after all, only an 'ordinary punk' – then 'the party' was over, the months of planning were wasted, there was nothing to do but turn and go. It mustn't happen; Dick returned to the station.

The door to the men's room was still bolted. He banged on it: 'For Christsake, Perry!'

'In a minute.'

'What's the matter? You sick?'

Perry gripped the edge of the washbasin and hauled himself to a standing position. His legs trembled; the pain in his knees made him perspire. He wiped his face with a paper towel. He unlocked the door and said, 'O.K. Let's go.'

Nancy's bedroom was the smallest, most personal room in the house – girlish, and as frothy as a ballerina's tutu. Walls, ceiling, and everything else except a bureau and a writing-desk, were pink or blue or white. The white-and-pink bed, piled with blue pillows, was dominated by a big pink-and-white Teddy bear – a shooting-gallery prize that Bobby had won at a county fair. A cork bulletin board, painted pink, hung above a white-skirted dressing-table; dry gardenias, the remains of some ancient corsage, were attached to it, and old valentines, newspaper recipes, and snapshots of her baby nephew and of Susan Kidwell and of Bobby Rupp, Bobby caught in a dozen actions – swinging a bat, dribbling a basketball, driving a tractor, wading, in bathing trunks, at the edge of McKinney Lake (which was as far as he dared go for he had never learned to swim). And there were photographs of the two together – Nancy and Bobby. Of these, she liked best one that showed them sitting in a leaf-dappled light amid picnic debris and looking at one another with expressions that, though unsmiling, seemed mirthful and full of delight. Other pictures, of horses, of cats deceased but unforgotten – like 'poor Boobs', who had died not long ago and most mysteriously (she suspected poison) – encumbered her desk.

Nancy was invariably the last of the family to retire; as she had once informed her friend and home-economics teacher, Mrs Polly Stringer, the midnight hours were her 'time to be selfish and vain'. It was then that she went through her beauty routine, a cleansing, creaming ritual, which on Saturday nights included washing her hair. Tonight, having dried and brushed her hair and bound it in a gauzy bandanna, she set out the clothes she intended to wear to church the next morning: nylons, black pumps, a red velveteen dress – her prettiest, which she herself had made. It was a dress in which she was to be buried.

Before saying her prayers, she always recorded in a diary a few occurrences ('Summer here. Forever, I hope. Sue over and we rode Babe down to the river. Sue played her flute. Fireflies') and an occasional outburst ('I love him, I do'). It was a five-year diary; in the four years of its existence she had never neglected to make an entry, though the splendour of several events (Eveanna's wedding, the birth of her nephew) and the drama of others (her 'first REAL quarrel with Bobby' – a page literally tear-stained) had caused her to usurp space allotted to the future. A different-tinted ink identified each year: 1956 was green and 1957 a ribbon of red, replaced the following year by bright lavender, and now, in 1959, she had decided upon a dignified blue. But as in every manifestation, she continued to tinker with her handwriting, slanting it to the right or to the left, shaping it roundly or steeply, loosely or stingily – as though she were asking, 'Is this Nancy? Or that? Or that? Which is me?'

(Once Mrs Riggs, her English teacher, had returned a theme with a scribbled comment: 'Good. But why written in three styles of script?' To which Nancy had replied: 'Because I'm not grown-up enough to be one person with one kind of signature'.) Still, she had progressed in recent months, and it was in a handwriting of emerging maturity that she wrote, 'Jolene K. came over and I showed her how to make a cherry-pie. Practised with Roxie. Bobby here and we watched TV. Left at eleven.'

'This is it, this is it, this has to be it, there's the school, there's the garage, now we turn south.' To Perry, it seemed as though Dick were muttering jubilant mumbo-jumbo. They left the highway, sped through a deserted Holcomb, and crossed the Santa Fe tracks. 'The bank, that must be the bank, now we turn west – see the trees? This is it, this has to be it.' The headlights disclosed a lane of Chinese elms; bundles of wind-blown thistle scurried across it. Dick doused the headlights, slowed down, and stopped until his eyes were adjusted to the moon-illuminated night. Presently, the car crept forward.

Holcomb is twelve miles east of the mountain time-zone border, a circumstance that causes some grumbling, for it means that at seven in the morning, and in winter at eight or after, the sky is still dark and the stars, if any, are still shining – as they were when the two sons of Vic Irsik arrived to do their Sunday-morning chores. But by nine, when the boys finished work – during which they noticed nothing amiss – the sun had risen, delivering another day of pheasant-season perfection. As they left the property and ran along the lane, they waved at an incoming car, and a girl waved back. She was a classmate of Nancy Clutter's, and her name was also Nancy – Nancy Ewalt. She was the only child of the man who was driving the car, Mr Clarence Ewalt, a middle-aged sugar-beet farmer. Mr Ewalt was not himself a churchgoer, nor was his wife, but every Sunday he dropped his daughter at River Valley Farm in order that she might accompany the Clutter family to Methodist services in

Garden City. The arrangement saved him 'making two back-and-forth trips to town'. It was his custom to wait until he had seen his daughter safely admitted to the house. Nancy, a clothes-conscious girl with a film-star figure, a bespectacled countenance, and a coy, tiptoe way of walking, crossed the lawn and pressed the front-door bell. The house had four entrances, and when, after repeated knockings, there was no response at this one, she moved on to the next – that of Mr Clutter's office. Here the door was partly open; she opened it somewhat more – enough to ascertain that the office was filled only with shadow – but she did not think the Clutters would appreciate her 'barging right in'. She knocked, rang, and at last walked around to the back of the house. The garage was there, and she noted that both cars were in it: two Chevrolet sedans. Which meant they *must* be home. However, having applied unavailingly at a third door, which led into a 'utility room', and a fourth, the door to the kitchen, she rejoined her father, who said, 'Maybe they're asleep.'

'But that's *im*possible. Can you imagine Mr Clutter missing church? Just to *sleep*?'

'Come on, then. We'll drive down to the Teacherage. Susan ought to know what's happened.'

The Teacherage, which stands opposite the up-to-date school, is an out-of-date edifice, drab and poignant. Its twenty-odd rooms are separated into grace-and-favour apartments for those members of the faculty unable to find, or afford, other quarters. Nevertheless, Susan Kidwell and her mother had managed to sugar the pill and install a cosy atmosphere in their apartment – three rooms on the ground floor. The very small living-room incredibly contained – aside from things to sit on – an organ, a piano, a garden of flowering flowerpots, and usually a darting little dog and a large, drowsy cat. Susan, on this Sunday morning, stood at the window of this room watching the street. She is a tall, languid young lady with a pallid, oval face and beautiful pale-blue-grey eyes; her hands are extraordinary – long-fingered, flexible, nervously elegant. She was dressed for church, and expected momentarily to see the Clutters' Chevrolet, for she, too, always attended services chaperoned by the Clutter family. Instead, the Ewalts arrived to tell their peculiar tale.

But Susan knew no explanation, nor did her mother, who said, 'If there was some change of plan, why, I'm sure they would have telephoned. Susan, why don't you call the house? They *could* be asleep – I suppose.'

'So I did,' said Susan, in a statement made at a later date. 'I called the house and let the phone ring – at least, I had the *impression* it was ringing – oh, a minute or more. Nobody answered, so Mr Ewalt suggested that we go to the house and try to 'wake them up'. But when we got there – I didn't want to do it. Go inside the house. I was frightened, and I don't know why, because it never occurred to me – well, something like that just doesn't. But the sun was so bright, everything looked too bright and quiet. And then I saw that all the cars were there, even Kenyon's old coyote wagon. Mr Ewalt was wearing work clothes; he had mud on his boots; he felt he wasn't properly dressed to go calling on the Clutters. Especially since he never had. Been in the house, I mean. Finally, Nancy said she would go with me. We went around to the kitchen door, and, of course, it wasn't locked; the only person who ever locked doors around there was Mrs Helm, the family never did. We walked in, and I saw right away that the Clutters hadn't eaten breakfast; there were no dishes, nothing on the stove. Then I noticed something funny: Nancy's purse. It was lying on the floor, sort of open. We passed on through the dining-room, and stopped at the bottom of the stairs. Nancy's room is just at the top. I called her name, and started up the stairs, and Nancy Ewalt followed. The sound of our footsteps frightened me more than anything, they were so loud and everything else was so silent. Nancy's door was open. The curtains hadn't been drawn, and the room was full of sunlight. I don't remember screaming. Nancy Ewalt says I did – screamed and screamed. I only remember Nancy's Teddy bear staring at me. And Nancy. And running. . . .'

In the interim, Mr Ewalt had decided that perhaps he ought not to have allowed the girls to enter the house alone. He was getting out of the car to go after them when he heard the screams, but before he could reach the house, the girls were running towards him. His daughter shouted, 'She's dead!' and flung herself into his arms. 'It's true, Daddy! Nancy's dead!'

Susan turned on her. 'No, she isn't. And don't you say it. Don't you dare. It's only a nosebleed. She has them all the time, terrible nosebleeds, and that's all it is.'

'There's too much blood. There's blood on the walls. You didn't really look.'

'I couldn't make head nor tails,' Mr Ewalt subsequently testified. 'I thought maybe the child was hurt. It seemed to me the first thing to do was call an ambulance. Miss Kidwell – Susan – she told me there was a telephone in the kitchen. I found it, right where she said. But the receiver was off the hook, and when I picked it up, I saw the line had been cut.'

Larry Hendricks, a teacher of English, aged twenty-seven, lived on the top floor of the Teacherage. He wanted to write, but his apartment was not the ideal lair for a would-be author. It was smaller than the Kidwells', and, moreover, he shared it with a wife, three active children, and a perpetually functioning television set. ('It's the only way we can keep the kids pacified.') Though as yet unpublished, young Hendricks, a he-mannish ex-sailor from Oklahoma who smokes a pipe and has a moustache and a crop of untamed black hair, at least looks literary – in fact, remarkably like youthful photographs of the writer he most admires, Ernest Hemingway. To supplement his teacher's salary, he also drove a school bus.

'Sometimes I cover sixty miles a day,' he said to an acquaintance. 'Which doesn't leave much time for writing. Except Sundays. Now, *that* Sunday, November fifteenth, I was sitting up here in the apartment going through the papers. Most of my ideas for stories, I get them out of the newspapers – you know? Well, the TV was on and the kids were kind of lively, but even so I could hear *voices*. From downstairs. Down at Mrs Kidwell's. But I didn't figure it was my concern, since I was new here – only came to Holcomb when school began. But then Shirley – she'd been out hanging up some clothes – my wife, Shirley, rushed in and said, "Honey, you better go downstairs. They're all hysterical." The two girls – now, they really were hysterical. Susan never has got over it. Never will, ask me. And poor Mrs Kidwell. Her health's not too good, she's high-strung to begin with. She kept saying – but it was only later I understood what she meant – she kept saying, "Oh Bonnie, Bonnie, what happened? You were so happy, you told me it was all over, you said you'd never be sick again." Words to that effect. Even Mr Ewalt, he was about as worked up as a man like that ever gets. He had the sheriff's office on the phone – the Garden City sheriff – and he was telling him that there was "something radically wrong over at the Clutter place". The sheriff promised to come straight out, and Mr Ewalt said fine, he'd meet him on the highway. Shirley came downstairs to sit with the women, try and calm them – as if anybody could. And I went with Mr Ewalt – drove with him out to the highway to wait for Sheriff Robinson. On the way, he told me what had happened. When he came to the part about finding the wires cut, right then I thought, Uh-uh, and decided I'd better keep my eyes open. Make a note of every detail. In case I was ever called on to testify in court.

'The sheriff arrived; it was nine thirty-five – I looked at my watch. Mr Ewalt waved at him to follow our car, and we drove out to the Clutters'. I'd never been there before, only seen it from a distance. Of course, I knew the family. Kenyon was in my sophomore English class, and I'd directed Nancy in the *Tom Sawyer* play. But they were such exceptional, unassuming kids you wouldn't have known they were rich or lived in such a big house – and the trees, the lawn, everything so tended and cared for. After we got there, and the sheriff had heard Mr Ewalt's story, he radioed his office and told them to send reinforcements, and an ambulance. Said, "There's been some kind of accident." Then we went in the house, the three of us. Went through the kitchen saw a lady's purse lying on the floor, and the phone where the wires had been cut. The sheriff was wearing a hip pistol, and when we started up the stairs, going to Nancy's room, I noticed he kept his hand on it, ready to draw.

'Well, it was pretty bad. That wonderful girl – but you would never have known her. She'd been shot in the back of the head with a shotgun held maybe two inches away. She was lying on her side, facing the wall, and the wall was covered with blood. The bedcovers were drawn up to her shoulders. Sheriff Robinson, he pulled them back, and we saw that she was wearing a bathrobe, pyjamas, socks, and slippers – like, whenever it happened, she hadn't gone to bed yet. Her hands were tied behind her, and her ankles were roped together with the kind of cord you see on Venetian blinds. Sheriff said, "Is this Nancy Clutter?" – he'd never seen the child before. And I said, "Yes. Yes, that's Nancy."

'We stepped back into the hall, and looked around. All the other doors were closed. We opened one, and that turned out to be a bathroom. Something about it seemed wrong. I decided it was because of the chair – a sort of dining-room chair, that looked out of place in a bathroom. The next door – we all agreed it must be Kenyon's room. A lot of boy-stuff around. And I recognized Kenyon's glasses – saw them on a bookshelf beside the bed. But the bed was empty, though it looked as if it had been slept in. So we walked to the end of the hall, the last door, and there, on her bed, that's where we found Mrs Clutter. She'd been tied, too. But differently – with her hands in front of her, so that she looked as though she were praying – and in one hand she was holding, *gripping*, a handkerchief. Or was it Kleenex? The cord around her wrists ran down to her ankles, which were bound together, and then ran down to the bottom of the bed, where it was tied to the footboard – a very complicated, artful piece of work. Think how long it took to do! And her lying there, scared out of her wits. Well, she was wearing some jewellery, two rings – which is one of the reasons why I've always discounted robbery as a motive – and a robe, and a white nightgown, and white socks. Her mouth had been taped with adhesive, but she'd been shot point-blank in the side of the head, and the blast – the impact – had ripped the tape loose. Her eyes were open. Wide open. As though she were still looking at the killer. Because she must have had to watch him do it – aim the gun. Nobody said anything. We were too stunned. I remember the sheriff searched around to see if he could find the discharged cartridge. But whoever had done it was much too smart and cool to have left behind any clues like that.

'Naturally, we were wondering where was Mr Clutter? And Kenyon? Sheriff said, "Let's try downstairs." The first place we tried was the master bedroom – the room where Mr Clutter slept. The bedcovers were drawn back, and lying there, towards the foot of the bed, was a billfold with a mess of cards spilling out of it, like somebody had shuffled through them hunting something particular – a note, an I.O.U., who knows? The fact that there wasn't any money in it didn't signify one way or the other. It was Mr Clutter's billfold, and he never did carry cash. Even I knew that, and I'd only been in Holcomb a little more than two months. Another thing I knew was that neither Mr Clutter nor Kenyon could see a darn without his glasses. And there were Mr Clutter's glasses sitting on a bureau. So I figured, wherever they were, they weren't there of their own accord. We looked all over, and everything was just as it should be – no sign of a struggle, nothing disturbed. Except the office, where the telephone was off the hook, and the wires cut, same as in the kitchen. Sheriff Robinson, he found some shotguns in a closet, and sniffed them to see if they had been fired recently. Said they hadn't, and – I never saw a more bewildered man – said, "Where the devil can Herb *be*?" About then we heard footsteps. Coming up the stairs from the basement. "Who's that?" said the sheriff, like he was ready to shoot. And a voice said, "It's me, Wendle." Turned out to be Wendle Meier, the undersheriff. Seems he had come to the house and hadn't seen us, so he'd gone investigating down in the basement. The sheriff told him – and it was sort of pitiful: "Wendle, I don't know what to make of it. There's two bodies upstairs." "Well," he said, Wendle did, "there's another one down here." So we followed him down to the basement. Or playroom, I guess you'd call it. It wasn't dark – there were windows that let in plenty of light. Kenyon was over in a corner, lying on a couch. He was gagged with adhesive tape and bound hand and foot, like the mother – the same intricate process of the cord leading from the hands to the feet, and finally tied to an arm of the couch. Somehow he haunts me the most, Kenyon does. I think it's because he was the most recognizable, the one that looked the most like himself – even though he'd been shot in the face, directly, head-on. He was wearing a T-shirt and blue jeans, and he was barefoot – as though he'd dressed in a hurry, just put on the first thing that came to hand. His head was propped by a couple of pillows, like they'd been stuffed under him to make an easier target.

'Then the sheriff said, "Where's this go to?" Meaning another door there in the basement. Sheriff led the way, but inside you couldn't see your hand until Mr Ewalt found the light switch. It was a furnace room, and very warm. Around here, people just install a gas furnace and pump the gas smack out of the ground. Doesn't cost them a nickel – that's why all the houses are overheated. Well, I took one look at Mr Clutter, and it was hard to look again. I knew plain shooting couldn't account for that much blood. And I wasn't wrong. He'd been shot, all right, the same as Kenyon – with the gun held right in front of his face. But probably he was dead before he was shot. Or, anyway, dying. Because his throat had been cut, too. He was wearing striped pyjamas – nothing else. His mouth was taped; the tape had been wound plumb around his head. His ankles were tied together, but not his hands – or, rather, he'd managed, God knows how, maybe in rage or pain, to break the cord binding his hands. He sprawled in front of the furnace. On a big cardboard box that looked as though it had been laid there specially. A mattress box. Sheriff said, "Look here, Wendle." What he was pointing at was a blood-stained footprint. On the mattress box. A half-sole footprint with circles – two holes in the centre like a pair of eyes. Then one of us – Mr Ewalt? I don't recall – pointed out something else. A thing I can't get out of my mind. There was a steampipe overhead, and knotted to it, dangling from it, was a piece of cord – the kind of cord the killer had used. Obviously, at some point Mr Clutter had been tied there, strung up by his hands, then cut down. But why? To torture him? I don't guess we'll ever know. Ever know who did it, or why, or what went on in that house that night.

'After a bit, the house began to fill up. Ambulances arrived, and the coroner, and the Methodist minister, a police photographer, state troopers, fellows from the radio and the newspaper. Oh, a bunch. Most of them had been called out of church, and acted as though they were still there. Very quiet. Whispery. It was like nobody could believe it. A state trooper asked me did I have any official business there, and said if not, then I'd better leave. Outside, on the lawn, I saw the undersheriff talking to a man – Alfred Stoecklein, the hired man. Seems Stoecklein lived not a hundred yards from the Clutter house, with nothing between his place and theirs except a barn. But he was saying as to how he hadn't heard a sound – said, "I didn't know a thing about it till five minutes ago, when one of my kids come running in and told us the sheriff was here. The Missis and me, we didn't sleep two hours last night, was up and down the whole time, on account of we got a sick baby. But the only thing we heard about ten-thirty, quarter to eleven, I heard a car drive away, and I made the remark to Missis, 'There goes Bob Rupp.'"' I started walking home, and on the way, about halfway down the lane, I saw Kenyon's old collie, and that dog was scared. Stood there with its tail between its legs, didn't bark or move. And seeing the dog – somehow that made me *feel* again. I'd been too dazed, too numb, to feel the full viciousness of it. The suffering. The horror. They were dead. a whole family. Gentle, kindly people, people *I* knew – *murdered*. You had to believe it, because it was really true.'

Eight non-stop passenger trains hurry through Holcomb every twenty-four hours. Of these, two pick up and deposit mail – an operation that, as the person in charge of it fervently explains, has its tricky side. 'Yessir, you've got to keep on your toes. Them trains come through here, sometimes they're going a hundred miles an hour. The breeze alone, why, it's enough to knock you down. And when those mail sacks come flying out – sakes alive! It's like playing tackle on a football team: Wham! *Wham!* WHAM! Not that I'm complaining, mind you. It's honest work, *government* work, and it keeps me young.' Holcomb's mail messenger, Mrs Sadie Truitt – or Mother Truitt, as the townspeople call her – does seem younger than her years, which amount to seventy-five. A stocky, weathered widow who wears babushka bandannas and cowboy boots ('Most comfortable things you can put on your feet, soft as a loon feather'), Mother Truitt is the oldest native-born Holcomite. 'Time was wasn't anybody here wasn't my kin. Them days, we called this place Sherlock. Then along came this stranger. By the name Holcomb. A *hog* raiser, he was. Made money, and decided the town ought to be called after him. Soon as it was, what did he do? Sold out. Moved to California. Not us. I was born here, my children was born here. And! Here! We! Are!' One of her children is Mrs Myrtle Clare, who happens to be the local postmistress. 'Only don't go thinking that's how I got this position with the government. Myrt didn't even want me to have it. But it's a job you *bid* for. Goes to whoever puts in the lowest bid. And I always do – so low a caterpillar could peak over it. Ha-ha! That sure does rile the boys. Lots of boys would like to be mail messenger, yes*sir*. But I don't know how much they'd like it when the snow's high as old Mr Primo Carnera, and the wind's blowing blue-hard, and those sacks come sailing – Ugh! Wham!'

In Mother Truitt's profession Sunday is a workday like any other. On November 15, while she was waiting for the westbound ten-thirty-two, she was astonished to see two ambulances cross the railroad tracks and turn towards the Clutter property. The incident provoked her into doing what she had never done before – abandon her duties. Let the mail fall where it may, this was news that Myrt must hear at once.

The people of Holcomb speak of their post office as 'the Federal Building', which seems rather too substantial a title to confer on a draughty and dusty shed. The ceiling leaks, the floorboards wobble, the mailboxes won't shut, the light bulbs are broken, the clock has stopped. 'Yes, it's a disgrace,'

agrees the caustic, somewhat original, and entirely imposing lady who presides over this litter. 'But the stamps work,
don't they? Anyhow, what do I care? Back here in *my* part
is real cosy. I've got my rocker, and a nice wood stove, and
a coffee pot, and plenty to read.'

Mrs Clare is a famous figure in Finney County. Her celeb-
rity derives not from her present occupation but a previous
one – dancehall hostess, an incarnation not indicated by
her appearance. She is a gaunt trouser-wearing, woollen-
shirted, cowboy-booted, ginger-coloured, gingery-tempered
woman of unrevealed age ('That's for me to know, and you
to guess') but promptly revealed opinions, most of which
are announced in a voice of rooster-crow altitude and pene-
tration. Until 1955 she and her late husband operated the
Holcomb Dance Pavilion, an enterprise that owing to its
uniqueness in the area, attracted from a hundred miles
around a fast-drinking, fancy-stepping clientele, whose behaviour, in turn, attracted the interest of the sheriff now
and then. 'We had some tough times, all right,' says Mrs
Clare, reminiscing. 'Some of those bowlegged country boys,
you give 'em a little hooch and they're like redskins – want
to scalp everything in sight. Course, we only sold setups,
never the hard stuff itself. Wouldn't have, even if it was legal.
My husband, Homer Clare, he didn't hold with it; neither
did I. One day Homer Clare – he passed on seven months
and twelve days ago today, after a five-hour operation out
in Oregon – he said to me, "Myrt, we've lived all our lives in
hell, now we're going to die in heaven." The next day we
closed the dance hall. I've never regretted it. Oh, along at
first I missed being a night owl – the tunes, the jollity. But
now that Homer's gone, I'm just glad to do my work here
at the Federal Building. Sit a spell. Drink a cup of coffee.'

In fact, on that Sunday morning Mrs Clare had just
poured herself a cup of coffee from a freshly brewed pot
when Mother Truitt returned.

'Myrt!' she said, but could say no more until she had
caught her breath. 'Myrt, there's two ambulances gone to
the Clutters'.'

Her daughter said, 'Where's the ten-thirty-two?'

'Ambulances. Gone to the Clutters' – '

'Well, what about it? It's only Bonnie. Having one of her spells. Where's the ten-thirty-two?'

Mother Truitt subsided; as usual, Myrt knew the answer, was enjoying the last word. Then a thought occurred to her. 'But, Myrt, if it's only Bonnie, why would there be *two* ambulances?'

A sensible question, as Mrs Clare, an admirer of logic, though a curious interpreter of it, was driven to admit. She said she would telephone Mrs Helm. 'Mabel will know,' she said.

The conversation with Mrs Helm lasted several minutes, and was most distressing to Mother Truitt, who could hear nothing of it except the non-committal monosyllabic responses of her daughter. Worse, when the daughter hung up, she did not quench the old woman's curiosity; instead, she placidly drank her coffee, went to her desk, and began to postmark a pile of letters.

'Myrt,' Mother Truit said. 'For heaven's sake. What did Mabel *say*?'

'I'm not surprised,' Mrs Clare said. 'When you think how Herb Clutter spent his whole life in a hurry, rushing in here to get his mail with never a minute to say good-morning-and-thank-you-dog, rushing around like a chicken with its head off – joining clubs, running everything, getting jobs maybe other people wanted. And now look – it's all caught up with him. Well, he won't be rushing *any* more.'

'Why, Myrt? Why won't he?'

Mrs Clare raised her voice. 'BECAUSE HE'S DEAD. And Bonnie, too. And Nancy. And the boy. Somebody shot them.'

'Myrt – don't say things like that. Who shot them?'

Without a pause in her postmarking activities, Mrs Clare replied, 'The man in the airplane. The one Herb sued for crashing into his fruit trees. If it wasn't him, maybe it was you. Or somebody across the street. All the neighbours are rattlesnakes. Varmints looking for a chance to slam the door in your face. It's the same the whole world over. You know that.'

'I don't,' said Mother Truitt, who put her hands over her ears. 'I don't know any such thing.'

'Varmints.'

'I'm scared, Myrt.'

'Of what? When your time comes, it comes. And tears won't save you.' She had observed that her mother had begun to shed a few. 'When Homer died, I used up all the fear I had in me, and all the grief, too. If there's somebody loose around here that wants to cut my throat, I wish him luck. What difference does it make? It's all the same in eternity. Just remember: If one bird carried every grain of sand, grain by grain, across the ocean, by the time he got them all on the other side, that would only be the beginning of eternity. So blow your nose.'

The grim information, announced from church pulpits, distributed over telephone wires, publicized by Garden City's radio station, KIUL ('A tragedy, unbelievable and shocking beyond words, struck four members of the Herb Clutter family late Saturday night or early today. Death, brutal and without apparent motive ...'), produced in the average recipient a reaction nearer that of Mother Truitt than that of Mrs Clare: amazement, shading into dismay; a shallow horror sensation that cold springs of personal fear swiftly deepened.

Hartman's Café, which contains four roughly made tables and a lunch counter, could accommodate but a fraction of the frightened gossips, mostly male, who wished to gather there. The owner, Mrs Bess Hartman, a sparsely fleshed, unfoolish lady with bobbed grey-and-gold hair and bright, authoritative green eyes, is a cousin of Postmistress Clare, whose style of candour Mrs Hartman can equal, perhaps surpass. 'Some people say I'm a tough old bird, but the Clutter business sure took the fly out of me,' she later said to a friend. 'Imagine anybody pulling a stunt like that! Time I heard it, when everybody was pouring in here talking all kinds of wild-eyed stuff, my first thought was Bonnie. Course, it was silly, but we didn't know the facts, and a lot of people thought *maybe* – on account of her spells. Now we don't know what to think. It must have been a grudge killing. Done by somebody who knew the house inside out. But who hated the Clutters? I never heard a word against them; they were about as popular as a family can be, and if something like this could happen to *them*, then who's safe, I ask you? One old man sitting here that Sunday, he put his finger right on it, the reason nobody can sleep; he said, "All we've got out here are our friends. There isn't anything else." In a way, that's the worst part of the crime. What a terrible thing when neighbours can't look at each other without kind of wondering! Yes, it's a hard fact to live with, but if they ever do find out who done it, I'm sure it'll be a bigger surprise than the murders themselves.'

Mrs Bob Johnson, the wife of the New York Life Insurance agent, is an excellent cook, but the Sunday dinner she had prepared was not eaten – at least, not while it was warm – for just as her husband was plunging a knife into the roast pheasant, he received a telephone call from a friend. 'And that,' he recalls, rather ruefully, 'was the first I heard of what had happened in Holcomb. I didn't believe it. I couldn't afford to. Lord, I had Clutter's cheque right here in my pocket. A piece of paper worth eighty thousand dollars. If what I'd heard was true. But I thought, It can't be, there must be some mistake, things like that don't *happen*, you don't sell a man a big policy one minute and he's dead the next. Murdered. Meaning double indemnity. I didn't know what to do. I called the manager of our office in Wichita. Told him how I had the cheque but hadn't put it through, and asked what was his advice? Well, it was a *del*icate situation. It appeared that *legally* we weren't obliged to pay. But *morally* – that was another matter. Naturally, we decided to do the moral thing.'

The two persons who benefited by this honourable attitude – Eveanna Jarchow and her sister Beverly, sole heirs to their father's estate – were, within a few hours of the awful discovery, on their way to Garden City, Beverly travelling from Winfield, Kansas, where she had been visiting her fiancé, and Eveanna from her home in Mount Carroll, Illinois. Gradually, in the course of the day, other relatives were notified, among them Mr Clutter's father, his two brothers, Arthur and Clarence, and his sister, Mrs Harry Nelson, all of Larned, Kansas, and a second sister, Mrs Elaine Selsor, of Palatka, Florida. Also, the parents of Bonnie Clutter, Mr and Mrs Arthur B. Fox, who lived in Pasadena, California, and her three brothers – Harold, of Visalia, California; Howard, of Oregon, Illinois; and Glenn, of Kansas City, Kansas. Indeed, the better part of those on the Clutters' Thanksgiving guest list were either telephoned or telegraphed, and the majority set forth at once for what was to be a family reunion not around a groaning board but at the graveside of a mass burial.

At the Teacherage, Wilma Kidwell was forced to control herself in order to control her daughter, for Susan, puffy-eyed, sickened by spasms of nausea, argued, inconsolably insisted, that she must go – must run – the three miles to the Rupp farm. 'Don't you see, Mother?' she said. 'If Bobby just *hears* it? He loved her. We both did. I *have* to be the one to tell him.'

But Bobby already knew. On his way home, Mr Ewalt had stopped at the Rupp farm and consulted with his friend Johnny Rupp, a father of eight, of whom Bobby is the third. Together, the two men went to the bunkhouse – a building separate from the farmhouse proper, which is too small to shelter all the Rupp children. The boys live in the bunkhouse, the girls 'at home'. They found Bobby making his bed. He listened to Mr Ewalt, asked no questions, and thanked him for coming. Afterwards, he stood outside in the sunshine. The Rupp property is on a rise, an exposed plateau, from which he could see the harvested, glowing land of River Valley Farm – scenery that occupied him for perhaps an hour. Those who tried to distract him could not. The dinner bell sounded, and his mother called to him to come inside – called until finally her husband said, 'No. I'd leave him alone.'

Larry, a younger brother, also refused to obey the summoning bell. He circled around Bobby, helpless to help but wanting to, even though he was told to 'go away'. Later, when his brother stopped standing and started to walk, heading down the road and across the fields towards Holcomb, Larry pursued him. 'Hey, Bobby. Listen. If we're going somewhere, why don't we go in the car?' His brother wouldn't answer. He was walking with purpose, running, really, but Larry had no difficulty in keeping stride. Though only fourteen, he was the taller of the two, the deeper-chested, the longer-legged, Bobby being, for all his athletic honours, rather less than medium-size – compact but slender, a finely made boy with an open, homely-handsome face. 'Hey, Bobby. Listen. They won't let you see her. It won't do any good.' Bobby turned on him, and said, 'Go back. Go home.' The younger brother fell behind, then followed at a distance. Despite the pumpkin-season temperature, the day's arid glitter, both boys were sweating as they approached a barricade that state troopers had erected at the entrance to River Valley Farm. Many friends of the Clutter family, and strangers from all over Finney County as well, had assembled at the site, but none was allowed past the barricade, which, soon after the arrival of the Rupp brothers, was briefly lifted to permit the exit of four ambulances, the number finally required to remove the victims, and a car filled with men from the sheriff's office – men who, even at that moment, were mentioning the name of Bobby Rupp. For Bobby, as he was to learn before nightfall, was their principal suspect.

From her parlour window, Susan Kidwell saw the white cortège glide past, and watched until it had rounded the corner and the unpaved street's easily airborne dust had landed again. She was still contemplating the view when Bobby, shadowed by his large little brother, became a part of it, a wobbly figure headed her way. She went out on the porch to meet him. She said, 'I wanted so much to tell you.' Bobby began to cry. Larry lingered at the edge of the Teacherage yard, hunched against a tree. He couldn't remember ever seeing Bobby cry, and he didn't want to, so he lowered his eyes.

Far off, in the town of Olathe, in a hotel room where window shades darkened the midday sun, Perry lay sleeping with a grey portable radio murmuring beside him. Except for taking off his boots, he had not troubled to undress. He had merely fallen face down across the bed, as though sleep were a weapon that had struck him from behind. The boots, black and silver-buckled, were soaking in a washbasin filled with warm, vaguely pink-tinted water.

A few miles north, in the pleasant kitchen of a modest farmhouse, Dick was consuming a Sunday dinner. The others at the table – his mother, his father, his younger brother – were not conscious of anything uncommon in his manner. He had arrived home at noon, kissed his mother, readily replied to questions his father put concerning his supposed overnight trip to Fort Scott, and sat down to eat, seeming quite his ordinary self. When the meal was over, the three male members of the family settled in the parlour to watch a televised basketball game. The broadcast had only begun when the father was startled to hear Dick snoring; as he remarked to the younger boy, he never thought he'd live to see the day when Dick would rather sleep than watch basketball. But, of course, he did not understand how very tired Dick was, did not know that his dozing son had, among other things, driven over eight hundred miles in the past twenty-four hours.

2

Persons Unknown

THAT Monday, the sixteenth of November, 1959, was still another fine specimen of pheasant weather on the high wheat plains of western Kansas – a day gloriously bright-skied, as glittery as mica. Often, on such days in years past, Andy Erhart had spent long pheasant-hunting afternoons at River Valley Farm, the home of his good friend Herb Clutter, and often, on these sporting expeditions, he'd been accompanied by three more of Herb's closest friends: Dr J. E. Dale, a veterinarian; Carl Myers, a dairy owner; and Everett Ogburn, a businessman. Like Erhart, the superintendent of the Kansas State University Agricultural Experiment Station, all were prominent citizens of Garden City.

Today this quartet of old hunting companions had once again gathered to make the familiar journey, but in an unfamiliar spirit and armed with odd, non-sportive equipment – mops and pails, scrubbing brushes, and a hamper heaped with rags and strong detergents. They were wearing their oldest clothes. For, feeling it their duty, a Christian task, these men had volunteered to clean certain of the fourteen rooms in the main house at River Valley Farm: rooms in which four members of the Clutter family had been murdered by, as their death certificates declared, 'a person or persons unknown'.

Erhart and his partners drove in silence. One of them later remarked, 'It just shut you up. The strangeness of it. Going out there, where we'd always had such a welcome.' On the present occasion a highway patrolman welcomed them. The patrolman, guardian of a barricade that the authorities had erected at the entrance to the farm, waved them on, and they drove a half-mile more, down the elm-shaded lane leading to the Clutter house. Alfred Stoecklein, the only employee who actually lived on the property, was waiting to admit them.

They went first to the furnace room in the basement, where the pyjama-clad Mr Clutter had been found sprawled atop the cardboard mattress box. Finishing there, they moved on to the playroom in which Kenyon had been shot to death. The couch, a relic that Kenyon had rescued and mended and that Nancy had slip-covered and piled with mottoed pillows, was a blood-splashed ruin; like the mattress box, it would have to be burned. Gradually, as the cleaning party progressed from the basement to the second-floor bedrooms where Nancy and her mother had been murdered in their beds, they acquired additional fuel for the impending fire – blood-soiled bedclothes, mattresses, a bed-side rug, a Teddy-bear doll.

Alfred Stoecklein, not usually a talkative man, had much to say as he fetched hot water and otherwise assisted in the cleaning-up. He wished 'folks would stop yappin' and try to understand' why he and his wife, though they lived scarcely a hundred yards from the Clutter home, had heard 'nary a nothin'' – not the slighest echo of gun thunder – of the violence taking place. 'Sheriff and all them fellas been out here fingerprintin' and scratchin' around, they got good sense, *they* understand how it was. How come we didn't hear. For one thing, the wind. A west wind, like it was, would carry the sound t'other way. Another thing, there's that big milo barn 'tween this house and our'n. That old barn 'ud soak up a lotta racket 'fore it reached us. And did you ever think of this? Him that done it, he must've *knowed* we wouldn't hear. Else he wouldn't have took the chance – shootin' off a shotgun four times in the middle of the night! Why, he'd be crazy. Course, you might say he must be crazy anyhow. To go doing what he did. But my opinion, him that done it had it figured out to the final T. He *knowed*. And there's one thing I know, too. Me and the Missis, we've slept our last night on this place. We're movin' to a house alongside the highway.'

The men worked from noon to dusk. When the time came to burn what they had collected, they piled it on a pickup truck and, with Stoecklein at the wheel, drove deep into the farm's north field, a flat place full of colour, though a single

colour – the shimmering tawny yellow of November wheat
stubble. There they unloaded the truck and made a pyra-
mid of Nancy's pillows, the bedclothes, the mattresses, the
playroom couch; Stoecklein sprinkled it with paraffin and
struck a match.

Of those present, none had been closer to the Clutter
family than Andy Erhart. Gentle, genially dignified, a
scholar with work-calloused hands and sunburned neck,
he'd been a classmate of Herb's at Kansas State University.
'We were friends for thirty years,' he said some time afterwards, and during those decades Erhart had seen his
friend evolve from a poorly paid County Agricultural Agent
into one of the region's most widely known and respected
farm ranchers: 'Everything Herb had, he earned – with the
help of God. He was a modest man but a proud man, as he
had a right to be. He raised a fine family. He made something of his life.' But that life, and what he'd made of it –
how could it happen, Erhart wondered as he watched the
bonfire catch. How was it possible that such effort, such
plain virtue, could overnight be reduced to this – smoke,
thinning as it rose and was received by the big, annihilat-
ing sky?

The Kansas Bureau of Investigation, a state-wide organization with headquarters in Topeka, had a staff of nineteen experienced detectives scattered through the state, and
the services of these men are available whenever a case
seems beyond the competence of local authorities. The
Bureau's Garden City representative, and the agent responsible for a sizeable portion of western Kansas, is a lean and
handsome fourth-generation Kansan of forty-seven named
Alvin Adams Dewey. It was inevitable that Earl Robinson,
the sheriff of Finney County, should ask Al Dewey to take
charge of the Clutter case. Inevitable, and appropriate. For
Dewey, himself a former sheriff of Finney County (from
1947 to 1955) and, prior to that, a Special Agent of the F.B.I.
(between 1940 and 1945 he had served in New Orleans, in San
Antonio, in Denver, in Miami, and in San Francisco), was
professionally qualified to cope with even as intricate an

affair as the apparently motiveless, all but clueless Clutter murders. Moreover, his attitude towards the crime made it, as he later said, 'a personal proposition'. He went on to say that he and his wife 'were real fond of Herb and Bonnie', and 'saw them every Sunday at church, visited a lot back and forth', adding, 'But even if I hadn't known the family, and liked them so well, I wouldn't feel any different. Because I've seen some bad things, I sure as hell have. But nothing so vicious as this. However long it takes, it may be the rest of my life, I'm going to know what happened in that house: the why and the who.'

Towards the end, a total of eighteen men were assigned to the case full time, among them three of the K.B.I.'s ablest investigators – Special Agents Harold Nye, Roy Church, and Clarence Duntz. With the arrival in Garden City of this trio, Dewey was satisfied that 'a strong team' had been assembled. 'Somebody better watch out,' he said.

The sheriff's office is on the third floor of the Finney County courthouse, an ordinary stone-and-cement building standing in the centre of an otherwise attractive tree-filled square. Nowadays, Garden City, which was once a rather raucous frontier town, is quite subdued. On the whole, the sheriff doesn't do much business, and his office, three sparsely furnished rooms, is ordinarily a quiet place popular with courthouse idlers; Mrs Edna Richardson, his hospitable secretary, usually has a pot of coffee going and plenty of time to 'chew the fat'. Or did, until, as she complained, 'this Clutter thing came along', bringing with it 'all these out-of-towners, all this *news*paper fuss'. The case, then commanding headlines as far east as Chicago, as far west as Denver, had indeed lured to Garden City a considerable press corps.

On Monday, at midday, Dewey held a press conference in the sheriff's office. 'I'll talk facts but not theories,' he informed the assembled journalists. 'Now, the big fact here, the thing to remember, is we're not dealing with one murder but four. And we don't know which of the four was the main target. The primary victim. It could have been Nancy or Kenyon, or either of the parents. Some people say, Well, it

must have been Mr Clutter. Because his throat was cut; he
was the most abused. But that's theory, not fact. It would
help if we knew in what order the family died, but the coroner can't tell us that; he only knows the murders happened some time between eleven p.m. Saturday and two
a.m. Sunday.' Then, responding to questions, he said no,
neither of the women had been 'sexually molested', and no,
as far as was presently known, nothing had been stolen
from the house, and yes, he did think it a 'queer coincidence'
that Mr Clutter should have taken out a forty-thousand-
dollar life-insurance policy, with double indemnity, within
eight hours of his death. However, Dewey was 'pretty darn
sure' that no connexion existed between this purchase and
the crime; how could there be one, when the only persons
who benefited financially were Mr Clutter's two surviving
children, the elder daughters, Mrs Donald Jarchow and
Miss Beverly Clutter? And yes, he told the reporters, he did
have an opinion on whether the murders were the work of
one man or two, but he preferred not to disclose it.

Actually, at this time, on this subject, Dewey was un-
decided. He still entertained a pair of opinions – or, to use
his word, 'concepts' – and, in reconstructing the crime, had
developed both a 'single-killer concept' and a 'double-killer
concept'. In the former, the murderer was thought to be a
friend of the family, or, at any rate, a man with more than
casual knowledge of the house and its inhabitants – someone who knew that the doors were seldom locked, that Mr
Clutter slept alone in the master bedroom on the ground
floor, that Mrs Clutter and the children occupied separate
bedrooms on the second floor. This person, so Dewey imagined, approached the house on foot, probably around
midnight. The windows were dark, the Clutters asleep, and
as for Teddy, the farm's watchdog – well, Teddy was fam-
ously gun-shy. He would have cringed at the sight of the
intruder's weapon, whimpered, and crept away. On entering the house, the killer first disposed of the telephone in-
stallations – one in Mr Clutter's office, the other in the
kitchen – and then, after cutting the wires, he went to Mr
Clutter's bedroom and awakened him. Mr Clutter, at the

mercy of the gun-bearing visitor, was forced to obey instructions – forced to accompany him to the second floor, where they aroused the rest of the family. Then, with cord and adhesive tape supplied by the killer, Mr Clutter bound and gagged his wife, bound his daughter (who, inexplicably, had not been gagged), and roped them to their beds. Next, father and son were escorted to the basement, and there Mr Clutter was made to tape Kenyon and tie him to the playroom couch. Then Mr Clutter was taken into the furnace room, hit on the head, gagged, and trussed. Now free to do as he pleased, the murderer killed them one by one, each time carefully collecting the discharged shell. When he had finished, he turned out all the lights and left.

It might have happened that way; it was *just* possible. But Dewey had doubts: 'If Herb had thought his family was in danger, mortal danger, he would have fought like a tiger. And Herb was no ninny – a strong guy in top condition. Kenyon too – big as his dad, bigger, a big-shouldered boy. It's hard to see how one man, armed or not, could have handled the two of them.' Moreover, there was reason to suppose that all four had been bound by the same person: in all four instances the same type of knot, a half-hitch, was used.

Dewey – and the majority of his colleagues, as well – favoured the second hypothesis, which in many essentials followed the first, the important difference being that the killer was not alone but had an accomplice, who helped subdue the family, tape, and tie them. Still, as a theory, this, too, had its faults. Dewey, for example, found it difficult to understand 'how two individuals could reach the same degree of rage, the kind of psychopathic rage it took to commit such a crime'. He went on to explain: 'Assuming the murderer was someone known to the family, a member of this community; assuming that he was an ordinary man, ordinary except that he had a quirk, an insane grudge against the Clutters, or one of the Clutters – where did he find a partner, someone crazy enough to help him? It doesn't add up. It doesn't make sense. But then, come right down to it, nothing does.'

After the news conference, Dewey retired to his office, a room that the sheriff had temporarily lent him. It contained a desk and two straight chairs. The desk was littered with what Dewey hoped would some day constitute courtroom exhibits: the adhesive tape and the yards of cord removed from the victims and now sealed in plastic sacks (as clues, neither item seemed very promising, for both were common-brand products, obtainable anywhere in the United States), and photographs taken at the scene of the crime by a police photographer – twenty blown-up glossy-print pictures of Mr Clutter's shattered skull, his son's demolished face, Nancy's bound hands, her mother's death-dulled, still-staring eyes, and so on. In days to come, Dewey was to spend many hours examining these photographs, hoping that he might 'suddenly see something', that a meaningful detail would declare itself: 'Like those puzzles. The ones that ask, "How many animals can you find in this picture?" In a way, that's what I'm trying to do. Find the hidden animals. I feel they must be there – if only I could see them.' As a matter of fact, one of the photographs, a close-up of Mr Clutter and the mattress box upon which he lay, had already provided a valuable surprise: footprints, the dusty trackings of shoes with diamond-patterned soles. The prints, not noticeable to the naked eye, registered on film; indeed, the delineating glare of a flashbulb had revealed their presence with superb exactness. These prints, together with another footmark found on the same cardboard cover – the bold and bloody impression of a Cat's Paw half sole – were the only 'serious clues' the investigators could claim. Not that they *were* claiming them; Dewey and his team had decided to keep secret the existence of this evidence.

Among the other articles on Dewey's desk was Nancy Clutter's diary. He had glanced through it, no more than that, and now he settled down to an earnest reading of the day-by-day entries, which began on her thirteenth birthday and ended some two months short of her seventeenth; the unsensational confidings of an intelligent child who adored animals, who liked to read, cook, sew, dance, ride horseback – a popular, pretty, virginal girl who thought it 'fun to flirt' but was nevertheless 'only really and truly in love with Bobby'. Dewey read the final entry first. It consisted of three lines written an hour or two before she died: 'Jolene K. came over and I showed her how to make a cherry-pie. Practised with Roxie. Bobby here and we watched TV. Left at eleven.'

Young Rupp, the last person known to have seen the family alive, had already undergone one extensive interrogation, and although he'd told a straightforward story of having passed 'just an ordinary evening' with the Clutters, he was scheduled for a second interview, at which time he was to be given a polygraph test. The plain fact was that the police were not quite ready to dismiss him as a suspect. Dewey himself did not believe the boy had 'anything to do with it'; still, it was true that at this early stage of the investigation, Bobby was the only person to whom a motive, however feeble, could be attributed. Here and there in the diary, Nancy referred to the situation that was supposed to have created the motive: her father's insistence that she and Bobby 'break off', stop 'seeing so much of each other', his objection being that the Clutters were Methodist, the Rupps Catholic – a circumstance that in his view completely cancelled any hope the young couple might have of one day marrying. But the diary notation that most tantalized Dewey was unrelated to the Clutter-Rupp Methodist-Catholic impasse. Rather, it concerned a cat, the mysterious demise of Nancy's favourite pet, Boobs, whom, according to an entry dated two weeks prior to her own death, she'd found 'lying in the barn', the victim, or so she suspected (without saying why), of a poisoner: 'Poor Boobs. I buried him in a special place.' On reading this, Dewey felt it could be 'very important'. If the cat had been poisoned, might not this act have been a small, malicious prelude to the murders? He determined to find the 'special place' where Nancy had buried her pet, even though it meant combing the vast whole of River Valley Farm.

While Dewey was occupying himself with the diary, his principal assistants, the Agents Church, Duntz, and Nye,

were criss-crossing the countryside, talking, as Duntz said,
'to anyone who could tell us anything': the faculty of the
Holcomb School, where both Nancy and Kenyon had been
honour-roll, straight-A students; the employees of River
Valley Farm (a staff that in spring and summer sometimes
amounted to as many as eighteen men but in the present
fallow season consisted of Gerald Van Vleet and three hired
men, plus Mrs Helm); friends of the victims; their neighbours; and, very particularly, their relatives. From far and
near, some twenty of the last had arrived to attend the
funeral services, which were to take place Wednesday
morning.

The youngest of the K.B.I. group, Harold Nye, who was
a peppy little man of thirty-four with restless, distrustful
eyes and a sharp nose, chin, and mind, had been assigned
what he called 'the damned delicate business' of inter-
viewing the Clutter kinfolk: 'It's painful for you and it's
painful for them. When it comes to murder, you can't respect grief. Or privacy. Or personal feelings. You've got to
ask the questions. And some of them cut deep.' But none of
the persons he questioned, and none of the questions he
asked ('I was exploring the emotional background. I
thought the answer might be another woman – a triangle.
Well, consider: Mr Clutter was a fairly young, very healthy
man, but his wife, she was a semi-invalid, she slept in a
separate bedroom ...'), produced useful information; not
even the two surviving daughters could suggest a cause for
the crime. In brief, Nye learned only this: 'Of all the people
in all the world, the Clutters were the least likely to be murdered.'

At the end of the day, when the three agents convened
in Dewey's office, it developed that Duntz and Church had
had better luck than Nye – brother Nye, as the others called
him. (Members of the K.B.I. are partial to nicknames; Duntz
is known as Old Man – unfairly, since he is not quite fifty, a
burly but light-footed man with a broad, tomcat face, and
Church, who is sixty or so, pink-skinned and professorial-
looking, but 'tough', according to his colleagues, and 'the
fastest draw in Kansas', is called Curly, because his head is

partly hairless.) Both men, in the course of their inquiries, had picked up 'promising leads'.

Duntz's story concerned a father and son who shall here be known as John Senior and John Junior. Some years earlier John Senior had conducted with Mr Clutter a minor business transaction, the outcome of which angered John Senior, who felt that Clutter had thrown him 'a queer ball'. Now, both John Senior and his son 'boozed'; indeed, John Junior was an often incarcerated alcoholic. One unfortunate day father and son, full of whisky courage, appeared at the Clutter home intending to 'have it out with Herb'. They were denied the chance, for Mr Clutter, an abstainer aggressively opposed to drink and drunkards, seized a gun and marched them off his property. This discourtesy the Johns had not forgiven; as recently as a month ago, John Senior had told an acquaintance, 'Every time I think of that bastard, my hands start to twitch. I just want to choke him.'

Church's lead was of a similar nature. He, too, had heard of someone admittedly hostile to Mr Clutter: a certain Mr Smith (though that is not his true name), who believed that the squire of River Valley Farm had shot and killed Smith's hunting dog. Church had inspected Smith's farm home and seen there, hanging from a barn rafter, a length of rope tied with the same kind of knot that was used to bind the four Clutters.

Dewey said, 'One of those, maybe that's our deal. A personal thing – a grudge that got out of hand.'

'Unless it was robbery,' said Nye, though robbery as the motive had been much discussed and then more or less dismissed. The arguments against it were good, the strongest being that Mr Clutter's aversion to cash was a county legend; he had no safe and never carried large sums of money. Also, if robbery were the explanation, why hadn't the robber removed the jewellery that Mrs Clutter was wearing – a gold wedding band and a diamond ring? Yet Nye was not convinced: 'The whole setup has that robbery smell. What about Clutter's wallet? Someone left it open and empty on Clutter's bed – I *don't* think it was the owner. And Nancy's purse. The purse was lying on the kitchen floor.

How did it get there? Yes, and not a dime in the house. Well – two dollars. We found two dollars in an envelope on Nancy's desk. And we *know* Clutter cashed a cheque for sixty bucks just the day before. We figure there ought to have been at least fifty of that left. So some say, "Nobody would kill four people for fifty bucks." And say, "Sure, maybe the killer did take the money – but just to try and mislead us, make us think robbery was the reason." I wonder.'

As darkness fell, Dewey interrupted the consultation to telephone his wife, Marie, at their home, and warn her that he wouldn't be home for dinner. She said, 'Yes. All right, Alvin,' but he noticed in her tone an uncharacteristic anxiety. The Deweys, parents of two young boys, had been married seventeen years, and Marie, a Louisiana-born former F.B.I. stenographer, whom he'd met while he was stationed in New Orleans, sympathized with the hardships of his profession – the eccentric hours, the sudden calls summoning him to distant areas of the state.

He said, 'Anything the matter?'

'Not a thing,' she assured him. 'Only, when you come home tonight, you'll have to ring the bell. I've had all the locks changed.'

Now he understood, and said, 'Don't worry, honey. Just lock the doors and turn on the porch light.'

After he'd hung up, a colleague asked, 'What's wrong? Marie scared?'

'Hell, yes,' Dewey said. 'Her, and everybody else.'

Not everybody. Certainly not Holcomb's widowed postmistress, the intrepid Mrs Myrtle Clare, who scorned her fellow townsmen as 'a lily-livered lot, shaking in their boots afraid to shut their eyes', and said of herself, 'This old girl, she's sleeping good as ever. Anybody wants to play a trick on me, let 'em try.' (Eleven months later a gun-toting team of masked bandits took her at her word by invading the post office and relieving the lady of nine hundred and fifty dollars.) As usual, Mrs Clare's notions conformed with those of very few. 'Around here,' according to the proprietor of one Garden City hardware store, 'locks and bolts are the fastest-going item. Folks ain't particular what brand they buy; they just want them to *hold*.' Imagination, of course, can open any door – turn the key and let terror walk right in. Tuesday, at dawn, a carload of pheasant hunters from Colorado – strangers, ignorant of the local disaster – were startled by what they saw as they crossed the prairies and passed through Holcomb: windows ablaze, almost every window in almost every house, and, in the brightly lit rooms, fully clothed people, even entire families, who had sat the whole night wideawake, watchful, listening. Of what were they frightened? 'It might happen again.' That, with variations, was the customary response. However, one woman, a schoolteacher, observed, 'Feeling wouldn't run half so high if this had happened to anyone *except* the Clutters. Anyone *less* admired. Prosperous. Secure. But that family represented everything people hereabouts really value and respect, and that such a thing could happen to them – well, it's like being told there is no God. It makes life seem pointless. I don't think people are so much frightened as they are deeply depressed.'

Another reason, the simplest, the ugliest, was that this hitherto peaceful congregation of neighbours and old friends had suddenly to endure the unique experience of distrusting each other; understandably, they believed that the murderer was among themselves, and, to the last man, endorsed an opinion advanced by Arthur Clutter, a brother of the deceased, who, while talking to journalists in the lobby of a Garden City hotel on November 17, had said, 'When this is cleared up, I'll wager whoever did it was someone within ten miles of where we now stand.'

Approximately four hundred miles east of where Arthur Clutter then stood, two young men were sharing a booth in the Eagle Buffet, a Kansas City diner. One – narrow-faced, and with a blue cat tattooed on his right hand – had polished off several chicken-salad sandwiches and was now eyeing his companion's meal: an untouched hamburger and a glass of root beer in which three aspirin were dissolving.

'Perry, baby,' Dick said, 'you don't want that burger. I'll take it.'

Perry shoved the plate across the table. 'Christ! Can't you let me concentrate?'

'You don't have to read it fifty times.'

The reference was to a front-page article in the 17 November edition of the Kansas City *Star*. Headlined CLUES ARE FEW IN SLAYING OF 4, the article, which was a follow-up of the previous day's initial announcement of the murders, ended with a summarizing paragraph:

'The investigators are left faced with a search for a killer or killers whose cunning is apparent if his (or their) motive is not. For this killer or killers: *Carefully cut the telephone cords of the home's two telephones. *Bound and gagged their victims expertly, with no evidence of a struggle with any of them. *Left nothing in the house amiss, left no indication they had searched for anything with the possible exception of [Clutter's] billfold. *Shot four persons in different parts of the house, calmly picking up the expended shotgun shells. *Arrived and left the home, presumably with the murder weapon, without being seen. *Acted without a motive, if you care to discount an abortive robbery attempt, which the investigators are wont to do.'

' "For this killer or killers," ' said Perry, reading aloud. 'That's incorrect. The grammar is. It ought to be "For this killer or *these* killers." ' Sipping his aspirin-spiked root beer, he went on, 'Anyway, I don't believe it. Neither do you. Own up, Dick. Be honest. You don't believe this no-clue stuff?'

Yesterday, after studying the papers, Perry had put the same question, and Dick, who thought he'd disposed of it ('Look. If those cowboys could make the slightest connexion, we'd have heard the sound of hoofs a hundred miles off'), was bored at hearing it again. Too bored to protest when Perry once more pursued the matter: 'I've always played my hunches. That's why I'm alive today. You know Willie-Jay? He said I was a natural-born "medium", and he knew about things like that, he was interested. He said I had a high degree of "extrasensory perception". Sort of like having built-in radar – you see things before you see them. The outlines of coming events. Take, like, my brother and his wife. Jimmy and his wife. They were crazy about each other, but he was jealous as hell, and he made her so miserable, being jealous and always thinking she was passing it out behind his back, that she shot herself, and the next day Jimmy put a bullet through his head. When it happened – this was 1949, and I was in Alaska with Dad up around Circle City – I told Dad, "Jimmy's dead." A week later we got the news. Lord's truth. Another time, over in Japan, I was helping load a ship, and I sat down to rest a minute. Suddenly a voice inside me said, "Jump!" I jumped I guess maybe ten feet, and just then, right where I'd been sitting, a ton of stuff came crashing down. I could give you a hundred examples. I don't care if you believe me or not. For instance, right before I had my motorcycle accident I saw the whole thing happen: saw it in my mind – the rain, the skid tracks, me lying there bleeding and my legs broken. That's what I've got now. A *pre*monition. Something tells me this is a trap.' He tapped the newspaper. 'A lot of *pre*varications.'

Dick ordered another hamburger. During the past few days he'd known a hunger that nothing – three successive steaks, a dozen Hershey bars, a pound of gumdrops – seemed to interrupt. Perry, on the other hand, was without appetite; he subsisted on root beer, aspirin, and cigarettes. 'No wonder you got leaps,' Dick told him. 'Aw, come on, baby. Get the bubbles out of your blood. We scored. It was perfect.'

'I'm surprised to hear that, all things considered,' Perry said. The quietness of his tone italicized the malice of his reply. But Dick took it, even smiled – and his smile was a skilful proposition. Here, it said, wearing a kid grin, was a very personable character, clean-cut, affable, a fellow any man might trust to shave him.

'O.K.' Dick said. 'Maybe I had some wrong information.'

'Hallelujah.'

'But on the whole it was perfect. We hit the ball right out of the park. It's lost. And it's gonna stay lost. There isn't a single connexion.'

'I can think of one.'

Perry had gone too far. He went further: 'Floyd – is that the name?' A bit below the belt, but then Dick deserved it, his confidence was like a kite that needed reeling in. Nevertheless, Perry observed with some misgiving the symptoms of fury rearranging Dick's expression: jaw, lips, the whole face slackened; saliva bubbles appeared at the corners of his mouth. Well, if it came to a fight, Perry could defend himself. He was short, several inches shorter than Dick, and his runty, damaged legs were unreliable, but he outweighed his friend, was thicker, had arms that could squeeze the breath out of a bear. To prove it, however – have a fight, a real falling-out – was far from desirable. Like Dick or not (and he didn't dislike Dick, though once he'd liked him better, respected him more), it was obvious they could not now safely separate. On that point they were in accord, for Dick had said, 'If we get caught, let's get caught together. Then we can back each other up. When they start pulling the confession crap, saying you said and I said.' Moreover, if he broke with Dick, it meant the end of plans still attractive to Perry, and still, despite recent reverses, deemed possible by both – a skin-diving, treasure-hunting life lived together among islands or along coasts south of the border.

Dick said, '*Mr* Wells!' He picked up a fork. 'It'd be worth it. Like if I was nabbed on a cheque charge, it'd be worth it. Just to get back in there.' The fork came down and stabbed the table. 'Right through the heart, honey.'

'I'm not saying he would,' said Perry, willing to make a concession now that Dick's anger had soared past him and struck elsewhere. 'He'd be too scared.'

'Sure,' said Dick. 'Sure. He'd be too scared.' A marvel, really, the ease with which Dick negotiated changes of mood; in a trice, all trace of meanness, of sullen bravura, had evaporated. He said, 'About that premonition stuff. Tell me this: If you were so damn sure you were gonna crack up, why didn't you call it quits? It wouldn't have happened if you'd stayed off your bike – right?'

That was a riddle that Perry had pondered. He felt he'd

solved it, but the solution, while simple, was also somewhat
hazy: 'No. Because once a thing is set to happen, all you
can do is hope it won't. Or will – depending. As long as you
live, there's always something waiting, and even if it's bad,
and you know it's bad, what can you do? You can't stop
living. Like my dream. Since I was a kid, I've had this same
dream. Where I'm in Africa. A jungle. I'm moving through
the trees towards a tree standing all alone. Jesus, it smells
bad, that tree; it kind of makes me sick, the way it stinks.
Only, it's beautiful to look at – it has blue leaves and diamonds hanging everywhere. Diamonds like oranges. That's
why I'm there – to pick myself a bushel of diamonds. But
I know the minute I try to, the minute I reach up, a snake
is gonna fall on me. A snake that guards the tree. This fat
sonofabitch living in the branches. I know this beforehand,
see? And Jesus, I don't know how to fight a snake. But I
figure, Well, I'll take my chances. What it comes down to is
I want the diamonds more than I'm afraid of the snake. So
I go to pick one, I have the diamond in my hand, I'm pulling
at it, when the snake lands on top of me. We wrestle around,
but he's a slippery sonofabitch and I can't get a hold, he's
crushing me, you can hear my legs cracking. Now comes
the part it makes me sweat even to think about. See, he
starts to swallow me. Feet first. Like going down in quick-
sand.' Perry hesitated. He could not help noticing that
Dick, busy gouging under his fingernails with a fork prong,
was uninterested in his dream.

Dick said, 'So? The snake swallows you? Or what?'

'Never mind. It's not important.' (But it was! The finale
was of great importance, a source of private joy. He'd once
told it to his friend Willie-Jay; he had described to him the
towering bird, the yellow 'sort of parrot'. Of course, Willie-
Jay was different – delicate-minded, 'a saint'. He'd understood. But Dick? Dick might laugh. And that Perry could
not abide: anyone's ridiculing the parrot, which had first
flown into his dreams when he was seven years old, a hated,
hating half-breed child living in a California orphanage
run by nuns – shrouded disciplinarians who whipped him
for wetting his bed. It was after one of these beatings, one

he could never forget ('She woke me up. She had a flashlight, and she hit me with it. Hit me and hit me. And when
the flashlight broke, she went on hitting me in the dark'),
that the parrot appeared, arrived while he slept, a bird
'taller than Jesus, yellow like a sunflower', a warrior-angel
who blinded the nuns with its beak, fed upon their eyes,
slaughtered them as they 'pleaded for mercy', then so gently
lifted him, enfolded him, winged him away to 'paradise'.

As the years went by, the particular torments from which
the bird delivered him altered; others – older children, his
father, a faithless girl, a sergeant he'd known in the Army
– replaced the nuns, but the parrot remained, a hovering
avenger. Thus, the snake, that custodian of the diamond-
bearing tree, never finished devouring him but was itself
always devoured. And afterwards the blessed ascent!
Ascension to a paradise that in one version was merely 'a
feeling', a sense of power, of unassailable superiority – sensations that in another version were transposed into 'A real
place. Like out of a movie. Maybe that's where I *did* see it –
remembered it from a movie. Because where else would
I have seen a garden like that? With white marble steps?
Fountains? And away down below, if you go to the edge of
the garden, you can see the ocean. Terrific! Like around
Carmel, California. The best thing, though – well, it's a long,
long table. You never imagined so much food. Oysters. Tur-
keys. Hot dogs. Fruit you could make into a million fruit
cups. And, listen – it's every bit *free*. I mean, I don't have to
be afraid to touch it. I can eat as much as I want, and it
won't cost a cent. That's how I know where I am.')

Dick said, 'I'm a normal. I only dream about blonde
chicken. Speaking of which, you hear about the nanny goat's
nightmare?' That was Dick – always ready with a dirty
joke on any subject. But he told the joke well, and Perry,
though he was in some measure a prude, could not help
laughing, as always.

Speaking of her friendship with Nancy Clutter, Susan
Kidwell said: 'We were like sisters. At least, that's how I felt
about her – as though she were my sister. I couldn't go to

school – not those first few days. I stayed out of school until after the funeral. So did Bobby Rupp. For a while Bobby and I were always together. He's a nice boy – he has a good heart – but nothing very terrible had ever happened to him before. Like losing anyone he'd loved. And then, on top of it, having to take a lie-detector test. I don't mean he was bitter about that; he realized the police were doing what they had to do. Some hard things, two or three, had already happened to me, but not to him, so it was a shock when he found out maybe life isn't one long basketball game. Mostly, we just drove around in his old Ford. Up and down the highway. Out to the airport and back. Or we'd go to the Cree-Mee – that's a drive-in – and sit in the car, order a Coke, listen to the radio. The radio was always playing; *we* didn't have anything to say ourselves. Except once in a while Bobby said how much he'd loved Nancy, and how he could never care about another girl. Well, I was sure Nancy wouldn't have wanted that, and I told him so. I remember – I think it was Monday – we drove down to the river. We parked on the bridge. You can see the house from there – the Clutter house. And part of the land – Mr Clutter's fruit orchard, and the wheat fields going away. Way off in one of the fields a bonfire was burning; they were burning stuff from the house. Everywhere you looked, there was something to remind you. Men with nets and poles were fishing along the banks of the river, but not fishing for fish. Bobby said they were looking for the weapons. The knife. The gun.

'Nancy loved the river. Summer nights we used to ride double on Nancy's horse, Babe – that old fat grey? Ride straight to the river and right into the water. Then Babe would wade along in the shallow part while we played our flutes and sang. Got cool. I keep wondering, Gosh, what will become of her? Babe. A lady from Garden City took Kenyon's dog. Took Teddy. He ran away – found his way back to Holcomb. But she came and got him again. And I have Nancy's cat – Evinrude. But Babe. I suppose they'll sell her. Wouldn't Nancy hate that? Wouldn't she be *furious*? Another day, the day before the funeral, Bobby and I were sitting by the railroad tracks. Watching the trains go by. Real stupid. Like sheep in a blizzard. When suddenly Bobby woke up and said, "We ought to go see Nancy. We ought to be with her." So we drove to Garden City – went to the Phillips' Funeral Home, there on Main Street. I think Bobby's kid brother was with us. Yes, I'm sure he was. Because I remember we picked him up after school. And I remember he said how there wasn't going to be any school the next day, so all the Holcomb kids could go to the funeral. And he kept telling us what the kids thought. He said the kids were convinced it was the work of "a hired killer". I didn't want to hear about it. Just gossip and talk – everything Nancy despised. Anyway, I don't much care who did it. Somehow it seems beside the point. My friend is gone. Knowing who killed her isn't going to bring her back. What else matters? They wouldn't let us. At the funeral parlour, I mean. They said no one could "view the family". Except the relatives. But Bobby insisted, and finally the undertaker – he knew Bobby, and, I guess, felt sorry for him – he said all right, be quiet about it, but come on in. Now I wish we hadn't.'

The four coffins, which quite filled the small, flower-crowded parlour, were to be sealed at the funeral services – very understandably, for despite the care taken with the appearance of the victims, the effect achieved was disquieting. Nancy wore her dress of cherry-red velvet, her brother a bright plaid shirt; the parents were more sedately attired, Mr Clutter in navy-blue flannel, his wife in navy-blue crêpe; and – and it was this, especially, that lent the scene an awful aura – the head of each was completely encased in cotton, a swollen cocoon twice the size of an ordinary blown-up balloon, and the cotton, because it had been sprayed with a glossy substance, twinkled like Christmas-tree snow.

Susan at once retreated. 'I went outside and waited in the car,' she recalled. 'Across the street a man was raking leaves. I kept looking at him. Because I didn't want to close my eyes. I thought, If I do I'll faint. So I watched him rake leaves and burn them. Watched, without really seeing him. Because all I could see was the dress. I knew it so well. I helped her pick the material. It was her own design, and she sewed it herself. I remember how excited she was the first time she wore it. At a party. All I could see was Nancy's red velvet. And Nancy in it. Dancing.'

The Kansas City *Star* printed a lengthy account of the Clutter funeral, but the edition containing the article was two days old before Perry, lying abed in a hotel room, got around to reading it. Even so, he merely skimmed through, skipped about among the paragraphs: 'A thousand persons, the largest crowd in the five-year history of the First Methodist Church, attended services for the four victims today. ... Several classmates of Nancy's from Holcomb High School wept as the Reverend Leonard Cowan said: "God offers us courage, love and hope even though we walk through the shadows of the valley of death. I'm sure he was with them in their last hours. Jesus has never promised us we would not suffer pain or sorrow but He has always said He would be there to help us bear the sorrow and the pain." ... On the unseasonably warm day, about six hundred persons went to the Valley View Cemetery on the north edge of this city. There, at graveside services, they recited the Lord's Prayer. Their voices, massed together in a low whisper, could be heard throughout the cemetery.'

A thousand people! Perry was impressed. He wondered how much the funeral had cost. Money was greatly on his mind, though not as relentlessly as it had been earlier in the day – a day he'd begun 'without the price of a cat's miaow'. The situation had improved since then; thanks to Dick, he and Dick now possessed 'a pretty fair stake' – enough to get them to Mexico.

Dick! Smooth. Smart. Yes, you had to hand it to him. Christ, it was incredible how he could 'con a guy'. Like the clerk in the Kansas City, Missouri, clothing store, the first of the places Dick had decided to 'hit'. As for Perry, he'd never tried to 'pass a cheque'. He was nervous, but Dick told him, 'All I want you to do is stand there. Don't laugh, and don't be surprised at anything I say. You got to play these things by ear.' For the task proposed, it seemed, Dick had perfect pitch. He breezed in, breezily introduced Perry to the clerk as 'a friend of mine about to get married', and went on, 'I'm his best man. Helping him kind of shop around for the clothes he'll want. Ha-ha, what you might say his – ha-ha – trousseau.' The salesman 'ate it up', and soon Perry, stripped of his denim trousers, was trying on a gloomy suit that the clerk considered 'ideal for an informal ceremony'. After commenting on the customer's oddly proportioned figure the oversized torso supported by the undersized legs – he added, 'I'm afraid we haven't anything that would fit without alteration.' Oh, said Dick, that was O.K., there was plenty of time – the wedding was 'a week tomorrow'. That settled, they then selected a gaudy array of jackets and slacks regarded as appropriate for what was to be, according to Dick, a Florida honeymoon. 'You know the Eden Rock?' Dick said to the salesman. 'In Miami Beach? They got reservations. A present from her folks – two weeks at forty bucks a day. How about that? An ugly runt like him, he's making it with a honey she's not only built but loaded. While guys like you and me, good-lookin' guys ...' The clerk presented the bill. Dick reached in his hip pocket, frowned, snapped his fingers, and said, 'Hot damn! I forgot my wallet.' Which to his partner seemed a ploy so feeble that it couldn't possibly 'fool a day-old nigger'. The clerk, apparently, was not of that opinion, for he produced a blank cheque, and when Dick made it out for eighty dollars more than the bill totalled, instantly paid over the difference in cash.

Outside, Dick said, 'So you're going to get married next week? Well, you'll need a ring.' Moments later, riding in Dick's aged Chevrolet, they arrived at a store named *Best Jewelry*. From there, after purchasing by cheque a diamond engagement ring and a diamond wedding band, they drove to a pawnshop to dispose of these items. Perry was sorry to see them go. He'd begun to half credit the make-believe bride, though in his conception of her, as opposed to Dick's, she was not rich, not beautiful; rather, she was nicely groomed, gently spoken, was conceivably 'a college graduate', in any event 'a very intellectual type' – a sort of girl he'd always wanted to meet but in fact never had.

Unless you counted Cookie, the nurse he'd known when he was hospitalized as a result of his motorcycle accident. A swell kid, Cookie, and she had liked him, pitied him, babied him, inspired him to read 'serious literature' – *Gone with the Wind, This Is My Beloved*. Sexual episodes of a strange and stealthy nature had occurred, and love had been mentioned, and marriage too, but eventually, when his injuries had mended, he'd told her good-bye and given her, by way of explanation, a poem he pretended to have written:

> There's a race of men that don't fit in,
>   A race that can't stay still;
> So they break the hearts of kith and kin;
>   And they roam the world at will.
> They range the field and they rove the flood,
>   And they climb the mountain's crest;
> Theirs is the curse of the gipsy blood,
>   And they don't know how to rest.
> If they just went straight they might go far;
>   They are strong and brave and true;
> But they're always tired of the things that are,
>   And they want the strange and new.

He had not seen her again, or even heard from or of her, yet several years later he'd had her name tattooed on his arm, and once, when Dick asked who 'Cookie' was, he'd said, 'Nobody. A girl I almost married.' (That Dick had been married – married twice – and had fathered three sons was something he envied. A wife, children – those were experiences 'a man ought to have', even if, as with Dick, they didn't 'make him happy or do him any good'.)

The rings were pawned for a hundred and fifty dollars. They visited another jewellery store, Goldman's, and sauntered out of there with a man's gold wristwatch. Next stop, an Elko Camera Store, where they 'bought' an elaborate motion-picture camera. 'Cameras are your best investment,' Dick informed Perry. 'Easiest thing to hock or sell. Cameras and TV sets.' This being the case, they decided to obtain several of the latter, and, having completed the mission, went on to attack a few more clothing emporiums – Sheperd & Foster's, Rothschild's, Shopper's Paradise. By sundown when the stores were closing, their pockets were filled with cash and the car was heaped with saleable, pawnable wares. Surveying this harvest of shirts and cigarette lighters, expensive machinery and cheap cuff-links, Perry felt elatedly tall – now Mexico, a new chance, a 'really living' life. But Dick seemed depressed. He shrugged off Perry's praises ('I mean it, Dick. You were amazing. Half the time I believed you myself'). And Perry was puzzled; he could not fathom why Dick, usually so full of himself, should suddenly, when he had good cause to gloat, be meek, look wilted and sad. Perry said, 'I'll stand you a drink.'

They stopped at a bar. Dick drank three Orange Blossoms. After the third, he abruptly asked, 'What about Dad? I feel – oh, Jesus, he's such a good old guy. And my mother – well, you saw her. What about *them*? Me, I'll be off in Mexico. Or wherever. But they'll be right here when those cheques start to bounce. I know Dad. He'll want to make them good. Like he tried to before. And he can't – he's old and he's sick, he ain't got anything.'

'I sympathize with that,' said Perry truthfully. Without being kind, he was sentimental, and Dick's affection for his parents, his professed concern for them, did indeed touch him. 'But hell, Dick. It's very simple,' Perry said. '*We* can pay off the cheques. Once we're in Mexico, once we get started down there, we'll make money. Lots of it.'

'How?'

'How?' – what could Dick mean? The question dazed Perry. After all, such a rich assortment of ventures had been discussed. Prospecting for gold, skin-diving for sunken treasure – these were but two of the projects Perry had ardently proposed. And there were others. The boat, for instance. They had often talked of a deep-sea-fishing boat, which they would buy, man themselves, and rent to vacationers – this though neither had ever skippered a canoe or hooked a guppy. Then, too, there was quick money to be made chauffeuring stolen cars across South American borders. ('You get paid five hundred bucks a trip,' or so Perry had read somewhere.) But of the many replies he might have made, he chose to remind Dick of the fortune awaiting them on Cocos Island, a land speck off the coast of Costa Rica. 'No fooling, Dick,' Perry said. 'This is authentic. I've got a map. I've got the whole history. It was buried there back in 1821 – Peruvian bullion, jewellery. Sixty million dollars – that's what they say it's worth. Even if we didn't find all of it, even if we found only some of it – Are you with me, Dick?' Heretofore, Dick had always encouraged him, listened attentively to his talk of maps, tales of treasure, but now – and it had not occurred to him before – he wondered if all along Dick had only been *pretending*, just kidding him.

The thought, acutely painful, passed, for Dick, with a wink and a playful jab, said, 'Sure, honey. I'm with you. All the way.'

It was three in the morning, and the telephone rang again. Not that the hour mattered. Al Dewey was wide-awake anyway, and so were Marie and their sons, nine-year-old Paul and twelve-year-old Alvin Adams Dewey, Jr. For who could sleep in a house – a modest one-storey house – where all night the telephone had been sounding every few minutes? As he got out of bed, Dewey promised his wife, 'This time I'll leave it off the hook.' But it was not a promise he dared keep. True, many of the calls came from news-hunting journalists, or would-be humorists, or theorists ('Al? Listen, fella, I've got this deal figured. It's suicide and murder. I happen to *know* Herb was in a bad way financially. He was spread pretty thin. So what does he do? He takes out this big insurance policy, shoots Bonnie and the kids, and kills himself with a bomb. A hand grenade stuffed with buckshot'), or anonymous persons with poison-pen minds ('Know them Ls? Foreigners? Don't work? Give parties? Serve *cock*tails? Where's the money come from? Wouldn't surprise me a darn if they ain't at the roots of this Clutter trouble'), or nervous ladies alarmed by the gossip going around, rumours that knew neither ceiling nor cellar ('Alvin, now, I've known you since you were a boy. And I want you to tell me straight out whether it's so. I loved and respected Mr Clutter, and I *refuse* to believe that that man, that Christian – I refuse to believe he was chasing after women...'). ˙

But most of those who telephoned were responsible citizens wanting to be helpful ('I wonder if you've interviewed Nancy's friend, Sue Kidwell? I was talking to the child, and she said something that struck me. She said the last time she ever spoke to Nancy, Nancy told her Mr Clutter was in a real bad mood. Had been the past three weeks. That she thought he was very worried about something, so worried he'd taken to smoking cigarettes...'). Either that or the callers were people officially concerned – law officers and sheriffs from other parts of the state ('This may be something, may not, but a bartender here says he overheard two fellows discussing the case in terms made it sound like they had a lot to do with it...'). And while none of these conversations had as yet done more than make extra work for the investigators, it was always possible that the next one might be, as Dewey put it, 'the break that brings down the curtain'.

On answering the present call, Dewey immediately heard 'I want to confess.'

He said, 'To whom am I speaking, please?'

The caller, a man, repeated his original assertion, and added, 'I did it. I killed them all.'

'Yes,' said Dewey. 'Now, if I could have your name and address...'

'Oh, no, you don't,' said the man, his voice thick with inebriated indignation. 'I'm not going to tell you anything. Not till I get the reward. You send the reward, then I'll tell you who I am. That's final.'

Dewey went back to bed. 'No, honey,' he said. 'Nothing important. Just another drunk.'

'What did he want?'

'Wanted to confess. Provided we sent the reward first.' (A Kansas paper, the Hutchinson *News*, had offered a thousand dollars for information leading to the solution of the crime.)

'Alvin, are you lighting another cigarette? Honestly, Alvin, can't you at least *try* to sleep?'

He was too tense to sleep, even if the telephone could be silenced – too fretful and frustrated. None of his 'leads' had led anywhere, except, perhaps, down a blind alley towards the blankest of walls. Bobby Rupp? The polygraph machine had eliminated Bobby, and Mr Smith, the farmer who tied rope knots indentical with those used by the murderer – he, too, was a discarded suspect, having established that on the night of the crime he'd been 'off in Oklahoma'. Which left the Johns, father and son, but they had also submitted provable alibis. 'So,' to quote Harold Nye, 'it all adds up to a nice round number. Zero.' Even the hunt for the grave of Nancy's cat had come to nothing.

Nevertheless, there had been one or two meaningful developments. First, while sorting Nancy's clothes, Mrs Elain Selsor, her aunt, had found tucked in the toe of a shoe, a gold wristwatch. Second, accompanied by a K.B.I. agent, Mrs Helm had explored every room at River Valley Farm, toured the house in the expectation that she might notice something awry or absent, and she had. It happened in Kenyon's room. Mrs Helm looked and looked, paced round and round the room with pursed lips, touching this and that – Kenyon's old baseball mitt, Kenyon's mud-spattered work boots, his pathetic abandoned spectacles. All the while she kept whispering, 'Something here is wrong, I feel it, I know it, but I don't know what it is.' And then she did know. 'It's the *radio*! Where is Kenyon's little radio?'

Taken together, these discoveries forced Dewey to consider again the possibility of 'plain robbery' as a motive. Surely that watch had not tumbled into Nancy's shoe by accident? She must, lying there in the dark, have heard sounds – footfalls, perhaps voices – that led her to suppose thieves were in the house, and so believing must have hurriedly hidden the watch, a gift from her father that she treasured. As for the radio, a grey portable made by Zenith – no doubt about it, the radio was gone. All the same, Dewey could not accept the theory that the family had been slaughtered for paltry profit – 'a few dollars and a radio'. To accept it would obliterate his image of the killer – or, rather, killers. He and his associates had definitely decided to pluralize the term. The expert execution of the crimes was proof enough that at least one of the pair commanded an immoderate amount of cool-headed slyness, and was – *must* be – a person too clever to have done such a deed without calculated motive. Then, too, Dewey had become aware of several particulars that reinforced his conviction that at least one of the murderers was emotionally involved with the victims, and felt for them, even as he destroyed them, a certain twisted tenderness. How else explain the mattress box?

The business of the mattress box was one of the things that most tantalized Dewey. Why had the murderers taken the trouble to move the box from the far end of the base-ment room and lay it on the floor in front of the furnace, unless the intention had been to make Mr Clutter more com-fortable – to provide him, while he contemplated the ap-proaching knife, with a couch less rigid than cold cement? And in studying the death-scene photographs Dewey had distinguished other details that seemed to support his notion of a murderer now and again moved by considerate im-pulses. 'Or' – he could never quite find the word he wanted – 'something fussy. And soft. Those bedcovers. Now, what kind of person would do that – tie up two women, the way Bonnie and the girl were tied, and then draw up the bed-covers, *tuck* them in, like sweet dreams and good night? Or the pillow under Kenyon's head. At first I thought maybe the pillow was put there to make his head a simpler target. Now I think, No, it was done for the same reason the mat-tress box was spread on the floor – to make the victim more comfortable.'

But speculations such as these, though they absorbed Dewey, did not gratify him or give him a sense of 'getting somewhere'. A case was seldom solved by 'fancy theories'; he put his faith in facts – 'sweated for and sworn to'. The quantity of facts to be sought and sifted, and the agenda planned to obtain them, promised perspiration aplenty, entailing, as it did, the tracking down, the 'checking out', of hundreds of people, among them all former River Valley Farm employees, friends and family, anyone with whom Mr Clutter had done business, much or little – a tortoise crawl into the past. For, as Dewey had told his team, 'we have to keep going till we know the Clutters better than they ever knew themselves. Until we see the connexion between what we found last Sunday morning and something that happened maybe five years ago. The link. Got to be one. Got to.'

Dewey's wife dozed, but she awakened when she felt him leave their bed, heard him once more answering the telephone, and heard, from the near-by room where her sons slept, sobs, a small boy crying. 'Paul?' Ordinarily, Paul was neither troubled nor troublesome – not a whiner, ever. He was too busy digging tunnels in the backyard or practising to be 'the fastest runner in Finney County'. But at breakfast that morning he'd burst into tears. His mother had not needed to ask him why; she knew that although he understood only hazily the reasons for the uproar round him, he felt endangered by it – by the harassing telephone, and the strangers at the door, and his father's worry-wearied eyes. She went to comfort Paul. His brother, three years older, helped. 'Paul,' he said, 'you take it easy now, and tomorrow I'll teach you to play poker.'

Dewey was in the kitchen; Marie, searching for him, found him there, waiting for a pot of coffee to percolate and with the murder-scene photographs spread before him on the kitchen table – bleak stains, spoiling the table's pretty fruit-patterned oilcloth. (Once he had offered to let her look at the pictures. She had declined. She had said, 'I want to remember Bonnie the way Bonnie was – and all of them.') He said, 'Maybe the boys ought to stay with Mother.' His mother, a widow, lived not far off, in a house she thought too spacious and silent; the grandchildren were always welcome. 'For just a few days. Until – well, until.'

'Alvin, do you think we'll ever get back to normal living?' Mrs Dewey asked.

Their normal life was like this: both worked, Mrs Dewey as an office secretary, and they divided between them the household chores, taking turns at the stove and the sink ('When Alvin was sheriff, I know some of the boys teased him. Used to say, "Lookayonder! Here comes Sheriff Dewey! Tough guy! Totes a six-shooter! But once he gets home, off comes the gun and on goes the apron!"') At that time they were saving to build a house on a farm that Dewey had bought in 1951 – two hundred and forty acres several miles north of Garden City. If the weather was fine, and especially when the days were hot and the wheat was high and ripe, he liked to drive out there and practise his draw – shoot crows, tin cans – or in his imagination roam through the house he hoped to have, and through the garden he meant to plant, and under trees yet to be seeded. He was very certain that some day his own oasis of oaks and elms would stand upon those shadeless plains: '*Some* day. God willing.'

A belief in God and the rituals surrounding that belief – church every Sunday, grace before meals, prayers before bed – were an important part of the Deweys' existence. 'I don't see how anyone can sit down to table without wanting to bless it,' Mrs Dewey once said. 'Sometimes, when I come home from work – well, I'm tired. But there's always coffee on the stove, and sometimes a steak in the icebox. The boys make a fire to cook the steak, and we talk, and tell each other our day, and by the time supper's ready I know we have good cause to be happy and grateful. So I say, Thank you, Lord. Not just because I should – because I want to.'

Now Mrs Dewey said, 'Alvin, answer me. Do you think we'll ever have a normal life again?'

He started to reply, but the telephone stopped him.

The old Chevrolet left Kansas City 21 November, Saturday night. Luggage was lashed to the fenders and roped to the roof; the trunk was so stuffed it could not be shut; inside, on the back seat, two television sets stood, one atop the other. It was a tight fit for the passengers: Dick, who was driving, and Perry, who sat clutching the old Gibson guitar, his most beloved possession. As for Perry's other belongings – a cardboard suitcase, a grey Zenith portable radio, a gallon jug of root-beer syrup (he feared that his favourite beverage might not be available in Mexico), and two big boxes containing books, manuscrips, cherished memorabilia (and hadn't Dick raised hell! Cursed, kicked the boxes, called them 'five hundred pounds of pig slop!') – these, too, were part of the car's untidy interior.

Around midnight they crossed the border into Oklahoma. Perry, glad to be out of Kansas, at last relaxed. Now it was true – they were on their way – On their way, and never coming back – without regret, as far as he was concerned, for he was leaving nothing behind, and no one who might deeply wonder into what thin air he'd spiralled. The same could not be said of Dick. There were those Dick claimed to love: three sons, a mother, a father, a brother – persons he hadn't dared confide his plans to, or bid goodbye, though he never expected to see them again – not in this life.

CLUTTER–ENGLISH VOWS GIVEN IN SATURDAY CEREMONY: that headline, appearing in the social page of the Garden City *Telegram* for 23 November, surprised many of its readers. It seemed that Beverly, the second of Mr Clutter's surviving daughters, had married Mr Vere Edward English, the young biology student to whom she had long been engaged. Miss Clutter had worn white, and the wedding, a full-scale affair ('Mrs Leonard Cowan was soloist, and Mrs Howard Blanchard organist'), had been 'solemnized at the First Methodist Church' – the church in which, three days earlier, the bride had formally mourned her parents, her brother, and her younger sister. However, according to the *Telegram*'s account, 'Vere and Beverly had planned to be married at Christmastime. The invitations were printed and her father had reserved the church for that date. Due to the unexpected tragedy and because of the many relatives being here from distant places, the young couple decided to have their wedding Saturday.'

The wedding over, the Clutter kinfolk dispersed. On Monday, the day the last of them left Garden City, the *Telegram* featured on its front page a letter written by Mr Howard Fox, of Oregon, Illinois, a brother of Bonnie Clutter. The letter, after expressing gratitude to the townspeople for having opened their 'homes and hearts' to the bereaved family, turned into a plea. 'There is much resentment in this community [that is, Garden City],' wrote Mr Fox. 'I have even heard on more than one occasion that the man, when found, should be hanged from the nearest tree. Let us not feel this way. The deed is done and taking another life cannot change it. Instead, let us forgive as God would have us do. It is not right that we should hold a grudge in our hearts. The doer of this act is going to find it very difficult indeed to live with himself. His only peace of mind will be when he gets to God for forgiveness. Let us not stand in the way but instead give prayers that he may find his peace.'

The car was parked on a promontory where Perry and Dick had stopped to picnic. It was noon. Dick scanned the view through a pair of binoculars. Mountains. Hawks wheeling in a white sky. A dusty road winding into and out of a white and dusty village. Today was his second day in Mexico, and so far he liked it fine – even the food. (At this very moment he was eating a cold, oily tortilla.) They had crossed the border at Laredo, Texas, the morning of 23 November, and spent the first night in a San Luis Potosí brothel. They were now two hundred miles north of their next destination, Mexico City.

'Know what I think?' said Perry. 'I think there must be something wrong with us. To do what we did.'

'Did what?'

'Out there.'

Dick dropped the binoculars into a leather case, a luxurious receptacle initialled H.W.C. He was annoyed. Annoyed as hell. Why the hell couldn't Perry shut up? Christ Jesus, what damn good did it do, always dragging the goddam thing up? It really was *annoying*. Especially since they'd agreed, sort of, not to talk about the goddam thing. Just forget it.

'There's got to be something wrong with somebody who'd do a thing like that,' Perry said.

'Deal me out, baby,' Dick said. 'I'm a normal.' And Dick meant what he said. He thought himself as balanced, as sane as anyone – maybe a bit smarter than the average fellow, that's all. But Perry – there *was*, in Dick's opinion, 'something wrong' with Little Perry. To say the least. Last spring, when they had celled together at Kansas State Penitentiary, he'd learned most of Perry's lesser peculiarities: Perry could be 'such a kid', always wetting his bed and crying in his sleep ('Dad, I been looking everywhere, where you been, Dad?'), and often Dick had seen him 'sit for hours just sucking his thumb and poring over them phony damn treasure guides'. Which was one side; there were others. In some ways old Perry was 'spooky as hell'. Take, for instance, that temper of his. He could slide into a fury 'quicker than ten drunk Indians'. And yet you wouldn't know it. 'He might be ready to kill you, but you'd never know it, not to look at or listen to,' Dick once said. For however extreme the inward rage, outwardly Perry remained a cool young tough, with eyes serene and slightly sleepy. The time had been when Dick had thought he could control, could regulate the temperature of these sudden cold fevers that burned and chilled his friend. He had been mistaken, and in the aftermath of that discovery, had grown very unsure of Perry, not at all certain what to think – except that he felt he ought to be afraid of him, and wondered really why he wasn't.

'Deep down,' Perry continued, 'way, way rock-bottom, I never thought I could do it. A thing like that.'

'How about the nigger?' Dick said. Silence. Dick realized that Perry was staring at him. A week ago, in Kansas City, Perry had bought a pair of dark glasses – fancy ones with silver-lacquered rims and mirrored lenses. Dick disliked them; he'd told Perry he was ashamed to be seen with 'anyone who'd wear that kind of flit stuff'. Actually, what irked him was the mirrored lenses; it was unpleasant having Perry's eyes hidden behind the privacy of those tinted, reflecting surfaces.

'But a nigger,' said Perry. 'That's different.'

The comment, the reluctance with which it was pronounced, made Dick ask, 'Or did you? Kill him like you said?' It was a significant question, for his original interest in Perry, his assessment of Perry's character and potentialities, was founded on the story Perry had once told him of how he had beaten a coloured man to death.

'Sure I did. Only – a nigger. It's not the same.' Then Perry said, 'Know what it is that really bugs me? About the other thing? It's just I don't believe it – that anyone can get away with a thing like that. Because I don't see how it's possible. To do what we did. And just one hundred per cent get away with it. I mean, that's what bugs me – I can't get it out of my head that something's got to happen.'

Though as a child he had attended church, Dick had never 'come near' a belief in God; nor was he troubled by superstitions. Unlike Perry, he was not convinced that a broken mirror meant seven years' misfortune, or that a young moon if glimpsed through glass portended evil. But Perry, with his sharp and scratchy intuitions, had hit upon Dick's one abiding doubt. Dick, too, suffered moments when that question circled inside his head: Was it possible – were the two of them 'honest to God going to get away with doing a thing like that'? Suddenly, he said to Perry, 'Now, just shut up!' Then he gunned the motor and backed the car off the promontory. Ahead of him, on the dusty road, he saw a dog trotting along in the warm sunshine.

Mountains. Hawks wheeling in a white sky.

When Perry asked Dick, 'Know what I think?' he knew he was beginning a conversation that would displease Dick, and one that, for that matter, he himself would just as soon avoid. He agreed with Dick: Why go on talking about it? But he could not always stop himself. Spells of helplessness occurred, moments when he 'remembered things' – blue light exploding in a black room, the glass eyes of a big toy bear – and when voices, a particular few words, started nagging his mind: 'Oh, no! Oh, please! No! No! No! No! Don't! Oh, please don't, please!' And certain sounds returned – a silver dollar rolling across a floor, boot steps on hardwood stairs, and the sounds of breathing, the gasps, the hysterical inhalations of a man with a severed windpipe.

When Perry said, 'I think there must be something wrong with us', he was making an admission he 'hated to make'. After all, it was 'painful' to imagine that one might be 'not just right' – particularly if whatever was wrong was not your own fault but 'maybe a thing you were born with'. Look at his family: Look at what had happened there! His mother, an alcoholic, had strangled to death on her own vomit. Of her children, two sons and two daughters, only the younger girl, Barbara, had entered ordinary life, married, begun raising a family. Fern, the other daughter, jumped out of a window of a San Francisco hotel. (Perry had ever since 'tried to believe she slipped', for he'd loved Fern. She was 'such a sweet person', so 'artistic', a 'terrific' dancer, and she could sing, too. 'If she'd ever had any luck at all, with her looks and all, she could have got somewhere, been somebody.' It was sad to think of her climbing over a window-sill and falling fifteen floors.) And there was Jimmy, the older boy – Jimmy, who had one day driven his wife to suicide and killed himself the next.

Then he heard Dick say, 'Deal me out, baby. I'm a normal.' Wasn't that a horse's laugh? But never mind, let it pass. 'Deep down,' Perry continued, 'way, way rock-bottom, I never thought I could do it. A thing like that.' And at once he recognized his error: Dick would, of course, answer by asking, 'How about the nigger?' When he'd told Dick that story, it was because he'd wanted Dick's friendship, wanted Dick to 'respect' him, think him 'hard', as much 'the masculine type' as he had considered Dick to be. And so one day after they had both read and were discussing a *Reader's Digest* article entitled 'How Good a Character Detective Are You?' ('As you wait in a dentist's office or a railway station, try studying the give-away signs in people around you. Watch the way they walk, for example. A stiff-legged gait can reveal a rigid, unbending personality; a shambling walk a lack of determination'), Perry had said 'I've always been an outstanding character detective, otherwise I'd be dead today. Like if I couldn't judge when to trust somebody. You never can much. But I've come to trust you, Dick. You'll see I do, because I'm going to put myself in your power. I'm going to tell you something I never told anybody. Not even Willie-Jay. About the time I fixed a guy.' And Perry saw, as he went on, that Dick was interested; he was really listening. 'It was a couple of summers ago. Out in Vegas. I was living in this old boarding-house – it used to be a fancy cathouse. But all the fancy was gone. It was a place they should have torn down ten years back; anyway, it was sort of coming down by itself. The cheapest rooms were in the attic, and I lived up there. So did this nigger. His name was King; he was a transient. We were the only two up there – us and a million *cucarachas*. King, he wasn't too young, but he'd done roadwork and other outdoor stuff – he had a good build. He wore glasses, and he read a lot. He never shut his door. Every time I passed by, he was always lying there buck-naked. He was out of work, and said he'd saved a few dollars from his last job, said he wanted to stay in bed awhile, read and fan himself and drink beer. The stuff he read, it was just junk – comic books and cowboy junk. He was O.K. Sometimes we'd have a beer together, and once he lent me ten dollars. I had no cause to hurt him. But one night we were sitting in the attic, it was so hot you couldn't sleep, so I said, "Come on, King, let's go for a drive." I had an old car I'd stripped and souped and painted silver – the Silver Ghost I called it. We went for a long drive. Drove way out in the desert. Out there it was cool. We parked and drank a few more beers. King got out of the car, and I followed after him. He didn't see I'd picked up this chain. A bicycle chain I kept under the seat. Actually, I had no real idea to do it till I did it. I hit him across the face. Broke his glasses. I kept right on. Afterwards, I didn't feel a thing. I left him there, and never heard a word about it. Maybe nobody ever found him. Just buzzards.'

There was some truth in the story. Perry had known, under the circumstances stated, a Negro named King. But if the man was dead today it was none of Perry's doing; he'd never raised a hand against him. For all he knew, King might still be lying abed somewhere, fanning himself and sipping beer.

'Or did you? Kill him like you said?' Dick asked.

Perry was not a gifted liar, or a prolific one; however, once he had told a fiction he usually stuck by it. 'Sure I did. Only – a nigger. It's not the same.' Presently, he said, 'Know what it is that really bugs me? About that other thing? It's just I don't believe it – that anyone can get away with a thing like that.' And he suspected that Dick didn't, either. For Dick was at least partly inhibited by Perry's mystical-moral apprehensions. Thus: 'Now, just shut up!'

The car was moving. A hundred feet ahead, a dog trotted along the side of the road. Dick swerved towards it. It was an old half-dead mongrel, brittle-boned and mangy, and the impact, as it met the car, was little more than what a bird might make. But Dick was satisfied. 'Boy!' he said – and it was what he always said after running down a dog, which was something he did whenever the opportunity arose. 'Boy! We sure splattered him!'

Thanksgiving passed, and the pheasant season came to a halt, but not the beautiful Indian summer, with its flow of clear, pure days. The last of the out-of-town newsmen, convinced that the case was never going to be solved, left Garden City. But the case was by no means closed for the people of Finney County, and least of all for those who patronized Holcomb's favourite meeting-place, Hartman's Café.

'Since the trouble started, we've been doing all the business we can handle,' Mrs Hartman said, gazing around her snug domain, every scrap of which was being sat or stood or leaned upon by tobacco-scented, coffee-drinking farmers, farm helpers, and ranch hands. 'Just a bunch of old women,' added Mrs Hartman's cousin, Postmistress Clare, who happened to be on the premises. 'If it was spring and work to be done, they wouldn't be here. But wheat's in, winter's on the way, they got nothing to do but sit around and scare each other. You know Bill Brown, down to the *Telegram*? See the editorial he wrote? That one he called it "Another Crime"? Said, "It's time for everyone to stop wagging loose tongues." Because that's a crime, too – telling plain-out lies. But what can you expect? Look around you. Rattlesnakes. Varmints. *Rumour*mongers. See anything else? Ha! Like dash you do.'

One rumour originating in Hartman's Café involved Taylor Jones, a rancher whose property adjoins River Valley Farm. In the opinion of a good part of the café's clientele, Mr Jones and his family, not the Clutters, were the murderer's intended victims. 'It makes harder sense,' argued one of those who held this view. 'Taylor Jones, he's a richer man than Herb Clutter ever was. Now, pretend the fellow who done it wasn't anyone from hereabouts. Pretend he'd been maybe hired to kill, and all he had was instructions on how to get to the house. Well, it would be mighty easy to make a mistake – take a wrong turn – and end up at Herb's place 'stead of Taylor's.' The 'Jones Theory' was much repeated – especially to the Joneses, a dignified and sensible family, who refused to be flustered.

A lunch counter, a few tables, an alcove harbouring a hot grill and an icebox and a radio – that's all there is to Hartman's Café. 'But our customers like it,' says the proprietress. 'Got to. Nowhere else for them to go. 'Less they drive seven miles one direction or fifteen the other. Anyway, we run a friendly place, and the coffee's good since Mabel came to work' – Mabel being Mrs Helm. 'After the tragedy, I said, "Mabel, now that you're out of a job, why don't you come give me a hand at the café. Cook a little. Wait counter." How it turned out – the only bad feature is, everybody comes in here, they pester her with questions. About the tragedy. But Mabel's not like Cousin Myrt. Or me. She's shy. Besides, she doesn't know anything special. No more than anybody else.' But by and large the Hartman congregation continued to suspect that Mabel Helm knew a thing or two that she was holding back. And, of course, she did. Dewey had had several conversations with her and had requested that everything they said be kept secret. Particularly, she was not to mention the missing radio or the watch found in Nancy's shoe. Which is why she said to Mrs Archibald

William Warren-Browne, 'Anybody reads the papers knows as much as I do. More. Because I don't read them.'

Square, squat, in the earlier forties, an Englishwoman fitted out with an accent almost incoherently upper-class, Mrs Archibald William Warren-Browne did not at all resemble the café's other frequenters, and seemed, within that setting, like a peacock trapped in a turkey pen. Once, explaining to an acquaintance why she and her husband had abandoned 'family estates in the North of England', exchanging the hereditary home – 'the jolliest, oh, the prettiest old priory' – for an old and highly unjolly farmhouse on the plains of western Kansas, Mrs Warren-Browne said: 'Taxes, my dear. Death duties. Enormous, *crim*inal death duties. That's what drove us out of England. Yes, we left a year ago. Without regrets. None. We love it here. *Just* adore it. Though, of course, it's very *dif*ferent from our other life. The life we've always known. Paris and Rome. Monte. London. I do – oc*cas*ionally – think of London. Oh, I don't *really* miss it – the frenzy, and never a cab, and always worrying how one looks. Positively not. We love it here. I suppose some people – those aware of our past, the life we've led – wonder aren't we the tiniest bit *lone*ly, out there in the wheat fields. Out West is where we meant to settle. Wyoming or Nevada – *la vraie chose*. We hoped when we got there some oil might stick to us. But on our way we stopped to visit friends in Garden City – friends *of* friends, *act*ually. But they couldn't have been kinder. In*sis*ted we linger on. And we thought, Well, why not? Why not hire a bit of land and start ranching? Or farming. Which is a decision we still haven't come to – whether to ranch or farm. Dr Austin asked if we didn't find it perhaps too quiet. *Act*ually, no. *Act*ually, I've never known such bedlam. It's noisier than a bomb raid. Train whistles. Coyotes. Monsters *howl*ing the bloody night long. A horrid racket. And since the murders it seems to bother me more. So many things do. Our house – what an old creaker it is! Mark you, I'm not complaining. Really, it's quite a serviceable house – has all the mod. cons. – but, oh, how it coughs and grunts! And after dark, when the wind commences, that *hate*ful prairie wind, one hears the most ap*pall*ing moans. I mean, if one's a bit nervy, one can't help imagining – silly things. Dear God! That poor family! No, we never met them. I *saw* Mr Clutter once. In the Federal Building.'

Early in December, in the course of a single afternoon, two of the café's steadiest customers announced plans to pack up and leave not merely Finney County but the state. The first was a tenant farmer who worked for Lester McCoy, a well-known western-Kansas landowner and businessman. He said, 'I had myself a talk with Mr McCoy. Tried to let him know what's going on out here in Holcomb and hereabouts. How a body can't sleep. My wife can't sleep, and she won't allow me. So I told Mr McCoy I like his place fine but he better hunt up another man. 'Count of we're movin' on. Down to east Colorado. Maybe then I'll get some rest.'

The second announcement was made by Mrs Hideo Ashida, who stopped by the café with three of her four red-cheeked children. She lined them up at the counter and told Mrs Hartman, 'Give Bruce a box of Cracker Jack. Bobby wants a Coke. Bonnie Jean? We know how you feel, Bonnie Jean, but come on, have a treat.' Bonnie Jean shook her head, and Mrs Ashida said, 'Bonnie Jean's sort of blue. She don't want to leave here. The school here. And all her friends.'

'Why, say,' said Mrs Hartman, smiling at Bonnie Jean. 'That's nothing to be sad over. Transferring from Holcomb to Garden City High. Lots more boys – '

Bonnie Jean said, 'You don't understand. Daddy's taking us away. To Nebraska.'

Bess Hartman looked at the mother, as if expecting her to deny the daughter's allegation.

'It's true, Bess,' Mrs Ashida said.

'I don't know what to say,' said Mrs Hartman, her voice indignantly astonished, and also despairing. The Ashidas were a part of the Holcomb community everyone appreciated – a family likeably high-spirited, yet hard-working and neighbourly and generous, though they didn't have much to be generous with.

Mrs Ashida said, 'We've been talking on it a long time. Hideo, he thinks we can do better somewhere else.'

'When you plan to go?'

'Soon as we sell up. But anyway not before Christmas. On account of a deal we've worked out with the dentist. About Hideo's Christmas present. Me and the kids, we've giving him three gold teeth. For Christmas.'

Mrs Hartman sighed. 'I don't know what to say. Except I wish you wouldn't. Just up and leave us.' She sighed again. 'Seems like we're losing everybody. One way and another.'

'Gosh, you think I want to leave?' Mrs Ashida said. 'Far as people go, this is the nicest place we ever lived. But Hideo, he's the man, and he says we can get a better farm in Nebraska. And I'll tell you something, Bess.' Mrs Ashida attempted a frown, but her plump, round, smooth face could not quite manage it. 'We used to argue about it. Then one night I said, "O.K., you're the boss, let's go." After what happened to Herb and his family, I felt something around here had come to an end. I mean personally. For me. And so I quit arguing. I said O.K.' She dipped a hand into Bruce's box of Cracker Jack. 'Gosh, I can't get over it. I can't get it off my mind. I *liked* Herb. Did you know I was one of the last to see him alive? Uh-huh. Me and the kids. We been to the 4-H meeting in Garden City and he gave us a ride home. The last thing I said to Herb, I told him how I couldn't imagine his ever being afraid. That no matter what the situation was, he could talk his way out of it.' Thoughtfully she nibbled a kernel of Cracker Jack, took a swig of Bobby's Coke, then said, 'Funny, but you know, Bess, I'll bet he *wasn't* afraid. I mean, however it happened, I'll bet right up to the last he didn't believe it would. Because it couldn't. Not to him.'

The sun was blazing. A small boat was riding at anchor in a mild sea: the *Estrellita*, with four persons aboard – Dick, Perry, a young Mexican, and Otto, a rich middle-aged German.

'Please. Again,' said Otto, and Perry, strumming his guitar, sang in a husky sweet voice a Smoky Mountains song:

'In this world today while we're living
Some folks say the worst of us they can,
But when we're dead and in our caskets,
They always slip some lilies in our hand.
Won't you give me flowers while I'm living . . .'

A week in Mexico City, and then he and Dick had driven
south – Cuernavaca, Taxco, Acapulco. And it was in Acapulco, in a 'jukebox honky-tonk', that they had met the
hairy-legged and hearty Otto. Dick had 'picked him up'.
But the gentleman, a vacationing Hamburg lawyer, 'already
had a friend' – a young native Acapulcan who called himself the Cowboy. 'He proved to be a trustworthy person,'
Perry once said of the Cowboy. 'Mean as Judas, some ways,
but oh, man, a funny boy, a real fast jockey. Dick liked him,
too. We got on great.'

The Cowboy found for the tattooed drifters a room in the
house of an uncle, undertook to improve Perry's Spanish,
and shared the benefits of his liaison with the holidaymaker
from Hamburg, in whose company and at whose expense
they drank and ate and bought women. The host seemed
to think his pesos well spent, if only because he relished
Dick's jokes. Each day Otto hired the *Estrellita*, a deep-sea-
fishing craft, and the four friends went trawling along the
coast. The Cowboy skippered the boat; Otto sketched and
fished; Perry baited hooks, daydreamed, sang, and sometimes fished; Dick did nothing – only moaned, complained
of the motion, lay about sun-drugged and listless, like a
lizard at siesta. But Perry said, 'This is finally it. The way it
ought to be.' Still, he knew that it couldn't continue – that
it was, in fact, destined to stop that very day. The next day
Otto was returning to Germany, and Perry and Dick were
driving back to Mexico City – at Dick's insistence. 'Sure,
baby,' he'd said when they were debating the matter. 'It's
nice and all. With the sun on your back. But the dough's
going-going-gone. And after we've sold the car, what have
we got left?'

The answer was that they had very little, for they had by
now mostly disposed of the stuff acquired the day of the
Kansas City cheque-passing spree – the camera, the cuff-

links, the television sets. Also, they had sold, to a Mexico City policeman with whom Dick had got acquainted, a pair of binoculars and a grey Zenith portable radio. 'What we'll do is, we'll go back to Mex, sell the car, and maybe I can get a garage job. Anyway, it's a better deal up there. Better opportunities. Christ, I sure could use some more of that Inez.' Inez was a prostitute who had accosted Dick on the steps of the Palace of Fine Arts in Mexico City (the visit was part of a sight-seeing tour taken to please Perry). She was eighteen, and Dick had promised to marry her. But he had also promised to marry Maria, a woman of fifty, who was the widow of a 'very prominent Mexican banker'. They had met in a bar, and the next morning she had paid him the equivalent of seven dollars. 'So how about it?' Dick said to Perry. 'We'll sell the wagon. Find a job. Save our dough. And see what happens.' As though Perry couldn't predict precisely what would happen. Suppose they got two or three hundred for the old Chevrolet. Dick, if he knew Dick, and he did – *now* he did – would spend it right away on vodka and women.

While Perry sang, Otto sketched him in a sketchbook. It was a passable likeness, and the artist perceived one not very obvious aspect of the sitter's countenance – its mischief, an amused, babyish malice that suggested some unkind cupid aiming envenomed arrows. He was naked to the waist. (Perry was 'ashamed' to take off his trousers, 'ashamed' to wear swimming trunks, for he was afraid that the sight of his injured legs would 'disgust people', and so, despite his under-water reveries, all the talk about skin-diving, he hadn't once gone into the water.) Otto reproduced a number of the tattoos ornamenting the subject's overmuscled chest, arms, and small and calloused but girlish hands. The sketchbook, which Otto gave Perry as a parting gift, contained several drawings of Dick – 'nude studies'.

Otto shut his sketchbook, Perry put down his guitar, and the Cowboy raised anchor, started the engine. It was time to go. They were ten miles out, and the water was darkening.

Perry urged Dick to fish. 'We may never have another chance,' he said.

'Chance?'

'To catch a big one.'

'Jesus, I've got the bastard kind,' Dick said. 'I'm sick.' Dick often had headaches of migraine intensity – 'the bastard kind'. He thought they were the result of his automobile accident. 'Please, baby. Let's be very, very quiet.'

Moments later Dick had forgotten his pain. He was on his feet, shouting with excitement. Otto and the Cowboy were shouting, too. Perry had hooked 'a big one'. Ten feet of soaring, plunging sailfish, it leaped, arched like a rainbow, dived, sank deep, tugged the line taut, rose, flew, fell, rose. An hour passed, and part of another, before the sweat-soaked sportsman reeled it in.

There is an old man with an ancient wooden box camera who hangs around the harbour in Acapulco, and when the *Estrellita* docked, Otto commissioned him to do six portraits of Perry posed beside his catch. Technically, the old man's work turned out badly – brown and streaked. Still, they were remarkable photographs, and what made them so was Perry's expression, his look of unflawed fulfilment, of beatitude, as though at last, and as in one of his dreams, a tall yellow bird had hauled him to heaven.

One December afternoon Paul Helm was pruning the patch of floral odds and ends that had entitled Bonnie Clutter to membership in the Garden City Garden Club. It was a melancholy task, for he was reminded of another afternoon when he'd done the same chore. Kenyon had helped him that day, and it was the last time he'd seen Kenyon alive, or Nancy, or any of them. The weeks between had been hard on Mr Helm. He was 'in poor health' (poorer than he knew; he had less than four months to live), and he was worried about a lot of things. His job, for one. He doubted he would have it much longer. Nobody seemed really to know, but he understood that 'the girls', Beverly and Eveanna, intended to sell the property – though, as he'd heard one of the boys at the café remark, 'ain't nobody gonna buy that spread, long as the mystery lasts'. It 'didn't do' to think about – strangers here, harvesting 'our' land. Mr Helm minded – he minded for Herb's sake. This was a place, he said, that 'ought to be kept in a man's family'. Once Herb had said to him, 'I hope there'll always be a Clutter here, and a Helm, too.' It was only a year ago Herb had said that. Lord, what was he to do if the farm got sold? He felt 'too old to fit in somewhere different'.

Still, he must work, and he wanted to. He wasn't, he said, the kind to kick off his shoes and sit by the stove. And yet it was true that the farm nowadays made him uneasy: the locked house, Nancy's horse forlornly waiting in a field, the odour of windfall apples rotting under the apple trees, and the absence of voices – Kenyon calling Nancy to the telephone, Herb whistling, his glad 'Good morning, Paul.' He and Herb had 'got along grand' – never a cross word between them. Why, then, did the men from the sheriff's office continue to question him? Unless they thought he had 'something to hide'? Maybe he ought never to have mentioned the Mexicans. He had informed Al Dewey that at approximately four o'clock on Saturday, 14 November, the day of the murders, a pair of Mexicans, one moustachioed and the other pockmarked, appeared at River Valley Farm. Mr Helm had seen them knock on the door of 'the office', seen Herb step outside and talk to them on the lawn, and, possibly ten minutes later, watched the strangers walk away, 'looking sulky'. Mr Helm figured that they had come asking for work and had been told there was none. Unfortunately, though he'd been called upon to recount his version of that day's events many times, he had not spoken of the incident until two weeks after the crime, because, as he explained to Dewey, 'I just suddenly recalled it.' But Dewey, and some of the other investigators, seemed not to credit his story, and behaved as though it were a tale he'd invented to mislead them. They preferred to believe Bob Johnson, the insurance salesman, who had spent all of Saturday afternoon conferring with Mr Clutter in the latter's office, and who was 'absolutely positive' that from two to ten past six he had been Herb's sole visitor. Mr Helm was equally definite: Mexicans, a moustache, pockmarks, four o'clock. Herb would have told them that he was speaking the truth, convinced them that he, Paul Helm, was a man

who 'said his prayers and earned his bread'. But Herb was
gone.

Gone. And Bonnie, too. Her bedroom window overlooked
the garden, and now and then, usually when she was 'having
a bad spell', Mr Helm had seen her stand long hours gazing
into the garden, as though what she saw bewitched her.
('When I was a girl,' she had once told a friend, 'I was ter-
ribly sure trees and flowers were the same as birds or people.
That they thought things, and talked among themselves.
And we could hear them if we really tried. It was just a
matter of emptying your head of all other sounds. Being
very quiet and listening very hard. Sometimes I still believe
that. But one can never get quiet enough . . .')

Remembering Bonnie at the window, Mr Helm looked
up, as though he expected to see her, a ghost behind the
glass. If he had, it could not have amazed him more than
what he did in fact discern – a hand holding back a curtain,
and eyes. 'But,' as he subsequently described it, 'the sun was
hitting that side of the house' – it made the window glass
waver, shimmeringly twisted what hung beyond it – and
by the time Mr Helm had shielded his eyes, then looked
again, the curtains had swung closed, the window was
vacant. 'My eyes aren't too good, and I wondered if they
had played me a trick,' he recalled. 'But I was pretty darn
certain that they hadn't. And I was pretty darn certain it
wasn't any spook. Because I don't believe in spooks. So who
could it be? Sneaking around in there. Where nobody's got
a right to go, except the law. And how did they get in? With
everything locked up like the radio was advertising tor-
nadoes. That's what I wondered. But I wasn't expecting to
find out – not by myself. I dropped what I was doing, and
cut across the fields to Holcomb. Soon as I got there, I
phoned Sheriff Robinson. Explained that there was somebody prowling around inside the Clutter house. Well, they
came raring right on out. State troopers. The sheriff and
his bunch. The K.B.I. fellows. Al Dewey. Just as they were
stringing themselves around the place, sort of getting ready
for action, the front door opened.' Out walked a person no
one present had ever seen before – a man in his middle

thirties, dull-eyed, wild-haired, and wearing a hip holster stocked with a .38-calibre pistol. 'I guess all of us there had the identical idea – this was him, the one who came and killed them,' Mr Helm continued. 'He didn't make a move. Stood quiet. Kind of blinking. They took the gun away, and started asking questions.'

The man's name was Adrian – Jonathan Daniel Adrian. He was on his way to New Mexico, and at present had no fixed address. For what purpose had he broken into the Clutter house, and how, incidentally, had he managed it? He showed them how. (He had lifted a lid off a water well and crawled through a pipe tunnel that led into the basement.) As for why, he had read about the case and was curious, just wanted to see what the place looked like. 'And then,' according to Mr Helm's memory of the episode, 'somebody asked him was he a hitchhiker? Hitchhiking his way to New Mexico? No, he said, he was driving his own car. And it was parked down the lane a piece. So everybody went to look at the car. When they found what was inside it, one of the men – maybe it was Al Dewey – said to him, told this Jonathan Daniel Adrian, "Well, mister, seems like we've got something to discuss." Because, inside the car, what they'd found was a .12-gauge shotgun. And a hunting knife.'

A room in a hotel in Mexico City. In the room was an ugly modern bureau with a lavender-tinted mirror, and tucked into a corner of the mirror was a printed warning from the Management:

> Su Día Termina a las 2 p.m.
> Your Day Ends at 2 p.m.

Guests, in other words, must vacate the room by the stated hour or expect to be charged another day's rent – a luxury that the present occupants were not contemplating. They wondered only whether they could settle the sum already owed. For everything had evolved as Perry had prophesied: Dick had sold the car, and three days later the money, slightly less than two hundred dollars, had largely vanished. On the fourth day Dick had gone out hunting honest work, and that night he had announced to Perry, 'Nuts! You know what they pay? What the *wages* are? For an *ex*pert mechanic? Two bucks a day. Mexico! Honey, I've had it. We got to make it out of here. Back to the States. No, now, I'm *not* going to listen. Diamonds. *Buried* treasure. Wake up, little boy. There ain't no caskets of gold. No sunken ship. And even if there was – hell, you can't even *swim*.' And the next day, having borrowed money from the richer of his two fiancées, the banker's widow, Dick bought bus tickets that would take them, via San Diego, as far as Barstow California. 'After that,' he said, 'we walk.'

Of course, Perry could have struck out on his own, stayed in Mexico, let Dick go where he damn well wanted. Why not? Hadn't he always been 'a loner', and without any 'real friends' (except the grey-haired, grey-eyed and 'brilliant' Willie-Jay)? But he was afraid to leave Dick; merely to consider it made him feel 'sort of sick', as though he were trying to make up his mind to 'jump off a train going ninety-nine miles an hour'. The basis of his fear, or so he himself seemed to believe, was newly grown superstitious certainty that 'whatever had to happen won't happen' as long as he and Dick 'stick together'. Then, too, the severity of Dick's 'wake-up' speech, the belligerence with which he'd proclaimed his theretofore concealed opinion of Perry's dreams and hope – all this, perversity being what it is, appealed to Perry, hurt and shocked him but charmed him, almost revived his former faith in the tough, the 'totally masculine', the pragmatic, the decisive Dick he'd once allowed to boss him. And so, since a sunrise hour on a chilly Mexico City morning in early December, Perry had been prowling about the unheated hotel room assembling and packing his possessions – stealthily, lest he waken the two sleeping shapes lying on one of the room's twin beds: Dick, and the younger of his betrotheds, Inez.

There was one belonging of his that need no longer concern him. On their last night in Acapulco, a thief had stolen the Gibson guitar – absconded with it from a waterfront café where he, Otto, Dick, and the Cowboy had been bidding one another a highly alcoholic goodbye. And Perry was bitter about it. He felt, he later said, 'real mean and low', explaining, 'You have a guitar long enough, like I had that one, wax and shine it, fit your voice to it, treat it like it was a girl you really had some use for – well, it gets to be kind of holy.' But while the purloined guitar presented no ownership problem, his remaining property did. As he and Dick would now be travelling by foot or thumb, they clearly could not carry with them more than a few shirts and socks. The rest of their clothing would have to be shipped – and, indeed, Perry had already filled a cardboard carton (putting into it – along with some bits of unlaundered laundry – two pairs of boots, one pair with soles that left a Cat's Paw print, the other pair with diamond-pattern soles) and addressed it to himself, care of General Delivery, Las Vegas, Nevada.

But the big question, and source of heartache, was what to do with his much-loved memorabilia – the two huge boxes heavy with books and maps, yellowing letters, song lyrics, poems, and unusual souvenirs (suspenders and a belt fabricated from the skins of Nevada rattlers he himself had slain; an erotic *netsuke* bought in Kyoto; a petrified dwarf tree, also from Japan; the foot of an Alaskan bear). Probably the best solution – at least, the best Perry could devise – was to leave the stuff with 'Jesus'. The 'Jesus' he had in mind tended bar in a café across the street from the hotel, and was, Perry thought, *muy simpático*, definitely someone he could trust to return the boxes on demand. (He intended to send for them as soon as he had a 'fixed address'.)

Still, there were some things too precious to chance losing, so while the lovers drowsed and time dawdled on towards 2 p.m., Perry looked through old letters, photographs, clippings, and selected from them those mementoes he meant to take with him. Among them was a badly typed composition entitled 'A History of My Boy's Life'. The author of this manuscript was Perry's father, who in an effort to help his son obtain a parole from Kansas State Penitentiary, had written it the previous December and mailed it to the Kansas State Parole Board. It was a document that

Perry had read at least a hundred times, never with in-difference:

'CHILDHOOD – Be glad to tell you, as I see it, both good and bad. Yes. Perry birth was *normal*. Healthy – yes. Yes, I was able to care for him properly until my wife turned out to be a disgraceful drunkard when my children were at school age. Happy disposition – *yes* and *no*, very serious if mistreated he never forgets. I also keep my promises and make him do so. My wife was different. We lived in the country. We are all truly outdoor people. I taught my children the Golden Rule. Live & let live and in many cases my children would tell on each other when doing wrong and the guilty one would always admit, and come forward, will-ing for a spanking. And promise to be good, and always done their work quickly and willing so they could be free to play. Always wash themselves first thing in the morning, dress in clean clothes, I was very strict about that, and wrong doings to others, and if wrong was done to them by other kids I made them quit playing with them. Our child-ren were no trouble to us as long as we were together. It all started when my wife wanted to go to the City and live a wild life – and ran away to do so. I let her go and said good-by as she took the car and left me behind (this was during depression). My children all cryed at the top of their voices. She only cussed them saying they would run away to come to me later. She got mad and then said she would turn the children to hate me, which she did, all but *Perry*. For the love of my children after several months I went to find them, located them in San Francisco, my wife not knowing. I tryed to see them in school. My wife had given orders to the teacher not to let me see them. However, I managed to see them while playing in the school yard and was surprised when they told me, "Mama told us not to talk to you." All but *Perry*. He was different. He put his arms around me and wanted to run away with me rite then. I told him *No*. But rite after school was out, he ran away to my lawyers office Mr *Rinso Turco*. I took my boy back to his mother and left the City. Perry later told me, his mother told him to find a new home. While my children were with her they run around as they pleased, I understand Perry got into trouble. I wanted *her* to ask for divorce, which she did after about a year or so. Her drinkin and stepin out, living with a young man. I contested the divorce and was granted full custody of the children. I took Perry to my home to live with me. The other children were put in homes as I could not manage to take them all in my home and them being part indian blood and welfare took care of them as I requested.

'This was during depression time. I was working on W.P.A. very small wages. I owned some property and small home at the time. Perry and I lived together peacefully. My heart was hurt, as I still loved my other children also. So I took to roaming to forget it all. I made a livin for us both. I sold my property and we lived in a "house car". Perry went to school often as possible. He didn't like school very well. He learns quick and never got into trouble with the other kids. Only when the *Bully Kid* picked on him. He was short and stocky a new kid in school they tried to mistreat him. They found him willing to fight for his rights. That was the way I raised my kids. I always told them dont start a fight, if you do, I'll give you a beaten when I find out. But if the other kids start a fight, do your best. One time a kid twice his age at school, run up and hit him, to his surprise Perry got him down and give him a good beating. I had given him some advice in wrestling. As I once used to Box & Wrestle. The lady principal of the school and all the kids watched this fight. The lady principal loved the big kid. To see him get whipped by my little boy Perry was more than she could take. After that Perry was King of the Kids at school. If any big kid tried to mistreat a small one, Perry would settle that rite now. Even the Big Bully was afraid of Perry now, and had to be good. But that hurt the lady principal so she came to me complaining about Perry fighting in school. I told her I knew all about it and that I didnt intend to let my boy get beat up by kids twice his size. I also asked her why she let that Bully Kid beat up on other kids. I told her that Perry had a rite to defend himself. Perry never started the trouble and that I would take a hand in this affair myself. I told her my son was well liked by all the neighbors, and their kids. I also told her I was going to take Perry out of her school real soon, move away to another state. Which I did. Perry is no Angel he has done wrong many times same as so many other kids. Rite is Rite and wrong is wrong. I don't stick up for his wrong doings. He must pay the *Hardway* when he does wrong, law is Boss he knows that by now.

'YOUTH – Perry joined the merchant Marines in second war. I went to Alaska, he came later and joined me there. I trapped furs and Perry worked with the Alaska Road Commission the first winter then he got work on the railroad for a short while. He couldn't get the work he liked to do. Yes – he give me $ now and then when he had it. He also sent me $30.00 a month while in Korea war while he was there from beginning until the end and was dischard in Seattle, Wash. Honorable as far as I know. He is mechanically inclined. Bulldozers, draglines, shovels, heavy duty trucks of all type is his desire. For the experience he has had he is real good. Somewhat reckless and speed crazy with motorcyles and light cars. But since he has had a good taste of what speed will do, and his both legs Broke & hip injury he now has slowed down on that I'm sure.

'RECREATION – INTERESTS. Yes he had several girl friends, soon as he found a girl to mistreat him or trifle, he would quit her. He never was married as far as I know. My troubles with his mother made him afraid of marriage somewhat. Im a *Sober man* and as far as I know Perry is also a person that dont like drunks. Perry is like myself a great deal. He likes Company of decent type – outdoors people, he like myself, likes to be by himself also he likes best to work for himself. As I do. I'm a jack of all trades, so to speak, master of few and so is Perry. I showed him how to make a living working for himself as a fur trapper, prospector, carpenter, woodsman, horses, etc. I know how to cook and so does he, not a professional cook just plane cooking for himself. Bake bread, etc. hunt, and fish, trap, do most anything else. As I said before, Perry likes to be his own Boss & if he is given a chance to work at a job he likes, tell him how you want it done, then leave him alone, he will take great pride in doing his work. If he sees the Boss appreciates his work he will go out of his way for him. But don't get *tuff with him*. Tell him in a pleasant way how you want to have it done. He is very *touchie*, his feeling is very easily hurt, and so are mine. I have quit several jobs & so has Perry on account of Bully Bosses. Perry does not have much schooling I dont either, I only had *second reader*. But dont let that make you think we are not *sharp*. Im a self taught man & so is Perry. A *White Colar* job is not for *Perry or me*. But outdoors jobs we can master & if we cant, show him or me how its done & in just a couple of days we can master a job or machine. Books are out. Actual experience we both catch on rite now, if we like to work at it. First of all we must like the job. But now hes a Cripple and almost middle-aged man. Perry knows he is not wanted now by Contracters, cripples can't get jobs on heavy equiptment, unless you are well known to the Contracter. He is beginning to realize that, he is beginning to think of a more easier way of supporting himself in line with my life. Im sure Im *correct*. I also think speed is no longer his desire. I notice all that now in his letters to me. He says "be careful Dad. Don't drive if you feel sleepy, better stop & rest by the road side". These are the same words I used to tell him. Now he's telling me. He's learned a lesson.

'As I see it – Perry has learned a lesson he will never forget. Freedom means everything to him you will never get him behind bars again. Im quite sure Im rite. I notice a big change in the way he talks. He deeply regrets his mistake he told me. I also know he feels ashamed to meet people he knows he will not tell them he was behind bars. He asked me not to mention where he is to his friends. When he wrote & told me he was behind bars, I told him let that be a lesson – that I was glad that it happened that way when it could have been worse. Someone could have shot him. I also told him to take his term behind bars with a smile U done it yourself. U know better. I didn't raise you to steal from others, so dont complain to me how tuff it is in prison. Be a good boy in prison. & he promised that he would. I hope he is a good prisoner. Im sure no one will talk him into stealing anymore. The *law is boss*, he knows that. He loves his Freedom.

'How well I know that Perry is goodhearted if you treat him rite. Treat him mean & you got a buzz saw to fight. You can trust him with any amount of $ if your his friend. He will do as you say he wont steal a cent from a friend or anyone else. Before this happened. And I sincerely hope he will live the rest of his life a honest man. He did steal something in Company with others when he was a little kid. Just ask Perry if I was a good father to him ask him if his mother was good to him in Frisco. Perry knows whats good for him. U got him whipped forever. He knows when he's beat. He's not a dunce. He knows life is too short to sweet to spend behind bars ever again.

'RELATIVES. One sister *Bobo* married, and me his father is all that is living of Perry. Bobo & her husband are self-supporting. Own their own home & I'm able & active to take care of myself also. I sold my lodge in Alaska two years ago. I intend to have another small place of my own next year. I located several mineral claims & hope to get something out of them. Besides that I have not give up prospecting. I am also asked to write a book on artistic wood carving, and the famous Trappers Den Lodge I build in Alaska once my homestead known by all tourists that travel by car to Anchorage and maybe I will. I'll share all I have with Perry. Anytime I eat he eats. As long as Im alive. & when I die Ive got life insurance that will be paid to him so he can start LIFE *Anew* when he gets free again. In case Im not alive then.'

The biography always set racing a stable of emotions – self-pity in the lead, love and hate running evenly at first, the latter ultimately pulling ahead. And most of the memories it released were unwanted, though not all. In fact, the first part of his life that Perry could remember was treasurable – a fragment composed of applause, glamour. He was perhaps three, and he was seated with his sisters and his older brother in the grandstand at an open-air rodeo; in the ring, a lean Cherokee girl rode a wild horse, a 'bucking bronc', and her loosened hair whipped back and forth, flew about like a flamenco dancer's. Her name was Flo Buckskin, and she was a professional rodeo performer, a 'champion bronc-rider'. So was her husband, Tex John Smith; it was while touring the Western rodeo circuit that the handsome Indian girl and the homely-handsome Irish cowboy had met, married, and had the four children sitting in the grandstand. (And Perry could remember many another rodeo spectacle – see again his father skipping about inside a circle of spinning lassos, or his mother, with silver and turquoise bangles jangling on her wrists, trick-riding at a desperado speed that thrilled her youngest child and caused crowds in towns from Texas to Oregon to 'stand up and clap'.)

Until Perry was five, the team of 'Tex & Flo' continued to work the rodeo circuit. As a way of life, it wasn't 'any gallon of ice cream', Perry once recalled: 'Six of us riding in an old truck, sleeping in it, too, sometimes, living off mush and Hershey kisses and condensed milk. Hawks Brand condensed milk it was called, which is what weakened my kidneys – the *sugar* content – which is why I was always wetting the bed.' Yet it was not an unhappy existence, especially for a little boy proud of his parents, admiring of their showmanship and courage – a happier life, certainly, than what replaced it. For Tex and Flo, both forced by ailments to retire from their occupation, settled near Reno, Nevada. They fought, and Flo 'took to whisky', and then, when Perry was six, she departed for San Francisco, taking the children with her. It was exactly as the old man had written: 'I let her go and said goodby as she took the car and left me behind (this was during depression). My children all cryed at the top of their voices. She only cursed them saying they would run away to come to me later.' And, indeed, over the course of the next three years Perry had on several occasions run off, set out to find his lost father, for he had lost his mother as well, learned to 'despise' her; liquor had blurred the face, swollen the figure of the once sinewy, limber Cherokee girl, had 'soured her soul', honed her

tongue to the wickedest point, so dissolved her self
that generally she did not bother to ask the names
stevedores and trolley-car conductors and such persons who
accepted what she offered without charge (except that she
insisted they drink with her first, and dance to the tunes of
a wind-up Victrola).

Consequently, as Perry recalled, 'I was always thinking
about Dad, hoping he could come take me away, and I remember, like a second ago, the time I saw him again. Standing in the schoolyard. It was like when the ball hits the bat
really solid. Di Maggio. Only Dad wouldn't help me. He
told me to be good and hugged me and went away. It was
not long afterward my mother put me to stay in a Catholic
orphanage. The one where the Black Widows were always
at me. Hitting me. Because of wetting the bed. Which is
one reason I have an aversion to nuns. *And* God. *And* religion. But later on I found there are people even more
evil. Because, after a couple of months, they tossed me out
of the orphanage, and she [his mother] put me some place
worse. A children's shelter operated by the Salvation Army.
They hated me, too. For wetting the bed. And being half-
Indian. There was this one nurse, she used to call me
"nigger" and say there wasn't any difference between niggers and Indians. Oh, Jesus, was she an Evil Bastard! In-
carnate. What she used to do, she'd fill a tub with ice-cold
water, put me in it, and hold me under till I was blue. Nearly
drowned. But she got found out, the bitch. Because I caught
pneumonia. I almost conked. I was in the hospital two
months. It was while I was so sick that Dad came back.
When I got well, he took me away.'

For almost a year father and son lived together in the
house near Reno, and Perry went to school. 'I finished the
third grade,' Perry recalled. 'Which *was* the finish. I never
went back. Because that summer Dad built a primitive sort
of trailer, what he called a "house car". It had two bunks
and a little cooking galley. The stove was good. You could
cook anything on it. Baked our own bread. I used to put up
preserves – picked apples, crab-apple jelly. Anyway, for
the next six years we shifted around the country. Never

stayed nowhere too long. When we stayed some place too long, people would begin to look at Dad, act like he was a character, and I hated that, it hurt me. Because I loved Dad then. Even though he could be rough on me. Bossy as hell. But I loved Dad then. So I was always glad when we moved on.' Moved on – to Wyoming, Idaho, Oregon, eventually Alaska. In Alaska, Tex taught his son to dream of gold, to hunt for it in the sandy beds of snow-water streams, and there, too, Perry learned to use a gun, skin a bear, track wolves and deer.

'Christ, it was cold,' Perry remembered. 'Dad and I slept hugged together, rolled up in blankets and bearskins. Mornings, before daylight, I'd hustle our breakfast, biscuits and syrup, fried meat, and off we went to scratch a living. It would have been O.K. if only I hadn't grown up; the older I got, the less I was able to appreciate Dad. He knew everything, one way, but he didn't know anything, another way. Whole sections of me Dad was ignorant of. Didn't understand an iota of. Like I could play a harmonica first time I picked one up. Guitar, too. I had this great natural musical ability. Which Dad didn't recognize. Or care about. I liked to read, too. Improve my vocabulary. Make up songs. And I could draw. But I never got any encouragement – from him or anybody else. Nights I used to lie awake – trying to control my bladder, partly, and partly because I couldn't stop thinking, Always, when it was too cold hardly to breathe, I'd think about Hawaii. About a movie I'd seen. With Dorothy Lamour. I wanted to go there. Where the sun was. And all you wore was grass and flowers.'

Wearing considerably more, Perry, one balmy evening in wartime 1945, found himself inside a Honolulu tattoo parlour having a snake-and-dagger design applied to his left forearm. He had got there by the following route: a row with his father, a hitchhike journey from Anchorage to Seattle, a visit to the recruiting offices of the Merchant Marine. 'But I never would have joined if I'd known what I was going up against,' Perry once said. 'I never minded the work, and I liked being a sailor – seaports, and all that. But the queens on ship wouldn't leave me alone. A sixteen-year-old kid, and a small kid. I could handle myself, sure. But a lot of queens aren't effeminate, you know. Hell, I've known queens could toss a pool table out the window. And the piano after it. Those kind of girls, they can give you an evil time, especially when there's a couple of them, they get together and gang up on you, and you're just a kid. It can make you practically want to kill yourself. Years later, when I went into the Army – when I was stationed in Korea – the same problem came up. I had a good record in the Army, good as anybody; they gave me the Bronze Star. But I never got promoted. After four years, and fighting through the whole goddam Korean war, I ought at least to have made corporal. But I never did. Know why? Because the sergeant we had was tough. Because I wouldn't roll over. Jesus, I hate that stuff. I can't stand it. Though – *I* don't know. Some queers I've really liked. As long as they didn't try anything. The most worthwhile friend I ever had, really sensitive and intelligent, he turned out to be queer.'

In the interval between quitting the Merchant Marine and entering the Army, Perry had made peace with his father, who, when his son left him, drifted down to Nevada, then back to Alaska. In 1952, the year Perry completed his military service, the old man was in the midst of plans meant to end his travels for ever. 'Dad was in a fever,' Perry recalled. 'Wrote me he had bought some land on the highway outside Anchorage. Said he was going to have a hunting lodge, a place for tourists. "Trapper's Den Lodge" – that was to be the name. And asked me to hurry on up there and help him build it. He was sure we'd make a fortune. Well, while I was still in the Army, stationed at Fort Lewis, Washington, I'd bought a motor-cycle (murdercycles, they ought to call them), and as soon as I got discharged I headed for Alaska. Got as far as Bellingham. Up there on the border. It was raining. My bike went into a skid.'

The skid delayed for a year the reunion with his father. Surgery and hospitalization account for six months of that year; the remainder he spent recuperating in the forest home, near Bellingham, of a young Indian logger and fisherman. 'Joe James. He and his wife befriended me. The difference in our age was only two or three years, but they took me into their home and treated me like I was one of their kids. Which was O.K. Because they took trouble with their kids and liked them. At the time they had four; the number finally went to seven. They were very good to me, Joe and his family. I was on crutches, I was pretty helpless. Just had to sit around. So to give me something to do, try to make myself useful, I started what became a sort of school. The pupils were Joe's kids, along with some of their friends, and we held classes in the parlour. I was teaching harmonica and guitar. Drawing. And penmanship. Everybody always remarks what a beautiful handwriting I have. I do, and it's because once I bought a book on the subject and practised till I could write same as in the book. Also, we used to read stories – the kids did, each one in turn, and I'd correct them as we went along. It was fun. I like kids. *Little* kids. And that was a nice time. But then the spring came. It hurt me to walk, but I could walk. And Dad was still waiting for me.'

Waiting, but not idly. By the time Perry arrived at the site of the proposed hunting lodge, his father, working alone, had finished the hardest chores – had cleared the ground, logged the necessary timber, cracked and carted wagonloads of native rock. 'But he didn't commence to build till I got there. We did every damn piece of it ourselves. With once in a while an Indian helper. Dad was like a maniac. It didn't matter what was happening – snowstorms, rainstorms, winds that could split a tree – we kept right at it. The day the roof was finished. Dad danced all over it, shouting and laughing, doing a regular jig. Well, it turned out quite an exceptional place. That could sleep twenty people. Had a big fireplace in the dining room. And there was a cocktail lounge. The Totem Pole Cocktail Lounge. Where I was to entertain the customers. Singing and so forth. We opened for business end of 1953.'

But the expected huntsmen did not materialize, and though ordinary tourists – the few that trickled along the highway – now and again paused to photograph the beyond-belief rusticity of Trapper's Den Lodge, they seldom stopped overnight. 'For a while we fooled ourselves. Kept thinking it would catch on. Dad tried to trick up the place. Made a Garden of Memories. With a Wishing Well. Put painted signs up and down the highway. But none of it meant a nickel more. When Dad realized that – saw it wasn't any use, all we'd done was waste ourselves and all our money – he began to take it out on me. Boss me around. Be spiteful. Say I didn't do my proper share of the work. It wasn't his fault, any more than it was mine. A situation like that, with no money and the grub getting low, we couldn't help but be on each other's nerves. The point came we were downright hungry. Which is what we fell out over. Ostensibly. A biscuit. Dad snatched a biscuit out of my hand, and said I ate too much, what a greedy, selfish bastard I was, and why didn't I get out, he didn't want me there no more. He carried on like that till I couldn't stand it. My hands got hold of his throat. *My* hands – but I couldn't control them. They wanted to choke him to death. Dad, though, he's slippery, a smart wrestler. He tore loose and ran to get his gun. Came back pointing it at me. He said, "Look at me, Perry. I'm the last thing living you're ever gonna see." I just stood my ground. And he pulled the trigger. And pulled again. And when he realized the gun wasn't even loaded he started to cry. Sat down and bawled like a kid. Then I guess I wasn't mad at him any more. I was sorry for him. For both of us. But it wasn't a bit of use – there wasn't anything I could say. I went out for a walk. This was April, but the woods were still deep in snow. I walked till it was almost night. When I got back, the lodge was dark, and all the doors were locked. And everything I owned was lying out there in the snow. Where Dad had thrown it. Books. Clothes. Everything. I just let it lie. Except my guitar. I picked up my guitar and started on down the highway. Not a dollar in my pocket. Around midnight a truck stopped to give me a lift. The driver asked where I was going. I told him, "Wherever you're headed, that's where I'm going." '

Several weeks later, after again sheltering with the James

family, Perry decided on a definite destination – Worcester, Massachusetts, the home town of an 'Army buddy' he thought might welcome him and help him find 'a good-paying job'. Various detours prolonged the eastward journey; he washed dishes in an Omaha restaurant, pumped gas at an Oklahoma garage, worked a month on a ranch in Texas. By July of 1955 he had reached, on the trek to Worcester, a small Kansas town, Phillipsburg, and there 'fate', in the form of 'bad company', asserted itself. 'His name was Smith,' Perry said. 'Same as me. I don't even recall his first name. He was just somebody I'd picked up with somewhere, and he had a car, and he said he'd give me a ride as far as Chicago. Anyway, driving through Kansas we came to this little Phillipsburg place and stopped to look at a map. Seems to me like it was a Sunday. Stores shut. Streets quiet. My friend there, bless his heart, he looked around and made a suggestion.' The suggestion was that they burglarize a near-by building, the Chandler Sales Company. Perry agreed, and they broke into the deserted premises and removed a quantity of office equipment (typewriters, adding machines). That might have been that if only, some days afterwards, the thieves hadn't ignored a traffic signal in the city of Saint Joseph, Missouri. 'The junk was still in the car. The cop that stopped us wanted to know where we got it. A little checking was done, and, as they say, we were "returned" to Phillipsburg, Kansas. Where the folks have a real cute jail. If you like jails.' Within forty-eight hours Perry and his companion had discovered an open window, climbed out of it, stolen a car, and driven northwest to McCook, Nebraska. 'Pretty soon we broke up, me and Mr Smith. I don't know what ever became of him. We both made the F.B.I.'s Wanted list. But far as I know, they never caught up with *him*.'

One wet afternoon the following November, a Greyhound bus deposited Perry in Worcester, a Massachusetts factory town of steep, up-and-down streets that even in the best of weathers seem cheerless and hostile. 'I found the house where my friend was supposed to live. My Army friend from Korea. But the people there said he'd left six months back and they had no idea where he'd gone. Too bad, big disappointment, end of the world, all that. So I found a liquor store and bought a half gallon of red wop and went back to the bus depot and sat there drinking my wine and getting a little warmer. I was really enjoying my-self till a man came along and arrested me for vagrancy.' The police booked him as 'Bob Turner' – a name he'd adopted because of being listed by the F.B.I. He spent four-teen days in jail, was fined ten dollars, and departed from Worcester on another wet November afternoon. 'I went down to New York and took a room in a hotel on Eighth Avenue,' Perry said. 'Near Forty-second Street. Finally, I got a night job. Doing odd jobs around a penny arcade. Right there on Forty-second Street, next to an Automat. Which is where I ate – *when* I ate. In over three months I practically never left the Broadway area. For one thing, I didn't have the right clothes. Just Western clothes – jeans and boots. But there on Forty-second Street nobody cares, it all rides – *any*thing. My whole life, I never met so many freaks.'

He lived out the winter in that ugly, neon-lit neighbour-hood, with its air full of the scent of popcorn, simmering hot dogs, and orange drink. But then, one bright March morning on the edge of spring, as he remembered it, 'two F.B.I. bastards woke me up. Arrested me at the hotel. Bang! – I was extradited back to Kansas. To Phillipsburg. That same cute jail. They nailed me to the cross – larceny, jailbreak, car theft. I got five to ten years. In Lansing. After I'd been there awhile, I wrote Dad. Let him know the news. And wrote Barbara, my sister. By now, over the years, that was all I had left me. Jimmy a suicide. Fern out the win-dow. My mother dead. Been dead eight years. Everybody gone but Dad and Barbara.'

A letter from Barbara was among the sheaf of selected matter that Perry preferred not to leave behind in the Mexico City hotel room. The letter, written in a pleasingly legible script, was dated April 28, 1958, at which time the recipient had been imprisoned for approximately two years:

Dearest Bro. Perry,

We got your 2nd letter today & forgive me for not writing sooner. Our weather here, as yours is, is turning warmer & maybe I am getting spring fever but I am going to try and do better. Your first letter was very disturbing, as I'm sure you must have suspected but that was not the reason I haven't written – it's true the children do keep me busy & it's hard to find time to sit and concentrate on a letter as I have wanted to write you for some time. Donnie has learned to open the doors and climb on the chairs & other furniture & he worries me constantly about falling.

I have been able to let the children play in the yard now & then – but I always have to go out with them as they can hurt themselves if I don't pay attention. But nothing is forever & I know I will be sorry when they start running the block & I don't know where they're at. Here are some statistics if you're interested –

	Height	Weight	Shoe Size
Freddie	36½ in.	26½ lb.	7½ narrow
Baby	37½ in.	29½ lb.	8 narrow
Donnie	34 in.	26 lb.	6½ wide

You can see that Donnie is a pretty big boy for 15 months & with his 16 teeth and his sparkling personality – people just can't help loving him. He wears the same size clothes as Baby and Freddie but the pants are too long as yet.

I am going to try & make this letter a long one so it will probably have a lot of interruptions such as right now it's time for Donnie's bath – Baby & Freddie had theirs this a.m. as it's quite cold today & I have had them inside. Be back soon –

About my typing – First – I cannot tell a lie! I am not a typist. I use from 1 to 5 fingers & although I can manage & do help Big Fred with his business affairs, what it takes me 1 hr. to do would probably take someone with the Know How – 15 minutes – Seriously, I do not have the time nor the *will* to learn professionally. But I think it is wonderful how you have stuck with it and become such an excellent typist. I do believe we all were very adaptable (Jimmy, Fern, you and myself) & we had all been blessed with a basic flair for the artistic – among other things. Even Mother & Dad were artistic.

I truthfully feel none of us have *anyone* to blame for *whatever* we have done with our own personal lives. It has been proven that at the age of 7 most of us have reached the *age of reason* – which means we *do*, at this age, *understand* & *know* the difference between right & wrong. Of course – environment plays an awfully important part in our lives such as the Convent in mine & in my case I am grateful for that influence. In Jimmy's case – he was the strongest of us all. I remember how he worked & went to school when there was no one to tell him & it was his own WILL to make something of himself. We will never know the reasons for what eventually happened, why he did what he did, but I still hurt thinking of it. It was such a waste. But we have very little control over our human weaknesses, & this applies also to Fern & the hundreds of thousands of other people including ourselves – for *we all* have weaknesses. In your case – I don't know what *your* weakness is but I do feel – IT IS NO SHAME TO HAVE A DIRTY FACE – THE SHAME COMES WHEN YOU KEEP IT DIRTY.

In all truthfulness & with love for you Perry, for you are my only living brother and the uncle of my children, I cannot say or feel your attitude towards our father or your imprisonment JUST or healthy. If you are getting your back up – better sim- mer down as I realize there are none of us who take criticism cheerfully & it is natural to feel a certain amount of resentment towards the one giving this criticism so I am prepared for one or two things – (a) Not to hear from you at all, or (b) a letter telling me exactly what you think of me.

I hope I'm wrong & I sincerely hope you will give this letter a lot of thought & *try* to see – how someone else feels. Please understand I know I am not an authority & I do not boast great intelligence or education but I do believe I am a normal in- dividual with basic reasoning powers & the will to live my life according to the laws of God & Man. It is also true that I have 'fallen' at times, as is normal – for as I said I am human & therefore I too have human weaknesses but the point is, again, There is no shame – having a dirty face – the shame comes when you keep it dirty. No one is more aware of my shortcomings and mistakes than myself so I won't bore you further.

Now, first & most important – Dad is *not* responsible for your wrong doings *or* your good deeds. What you have done, whether *right* or *wrong*, is *your own doing*. From what I per- sonally know, you have lived your life exactly as you pleased *without* regard to circumstances or persons who loved you – who might be hurt. Whether you realize it or not – your present confinement is embarrassing to me as well as Dad – not because of what you did but the fact that you don't show me any signs of SINCERE regret and seem to show no *respect* for any laws, people or anything. Your letter implies that the blame of all your problems is that of someone else, but never you. I do admit that you are intelligent & your vocabulary is excellent & I do feel you can do anything you decide to do & do it well but what exactly do you want to do & are you willing to *work* & make an *honest* effort to attain whatever it is you choose to do? Nothing good comes easy & I'm sure you've heard this many times but once more won't hurt.

In case you want the truth about Dad – his heart is broken because of you. He would give anything to get you out so he can have his son back – but I am afraid you would only hurt him worse if you could. He is not well and is getting older &, as the saying goes, he cannot – 'Cut the Mustard' as in the old days. He has been wrong at times & he realizes this but whatever he had and wherever he went he shared his life & belongings with you when he wouldn't do this for anyone else. Now I don't say you owe him *undying gratitude* or your *life* but you do owe him RESPECT and COMMON DECENCY. I, personally, am proud of Dad. I love him & Respect him as my Dad & I am only sorry he chose to be the Lone Wolf with his son, or he might be living with us and share our love instead of alone in his little trailer & longing & waiting & lonesome for you, his son. I worry for him & when I say *I* I mean my husband too for my husband respects our Dad. Because he is a MAN. It's true that Dad did not have a great extensive education but in school we only learn to recognize the words and to spell but the *application* of these words to *real life* is another thing that only LIFE & LIVING can give us. Dad has lived & you show ignorance in calling him uneducated & unable to understand 'the scientific meaning etc' of life's problems. A mother is still the only one who can kiss a boo-boo and make it all well – explain that *scientifically*.

I'm sorry to let you have it so strong but I feel I must speak my piece. I am sorry that this must be censored [by the prison authorities], & I sincerely hope this letter is not detrimental towards your eventual release but I feel you should know & realize what terrible hurt you have done. Dad is the important one as I am dedicated to my family but you are the only one Dad loves – in short, his 'family'. He knows I love him, of course, but the closeness is not there, as you know.

Your confinement is nothing to be proud of and you will have to live with it & try & live it down & it can be done but not with your attitude of feeling everyone is stupid & uneducated & un-

understanding. You are a human being with a *free will*. Which puts you above the animal level. But if you live your life without feeling and compassion for your fellow-man – you are as an animal – 'an eye for an eye, a tooth for a tooth' & happiness & peace of mind is not attained by living thus.

As far as responsibility goes, no one really wants it – but all of us are responsible to the community we live in & its laws. When the time comes to assume the responsibility of a home and children or business, this is the seeding of the boys from the Men – for surely you can realize what a mess the world would be if everyone in it said, 'I want to be an individual, without responsibilities, & be able to speak my mind freely & do as *I* alone will.' We are all free to speak & do as we individually will – *providing* this 'freedom' of Speech & Deed are not injurious to our fellow-man.

Think about it, Perry. You are above average in intelligence, but somehow your reasoning is off the beam. Maybe it's the strain of your confinement. Whatever it is – remember – you & only you are responsible and it is up to you and you alone to overcome this part of your life. Hoping to hear from you soon.

> With Love & Prayers,
> Your sister & Bro. in Law
> Barbara & Frederic & Family

In preserving this letter, and including it in his collection of particular treasures, Perry was not moved by affection. Far from it. He 'loathed' Barbara, and just the other day he had told Dick, 'The only *real* regret I have – I wish the hell my sister had been in that house.' (Dick had laughed, and confessed to a similar yearning: 'I keep thinking what fun if my second wife had been there. Her, and all her goddam family.') No, he valued the letter merely because his prison friend, the 'super-intelligent' Willie-Jay, had written for him a 'very sensitive' analysis of it, occupying two single-spaced typewritten pages, with the title 'Impressions I Garnered from the Letter' at the top:

IMPRESSIONS I GARNERED FROM THE LETTER

(1) When she began this letter, she intended that it should be a compassionate demonstration of Christian principles. That is to say that in return for your letter to her, which apparently annoyed her, she meant to turn the other cheek hoping in this

way to incite regret for your previous letter and to place you on the defensive in your next.

However few people can successfully demonstrate a principle in common ethics when their deliberation is festered with emotionalism. Your sister substantiates this failing for as her letter progresses her judgement gives way to temper – her thoughts are good, lucid, the products of intelligence, but it is not now an unbiased, impersonal intelligence. It is a mind propelled by emotional response to memory and frustration; consequently, however wise her admonishments might be, they fail to inspire resolve, unless it would be the resolve to retaliate by hurting her in your next letter. Thus commencing a cycle that can only culminate in further anger and distress.

(2) It is a foolish letter, but born of human failing.

Your letter to her, and this, her answer to you, failed in their objectives. Your letter was an attempt to explain your outlook on life, as you are necessarily affected by it. It was destined to be misunderstood, or taken too literally because your ideas are opposed to conventionalism. What could be *more* conventional than a housewife with three children, who is 'dedicated' to her family ? ? ? ? What could be more natural than that she would resent an unconventional person? There is considerable hypocrisy in conventionalism. Any thinking person is aware of this paradox; but in dealing with conventional people it is advantageous to treat them as though they were not hypocrites. It isn't a question of faithfulness to your own concepts; it is a matter of compromise so that you *can* remain an individual without the constant threat of conventional pressures. Her letter failed because she couldn't conceive of the profundity of your problem – she couldn't fathom the pressures brought to bear upon you because of environment, intellectual frustration and a growing tendency towards isolationism.

(3) She feels that:

(a) You are leaning too heavily towards self-pity.

(b) That you are too calculating.

(c) That you are really undeserving of an 8 page letter written in between motherly duties.

(4) On page 3 she writes: 'I truthfully feel none of us has anyone to blame etc.' Thus vindicating those who bore influence in her formative years. But is this the whole truth? She is a wife and mother. Respectable and more or less secure. It is easy to ignore the rain if you have a raincoat. But how would she feel if she were compelled to hustle her living on the streets? Would

she still be all-forgiving about the people in her past? Absolutely not. Nothing is more usual than to feel that others have shared in our failures, just as it is an ordinary reaction to forget those who have shared in our achievements.

(5) Your sister respects your Dad. She also resents the fact that you have been preferred. Her jealousy takes a subtle form in this letter. Between the lines she is registering a question: 'I love Dad and have tried to live so he could be proud to own me as his daughter. But I have had to content myself with the crumbs of his affection. Because it is you he loves, and why should it be so?'

Obviously over the years your Dad has taken advantage of your sister's emotional nature via the mails. Painting a picture that justifies her opinion of him – an underdog cursed with an ungrateful son upon whom he has showered love and concern, only to be infamously treated by that son in return.

On page 7 she says she is sorry that her letter must be censored. But she is really not sorry at all. She is glad it passes through a censor. Subconsciously she has written it with the censor in mind, hoping to convey the idea that the Smith family is really a well-ordered unit: *'Please do not judge us all by Perry.'*

About the mother kissing away her child's boo-boo. This is a woman's form of sarcasm.

(6) You write to her because:
    (a) You love her after a fashion.
    (b) You feel a need for this contact with the outside world.
    (c) You can use her.

Prognosis: Correspondence between you and your sister cannot serve anything but a purely social function. Keep the theme of your letters within the scope of her understanding. Do not unburden your private conclusions. Do not put her on the defensive and do not permit her to put you on the defensive. Respect her limitations to comprehend your objectives, and remember that she is touchy towards criticism of your Dad. Be consistent in your attitude towards her and do not add anything to the impression she has that you are weak, not because you need her good-will but because you can expect more letters like this, and *they can only serve to increase your already dangerous anti-social instincts.*

FINISH

As Perry continued to sort and choose, the pile of

material he thought too dear to part with, even temporarily, assumed a tottering height. But what was he to do? He couldn't risk losing the Bronze Medal earned in Korea, or his high-school diploma (issued by the Leavenworth County Board of Education as a result of his having, while in prison, resumed his long-recessed studies). Nor did he care to chance the loss of a manila envelope fat with photographs – primarily of himself, and ranging in time from a pretty-little-boy portrait made when he was in the Merchant Marine (and on the back of which he had scribbled, '16 yrs. old. Young, happy-go-lucky & Innocent') to the recent Acapulco pictures. And there were half a hundred other items he had decided he must take with him, among them his treasure maps, Otto's sketchbook, and two thick notebooks, the thicker of which constituted his personal dictionary, a non-alphabetically listed miscellany of words he believed 'beautiful' or 'useful', or at least 'worth memorizing'. (Sample page: 'Thanatoid = deathlike; Omnilingual = versed in languages; Amerce = punishment, amount fixed by court; Nescient = ignorance; Facinorous = atrociously wicked; Hagiophobia = a morbid fear of holy places & things; Lapidicolous = living under stones, as certain blind beetles; Dyspathy = lack of sympathy, fellow feeling; Psilopher = a fellow who fain would pass as a philosopher; Omophagia = eating raw flesh, the rite of some savage tribes; Depredate=to pillage, rob and prey upon; Aphrodisiac=a drug or the like which excites sexual desire; Megalodactylous = having abnormally large fingers; Myrtophobia=fear of night and darkness.')

On the cover of the second notebook, the handwriting of which he was so proud, a script abounding in curly, feminine flourishes, proclaimed the contents to be 'The Private Diary of Perry Edward Smith' – an inaccurate description, for it was not in the least a diary, but rather a form of anthology consisting of obscure facts ('Every fifteen years Mars gets closer. 1958 is a close year'), poems and literary quotations ('No man is an island, Entire of itself.'), and passages from newspapers and books paraphrased or quoted. For example:

'My acquaintances are many, my friends are few; those who really know me fewer still.

'Heard about a new rat poison on the market. Extremely potent, odourless, tasteless, is so completely absorbed once swallowed that no trace could ever be found in a dead body.

'If called upon to make a speech: "I can't remember what I was going to say for the life of me – I don't think that ever before in my life have so many people been so directly responsible for my being so very, very glad. It's a wonderful moment and a rare one and I'm certainly indebted. Thank you!"

'Read interesting article Feb. issue of *Man to Man*: "I Knifed My Way to a Diamond Pit."

' "It is almost impossible for a man who enjoys freedom with all its prerogatives, to realize what it means to be deprived of that freedom." – Said by Erle Stanley Gardner.

' "What is life? It is the flash of a firefly in the night. It is a breath of a buffalo in the wintertime. It is as the little shadow that runs across the grass and loses itself in the sunset." – Said by Chief Crowfoot, Blackfoot Indian Chief.'

This last entry was written in red ink and decorated with a border of green-ink stars; the anthologist wished to emphasize its 'personal significance'. 'A breath of a buffalo in the wintertime' – that exactly evoked his view of life. Why worry? What was there to 'sweat about'? Man was nothing, a mist, a shadow absorbed by shadows.

But, damn it, you do worry, scheme, fret over your fingernails and the warnings of hotel managements– 'Su Día Termina a las 2 p.m.'

'Dick? You hear me?' Perry said. 'It's almost one o'clock.'

Dick was awake. He was rather more than that; he and Inez were making love. As though reciting a rosary, Dick incessantly whispered: 'Is it good, baby? Is it good?' But Inez, smoking a cigarette, remained silent. The previous midnight, when Dick had brought her to the room and told Perry that she was going to sleep there, Perry, though disapproving, had acquiesced, but if they imagined that their conduct stimulated him, or seemed to him anything other than a 'nuisance', they were wrong. Nevertheless, Perry felt sorry for Inez. She was such a 'stupid kid' – she really believed that Dick meant to marry her, and had no idea he was planning to leave Mexico that very afternoon.

'Is it good, baby? Is it good?'

Perry said: 'For Christsake, Dick. Hurry it up, will you? Our day ends at two p.m.'

It was Saturday, Christmas was near, and the traffic crept along Main Street. Dewey, caught in the traffic, looked up at the holly garlands that hung above the street – swags of gala greenery trimmed with scarlet paper bells – and was reminded that he had not yet bought a single gift for his wife or his sons. His mind automatically rejected problems not concerned with the Clutter case. Marie and many of their friends had begun to wonder at the completeness of his fixation.

One close friend, the young lawyer Clifford R. Hope, Jr, had spoken plainly: 'Do you know what's happening to you, Al? Do you realize you never talk about anything else?' 'Well,' Dewey had replied, 'that's all I think about. And there's the chance that just while talking the thing over, I'll hit on something I haven't thought of before. Some new angle. Or maybe *you* will. Damn it, Cliff, what do you suppose my life will be if this thing stays in the Open File? Years from now I'll still be running down tips, and every time there's a murder, a case anywhere in the country even remotely similar, I'll have to horn right in, check, see if there could be any possible connexion. But it isn't only that. The real thing is I've come to feel I know Herb and the family better than they ever knew themselves. I'm haunted by them. I guess I always will be. Until I know what happened.'

Dewey's dedication to the puzzle had resulted in an uncharacteristic absent-mindedness. Only that morning Marie had asked him please, would he please, *please,* not forget to ... But he couldn't remember, or didn't, until, free of the shopping-day traffic and racing along Route 50 towards Holcomb, he passed Dr I. E. Dale's veterinarian establishment.

Of *course*. His wife had asked him to be sure and collect the family cat, Courthouse Pete. Pete, a tiger-striped tom weighing fifteen pounds, is a well-known character around Garden City, famous for his pugnacity, which was the cause of his current hospitalization; a battle lost to a boxer dog had left him with wounds necessitating both stitches and antibiotics. Released by Dr Dale, Pete settled down on the front seat of his owner's automobile and purred all the way to Holcomb.

The detective's destination was River Valley Farm, but wanting something warm – a cup of hot coffee – he stopped off at Hartman's Café.

'Hello, handsome,' said Mrs Hartman. 'What can I do for you?'

'Just coffee, ma'am.'

She poured a cup. 'Am I wrong? Or have you lost a lot of weight?'

'Some.' In fact, during the past three weeks Dewey had dropped twenty pounds. His suits fitted as though he had borrowed them from a stout friend, and his face, seldom suggestive of his profession, was now not at all so; it could have been that of an ascetic absorbed in occult pursuits.

'How do you feel?'

'Mighty fine.'

'You *look* awful.'

Unarguably. But no worse than the other members of the K.B.I. entourage – Agents Duntz, Church, and Nye. Certainly he was in better shape than Harold Nye, who, though full of flu and fever, kept reporting for duty. Among them, the four tired men had 'checked out' some seven hundred tips and rumours. Dewey, for example, had spent two wearying and wasted days trying to trace that phantom pair, the Mexicans sworn by Paul Helm to have visited Mr Clutter on the eve of the murders.

'Another cup, Alvin?'

'Don't guess I will. Thank you, ma'am.'

But she had already fetched the pot. 'It's on the house, Sheriff. How you look, you need it.'

At a corner table two whiskery ranch hands were

playing draughts. One of them got up and came over to the counter where Dewey was seated. He said, 'Is it true what we heard?'

'Depends.'

'About that fellow you caught? Prowling in the Clutter house? He's the one responsible. That's what we heard.'

'I think you heard wrong, old man. Yes, sir, I do.'

Although the past life of Jonathan Daniel Adrian, who was then being held in the county jail on a charge of carrying a concealed weapon, included a period of confinement as a mental patient in Topeka State Hospital, the data assembled by the investigators indicated that in relation to the Clutter case he was guilty only of an unhappy curiosity.

'Well, if he's the wrong un, why the hell don't you find the right un? I got a houseful of women won't go to the *bath*-room alone.'

Dewey had become accustomed to this brand of abuse; it was a routine part of his existence. He swallowed the second cup of coffee, sighed, smiled.

'Hell, I'm not cracking jokes. I mean it. Why don't you arrest somebody? That's what you're paid for.'

'Hush your meanness,' said Mrs Hartman. 'We're all in the same boat. Alvin's doing good as he can.'

Dewey winked at her. 'You tell him, ma'am. And much obliged for the coffee.'

The ranch hand waited until his quarry had reached the door, then fired a farewell volley. 'If you ever run for sheriff again, just forget my vote. 'Cause you *ain't* gonna get it.'

'Hush your meanness,' said Mrs Hartman.

A mile separates River Valley Farm from Hartman's Café. Dewey decided to walk it. He enjoyed hiking across wheat fields. Normally, once or twice a week he went for long walks on his own land, the well-loved piece of prairie where he had always hoped to build a house, plant trees, eventually entertain great-grandchildren. That was the dream, but it was one his wife had lately warned him she no longer shared; she had told him that never now would she consider living all alone 'way out there in the country'. Dewey knew that even if he were to snare the murderers the next day, Marie would not change her mind – for once an awful fate had befallen friends who lived in a lonely country house.

Of course, the Clutter family were not the first persons ever murdered in Finney County, or even in Holcomb. Senior members of that small community can recall 'a wild goings-on' of more than forty years ago – the Hefner Slaying. Mrs Sadie Truitt, the hamlet's septuagenarian mail messenger, who is the mother of Postmistress Clare, is expert on this fabled affair: 'August, it was. 1920. Hot *as* Hades. A fellow called Tunif was working on the Finnup ranch. *Walter* Tunif. He had a car, turned out to be stolen. Turned out he was a soldier AWOL from Fort Bliss, over there in Texas. He was a rascal, sure enough, and a lot of people suspected him. So one evening the sheriff – them days that was Orlie Hefner, such a fine singer, don't you know he's part of the Heavenly Choir? – one evening he rode out to the Finnup ranch to ask Tunif a few straightforward questions. Third of August. Hot *as* Hades. Outcome of it was, Walter Tunif shot the sheriff right through the heart. Poor Orlie was gone 'fore he hit the ground. The devil who done it, he lit out of there on one of the Finnup horses, rode east along the river. Word spread, and men for miles around made up a posse. Along about the next morning, they caught up with him; old *Wal*ter Tunif. He didn't get the chance to say how d'you do? On account of the boys were pretty irate. They just let the buckshot fly.'

Dewey's own initial contact with foul play in Finney County occurred in 1947. The incident is noted in his files as follows: 'John Carlyle Polk, a Creek Indian, 25 years of age, resident Muskogee, Okla., killed Mary Kay Finley, white female, 40 years of age, a waitress residing in Garden City. Polk stabbed her with the jagged neck of a beer bottle in a room in the Copeland Hotel, Garden City, Kansas, 5-9-47.' A cut-and-dried description of an open-and-shut case. Of three other murders Dewey had since investigated, two were equally obvious (a pair of railroad workers robbed and killed an elderly farmer, 11-1-52; a drunken husband beat and kicked his wife to death, 6–7–56), but the third case, as it was once conversationally narrated by Dewey, was not without several original touches. 'It all started out at Stevens Park. Where they have a bandstand, and under the bandstand a men's room. Well, this man named Mooney was walking around the park. He was from North Carolina somewhere, just a stranger passing through town. Anyway, he went to the rest room, and somebody followed him inside – a boy from hereabouts, Wilmer Lee Stebbins, twenty years old. Afterwards, Wilmer Lee always claimed Mr Mooney made him an unnatural suggestion. And that was why he robbed Mr Mooney, and knocked him down, and banged his head on the cement floor, and why, when *that* didn't finish him, he stuck Mr Mooney's head in a toilet bowl and kept on flushing till he drowned him. Maybe so. But nothing can explain the rest of Wilmer Lee's behaviour. First off, he buried the body a couple of miles northeast of Garden City. Next day he dug it up and put it down fourteen miles the other direction. Well, it went on like that, burying reburying. Wilmer Lee was like a dog with a bone – he just wouldn't let Mr Mooney rest in peace. Finally, he dug one grave too many; somebody saw him.' Prior to the Clutter mystery, the four cases cited were the sum of Dewey's experience with murder, and measured against the case confronting him, were as squalls preceding a hurricane.

Dewey fitted a key into the front door of the Clutter house. Inside, the house was warm, for the heat had not been turned off, and the shiny-floored rooms, smelling of a lemon-scented polish, seemed only temporarily untenanted; it was as though today were Sunday and the family might at any moment return from church. The heirs, Mrs English and Mrs Jarchow, had removed a vanload of clothing and furniture, yet the atmosphere of a house still humanly inhabited had not thereby been diminished. In the parlour, a sheet of music, 'Comin' Thro' the Rye' stood open on the piano rack. In the hall, a sweat-stained gray Stetson hat – Herb's – hung on a hat peg. Upstairs in Kenyon's room, on a shelf above his bed, the lenses of the dead boy's spectacles gleamed with reflected light.

The detective moved from room to room. He had toured the house many times; indeed, he went out there almost every day, and, in one sense, could be said to find these visits pleasurable, for the place, unlike his own home, or the sheriff's office, with its hullabaloo, was peaceful. The telephones, their wires still severed, were silent. The great quiet of the prairies surrounded him. He could sit in Herb's parlour rocking-chair, and rock and think. A few of his conclusions were unshakeable: he believed that the death of Herb Clutter had been the criminals' main objective, the motive being a psychopathic hatred, or possibly a combination of hatred and thievery, and he believed that the commission of the murders had been a leisurely labour, with perhaps two or more hours elapsing between the entrance of the killers and their exit. (The coroner, Dr Robert Fenton, reported an appreciable difference in the body temperatures of the victims, and on this basis, theorized that the order of execution had been: Mrs Clutter, Nancy, Kenyon, and Mr Clutter.) Attendant upon these beliefs was his conviction that the family had known very well the persons who destroyed them.

During this visit Dewey paused at an upstairs window, his attention caught by something seen in the near distance – a scarecrow amid the wheat stubble. The scarecrow wore a man's hunting-cap and a dress of weather-faded flowered calico. (Surely an old dress of Bonnie Clutter's?) Wind frolicked the skirt and made the scarecrow sway – made it seem a creature forlornly dancing in the cold December field. And Dewey was somehow reminded of Marie's dream. One recent morning she had served him a bungled breakfast of sugared eggs and salted coffee, then blamed it all on 'a silly dream' – but a dream the power of daylight had not dispersed. 'It was so real, Alvin,' she said. 'As real as this kitchen. That's where I was. Here in the kitchen. I was cooking supper, and suddenly Bonnie walked through the door. She was wearing a blue angora sweater, and she looked so sweet and pretty. And I said, "Oh,

Bonnie ... Bonnie, dear ... I haven't seen you since that terrible thing happened." But she didn't answer, only looked at me in that shy way of hers, and I didn't know how to go on. Under the circumstances. So I said, "Honey, come see what I'm making Alvin for his supper. A pot of gumbo. With shrimp and fresh crabs. It's just about ready. Come on, honey, have a taste." But she wouldn't. She stayed by the door looking at me. And then – I don't know how to tell you exactly, but she shut her eyes, she began to shake her head, very slowly, and wring her hands, *very* slowly, and to whimper, or whisper. I couldn't understand *what* she was saying. But it broke my heart, I never felt so sorry for anyone, and I hugged her. I said, "Please, Bonnie! Oh, don't, darling, don't! If ever anyone was prepared to go to God, it was you, Bonnie." But I couldn't comfort her. She shook her head, and wrung her hands, and then I heard what she was saying. She was saying, "To be murdered. To be murdered. No. No. There's nothing worse. Nothing worse than that. Nothing." '

It was midday deep in the Mojave Desert. Perry, sitting on a straw suitcase, was playing a harmonica. Dick was standing at the side of a black-surfaced highway, Route 66, his eyes fixed upon the immaculate emptiness as though the fervour of his gaze could force motorists to materialize. Few did, and none of those stopped for the hitchhikers. One truck driver, bound for Needles, California, had offered a lift, but Dick had declined. That was not the sort of 'setup' he and Perry wanted. They were waiting for some solitary traveller in a decent car and with money in his billfold – a stranger to rob, strangle, discard on the desert.

In the desert, sound often precedes sight. Dick heard the dim vibrations of an oncoming, not yet visible car. Perry heard it, too; he put the harmonica in his pocket, picked up the straw suitcase (this, their only luggage, bulged and sagged with the weight of Perry's souvenirs, plus three shirts, five pairs of white socks, a box of aspirin, a bottle of tequila, scissors, a safety razor, and a fingernail file; all their other belongings had either been pawned or been left with the Mexican bartender or been shipped to Las Vegas), and joined Dick at the side of the road. They watched. Now the car appeared, and grew until it became a blue Dodge sedan with a single passenger, a bald, skinny man. Perfect. Dick raised his hand and waved. The Dodge slowed down, and Dick gave the man a sumptuous smile. The car almost, but not quite, came to a stop, and the driver leaned out the window, looking them up and down. The impression they made was evidently alarming. (After a fifty-hour bus ride from Mexico City to Barstow, California, and half a day of trekking across the Mojave, both hikers were bearded, stark, dusty figures.) The car leaped forward and sped on. Dick cupped his hands around his mouth and called out, 'You're a lucky bastard!' Then he laughed and hoisted the suitcase to his shoulder. Nothing could get him really angry, because as he later recalled, he was 'too glad to be back in the good ol' U.S.A.' Anyway, another man in another car would come along.

Perry produced his harmonica (his since yesterday, when he stole it from a Barstow variety store) and played opening bars of what had come to be their 'marching music'; the song was one of Perry's favourites, and he had taught Dick all five stanzas. In step, and side by side, they swung along the highway, singing, 'Mine eyes have seen the glory of the coming of the Lord; He is trampling out the vintage where the grapes of wrath are stored.' Through the silence of the desert, their hard, young voices rang: 'Glory! Glory! Hallelujah! Glory! Glory! Hallelujah!'

3

Answer

THE young man's name was Floyd Wells, and he was short and nearly chinless. He had attempted several careers, as soldier, ranch hand, mechanic, thief, the last of which had earned him a sentence of three to five years in Kansas State Penitentiary. On the evening of Tuesday, November 17, 1959, he was lying in his cell with a pair of radio earphones clamped to his head. He was listening to a news broadcast, but the announcer's voice and the drabness of the day's events ('Chancellor Konrad Adenauer arrived in London today for talks with Prime Minister Harold Macmillan. ... President Eisenhower put in seventy minutes going over space problems and the budget for space exploration with Dr T. Keith Glennan') were luring him towards sleep. His drowsiness instantly vanished when he heard, 'Officers investigating the tragic slaying of four members of the Herbert W. Clutter family have appealed to the public for any information which might aid in solving this baffling crime. Clutter, his wife, and their two teen-age children were found murdered in their farm home near Garden City early last Sunday morning. Each had been bound, gagged, and shot through the head with a .12-gauge shotgun. Investigating officials admit they can discover no motive for the crime, termed by Logan Sanford, Director of the Kansas Bureau of Investigation, as the most vicious in the history of Kansas. Clutter, a prominent wheat grower and former Eisenhower appointee to the Federal Farm Credit Board ...'

Wells was stunned. As he was eventually to describe his reaction, he 'didn't hardly believe it'. Yet he had good reason to, for not only had he known the murdered family, he knew very well who had murdered them.

It had begun a long time ago – eleven years ago, in the autumn of 1948, when Wells was nineteen. He was 'sort of drifting around the country, taking jobs as they came', as he recalled it. 'One way and another, I found myself out there in western Kansas. Near the Colorado border. I was hunting work, and asking round, I heard maybe they could use a hand over to River Valley Farm – that's how he called his place, Mr Clutter did. Sure enough, he put me on. I stayed there I guess a year – all that winter, anyway – and when I left it was just 'cause I was feeling kind of footy. Wanted to move on. Not account of any quarrel with Mr Clutter. He treated me fine, same as he treated everybody that worked for him; like, if you was a little short before payday, he'd always hand you a ten or a five. He paid good wages, and if you deserved it he was quick to give you a bonus. The fact is, I liked Mr Clutter much as any man I ever met. The whole family. Mrs Clutter and the four kids. When I knew them, the youngest two, the ones that got killed – Nancy and the little boy what wore glasses – they were only babies, maybe five or six years old. The other two – one was called Beverly, the other girl I don't remember her name – they were already in high school. A nice family, *real* nice. I never forgot them. When I left there, it was sometime in 1949. I got married, I got divorced, the Army took me, other stuff happened, time went by, you might say, and in 1959 – June 1959, ten years since I last seen Mr Clutter – I got sent to Lansing. Because of breaking into this appliance store. Electrical appliances. What I had in mind was, I wanted to get hold of some electrical lawn mowers. Not to sell. I was going to start a lawn-mower rental service. That way, see, I'd have had my own permanent little business. Course nothing come of it – 'cept I drew a three-to-five. If I hadn't, then I never would have met Dick, and maybe Mr Clutter wouldn't be in his grave. But there you are. There it is. I come to meet Dick.

'He was the first fellow I celled with. We celled together I guess a month. June and part of July. He was just finishing a three-to-five – due for parole in August. He talked a lot about what he planned to do when he got out. Said he thought he might go to Nevada, one of them missile-base towns, buy hisself a uniform, and pass hisself off as a Air Force officer. So he could hang out a regular washline of hot paper. That was one idea he told me. (Never thought much of it myself. He was smart, I don't deny, but he didn't *look* the part. Like no Air Force officer.) Other times, he mentioned this friend of his. Perry. A half-Indian fellow he used to cell with. And the big deals him and Perry might pull when they got together again. I never met him – Perry. Never saw him. He'd already left Lansing, was out on parole. But Dick always said if the chance of a real big score came up, he could rely on Perry Smith to go partners.

'I don't exactly recall how Mr Clutter first got mentioned. It must have been when we were discussing jobs, different kinds of work we'd done. Dick, he was a trained car mechanic, and mostly that was the work he'd done. Only, once he'd had a job driving a hospital ambulance. He was full of brag about that. About nurses, and all what he'd done with them in the back of the ambulance. Anyway, I informed him how I'd worked a year on a considerable wheat spread in western Kansas. For Mr Clutter. He wanted to know if Mr Clutter was a wealthy man. Yes, I said. Yes, he was. In fact, I said, Mr Clutter had once told me that he got rid of ten thousand dollars in one week. I mean, said it sometimes cost him ten thousand dollars a week to run his operation. After that, Dick never stopped asking me about the family. How many was they? What ages would the kids be now? Exactly how did you get to the house? How was it laid out? Did Mr Clutter keep a safe? I won't deny it – I told him he did. Because I seemed to remember a sort of cabinet, or safe, or *some*thing, right behind the desk in the room Mr Clutter used as an office. Next thing I knew, Dick was talking about killing Mr Clutter. Said him and Perry was gonna go out there and rob the place, and they was gonna kill all witnesses – the Clutters, and anybody else that happened to be around. He described to me a dozen times how he was gonna do it, how him and Perry was gonna tie them people up and gun them down. I told him, "Dick, you'll never get by with it." But I can't honestly say I tried to persuade him different. Because I never for a minute believed he meant to carry it out. I thought it was just talk. Like you hear plenty of in Lansing. That's about all you *do* hear: what a fellow's gonna do when he gets out – the holdups and robberies and so forth. It's nothing but brag, mostly. Nobody takes it serious. That's why, when I heard what I heard on the earphones – well, I didn't hardly believe it. Still and all, it happened. Just like Dick said it would.'

That was Floyd Wells' story, though as yet he was far from telling it. He was afraid to, for if the other prisoners heard of his bearing tales to the warden, then his life, as he put it, 'wouldn't be worth a dead coyote'. A week passed. He monitored the radio, he followed the newspaper accounts – and in one of them read that a Kansas paper, the Hutchinson *News,* was offering a reward of one thousand dollars for any information leading to the capture and conviction of the person or persons guilty of the Clutter murders. An interesting item; it almost inspired Wells to speak. But he was still too much afraid, and his fear was not solely of the other prisoners. There was also the chance that the authorities might charge him with being an accessory to the crime. After all, it was he who had guided Dick to the Clutters' door; certainly it could be claimed that he had been aware of Dick's intentions. However one viewed it, his situation was curious, his excuses questionable. So he said nothing, and ten more days went by. December replaced November, and those investigating the case remained, according to increasingly brief newspaper reports (radio newscasters had ceased to mention the subject), as bewildered, as virtually clueless, as they had been the morning of the tragic discovery.

But *he* knew. Presently, tortured by a need to 'tell somebody', he confided in another prisoner. 'A particular friend. A Catholic. Kind of very religious. He asked me, "Well, what are you gonna do, Floyd?" I said, Well, I didn't rightly know – what did he think I ought to do? Well, he was all for me going to the proper people. Said he didn't think I ought to live with something like that on my mind. And he said I could do it without anybody inside guessing I was the one told. Said he'd fix it. So the next day he got word to the deputy warden – told him I wanted to be "called out". Told the deputy if he called me to his office on some pretext or other, maybe I could tell him who killed the Clutters. Sure enough, the deputy sent for me. I was scared, but I remembered Mr Clutter, and how he'd never done me no harm, how at Christmas he'd give me a little purse with fifty dollars in it. I talked to the deputy. Then I told the warden hisself. And while I was still sitting there, right there in Warden Hand's office, he picked up the telephone – '

The person to whom Warden Hand telephoned was Logan Sanford. Sanford listened, hung up, issued several orders, then placed a call of his own to Alvin Dewey. That evening, when Dewey left his office in the courthouse at Garden City, he took home with him a manila envelope.

When Dewey got home, Marie was in the kitchen preparing supper. The moment he appeared, she launched into an account of household upsets. The family cat had attacked the cocker spaniel that lived across the street, and now it seemed as if one of the spaniel's eyes might be seriously damaged. And Paul, their nine-year-old, had fallen out of a tree. It was a wonder he was alive. And then their twelve-year-old, Dewey's namesake, had gone into the yard to burn rubbish and started a blaze that had threatened the neighbourhood. Someone – she didn't know who – had actually called the Fire Department.

While his wife described these unhappy episodes, Dewey poured two cups of coffee. Suddenly, Marie stopped in the middle of a sentence and stared at him. His face was flushed, and she could tell that he was elated. She said, 'Alvin. Oh, honey. Is it good news?' Without comment, he gave her the manila envelope. Her hands were wet; she dried them, sat down at the kitchen table, sipped her coffee, opened the envelope, and took out photographs of a blond young man and a dark-haired, dark-skinned young man – police-made 'mug-shots'. A pair of semi-coded dossiers accompanied the photographs. The one for the fair-headed man read:

Hickock, Richard Eugene (WM) 28. KBI 97 093; FBI 859 273 A. Address: Edgerton, Kansas. Birthdate 6-6-31. Birthplace: K.C., Kans. Height: 5-10. Weight: 175. Hair: Blond. Eyes: Blue. Build: Stout. Comp: Ruddy. Occup: Car Painter. Crime: Cheat & Defr. & Bad Cheques. Paroled: 8-13-59. By: So. KCK.

The second description read:

Smith, Perry Edward (WM) 27-59. Birthplace: Nevada. Height: 5-4. Weight: 156. Hair: D. Brn. Crime: B&E. Arrested: (blank). By: (blank). Disposition: Sent KSP 3-13-56 from Phillips Co. 5-10 yrs. Rec. 3-14-56. Paroled: 7-6-59.

Marie examined the front-view and profile photographs of Smith: an arrogant face, tough, yet not entirely, for there was about it a peculiar refinement; the lips and nose seemed nicely made, and she thought the eyes, with their moist, dreamy, expression, rather pretty – rather, in an actorish way, sensitive. Sensitive, and something more: 'mean'. Though not as mean, as forbiddingly 'criminal', as the eyes of Hickock, Richard Eugene. Marie, transfixed by Hickocks' eyes, was reminded of a childhood incident – of a bobcat she'd once seen caught in a trap, and of how, though she'd wanted to release it, the cat's eyes, radiant with pain and hatred, had drained her of pity and filled her with terror. 'Who are they?' Marie asked.

Dewey told her Floyd Wells' story, and at the end he said, 'Funny. The past three weeks, that's the angle we've concentrated on. Tracking down every man who ever worked on the Clutter place. Now, the way it's turned out, it just seems like a piece of luck. But a few days more and we would've hit this Wells. Found he was in prison. We would've got the truth then. Hell, yes.'

'Maybe it isn't the truth,' Marie said. Dewey and the eighteen men assisting him had pursued hundreds of leads to barren destinations, and she hoped to warn him against another disappointment, for she was worried about his health. His state of mind was bad; he was emaciated; and he was smoking sixty cigarettes a day.

'No. Maybe not,' Dewey said. 'But I have a hunch.'

His tone impressed her; she looked again at the faces on the kitchen table. 'Think of him,' she said, placing a finger against the front-view portrait of the blond young man. 'Think of those eyes. Coming towards you.' Then she pushed the pictures back into their envelope. 'I wish you hadn't shown me.'

Later that same evening, another woman, in another kitchen, put aside a sock she was darning, removed a pair of plastic-rimmed spectacles and levelling them at a visitor, said, 'I hope you find him, Mr Nye. For his own sake. We have two sons, and he's one of them, our first-born. We love him. But . . . Oh, I realized. I realized he wouldn't have packed up. Run off. Without a word to anybody – his daddy or his brother. Unless he was in trouble again. What makes him do it? Why?' She glanced across the small, stove-warmed room at a gaunt figure hunched in a rocking-chair – Walter Hickock, her husband and the father of Richard Eugene. He was a man with faded, defeated eyes and rough hands; when he spoke, his voice sounded as if it were seldom used.

'Was nothing wrong with my boy, Mr Nye,' Mr Hickock said. 'An outstanding athlete – always on the first team at school. Basketball! Baseball! Football! Dick was always the star player. A pretty good student, too, with A marks in several subjects. History. Mechanical drawing. After he graduated from high school – June 1949 – he wanted to go on to college. Study to be an engineer. But we couldn't do it. Plain didn't have the money. Never have had any money. Our farm here, it's only forty-four acres – we hardly can scratch a living. I guess Dick resented it, not getting to college. The first job he had was with Santa Fe Railways, in Kansas City. Made seventy-five dollars a week. He figured that was enough to get married on, so him and Carol got married. She wasn't but sixteen; he wasn't but nineteen hisself. I never thought nothing good would come of it. Didn't, neither.'

Mrs Hickock, a plump woman with a soft, round face unmarred by a lifetime of dawn-to-dark endeavour, reproached him. 'Three precious little boys, our grand-children – there, that's what came of it. And Carol is a lovely girl. She's not to blame.'

Mr Hickock continued, 'Him and Carol rented a good-size house, bought a fancy car – they was in debt all the time. Even though pretty soon Dick was making better money driving a hospital ambulance. Later on, the Markl Buick Company, a big outfit there in Kansas City, they hired him. As a mechanic and car painter. But him and Carol lived too high, kept buying stuff they couldn't nohow afford, and Dick got to writing cheques. I still think the reason he started doing stunts such as that was connected with the smash-up. Concussed his head in a car smash-up. After that, he wasn't the same boy. Gambling, writing bad cheques. I never knew him to do them things before. And it was along about then he took up with this older gal. The one he divorced Carol for, and was his second wife.'

Mrs Hickock said, 'Dick couldn't help that. You remember how Margaret Edna was attracted to him.'

' 'Cause a woman likes you, does that mean you got to get caught?' Mr Hickock said. 'Well, Mr Nye, I expect you know as much about it as we do. Why our boy was sent to prison. Locked away seventeen months, and all he done was bor-row a hunting rifle. From the house of a neighbour here. He had no idea to steal it, I don't give a damn what nobody says. And that was the ruination of him. When he came out of Lansing, he was a plain stranger to me. You couldn't talk to him. The whole world was against Dick Hickock – that's how he figured. Even the second wife, she left him – filed for divorce while he was in prison. Just the same, lately there, he seemed to be settling down. Working for the Bob Sands' Body Shop, over in Olathe. Living here at home with us, getting to bed early, not violating his parole any shape or fashion. I'll tell you, Mr Nye, I've not got long, I'm with cancer, and Dick knowed that – leastways, he knowed I'm sickly – and not a month ago, right before he took off, he told me, "Dad, you've been a pretty good old dad to me. I'm not ever gonna do nothing more to hurt you." He meant it, too. That boy has plenty of good inside him. If ever you seen him on a football field, if ever you seen him play with his children, you wouldn't doubt me. Lord, I wish the Lord could tell me, because I don't know what happened.'

His wife said, 'I do,' resumed her darning, and was forced by tears to stop. 'That friend of his. That's what happened.'

The visitor, K.B.I. Agent Harold Nye, busied himself scribbling in a shorthand notebook – a notebook already well filled with the results of a long day spent probing the accusations of Floyd Wells. Thus far the facts ascertained corroborated Wells' story most persuasively. On November 20 the suspect Richard Eugene Hickock had gone on a Kansas City shopping spree during which he had passed not fewer than 'seven pieces of hot paper'. Nye had called on all the reported victims – salesmen of cameras and of radio and television equipment, the proprietor of a jewellery shop, a clerk in a clothing store – and when in each instance the witness was shown photographs of Hickock and Perry Edward Smith, he had identified the former as the author of the spurious cheques, the latter as his 'silent' accomplice. (One deceived salesman said, 'He [Hickock] did the work. A very smooth talker, very convincing. The other one – I thought he might be a foreigner, a Mexican maybe – he never opened his mouth.')

Nye had next driven to the suburban village of Olathe, where he interviewed Hickock's last employer, the owner of the Bob Sands' Body shop. 'Yes, he worked here', said Mr. Sands. 'From August until – Well, I never saw him after the nineteenth of November, or maybe it was the twentieth. He left without giving me any notice whatever. Just took off – I don't know where to, and neither does his dad. Surprised? Well, yes. Yes, I was. We were on a fairly friendly basis. Dick kind of has a way with him, you know. He can be very likeable. Once in a while he used to come to our house. Fact is, a week before he left, we had some people over, a little party, and Dick brought this friend he had visiting him, a boy from Nevada – Perry Smith was his name. He could play the guitar real nice. He played the guitar and sang some songs, and him and Dick entertained everybody with a weight-lifting act. Perry Smith, he's a little fellow, not much over five feet high, but he could just about pick up a horse. No, they didn't seem nervous, neither one. I'd say they were enjoying themselves. The exact date? Sure I remember. It was the thirteenth. Friday, the thirteenth of November.'

From there, Nye steered his car northwards along raw country roads. As he neared the Hickock farm, he stopped at several neighbouring homesteads, ostensibly to ask directions, actually to make inquiries concerning the suspect. One farmer's wife said, 'Dick Hickock! Don't talk to me about Dick Hickock! If ever I met the devil! Steal? Steal the weights off a dead man's eyes! His mother, though, Eunice, she's a fine woman. Heart big as a barn. His daddy, too. Both of them plain, honest people. Dick would've gone to jail more times than you can count, except nobody around here ever wanted to prosecute. Out of respect for his folks.'

Dusk had fallen when Nye knocked at the door of Walter Hickock's weather-greyed four-room farmhouse. It was as though some such visit had been expected. Mr Hickock invited the detective into the kitchen, and Mrs Hickock offered him coffee. Perhaps if they had known the true meaning of the caller's presence, the reception tendered him would have been less gracious, more guarded. But they did not know, and during the hours the three sat conversing, the name Clutter was never mentioned, or the word murder. The parents accepted what Nye implied – that parole violation and financial fraud were all that motivated his pursuit of their son.

'Dick brought him [Perry] home one evening, and told us he was a friend just off a bus from Las Vegas, and he wanted to know couldn't he sleep here, stay here awhile,' Mrs Hickock said. 'No, sir, I wouldn't have him in the house. One look and I saw what he was. With his perfume. And his oily hair. It was clear as day where Dick had met him. According to the conditions of his parole, he wasn't supposed to associate with anybody he'd met up there [Lansing]. I warned Dick, but he wouldn't listen. He found a room for his friend at the Hotel Olathe, in Olathe, and after that Dick was with him every spare minute. Once they went off on a weekend trip. Mr Nye, certain as I'm sitting, here, Perry Smith was the one put him up to writing them cheques.'

Nye shut his notebook and put his pen in his pocket, and both his hands as well, for his hands were shaking from excitement. 'Now, on this weekend trip. Where did they go?'

'Fort Scott,' Mr Hickock said, naming a Kansas town with a military history. 'The way I understood it, Perry Smith has a sister lives in Fort Scott. She was supposed to be holding a piece of money belonged to him. Fifteen hundred dollars was the sum mentioned. That was the main reason he'd come to Kansas, to collect his money his sister was holding. So Dick drove him down there to get it. It was only an overnight trip. He was back home a little before noon Sunday. Time for Sunday dinner.

'I see,' said Nye. 'An overnight trip. Which means they left here some time Saturday. That would be Saturday, November fourteenth?'

The old man agreed.

'And returned Sunday, November fifteenth?'

'Sunday noon.'

Nye pondered the mathematics involved, and was encouraged by the conclusion he came to: that within a time span of twenty or twenty-four hours, the suspects could have made a round-trip journey of rather more than eight hundred miles, and, in the process, murdered four people.

'Now, Mr Hickock,' Nye said. 'On Sunday, when your son came home, was he alone? Or was Perry Smith with him?'

'No, he was alone. He said he'd left Perry off at the Hotel Olathe.'

Nye, whose normal voice is cuttingly nasal and naturally intimidating, was attempting a subdued timbre, a disarming, throwaway style. 'And do you remember – did anything in his manner strike you as unusual? Different?'

'Who?'

'Your son.'

'When?'

'When he returned from Fort Scott.'

Mr Hickock ruminated. Then he said, 'He seemed the same as ever. Soon as he came in, we sat down to dinner. He was mighty hungry. Started piling his plate before I'd finished the blessing. I remarked on it, said, "Dick, you're shovelling it in as fast as you can work your elbow. Don't you mean to leave nothing for the rest of us?" 'Course, he's always been a big eater. Pickles. He can eat a whole tub of pickles.'

'And after dinner what did he do?'

'Fell asleep,' said Mr Hickock, and appeared to be moderately taken aback by his own reply. 'Fell fast asleep. And I guess you could say that was unusual. We'd gathered round to watch a basketball game. On the TV. Me and Dick and our other boy, David. Pretty soon Dick was snoring like a buzz saw, and I said to his brother, "Lord, I never thought I'd live to see the day Dick would go to sleep at a basketball game." Did, though. Slept straight through it. Only woke up long enough to eat some cold supper, and right after went off to bed.'

Mrs Hickock rethreaded her darning needle; her husband rocked his rocker and sucked on an unlit pipe. The detective's trained eyes roamed the scrubbed and humble room. In a corner, a gun stood propped against the wall; he had noticed it before. Rising, reaching for it, he said, 'You do much hunting, Mr. Hickock?'

'That's his gun. Dick's. Him and David go out once in a while. After rabbits, mostly.'

It was a .12-gauge Savage shotgun, Model 300; a delicately etched scene of pheasants in flight ornamented the handle.

'How long has Dick had it?'

The question aroused Mrs Hickock. 'That gun cost over a hundred dollars. Dick bought it on credit, and now the store won't have it back, even though it's not hardly a month old and only been used the one time – the start of November, when him and David went to Grinnell on a pheasant shoot. He used our names to buy it – his daddy let him – so here we are, liable for the payments, and when you think of Walter, sick as he is, and all the things we need, all we do without ...' She held her breath, as though trying to halt an attack of hiccups. 'Are you sure you won't have a cup of coffee, Mr Nye? It's no trouble.'

The detective leaned the gun against the wall, relinquishing it, although he felt certain it was the weapon that had killed the Clutter family. 'Thank you, but it's late, and I have to drive to Topeka,' he said, then, consulting his notebook, 'Now, I'll just run through this, see if I have it straight. Perry Smith arrived in Kansas Thursday the twelfth of November. Your son claimed this person came here to collect a sum of money from a sister residing in Fort Scott. That Saturday the two drove to Fort Scott, where they remained overnight – I assume in the home of the sister?'

Mr Hickock said, 'No. They never could find her. Seems like she'd moved.'

Nye smiled. 'Nevertheless, they stayed away overnight. And during the week that followed – that is, from the fifteenth to the twenty-first – Dick continued to see his friend Perry Smith, but otherwise, or as far as you know, he maintained a normal routine: lived at home and reported to work every day. On the twenty-first he disappeared, so did Perry Smith. And since then you've not heard from him? He hasn't written you?'

'He's afraid to,' said Mrs Hickock. 'Ashamed and afraid.'

'Ashamed?'

'Of what he's done. Of how he's hurt us again. And afraid because he thinks we won't forgive him. Like we always have. And will. You have children, Mr Nye?'

He nodded.

'Then you know how it is.'

'One thing more. Have you any idea, any at all, where your son might have gone?'

'Open a map,' said Mr Hickock. 'Point your finger – maybe that's it.'

It was late afternoon, and the driver of the car, a middle-aged travelling salesman who shall here be known as Mr

Bell, was tired. He longed to stop for a short nap. However, he was only a hundred miles from his destination – Omaha, Nebraska, the headquarters of the large meat-packing company for which he worked. A company rule forbade its salesmen to pick up hitchhikers, but Mr Bell often disobeyed it, particularly if he was bored and drowsy, so when he saw the two young men standing by the side of the road, he immediately braked his car.

They looked to him like 'O.K. boys'. The taller of the two, a wiry type with dirty-blond, crew-cut hair, had an engaging grin and a polite manner, and his partner, the 'runty' one, holding a harmonica in his right hand, and, in his left, a swollen straw suitcase, seemed 'nice enough', shy but amiable. In any event, Mr Bell, entirely unaware of his guests' intentions, which included throttling him with a belt and leaving him, robbed of his car, his money, and his life, concealed in a prairie grave, was glad to have company, somebody to talk to and keep him awake until he arrived at Omaha.

He introduced himself, then asked them their names. The affable young man with whom he was sharing the front seat said his name was Dick. 'And that's Perry,' he said, winking at Perry, who was seated directly behind the driver.

'I can ride you boys as far as Omaha.'

Dick said, 'Thank you, sir. Omaha's where we were headed. Hoped we might find some work.'

What kind of work were they hunting? The salesman thought perhaps he could help.

Dick said, 'I'm a first-class car painter. Mechanic, too. I'm used to making real money. My buddy and me, we just been down in Old Mexico. Our idea was, we wanted to live there. But hell, they don't pay any wages. Nothing a white man could live off.'

Ah, Mexico. Mr Bell explained that he had honeymooned in Cuernavaca. 'We always wanted to go back. But it's hard to move around when you've got five kids.'

Perry, as he later recalled, thought, Five kids – well, too bad. And listening to Dick's conceited chatter, hearing him start to describe his Mexican 'amorous conquests', he thought how 'queer' it was, 'egomaniacal'. Imagine going all out to impress a man you were going to kill, a man who wouldn't be alive ten minutes from now – not if the plan he and Dick had devised went smoothly. And why shouldn't it? The setup was ideal – exactly what they had been look-ing for during the three days it had taken them to hitch-hike from California to Nevada and across Nevada and Wyoming into Nebraska. Until now, however, a suitable victim had eluded them. Mr Bell was the first prosperous-seeming solitary traveller to offer them a lift. Their other hosts had been either truck drivers or soldiers – and, once, a pair of Negro prize-fighters driving a lavender Cadillac. But Mr Bell was perfect. Perry felt inside a pocket of the leather windbreaker he was wearing. The pocket bulged with a bottle of Bayer aspirin and with a jagged, fist-size rock wrapped in a yellow cotton cowboy handkerchief. He unfastened his belt, a Navajo belt, silver-buckled and stud-ded with turquoise beads; he took it off, flexed it, placed it across his knees. He waited. He watched the Nebraska prairie rolling by, and fooled with his harmonica – made up a tune and played it and waited for Dick to pronounce the agreed-upon signal: 'Hey, Perry, pass me a match.' Whereupon Dick was supposed to seize the steering wheel, while Perry, wielding his handkerchief-wrapped rock, be-laboured the salesman's head – 'opened it up'. Later, along the same quiet side road, use would be made of the belt with the sky-blue beads.

Meanwhile, Dick and the condemned man were trading dirty jokes. Their laughter irritated Perry; he especially disliked Mr Bell's outbursts – hearty barks that sounded very much like the laughter of Tex John Smith, Perry's father. The memory of his father's laughter increased his tension; his head hurt, his knees ached. He chewed three aspirin and swallowed them dry. Jesus! He thought he might vomit, or faint; he felt certain he would if Dick de-layed 'the party' much longer. The light was dimming, the road was straight, with neither house nor human being in view – nothing but land winter-stripped and as sombre as sheet iron. Now was the time, *now*. He stared at Dick, as though to communicate this realization, and a few small signs – a twitching eyelid, a moustache of sweat drops – told him that Dick had already reached the same conclusion.

And yet when Dick next spoke, it was only to launch another joke. 'Here's a riddle. The riddle is: What's the similarity between a trip to the bathroom and a trip to the cemetery?' He grinned. 'Give up?'

'Give up.'

'When you gotta go, you gotta go!'

Mr Bell barked.

'Hey, Perry, pass me a match.'

But just as Perry raised his hand, the rock was on the verge of descent, something extraordinary occurred – what Perry later called 'a goddam miracle'. The miracle was the sudden appearance of a third hitchhiker, a Negro soldier, for whom the charitable salesman stopped. 'Say, that's pretty cute,' he said as his saviour ran towards the car. 'When you gotta go, you gotta go!'

16 December 1959, Las Vegas, Nevada. Age and weather had removed the first letter and the last – an R and an S – thereby coining a somewhat ominous word: OOM. The word, faintly present upon a sun-warped sign, seemed appropriate to the place it publicized, which was, as Harold Nye wrote in his official K.B.I. report, 'run-down and shabby, the lowest type of hotel or rooming house'. The report continued: 'Until a few years ago (according to information supplied by the Las Vegas police), it was one of the biggest cathouses in the West. Then fire destroyed the main building, and the remaining portion was converted into a cheap-rent rooming house.' The 'lobby' was unfurnished, except for a cactus plant six feet tall and a makeshift reception desk; it was also uninhabited. The detective clapped his hands. Eventually, a voice, female, but not very feminine, shouted, 'I'm coming', but it was five minutes before the woman appeared. She wore a soiled housecoat and high-heeled gold leather sandals. Curlers pinioned

her thinning yellowish hair. Her face was broad, muscular, rouged, powdered. She was carrying a can of Miller High Life beer; she smelled of beer and tobacco and recently applied nail varnish. She was seventy-four years old, but in Nye's opinion, 'looked younger – maybe ten minutes younger'. She stared at him, his trim brown suit, his brown snapbrim hat. When he displayed his badge, she was amused; her lips parted, and Nye glimpsed two rows of fake teeth. 'Uh-huh. That's what I figured,' she said. 'O.K. Let's hear it.'

He handed her a photograph of Richard Hickock. 'Know him?'

A negative grunt.

'Or him?'

She said, 'Uh-huh. He's stayed here a coupla times. But he's not here now. Checked out over a month ago. You wanna see the register?'

Nye leaned against the desk and watched the landlady's long and lacquered fingernails search a page of pencil-scribbled names. Las Vegas was the first of these places that his employers wished him to visit. Each had been chosen because of its connexion with the history of Perry Smith. The two others were Reno, where it was thought that Smith's father lived, and San Francisco, the home of Smith's sister, who shall here be known as Mrs Frederic Johnson. Though Nye planned to interview these relatives, and anyone else who might have knowledge of the suspect's whereabouts, his main objective was to obtain the aid of the local law agencies. On arriving in Las Vegas, for example, he had discussed the Clutter case with Lieutenant B. J. Handlon, Chief of the Detective Division of the Las Vegas Police Department. The lieutenant had then written a memorandum ordering all police personnel to be on the alert for Hickock and Smith: 'Wanted in Kansas for parole violation, and said to be driving a 1949 Chevrolet bearing Kansas licence JO-58269. These men are probably armed and should be considered dangerous.' Also, Handlon had assigned a detective to help Nye 'case the pawnbrokers'; as he said, there was 'always a pack of them in any gambling town'. Together, Nye and the Las Vegas detective had checked every pawn ticket issued during the past month. Specifically, Nye hoped to find a Zenith portable radio believed to have been stolen from the Clutter house on the night of the crime, but he had no luck with that. One broker, though, remembered Smith ('He's been in and out of here going on a good ten years'), and was able to produce a ticket for a bearskin rug pawned during the first week in November. It was from this ticket that Nye had obtained the address of the rooming house.

'Registered October thirtieth,' the landlady said. 'Pulled out November eleventh.' Nye glanced at Smith's signature. The ornateness of it, the mannered swoops and swirls, surprised him – a reaction that the landlady apparently divined, for she said, 'Uh-huh. And you oughta hear him talk. Big, long words coming at you in this kinda lispy, whisperry voice. Quite a personality. What you got against him – a nice little punk like that?'

'Parole violation.'

'Uh-huh. Came all the way from Kansas on a parole case. Well, I'm just a dizzy blonde. I believe you. But I wouldn't tell that tale to any brunettes.' She raised the beer can, emptied it, then thoughtfully rolled the empty can between her veined and freckled hands. 'Whatever it is, it ain't nothing big-big. Couldn't be. I never saw the man yet I couldn't gauge his shoe size. This one, he's only a punk. Little punk tried to sweet-talk me out of paying rent the last week he was here.' She chuckled, presumably at the absurdity of such an ambition.

The detective asked how much Smith's room had cost.

'Regular rate. Nine bucks a week. Plus a fifty-cent key deposit. Strictly cash. Strictly in advance.'

'While he was here, what did he do with himself? Does he have any friends?' Nye asked.

'You think I keep an eye on every crawly that comes in here?' the landlady retorted. 'Bums. Punks. I'm not interested. I got a daughter married big-big.' Then she said, 'No, he doesn't have any friends. Least, I never noticed him run around with anybody special. This last time he was here, he spent most every day tinkering with his car. Had it parked out front here. An old Ford. Looked like it was made before he was born. He gave it a paint job. Painted the top part black and the rest silver. Then he wrote "For Sale" on the windshield. One day I heard a sucker stop and offer him forty bucks – that's forty more than it was worth. But he allowed he couldn't take less than ninety. Said he needed the money for a bus ticket. Just before he left I heard some coloured man bought it.'

'He said he needed the money for a bus ticket. But you don't know where it was he wanted to go?'

She pursed her lips, hung a cigarette between them, but her eyes stayed on Nye. 'Play fair. Any money on the table? A reward?' She waited for an answer; when none arrived, she seemed to weigh the probabilities and decide in favour of proceeding. 'Because I got the impression wherever he was going he didn't mean to stay long. That he meant to cut back here. Sorta been expecting him to turn up any day.' She nodded towards the interior of the establishment. 'Come along, and I'll show you why.'

Stairs. Grey halls. Nye sniffed the odours, separating one from another: lavatory disinfectant, alcohol, dead cigars. Beyond one door, a drunken tenant wailed and sang in the firm grip of either gladness or grief. 'Boil down, Dutch! Turn it off or out you go!' the woman yelled. 'Here,' she said to Nye, leading him into a darkened storage room. She switched on a light. 'Over there. That box. He asked would I keep it till he came back.'

It was a cardboard box, unwrapped but tied with cord. A declaration, a warning somewhat in the spirit of an Egyptian curse, was crayoned across the top: '*Beware!* Property of Perry E. Smith! *Beware!*' Nye undid the cord; the knot, he was unhappy to see, was not the same as the half hitch that the killers had used when binding the Clutter family. He parted the flaps. A cockroach emerged, and the landlady stepped on it, squashing it under the heel of her gold leather sandal. 'Hey!' she said as he carefully extracted and slowly examined Smith's possessions. 'The sneak. That's *my* towel.' In addition to the towel, the meticulous

Nye listed in his notebook: 'One dirty pillow, "Souvenir of Honolulu"; one pink baby blanket; one pair khaki trousers; one aluminium pan with pancake turner.' Other oddments included a scrapbook thick with photographs clipped from physical-culture magazines (sweaty studies of weight-lifting weight-lifters) and, inside a shoebox, a collection of medicines: rinses and powders employed to combat trench mouth, and also a mystifying amount of aspirin – at least a dozen containers, several of them empty.

'Junk,' the landlady said. 'Nothing but trash.'

True, it was valueless stuff even to a clue-hungry detective. Still, Nye was glad to have seen it; each item – the palliatives for sore gums, the greasy Honolulu pillow – gave him a clearer impression of the owner and his lonely, mean life.

The next day in Reno, preparing his official notes, Nye wrote: 'At 9 a.m. the reporting agent contacted Mr Bill Driscoll, chief criminal investigator, Sheriff's Office, Washoe County, Reno, Nevada. After being briefed on the circumstances of this case, Mr Driscoll was supplied with photographs, fingerprints and warrants for Hickock and Smith. Stops were placed in the files on both these individuals as well as the automobile. At 10.30 a.m. the reporting agent contacted Sgt Abe Feroah, Detective Division, Police Department, Reno, Nevada. Sgt Feroah and the reporting agent checked the police files. Neither the name of Smith or Hickock was reflected in the felon registration file. A check of the pawnshop-ticket files failed to reflect any information about the missing radio. A permanent stop was placed in these files in the event the radio is pawned in Reno. The detective handling the pawnshop detail took photographs of Smith and Hickock to each of the pawnshops in town and also made a personal check of each shop for the radio. These pawnshops made an identification of Smith as being familiar, but were unable to furnish any further information.'

Thus the morning. That afternoon Nye set forth in search of Tex John Smith. But at his first stop, the post office, a clerk at the General Delivery window told him he need look no farther – not in Nevada – for 'the individual' had left there the previous August and now lived in the vicinity of Circle City, Alaska. That, anyway, was where his mail was being forwarded.

'Gosh! Now, there's a tall order,' said the clerk in response to Nye's request for a description of the elder Smith. 'The guy's out of a book. He calls himself the Lone Wolf. A lot of his mail comes addressed that way – the Lone Wolf. He doesn't receive many letters, no, but bales of catalogues and advertising pamphlets. You'd be surprised the number of people send away for that stuff – just to get some mail, must be. How old? I'd say sixty. Dresses Western – cowboy boots and a big ten-gallon hat. He told me he used to be with the rodeo. I've talked to him quite a bit. He's been in here almost every day the last few years. Once in a while he'd disappear, stay away a month or so – always claimed he'd been off prospecting. One day last August a young man came here to the window. He said he was looking for his father, Tex John Smith, and did I know where he could find him. He didn't look much like his dad; the Wolf is so thin-lipped and Irish, and this boy looked almost pure Indian – hair black as boot polish, with eyes to match. But next morning in walks the Wolf and confirms it; he told me his son had just got out of the Army and that they were going to Alaska. He's an old Alaska hand. I think he once owned a hotel there, or some kind of hunting lodge. He said he expected to be gone about two years. Nope, never seen him since, him or his boy.'

The Johnson family were recent arrivals in their San Francisco community – a middle-class, middle-income real-estate development high in the hills north of the city. On the afternoon of 18 December 1959, young Mrs Johnson was expecting guests; three women of the neighbourhood were coming by for coffee and cake and perhaps a game of cards. The hostess was tense; it would be the first time she had entertained in her new home. Now, while she was listening for the doorbell, she made a final tour, pausing to dispose of a speck of lint or alter an arrangement of Christmas poinsettias. The house, like the others on the slanting hillside street, was a conventional suburban ranch house, pleasant and commonplace. Mrs Johnson loved it; she was in love with the redwood panelling, the wall-to-wall carpeting, the picture windows fore and aft, the view that the rear window provided – hills, a valley, then sky and ocean. And she was proud of the small back garden; her husband – by profession an insurance salesman, by inclination a carpenter – had built around it a white picket fence, and inside it a house for the family dog, and a sand-box and swings for the children. At the moment, all four – dog, two little boys, and a girl – were playing there under a mild sky; she hoped they would be happy in the garden until the guests had gone. When the doorbell sounded and Mrs Johnson went to the door, she was wearing what she considered her most becoming dress, a yellow knit that hugged her figure and heightened the pale-tea shine of her Cherokee colouring and the blackness of her feather-bobbed hair. She opened the door, prepared to admit three neighbours; instead, she discovered two strangers – men who tipped their hats and flipped open badge-studded billfolds. 'Mrs Johnson?' one of them said. 'My name is Nye. This is Inspector Guthrie. We're attached to the San Francisco police, and we've just received an inquiry from Kansas concerning your brother, Perry Edward Smith. It seems he hasn't been reporting to his parole officer, and we wondered if you could tell us anything of his present whereabouts.'

Mrs Johnson was not distressed – and definitely not surprised – to learn that the police were once more interested in her brother's activities. What did upset her was the prospect of having guests arrive to find her being questioned by detectives. She said, 'No. Nothing. I haven't seen Perry in four years.'

'This is a serious matter, Mrs Johnson,' Nye said. 'We'd like to talk it over.'

Having surrendered, having asked them in and offered them coffee (which was accepted), Mrs Johnson said, 'I haven't seen Perry in four years. Or heard from him since he was paroled. Last summer, when he came out of prison, he visited my father in Reno. In a letter, my father told me he was returning to Alaska and taking Perry with him. Then he wrote again, I think in September, and he was very angry. He and Perry had quarrelled and separated before they reached the border. Perry turned back; my father went on to Alaska alone.'

'And he hasn't written you since?'

'No.'

'Then it's possible your brother may have joined him recently. Within the last month.'

'I don't know. I don't care.'

'On bad terms?'

'With Perry? Yes, I'm afraid of him.'

'But while he was in Lansing you wrote him frequently. Or so the Kansas authorities tell us,' Nye said. The second man, Inspector Guthrie, seemed content to occupy the sidelines.

'I wanted to help him. I hoped I might change a few of his ideas. Now I know better. The rights of other people mean nothing to Perry. He has no respect for anyone.'

'About friends. Do you know of any with whom he might be staying?'

'Joe James,' she said, and explained that James was a young Indian logger and fisherman who lived in the forest near Bellingham, Washington. No, she was not personally acquainted with him, but she understood that he and his family were generous people who had often been kind to Perry in the past. The only friend of Perry's she had ever *met* was a young lady who had appeared on the Johnsons' doorstep in June 1955, bringing with her a letter from Perry in which he introduced her as his wife. 'He said he was in trouble, and asked if I would take care of his wife until he could send for her. The girl looked twenty; it turned out she was fourteen. And of course she wasn't anyone's wife. But at the time I was taken in. I felt sorry for her, and asked her to stay with us. She did, though not for long. Less than a week. And when she left, she took our suitcases and everything they could hold – most of my clothes and most of my husband's, the silver, even the kitchen clock.'

'When this happened, where were you living?'

'Denver.'

'Have you ever lived in Fort Scott, Kansas?'

'Never. I've never been to Kansas.'

'Have you a sister who lives in Fort Scott?'

'My sister is dead. My only sister.'

Nye smiled. He said, 'You understand, Mrs Johnson, we're working on the assumption that your brother will contact you. Write or call. Or come to see you.'

'I hope not. As a matter of fact, he doesn't know we've moved. He thinks I'm still in Denver. Please, if you do find him, don't give him my address. I'm afraid.'

'When you say that, is it because you think he might harm you? Hurt you physically?'

She considered, and unable to decide, said she didn't know. 'But I'm afraid of him. I always have been. He can *seem* so warm-hearted and sympathetic. Gentle. He cries so easily. Sometimes music sets him off, and when he was a little boy he used to cry because he thought a sunset was beautiful. Or the moon. Oh, he can fool you. He can make you feel so sorry for him – '

The doorbell rang. Mrs Johnson's reluctance to answer conveyed her dilemma, and Nye (who later wrote of her, 'Throughout the interview she remained composed and most gracious. A person of exceptional character') reached for his brown snapbrim. 'Sorry to have troubled you, Mrs Johnson. But if you hear from Perry, we hope you'll have the good sense to call us. Ask for Inspector Guthrie.'

After the departure of the detectives, the composure that had impressed Nye faltered; a familiar despair impended. She fought it, delayed its full impact until the party was done and the guests had gone, until she'd fed the children and bathed them and heard their prayers. Then the mood, like the evening ocean fog now clouding the street lamps, closed round her. She had said she was afraid of Perry, and she was, but was it simply Perry she feared, or was it a configuration of which he was part – the terrible destinies that seemed promised the four children of Florence Buckskin and Tex John Smith? The eldest, the brother she loved, had shot himself; Fern had fallen out of a window, or jumped; and Perry was committed to violence, a criminal. So, in a sense, she was the only survivor; and what tormented her was the thought that in time she, too, would be overwhelmed: go mad, or contract an incurable illness, or in a fire lose all she valued – home, husband, children.

Her husband was away on a business trip, and when she was alone, she never thought of having a drink. But tonight she fixed a strong one, then lay down on the living-room couch, a picture album propped against her knees.

A photograph of her father dominated the first page – a studio portrait taken in 1922, the year of his marriage to the young Indian rodeo rider Miss Florence Buckskin. It was a photograph that invariably transfixed Mrs Johnson. Because of it, she could understand why, when essentially they were so mismatched, her mother had married her father. The young man in the picture exuded virile allure. Everything – the cocky tilt of his ginger-haired head, the squint of his left eye (as though he were sighting a target), the tiny cowboy scarf knotted round his throat – was abundantly attractive. On the whole, Mrs Johnson's attitude towards her father was ambivalent, but one aspect of him she had always respected – his fortitude. She well knew how eccentric he seemed to others; he seemed so to her, for that matter. All the same, he was 'a real man'. He did things, did them easily. He could make a tree fall precisely where he wished. He could skin a bear, repair a watch, build a house, bake a cake, darn a sock, or catch a trout with a bent pin and a piece of string. Once he had survived a winter alone in the Alaskan wilderness.

Alone: in Mrs Johnson's opinion, that was how such men should live. Wives, children, a timid life are not for them.

She turned over some pages of childhood snapshots – pictures made in Utah and Nevada and Idaho and Oregon. The rodeo careers of 'Tex & Flo' were finished, and the family, living in an old truck, roamed the country hunting work, a hard thing to find in 1933. 'Tex John Smith Family picking berries in Oregon, 1933' was the caption under a snapshot of four barefooted children wearing overalls and cranky, uniformly fatigued expressions. Berries or stale bread soaked in sweet condensed milk was often all they had to eat. Barbara Johnson remembered that once the family had lived for days on rotten bananas, and that, as a result, Perry had got colic; he had screamed all night, while Bobo, as Barbara was called, wept for fear he was dying.

Bobo was three years older than Perry, and she adored him; he was her only toy, a doll she scrubbed and combed and kissed and sometimes spanked. Here was a picture of the two together bathing naked in a diamond-watered Colorado creek, the brother, a pot-bellied, sun-blackened cupid, clutching his sister's hand and giggling, as though the tumbling stream contained ghostly tickling fingers. In another snapshot (Mrs Johnson was unsure, but she thought probably it was taken at a remote Nevada ranch where the family was staying when a final battle between the parents, a terrifying contest in which horsewhips and scalding water and kerosene lamps were used as weapons, had brought the marriage to a stop), she and Perry are astride a pony, their heads are together, their cheeks touch; beyond them dry mountains burn.

Later, when the children and their mother had gone to live in San Francisco, Bobo's love for the little boy weakened until it went quite away. He wasn't her baby any more but a wild thing, a thief, a robber. His first recorded arrest was on 27 October 1936 – his eighth birthday. Ultimately, after several confinements in institutions and children's detention centres, he was returned to the custody of his father, and it was many years before Bobo saw him again, except in photographs that Tex John occasionally sent his other children – pictures that, pasted above white-ink captions, were part of the album's contents. There was 'Perry, Dad, and their Husky Dog', 'Perry and Dad Panning for Gold', 'Perry Bear-Hunting in Alaska'. In this last, he was a fur-capped boy of fifteen standing on the snowshoes among snow-weighted trees, a rifle hooked under his arm; the face was drawn and the eyes were sad and very tired, and Mrs Johnson, looking at the picture, was reminded of a 'scene' that Perry had made once when he had visited her in Denver. Indeed, it was the last time she had ever seen him – the spring of 1955. They were discussing his child-hood with Tex John, and suddenly Perry, who had too much drink inside him, pushed her against a wall and held her there. 'I was his nigger,' Perry said. 'That's all. Somebody he could work their guts out and never have to pay them one hot dime. No, Bobo, *I'm* talking. Shut up, or I'll throw you in the river. Like once when I was walking across a bridge in Japan, and a guy was standing there, I never saw him before, I just picked him up and threw him in the river.

'Please, Bobo. Please listen. You think I *like* myself? Oh, the man I could have been! But that bastard never gave me a chance. He wouldn't *let* me go to school. O.K. O.K. I was a bad kid. But the time came I begged to go to school. I happen to have a brilliant mind. In case you don't know. A brilliant mind and talent plus. But no education, because he didn't want me to learn anything, only how to tote and carry for him. Dumb. Ignorant. That's the way he wanted me to be. So that I could never escape him. But you, Bobo. *You* went to school. You and Jimmy and Fern. Every damn one of you got an education. Everybody but me. And I hate you, all of you – Dad and everybody.'

As though for his brother and sisters life had been a bed of roses! Maybe so, if that meant cleaning up Mama's drunken vomit, if it meant never anything nice to wear or enough to eat. Still, it was true, all three had finished high school. Jimmy, in fact, had graduated at the top of his class – an honour he owed entirely to his own will power. That, Barbara Johnson felt, was what made his suicide so omin-ous. Strong character, high courage, hard work – it seemed that none of these were determining factors of the fates of Tex John's children. They shared a doom against which virtue was no defence. Not that Perry was virtuous, or Fern. When Fern was fourteen, she changed her name, and for the rest of her short life she tried to justify the replace-ment: Joy. She was an easygoing girl, 'everybody's sweet-heart' – rather too much everybody's, for she was partial to men, though somehow she hadn't much luck with them.

Somehow, the kind of man she liked always let her down. Her mother had died in an alcoholic coma, and she was afraid of drink – yet she drank. Before she was twenty, Fern-Joy was beginning the day with a bottle of beer. Then, one summer night, she fell from the window of a hotel room. Falling, she struck a theatre marquee, bounced off it, and rolled under the wheels of a taxi. Above, in the vacated room, police found her shoes, a moneyless purse, an empty whisky bottle.

One could understand Fern and forgive her, but Jimmy was a different matter. Mrs Johnson was looking at picture of him in which he was dressed as a sailor; during the war he had served in the Navy. Slender, a pale young seafarer with an elongated face of slightly dour saintliness, he stood with an arm around the waist of the girl he had married and, in Mrs Johnson's estimation, ought not to have, for they had nothing in common – the serious Jimmy and his teenage San Diego fleet-follower whose glass beads reflected a now long-faded sun. And yet what Jimmy had felt for her was beyond normal love; it was passion – a passion that was in part pathological. As for the girl, she *must* have loved him, and loved him completely, or she would not have done as she did. If only Jimmy had believed that! Or been capable of believing it. But jealousy imprisoned him. He was mortified by thoughts of the men she had slept with before their marriage; he was convinced, moreover, that she remained promiscuous – that every time he went to sea, or even left her alone for the day, she betrayed him with a multitude of lovers, whose existence he unendingly demanded that she admit. Then she aimed a shotgun at a point between her eyes and pressed the trigger with her toe. When Jimmy found her, he didn't call the police. He picked her up and put her on the bed and lay down beside her. Some time around dawn of the next day, he reloaded the gun and killed himself.

Opposite the picture of Jimmy and his wife was a photograph of Perry in uniform. It had been clipped from a newspaper, and was accompanied by a paragraph of text: 'Headquarters, United States Army, Alaska, Pvt. Perry E.

Smith, 23, first Army Korean combat veteran to return to the Anchorage, Alaska, area, is greeted by Captain Mason, Public Information Officer, upon arrival at Elmendorf Air Force Base. Smith served 15 months with the 24th Division as a combat engineer. His trip from Seattle to Anchorage was a gift from Pacific Northern Airlines. Miss Lynn Marquis, airline hostess, smiles approval at welcome. (Official U.S. Army Photo).' Captain Mason, with hand extended, is looking at Private Smith, but Private Smith is looking at the camera. In his expression Mrs Johnson saw, or imagined she saw, not gratitude but arrogance, and, in place of pride, immense conceit. It wasn't incredible that he had met a man on a bridge and thrown him off it. Of course he had. She had never doubted it.

She shut the album and switched on the television, but it did not console her. Suppose he did come? The detectives had found her; why shouldn't Perry? He need not expect her to help him; she wouldn't even let him in. The front door was locked but not the door to the garden. The garden was white with sea-fog; it might have been an assembly of spirits: Mama and Jimmy and Fern. When Mrs Johnson bolted the door, she had in mind the dead as well as the living.

A cloudburst. Rain. Buckets of it. Dick ran. Perry ran too, but he could not run as fast; his legs were shorter, and he was lugging the suitcase. Dick reached shelter – a barn near the highway – long before him. On leaving Omaha, after a night spent in a Salvation Army dormitory, a truck driver had given them a ride across the Nebraska border into Iowa. The past several hours, however, had found them afoot. The rain came when they were sixteen miles north of an Iowa settlement called Tenville Junction.

The barn was dark.

'Dick?' Perry said.

'Over here,' Dick said. He was sprawled on a bed of hay.

Perry, drenched and shaking, dropped beside him. 'I'm so cold,' he said, burrowing in the hay, 'I'm so cold I wouldn't give a damn if this caught fire and burned me alive.' He was hungry, too. Starved. Last night they had dined on bowls of Salvation Army soup, and today the only nourishment they'd had was some chocolate bars and chewing-gum that Dick had stolen from a drugstore candy counter. 'Any more Hershey?' Perry asked.

No, but there was still a pack of chewing-gum. They divided it, then settled down to chewing it, each chomping on two and a half sticks of Doublemint, Dick's favourite flavour (Perry preferred Juicy Fruit). Money was the problem. Their utter lack of it had led Dick to decide that their next move should be what Perry considered 'a crazy-man stunt' – a return to Kansas City. When Dick had first urged the return, Perry said, 'You ought to see a doctor.' Now, huddled together in the cold darkness, listening to the dark, cold rain, they resumed the argument, Perry once more listing the dangers of such a move, for surely by this time Dick was wanted for parole violation – '*if* nothing more'. But Dick was not to be dissuaded. Kansas City, he again insisted, was the one place he was certain he could successfully 'hang a lot of hot paper. Hell, I know we've got to be careful. I know they've got a warrant out. Because of the paper we hung before. But we'll move fast. One day – that'll do it. If we grab enough, maybe we ought to try Florida. Spend Christmas in Miami – stay the winter if it looks good.' But Perry chewed his gum and shivered and sulked. Dick said, 'What is it, honey? That other deal? Why the hell can't you forget it? They never made any connexion. They never will.'

Perry said, 'You could be wrong. And if you are, it means The Corner.' Neither one had ever before referred to the ultimate penalty in the State of Kansas – the gallows, or death in The Corner, as the inmates of Kansas State Penitentiary have named the shed that houses the equipment required to hang a man.

Dick said, 'The comedian. You kill me.' He struck a match, intending to smoke a cigarette, but something seen by the light of the flaring match brought him to his feet carried him across the barn to a cow stall. A car was parked

inside the stall, a black-and-white two-door 1956 Chevrolet.
The key was in the ignition.

Dewey was determined to conceal from 'the civilian
population' any knowledge of a major break in the Clutter
case – so determined that he decided to take into his confidence Garden City's two professional town criers: Bill
Brown, editor of the Garden City *Telegram*, and Robert
Wells, manager of the local radio station, KIUL. In outlining the situation, Dewey emphasized his reasons for considering secrecy of the first importance: 'Remember, there's
a possibility these men are innocent.'

It was a possibility too valid to dismiss. The informer,
Floyd Wells, might easily have invented his story; such
tale-telling was not infrequently undertaken by prisoners
who hoped to win favour or attract official notice. But even
if the man's every word was gospel, Dewey and his colleagues had not yet unearthed one bit of solid supporting
evidence – 'courtroom evidence'. What had they discovered
that could not be interpreted as plausible, though exceptional, coincidence? Just because Smith had travelled to
Kansas to visit his friend Hickock, and just because Hickock possessed a gun of the calibre used to commit the
crime, and just because the suspects had arranged a false
alibi to account for their whereabouts the night of 14
November, they were not necessarily mass murderers. 'But
we're pretty sure this is it. We all think so. If we didn't, we
wouldn't have set up a seventeen-state alarm, from Arkansas to Oregon. But keep in mind: It could be years before
we catch them. They may have separated. Or left the country. There's a chance they've gone to Alaska – not hard to
get lost in Alaska. The longer they're free, the less of a case
we'll have. Frankly, as matters stand, we don't have much
of a case anyhow. We could nab those sonsabitches tomorrow, and never be able to prove spit.'

Dewey did not exaggerate. Except for two sets of boot
prints, one bearing a diamond pattern and the other a Cat's
Paw design, the slayers had left not a single clue. Since they
seemed to take such care, they had undoubtedly got rid of

the boots long ago. And the radio, too – assuming that it was they who had stolen it, which was something Dewey still hesitated to do, for it appeared to him 'ludicrously inconsistent' with the magnitude of the crime and the manifest cunning of the criminals, and 'inconceivable' that these men had entered a house expecting to find a money-filled safe, and then, not finding it, had thought it expedient to slaughter the family for perhaps a few dollars and a small portable radio. 'Without a confession, we'll never get a conviction,' he said. 'That's my opinion. And that's why we can't be too cautious. They think they've got away with it. Well, we don't want them to know any different. The safer they feel, the sooner we'll grab them.'

But secrets are an unusual commodity in a town the size of Garden City. Anyone visiting the sheriff's office, three under-furnished, overcrowded rooms on the third floor of the county courthouse, could detect an odd, almost sinister atmosphere. The hurry-scurry, the angry hum of recent weeks had departed; a quivering stillness now permeated the premises. Mrs Richardson, the office secretary and a very down-to-earth person, had acquired overnight a dainty lot of whispery, tiptoe mannerisms, and the men she served, the sheriff and his staff, Dewey and the imported team of K.B.I. agents, crept about conversing in hushed tones. It was as though, like huntsmen hiding in a forest, they were afraid that any abrupt sound or movement would warn away approaching beasts.

People talked. The Trail Room of the Warren Hotel, a coffee shop that Garden City businessmen treat as though it were a private club, was a murmuring cave of speculation and rumour. An eminent citizen, so one heard, was on the point of arrest. Or it was now known that the crime was the work of killers hired by enemies of the Kansas Wheat Growers' Association, a progressive organization in which Mr Clutter had played a large role. Of the many stories circulating, the most nearly accurate was contributed by a prominent car dealer (who refused to disclose its source): 'Seems there was a man who worked for Herb way back yonder around '47 or '48. Ordinary ranch hand. Seems he went to prison, state prison, and while he was there he got to thinking what a rich man Herb was. So about a month ago, when they let him loose, the first thing he did was come on out here to rob and kill those people.'

But seven miles westward, in the village of Holcomb, not a hint was heard of impending sensations, one reason being that for some while the Clutter tragedy had been a banned topic at both of the community's principal gossip-dispensaries – the post office and Hartman's Café. 'Myself, I don't want to hear another word,' said Mrs Hartman. 'I told them, We can't go on like this. Distrusting everybody, scaring each other to death. What I say is, if you want to talk about it, stay out of my place.' Myrt Clare took quite as strong a stand. 'Folks come in here to buy a nickel's worth of postage and they think they can spend the next three hours and thirty-three minutes turning the Clutters inside out. Pickin' the wings off other people. Rattlesnakes, that's all they are. I don't have the time to listen. I'm in business – I'm a representative of the government of the United States. Anyway, it's morbid. Al Dewey and those hot-shot cops from Topeka and Kansas City – supposed to be sharp as turpentine. But I don't know a soul who still thinks they've got hell's chance of catching the one done it. So I say the sane thing to do is shut up. You live until you die, and it doesn't matter *how* you go; dead's dead. So why carry on like a sackful of sick cats just because Herb Clutter got his throat cut? Anyway, it's morbid. Polly Stringer, from over at the schoolhouse? Polly Stringer was in here this morning. She said it's only now, after over a month, only now those kids are beginning to quiet down. Which made me think: What if they *do* arrest somebody? If they do, it's bound to be somebody everybody knows. And that would fan the fire for sure, get the pot boiling just when it had started to cool off. Ask me, we've had enough excitement.'

It was early, not yet nine, and Perry was the first customer at the Washateria, a self-service laundry. He opened his fat straw suitcase, extracted a wad of briefs and socks and shirts (some his, some Dick's), tossed them into a washer, and fed the machine a lead slug – one of many bought in Mexico.

Perry was well acquainted with the workings of such emporiums, having often patronized them, and happily, since usually he found it 'so relaxing' to sit quietly and watch clothes get clean. Not today. He was too apprehensive. Despite his warnings, Dick had won out. Here they were, back in Kansas City – dead broke, to boot, and driving a stolen car! All night they had raced the Iowa Chevrolet through thick rain, stopping twice to siphon gas, both times from vehicles parked on the empty streets of small sleeping towns. (This was Perry's job, one at which he judged himself 'absolutely tops. Just a short piece of rubber hose, that's my cross-country credit card.') On reaching Kansas City at sunrise, the travellers had gone first to the airport, where in the men's lavatory they washed and shaved and brushed their teeth; two hours later, after a nap in the airport lounge, they returned to the city. It was then that Dick had dropped his partner at the Washateria, promising to come back for him within the hour.

When the laundry was clean and dry, Perry repacked the suitcase. It was past ten. Dick, supposedly off somewhere 'hanging paper', was overdue. He sat down to wait, choosing a bench on which, an arm's length away, a woman's purse rested – tempting him to snake his hand around inside it. But the appearance of its owner, the burliest of several women now employing the establishment's facilities, deterred him. Once, when he was a running-wild child in San Francisco, he and a 'Chink kid' (Tommy Chan? Tommy Lee?) had worked together as a 'purse-snatching team'. It amused Perry – cheered him up – to remember some of their escapades. 'Like one time we sneaked up on an old lady, really old, and Tommy grabbed her handbag, but she wouldn't let go, she was a regular tiger. The harder he tugged one way, the harder she tugged the other. Then she saw me, and said, "Help me! Help me!" and I said, "Hell, lady, I'm helping *him*!" – and bopped her good. Put her on the pavement. Ninety cents was all we got – I remember exactly. We went to a Chink restaurant and ate ourselves under the table.

Things hadn't changed much. Perry was twenty-odd years older and a hundred pounds heavier, and yet his material situation had improved not at all. He was still (and wasn't it incredible, a person of his intelligence, his talents?) an urchin dependent, so to say, on stolen coins.

A clock on the wall kept catching his eye. At half past ten he began to worry; by eleven his legs were pulsing with pain, which was always, with him, a sign of approaching panic – 'bubbles in my blood'. He ate an aspirin, and tried to blot out – blur, at least – the brilliantly vivid cavalcade gliding across his mind, a procession of dire visions: Dick in the hands of the law, perhaps arrested while writing a phony cheque, or for committing a minor traffic violation (and found to be driving a 'hot' car). Very likely, at this very instant Dick sat trapped inside a circle of red-necked detectives. And they weren't discussing trivialities – bad cheques or stolen automobiles. Murder, that was the topic, for somehow the connexion that Dick had been so certain no one could make had been made. And right *now* a carload of Kansas City police were on their way to the Washateria.

But, no, he was imagining too much. Dick would never do that – 'spill his guts'. Think of how often he had heard him say, 'They can beat me blind, I'll never tell them anything.' Of course, Dick was a 'blowhard'; his toughness, as Perry had come to know, existed solely in situations where he unarguably had the upper hand. Suddenly, gratefully, he thought of a less desperate reason for Dick's prolonged absence. He'd gone to visit his parents. A risky thing to do, but Dick was 'devoted' to them, or claimed to be, and last night during the long rainy ride he had told Perry, 'I'd sure like to see my folks. They wouldn't mention it. I mean, they wouldn't tell the parole officer – do anything to get us into trouble. Only I'm ashamed to. I'm afraid of what my mother would say. About the cheques. And going off like we did. But I wish I could call them, hear how they are.' However, that was not possible, for the Hickock home was

without a telephone; otherwise, Perry would have rung up
to see if Dick was there.

Another few minutes, and he was again convinced that
Dick was under arrest. His leg pains flared up, flashed
through his body, and the laundry odours, the steamy
stench, all at once sickened him, picked him up and propelled him out the door. He stood at the kerb retching like
'a drunk with the dry heaves'. Kansas City! Hadn't he
known Kansas City was bad luck, and *begged* Dick to keep
away? Now, maybe now, Dick was sorry he hadn't listened.
And he wondered: But what about me, 'with a dime or two
and a bunch of lead slugs in my pocket'? Where could he
go? Who would help him? Bobo? Fat chance! But her husband might. If Fred Johnson had followed his own inclination, he would have guaranteed employment for Perry
after he left prison, thus helping him obtain a parole. But
Bobo wouldn't permit it; she had said it would only lead to
trouble and possibly danger. Then she had written to Perry
to tell him precisely that. One fine day he'd pay her back,
have a little fun – talk to her, advertise his abilities, spell
out in detail the things he was capable of doing to people
like her, respectable people, safe and smug people, exactly
like Bobo. Yes, let her know just how dangerous he could
be, and watch her eyes. Surely that was worth a trip to Denver? Which was what he'd do – go to Denver and visit the
Johnsons. Fred Johnson would stake him to a new start in
life; he'd have to, if he wanted ever to be rid of him.

Then Dick came up to him at the kerb. 'Hey, Perry,' he
said. 'You sick?'

The sound of Dick's voice was like an injection of some
potent narcotic, a drug that, invading his veins, produced a
delirium of colliding sensations: tension and relief, fury
and affection. He advanced towards Dick with clenched
fists. 'You sonofabitch,' he said.

Dick grinned, and said, 'Come on. We're eating again.'

But explanations were in order – apologies, too – and over
a bowl of chili at the Kansas City hash house that Dick
liked best, the Eagle Buffet, Dick supplied them. 'I'm sorry,
honey. I knew you'd get the bends. Think I'd tangled with

a bull. But I was having such a run of luck it seemed like I ought to let it ride.' He explained that after leaving Perry he had gone to the Markl Buick Company, the firm that had once employed him, hoping to find a set of licence plates to substitute for the hazardous Iowa plates on the abducted Chevrolet. 'Nobody saw me come or go. Markl used to do a considerable wrecked-car trade. Sure enough, out back there was a smashed-up De Soto with Kansas tags.' And where were they now? 'On our buggy, pal.'

Having made the switch, Dick had dropped the Iowa plates in a municipal reservoir. Then he'd stopped at a filling station where a friend worked, a former high-school classmate named Steve, and persuaded Steve to cash a cheque for fifty dollars, which was something he'd not done before – 'rob a buddy'. Well, he'd never see Steve again. He was 'cutting out' of Kansas City tonight, this time really for ever. So why not fleece a few old friends? With that in mind, he'd called on another ex-classmate, a drugstore clerk. The take was thereby increased to seventy-five dollars. 'Now, this afternoon, we'll roll that up to a couple hundred. I've made a list of place to hit. Six or seven, starting right here,' he said, meaning the Eagle Buffet, where everybody – the bartender and waiters – knew and liked him, and called him Pickles (in honour of his favourite food). 'Then Florida, here we come. How about it, honey? Didn't I promise you we'd spend Christmas in Miami? Just like all the millionaires?'

Dewey and his colleague K.B.I. Agent Clarence Duntz stood waiting for a free table in the Trail Room. Looking around at the customary exhibit of lunch-hour faces – soft-fleshed businessmen and ranchers with sun-branded, coarse complexions – Dewey acknowledged particular acquaintances: the county coroner, Dr Fenton; the manager of the Warren, Tom Mahar; Harrison Smith, who had run for county attorney last year and lost the election to Duane West; and also Herbert W. Clutter, the owner of River Valley Farm and member of Dewey's Sunday School class. *Wait a minute!* Wasn't Herb Clutter dead? And hadn't Dewey attended his funeral? Yet there he was, sitting in the Trail Room's circular corner booth, his lively brown eyes, his square-jawed, genial good looks unchanged by death. But Herb was not alone. Sharing the table were two young men, and Dewey, recognizing them, nudged Agent Duntz.

'Look.'

'Where?'

'The corner.'

'I'll be damned.'

Hickock and Smith! But the moment of recognition was mutual. Those boys smelled danger. Feet first, they crashed through the Trail Room's plate-glass window, and with Duntz and Dewey leaping after them, sped along Main Street, past Palmer Jewelry, Norris Drugs, the Garden Café, then around the corner and down to the depot and in and out, hide-and-seek, among the congregation of white grain-storage towers. Dewey drew a pistol, and so did Duntz, but as they took aim, the supernatural intervened. Abruptly, mysteriously (it was like a dream!), everyone was swimming – the pursued, the pursuers – stroking the awesome width of water that the Garden City Chamber of Commerce claims is the 'World's Largest FREE Swimpool'. As the detectives drew abreast of their quarry, why, once more (How did it happen? *Could* he be dreaming?) the scene faded out, and faded in upon another landscape: Valley View Cemetery, that grey-and-green island of tombs and trees and flowered paths, a restful, leafy, whispering oasis lying like a cool piece of cloud shade on the luminous wheat plains north of town. But now Duntz had disappeared, and Dewey was alone with the hunted men. Though he could not see them, he was certain they were hiding among the dead, crouching there behind a headstone, perhaps the headstone of his own father: 'Alvin Adams Dewey, 6 September 1879–26 January 1948.' Gun drawn, he crept along the solemn lanes until, hearing laughter and tracing its sound, he saw that Hickock and Smith were not hiding at all but standing astride the as yet unmarked mass grave of Herb and Bonnie and Nancy and Kenyon, standing legs apart, hands on hips, heads flung

back, laughing. Dewey fired ... and again ... and again ...
Neither man fell, though each had been shot through the
heart three times; they simply rather slowly turned trans-
parent, by degress grew invisible, evaporated, though the
loud laughter expanded until Dewey bowed before it, ran
from it, filled with a despair so mournfully intense that it
awakened him.

When he awoke, it was as though he were a feverish,
frightened ten-year-old; his hair was wet, his shirt cold-
damp and clinging. The room – a room in the sheriff's
office, into which he'd locked himself before falling asleep
at a desk – was dull with near-darkness. Listening, he could
hear Mrs Richardson's telephone ringing in the adjacent
office. But she was not there to answer it; the office was
closed. On his way out he walked past the ringing phone
with determined indifference, and then hesitated. It might
be Marie, calling to ask if he was still working and should
she wait dinner.

'Mr A. A. Dewey, please. Kansas City calling.'

'This is Mr Dewey.'

'Go ahead, Kansas City. Your party is on the line.'

'Al? Brother Nye.'

'Yes, Brother.'

'Get ready for some very big news.'

'I'm ready.'

'Our friends are here. Right here in Kansas City.'

'How do you know?'

'Well, they aren't exactly keeping it a secret. Hickock's
written cheques from one side of town to the other. Using
his own name.'

'His own name. That must mean he doesn't plan to
hang around long – either that or he's feeling awful damn
sure of himself. So Smith's still with him?'

'Oh, they're together O.K. But driving a different car. A
1956 Chevy – black-and-white two-door job.'

'Kansas tags?'

'Kansas tags. And listen, Al – are we lucky! They bought
a television set, see? Hickock gave the salesman a cheque.
Just as they were driving off, the guy had the sense to write

down the licence number. Jot it on the back of the cheque. Johnson County Licence 16212.'

'Checked the registration?'

'Guess what?'

'It's a stolen car.'

'Undoubtedly. But the tags were definitely lifted. Our friends took them off a wrecked De Soto in a K.C. garage.'

'Know when?'

'Yesterday morning. The boss [Logan Sanford] sent out an alert with the new licence number and a description of the car.'

'How about the Hickock farm? If they're still in the area, it seems to me sooner or later they'll go there.'

'Don't worry. We're watching it. Al—'

'I'm here.'

'That's what I want for Christmas. All I want. To wrap this up. Wrap it up and sleep till New Year's. Wouldn't that be one hell of a present?'

'Well, I hope you get it.'

'Well, I hope we both do.'

Afterwards, as he crossed the darkening courthouse square, pensively scuffing through dry mounds of unraked leaves, Dewey wondered at his lack of elation. Why, when he now knew that the suspects were not for ever lost in Alaska or Mexico or Timbuctoo, when the next second an arrest might be made – why was it he felt none of the excitement he ought to feel? The dream was at fault, for the treadmill mood of it had lingered, making him question Nye's assertions – in a sense, disbelieve them. He did not believe that Hickock and Smith would be caught in Kansas City. They were invulnerable.

In Miami Beach, 335 Ocean Drive is the address of the Somerset Hotel, a small, square building painted more or less white, with many lavender touches, among them a lavender sign that reads, 'VACANCY – LOWEST RATES – BEACH FACILITIES – ALWAYS A SEA-BREEZE.' It is one of a row of little stucco-and-cement hotels lining a white, melancholy street. In December 1959, the Somerset's 'beach facilities' consisted of two beach umbrellas stuck in a strip of sand at the rear of the hotel. One umbrella, pink, had written upon it, 'We Serve Valentine Ice-Cream.' At noon on Christmas Day, a quartet of women lay under and around it, a transistor radio serenading them. The second umbrella, blue and bearing the command 'Tan with Coppertone', sheltered Dick and Perry, who for five days had been living at the Somerset, in a double room renting for eighteen dollars weekly.

Perry said, 'You never wished me a Merry Christmas.'

'Merry Christmas, honey. And a Happy New Year.'

Dick wore bathing trunks, but Perry, as in Acapulco, refused to expose his injured legs – he feared the sight might 'offend' other beach-goers – and therefore sat fully clothed, wearing even socks and shoes. Still, he was comparatively content, and when Dick stood up and started performing exercises – headstands, meant to impress the ladies beneath the pink umbrella – he occupied himself with the Miami *Herald*. Presently he came across an inner-page story that won his entire attention. It concerned murder, the slaying of a Florida family, a Mr and Mrs Clifford Walker, their four-year-old son, and their two-year-old daughter. Each of the victims, though not bound or gagged, had been shot through the head with a .22 weapon. The crime, clueless and apparently motiveless, had taken place Saturday night, 19 December, at the Walker home, on a cattle-raising ranch not far from Tallahassee.

Perry interrupted Dick's athletics to read the story aloud, and said, 'Where were we last Saturday night?'

'Tallahassee?'

'I'm asking you.'

Dick concentrated. On Thursday night, taking turns at the wheel, they had driven out of Kansas and through Missouri into Arkansas and over the Ozarks, 'up' to Louisiana, where a burned-out generator stopped them early Friday morning. (A second-hand replacement, bought in Shreveport, cost twenty-two fifty.) That night they'd slept parked by the side of the road somewhere near the Alabama-Florida border. The next day's journey, an unhurried affair, had included several touristic diversions – visits to an alligator farm and a rattlesnake ranch, a ride in a glass-bottomed boat over a silvery-clear swamp lake, a late and long and costly broiled-lobster lunch at a roadside seafood restaurant. Delightful day! But both were exhausted when they arrived at Tallahassee, and decided to spend the night there. 'Yes, Tallahassee,' Dick said.

'Amazing!' Perry glanced through the article again. 'Know what I wouldn't be surprised? If this wasn't done by a lunatic. Some nut that read about what happened out in Kansas.'

Dick, because he didn't care to hear Perry 'get going on that subject', shrugged and grinned and trotted down to the ocean's edge, where he ambled awhile over the surf-drenched sand, here and there stooping to collect a sea-shell. As a boy he'd so envied the son of a neighbour who had gone to the Gulf Coast on holiday and returned with a box full of shells – so hated him – that he'd stolen the shells and one by one crushed them with a hammer. Envy was constantly with him; the Enemy was anyone who was someone he wanted to be or who had anything he wanted to have.

For instance, the man he had seen by the pool at the Fontainebleau. Miles away, shrouded in a summery veil of heat-haze and sea-sparkle, he could see the towers of the pale, expensive hotels – the Fontainebleau, the Eden Roc, the Roney Plaza. On their second day in Miami he had suggested to Perry that they invade these pleasure-domes. 'Maybe pick up a coupla rich women,' he had said. Perry had been most reluctant; he felt people would stare at them because of their khaki trousers and T-shirts. Actually, their tour of the Fontainebleaus' gaudy premises went unnoticed, amid the men striding about in Bermuda shorts of candy-striped raw silk, and the women wearing bathing suits and mink stoles simultaneously. The trespassers had loitered in the lobby, strolled in the garden, lounged by the swimming pool. It was there that Dick saw the man, who was his own age – twenty-eight or thirty. He could have been a 'gambler or lawyer or maybe a gangster from Chicago'.

Whatever he was, he looked as though he knew the glories of money and power. A blonde who resembled Marilyn Monroe was kneading him with suntan oil, and his lazy, beringed hand reached for a tumbler of iced orange juice. All that belonged to him, Dick, but he would never have it. Why should that sonofabitch have everything, while he had nothing? Why should that 'big-shot bastard' have all the luck? With a knife in his hand, he, Dick, had power. Big-shot bastards like that had better be careful or he might 'open them up and let a little of their luck spill on the floor'. But Dick's day was ruined. The beautiful blonde rubbing on the suntan oil had ruined it. He'd said to Perry, 'Let's pull the hell out of here.'

Now a young girl, probably twelve, was drawing figures in the sand, carving out big, crude faces with a piece of driftwood. Dick, pretending to admire her art, offered the shells he had gathered. 'They make good eyes,' he said. The child accepted the gift, whereupon Dick smiled and winked at her. He was sorry he felt as he did about her, for his sexual interest in female children was a failing of which he was 'sincerely ashamed' – a secret he'd not confessed to anyone and hoped no one suspected (though he was aware that Perry had reason to), because other people might not think it 'normal'. That, to be sure, was something he was certain he was – 'a normal'. Seducing pubescent girls, as he had done 'eight or nine' times in the last several years, did not disprove it, for if the truth were known, most real men had the same desires he had. He took the child's hand and said, 'You're my baby girl. My little sweetheart.' But she objected. Her hand, held by his, twitched like a fish on a hook, and he recognized the astounded expression in her eyes from earlier incidents in his career. He let go, laughed lightly, and said, 'Just a game. Don't you like games?'

Perry, still reclining under the blue umbrella, had observed the scene and realized Dick's purpose at once, and despised him for it; he had 'no respect for people who can't control themselves sexually', especially when the lack of control involved what he called 'pervertiness' – 'bothering kids', 'queer stuff', rape. And he thought he had made his views obvious to Dick; indeed, hadn't they almost had a fist fight when quite recently he had prevented Dick from raping a terrified young girl? However, he wouldn't care to repeat that particular test of strength. He was relieved when he saw the child walk away from Dick.

Christmas carols were in the air; they issued from the radio of the four women and mixed strangely with Miami's sunshine and the cries of the querulous, never thoroughly silent seagulls. 'Oh, come let us adore Him, Oh, come let us adore Him': a cathedral choir, an exalted music that moved Perry to tears – which refused to stop, even after the music did. And as was not uncommon when he was thus afflicted, he dwelt upon a possibility that had for him 'tremendous fascination': suicide. As a child he had often thought of killing himself, but those were sentimental reveries born of a wish to punish his father and mother and other enemies. From young manhood onward, however, the prospect of ending his life had more and more lost its fantastic quality. That, he must remember, was Jimmy's 'solution', and Fern's, too. And lately it had come to seem not just an alternative but the specific death awaiting him.

Anyway, he couldn't see that he had 'a lot to live for'. Hot islands and buried gold, diving deep in fire-blue seas towards sunken treasure – such dreams were gone. Gone, too, was 'Perry O'Parsons', the name invented for the singing sensation of stage and screen that he'd half-seriously hoped some day to be. Perry O'Parsons had died without having ever lived. What was there to look forward to? He and Dick were 'running a race without a finish line' – that was how it struck him. And now, after not quite a week in Miami, the long ride was to resume. Dick, who had worked one day at the ABC auto-service company for sixty-five cents an hour, had told him, 'Miami's worse than Mexico. Sixty-five cents! Not me. I'm white.' So tomorrow, with only twenty-seven dollars left of the money raised in Kansas City, they were heading west again, to Texas, to Nevada – 'nowhere definite'.

Dick, who had waded into the surf, returned. He fell, wet and breathless, face down on the sticky sand.

'How was the water?'

'Wonderful.'

The closeness of Christmas to Nancy Clutter's birthday, which was right after New Year's, had always created problems for her boy friend, Bobby Rupp. It had strained his imagination to think of two suitable gifts in such quick succession. But each year, with money made working summers on his father's sugar-beet farm, he had done the best he could, and on Christmas morning he had always hurried to the Clutter house carrying a package that his sisters had helped him wrap and that he hoped would surprise Nancy and delight her. Last year he had given her a small heart-shaped gold locket. This year, as forehanded as ever, he'd been wavering between the imported perfumes on sale at Norris Drugs and a pair of riding boots. But then Nancy had died.

On Christmas morning, instead of racing off to River Valley Farm, he remained at home, and later in the day he shared with his family the splendid dinner his mother had been a week preparing. Everybody – his parents and every one of his seven brothers and sisters – had treated him gently since the tragedy. All the same, at mealtimes he was told again and again that he must please eat. No one comprehended that really he was ill, that grief had made him so, that grief had drawn a circle around him he could not escape from and others could not enter – except possibly Sue. Until Nancy's death he had not appreciated Sue, never felt altogether comfortable with her. She was too different – took seriously things that even girls ought not to take very seriously: paintings, poems, the music she played on the piano. And, of course, he was jealous of her; her position in Nancy's esteem, though of another order, had been at least equal to his. But that was why she was able to understand his loss. Without Sue, without her almost constant presence, how could he have withstood such an avalanche of shocks – the crime itself, his interviews with Mr

Dewey, the pathetic irony of being for a while the principal suspect?

Then, after about a month, the friendship waned. Bobby went less frequently to sit in the Kidwells' tiny, cosy parlour, and when he did go, Sue seemed not as welcoming. The trouble was that they were forcing each other to mourn and remember what in fact they wanted to forget. Sometimes Bobby could: when he was playing basketball or driving his car over country roads at eighty miles an hour, or when, as part of a self-imposed athletic programme (his ambition was to be a high-school gymnastics instructor), he took long-distance jog-trots across flat yellow fields. And now, after helping clear the dining-table of all its holiday dishes, that was what he decided to do – put on a sweatshirt and go for a run.

The weather was remarkable. Even for western Kansas, renowned for the longevity of its Indian summers, the current sample seemed far-fetched – dry air, bold sun, azure sky. Opimistic ranchers were predicting an 'open winter' – a season so bland that cattle could graze during the whole of it. Such winters are rare, but Bobby could remember one – the year he had started to court Nancy. They were both twelve, and after school he used to carry her book satchel the mile separating the Holcomb schoolhouse from her father's farm ranch. Often, if the day was warm and sun-kindled, they stopped along the way and sat by the river, a snaky, slow-moving, brown piece of the Arkansas.

Once Nancy had said to him, 'One summer, when we were in Colorado, I saw where the Arkansas begins. The exact place. You wouldn't believe it, though. That it was our river. It's not the same colour. But pure as drinking water. And fast. And full of rocks. Whirlpools. Daddy caught a trout.' It had stayed with Bobby, her memory of the river's source, and since her death ... Well, he couldn't explain it, but whenever he looked at the Arkansas, it was for an instant transformed, and what he saw was not a muddy stream meandering across the Kansas plains, but what Nancy had described – a Colorado torrent, a chilly, crystal trout river speeding down a mountain valley. That was how Nancy had been: like young waters – energetic, joyous.

Usually, though, western-Kansas winters are imprisoning, and usually frost on the fields and razory winds have altered the climate before Christmas. Some years back snow had fallen on Christmas Eve and continued falling, and when Bobby set out the next morning for the Clutter property, a three-mile walk, he had had to fight through deep drifts. It was worth it, for though he was numbed and scarlet, the welcome he got thawed him thoroughly. Nancy was amazed and proud, and her mother, often so timid and distant, had hugged and kissed him, insisting that he wrap up in a quilt and sit close to the parlour fire. While the women worked in the kitchen, he and Kenyon and Mr Clutter had sat around the fire cracking walnuts and pecans, and Mr Clutter said he was reminded of another Christmas, when he was Kenyon's age: 'There were seven of us. Mother, my father, the two girls, and us three boys. We lived on a farm a good ways from town. For that reason it was the custom to do our Christmas buying in a bunch – make the trip once and do it all together. The year I'm thinking of, the morning we were supposed to go, the snow was high as today, higher, and still coming down – flakes like saucers. Looked like we were in for a snowbound Christmas with no presents under the tree. Mother and the girls were heartbroken. Then I had an idea.' He would saddle their huskiest plough horse, ride into town, and shop for everybody. The family agreed. All of them gave him their Christmas savings and a list of the things they wished him to buy: four yards of calico, a football, a pin-cushion, shotgun shells – an assortment of orders that took until nightfall to fill. Heading homeward, the purchases secure inside a tarpaulin sack, he was grateful that his father had forced him to carry a lantern, and glad, too, that the horses harness was strung with bells, for both their jaunty racket and the careening light of the paraffin lantern were a comfort to him.

'The ride in, that was easy, a piece of cake. But now the road was gone, and every landmark.' Earth and air – all was snow. The horse, up to his haunches in it, slipped side-wise. 'I dropped our lamp. We were lost in the night. It was just a question of time before we fell asleep and froze. Yes, I was afraid. But I prayed. And I felt God's presence ...' Dogs howled. He followed the noise until he saw the windows of a neighbouring farmhouse. 'I ought to have stopped there. But I thought of the family – imagined my mother in tears, Dad and the boys getting up a search party, and I pushed on. So, naturally, I wasn't too happy when finally I reached home and found the house dark. Doors locked. Found everybody had gone to bed and plain forgot me. None of them could understand why I was so put out. Dad said, "We were sure you'd stay the night in town. Good grief, boy! Who'd have thought you hadn't better sense than to start home in a perfect blizzard?"'

The cider-tart odour of spoiling apples. Apple trees and pear trees, peach and cherry: Mr Clutter's orchard, the treasured assembly of fruit trees he had planted. Bobby, running mindlessly, had not meant to come here, or to any other part of River Valley Farm. It was inexplicable, and he turned to leave, but he turned again and wandered towards the house – white and solid and spacious. He had always been impressed by it, and pleased to think that his girl friend lived there. But now that it was deprived of the late owner's dedicated attention, the first threads of decay's cobweb were being spun. A gravel rake lay rusting in the driveway; the lawn was parched and shabby. That fateful Sunday, when the sheriff summoned ambulances to remove the murdered family, the ambulances had driven across the grass straight to the front door, and the tyre tracks were still visible.

The hired man's house was empty, too; he had found new quarters for his family nearer Holcomb – to no one's surprise, for nowadays, though the weather was glittering, the Clutter place seemed shadowed, and hushed, and motion-less. But as Bobby passed a storage barn, and beyond that, a livestock corral, he heard a horse's tail swish. It was Nancy's Babe, the obedient old dappled mare with flaxen

mane and dark-purple eyes like magnificent pansy blossoms.
Clutching her mane, Bobby rubbed his cheek along Babe's
neck – something Nancy used to do. And Babe whinnied.
Last Sunday, the last time he had visited the Kidwells, Sue's
mother had mentioned Babe. Mrs Kidwell, a fanciful
woman, had been standing at a window watching dusk tint
the outdoors, the sprawling prairie. And out of the blue she
said, 'Susan? You know what I keep seeing? Nancy. On
Babe. Coming this way.'

Perry noticed them first – hitchhikers, a boy and an old
man, both carrying homemade knapsacks, and despite
the blowy weather, a gritty and bitter Texas wind, wearing
only overalls and a thin denim shirt. 'Let's give them a lift,'
Perry said. Dick was reluctant; he had no objection to assisting hitchhikers, provided they looked as if they could pay
their way – at least 'chip in a couple of gallons of gas'. But
Perry, little old big-hearted Perry, was always pestering
Dick to pick up the damnedest, sorriest-looking people.
Finally Dick agreed, and stopped the car.

The boy – a stocky, sharp-eyed, talkative towhead of
about twelve – was exuberantly grateful, but the old man,
whose face was seamed and yellow, feebly crawled into the
back seat and slumped there silently. The boy said, 'We sure
do appreciate this. Johnny was ready to drop. We ain't
had a ride since Galveston.'

Perry and Dick had left that port city an hour earlier,
having spent a morning there applying at various shipping
offices for jobs as able-bodied seamen. One company offered
them immediate work on a tanker bound for Brazil, and,
indeed, the two would now have been at sea if their prospective employer had not discovered that neither man
possessed union papers or a passport. Strangely, Dick's disappointment exceeded Perry's: 'Brazil! That's where they're
building a whole new capital city. Right from scratch.
Imagine getting in on the ground floor of something like
that! Any fool could make a fortune.'

'Where you headed?' Perry asked the boy.

'Sweetwater.'

'Where's Sweetwater?'

'Well, it's along in this direction somewhere. It's somewhere in Texas. Johnny, here, he's my gramp. And he's got a sister lives in Sweetwater. Least, I sure Jesus hope she does. We thought she lived in Jasper, Texas. But when we got to Jasper, folks told us her and her people moved to Galveston. But she wasn't in Galveston – lady there said she was gone to Sweetwater. I sure Jesus hope we find her. Johnny,' he said, rubbing the old man's hands, as if to thaw them, 'you hear me, Johnny? We're riding in a nice warm Chevrolet – '56 model.'

The old man coughed, rolled his head slightly, opened and closed his eyes, and coughed again.

Dick said, 'Hey, *listen*. What's wrong with him?'

'It's the change,' the boy said. 'And the walking. We been walking since before Christmas. Seems to me we covered the better part of Texas.' In the most matter-of-fact voice, and while continuing to massage the old man's hands, the boy told them that up to the start of the present journey he and his grandfather and an aunt had lived alone on a farm near Sheveport, Louisiana. Not long ago the aunt had died. 'Johnny's been poorly about a year, and Auntie had all the work to do. With only me to help. We were chopping firewood. Chopping up a stump. Right in the middle of it, Auntie said she was wore out. Ever seen a horse just lay down and never get up? I have. And that's like what Auntie did.' A few days before Christmas the man from whom his grandfather rented the farm 'turned us off the place', the boy continued. 'That's how come we started out for Texas. Looking to find Mrs Jackson. I never seen her, but she's Johnny's own blood sister. And somebody's got to take us in. Leastways, him. He can't go a lot more. Last night it rained on us.'

The car stopped. Perry asked Dick why he had stopped it.

'That man's very sick,' Dick said.

'Well? What do you want to do? Put him out?'

'Use your head. Just for once.'

'You really are a mean bastard.'

'Suppose he dies?'

The boy said, 'He won't die. We've got this far, he'll wait now.'

Dick persisted. 'Suppose he dies? Think of what could happen. The questions.'

'Frankly, I don't give a damn. You want to put them out? Then by all means.' Perry looked at the invalid, still somnolent, dazed, deaf, and he looked at the boy, who returned his gaze calmly, not begging, not 'asking for anything', and Perry remembered himself at that age, his own wanderings with an old man. 'Go ahead. Put them out. But I'll be getting out, too.'

'O.K. O.K. O.K. Only don't forget,' said Dick. 'It's your damn fault.'

Dick shifted gears. Suddenly as the car began to move again, the boy hollered, 'Hold it!' Hopping out, he hurried along the edge of the road, stopped, stooped, picked up one, two, three, four empty Coca-Cola bottles, ran back, and hopped in, happy and grinning. 'There's plenty of money in bottles,' he said to Dick. 'Why, mister, if you was to drive kind of slow, I guarantee you we can pick us up a big piece of change. That's what me and Johnny been eating off. *Re*-fund money.'

Dick was amused, but he was also interested, and when next the boy commanded him to halt, he at once obeyed. The commands came so frequently that it took them an hour to travel five miles, but it was worth it. The kid had an 'honest-to-God genius' for spotting, amid the roadside rocks and grassy rubble, and the brown glow of thrown-away beer bottles, the emerald daubs that had once held 7-UP and Canada Dry. Perry soon developed his own personal gift for spying out bottles. At first he merely indicated to the boy the whereabouts of his finds; he thought it too undignified to scurry about collecting them himself. It was all 'pretty silly', just 'kid stuff'. Nevertheless, the game generated a treasure-hunt excitement, and presently he, too, succumbed to the fun, the fervour of this quest for refundable empties. Dick, too, but Dick was in dead earnest. Screwy as it seemed, maybe this *was* a way to make some money – or, at any rate, a few bucks. Lord knows, he and Perry could use them; their combined finances amounted at the moment to less than five dollars.

Now all three – Dick and the boy and Perry – were piling out of the car and shamelessly, though amiably, competing with one another. Once Dick located a cache of wine and whisky bottles at the bottom of a ditch, and was chagrined to learn that his discovery was valueless. 'They don't give no refund on liquor empties,' the boy informed him. 'Even some of the beers ain't no good. I don't mess with them usually. Just stick with the surefire things. Dr Pepper. Pepsi. Coke. White Rock. Nehi.'

Dick said, 'What's your name?'

'Bill,' the boy said.

'Well, Bill. You're a regular education.'

Nightfall came, and forced the hunters to quit – that, and lack of space, for they had amassed as many bottles as the car could contain. The trunk was filled, the back seat seemed a glittering dump heap; unnoticed, unmentioned by even his grandson, the ailing old man was all but hidden under the shifting, dangerously chiming cargo.

Dick said, 'Be funny if we had a smash-up.'

A bunch of lights publicized the New Hotel, which proved to be, as the travellers neared it, an impressive compound consisting of bungalows, a garage, a restaurant, and a cocktail lounge. Taking charge, the boy said to Dick, 'Pull in there. Maybe we can make a deal. Only let me talk. I've had the experience. Sometimes they try to cheat.' Perry could not imagine 'anyone smart enough to cheat that kid,' he said later. 'It didn't shame him a bit going in there with all those bottles. Me, I never could've, I'd have felt so ashamed. But the people at the motel were nice about it; they just laughed. Turned out the bottles were worth twelve dollars and sixty cents.'

The boy divided the money evenly, giving half to him-self, the rest to his partners, and said, 'Know what? I'm gonna blow me and Johnny to a good feed. Ain't you fellows hungry?'

As always, Dick was. And after so much activity, even

Perry felt starved. As he later told about it, 'We carted the old man into the restaurant and propped him up at a table. He looked exactly the same – thanatoid. And he never said one word. But you should have seen him shovel it in. The kid ordered him pancakes; he said that was what Johnny liked best. I swear he ate something like thirty pancakes. With maybe two pounds of butter, and a quart of syrup. The kid could put it down himself. Potato chips and ice cream, that was all he wanted, but he sure ate a lot of them. I wonder it didn't make him sick.'

During the dinner party, Dick, who had consulted a map, announced that Sweetwater was a hundred or more miles west of the route he was driving – the route that would take him across New Mexico and Arizona to Nevada – to Las Vegas. Though this was true, it was clear to Perry that Dick simply wanted to rid himself of the boy and the old man. Dick's purpose was obvious to the boy, too, but he was polite and said, 'Oh, don't you worry about us. Plenty of traffic must stop here. We'll get a ride.'

The boy walked with them to the car, leaving the old man to devour a fresh stack of pancakes. He shook hands with Dick and with Perry, wished them a Happy New Year, and waved them away into the dark.

The evening of Wednesday, December 30, was a memorable one in the household of Agent A. A. Dewey. Remembering it later, his wife said, 'Alvin was singing in the bath. "The Yellow Rose of Texas". The kids were watching TV. And I was setting the dining-room table. For a buffet. I'm from New Orleans; I love to cook and entertain, and my mother had just sent us a crate of avocados and black-eyed peas, and – oh, a heap of real nice things. So I decided: We're going to have a buffet, invite some friends over – the Murrays, and Cliff and Dodie Hope. Alvin didn't want to, but I was determined. My goodness! The case could go on for ever, and he hadn't taken hardly a minute off since it began. Well, I was setting the table, so when I heard the phone I asked one of the boys to answer it – Paul. Paul said it was for Daddy, and I said, "You tell them he's in the bath," but Paul said he wondered if he ought to do that, because it was Mr Sanford calling from Topeka. Alvin's boss. Alvin took the call with just a towel around him. Made me so mad – dripping puddles everywhere. But when I went to get a mop I saw something worse – that cat, that fool Pete, up on the kitchen table gorging crabmeat salad. My avocado stuffing.

'The next thing was, suddenly Alvin had hold of me, he was hugging me, and I said, "Alvin Dewey, have you lost your mind?" Fun's fun, but the man was wet as a pond, he was ruining my dress, and I was already dressed for company. Of course, when I understood why he was hugging me I hugged him right back. You can imagine what it meant to Alvin to know those men had been arrested. Out in Las Vegas. He said he had to leave for Las Vegas straight away, and I asked him hadn't he ought to put on some clothes first, and Alvin, he was so excited, he said, "Gosh, honey, I guess I've spoiled your party!" I couldn't think of a happier way of having it spoiled – not if this meant that maybe one day soon we'd be back living an ordinary life. Alvin laughed – it was just beautiful to hear him. I mean, the past two weeks had been the worst of all. Because the week before Christmas those men turned up in Kansas City – came and went without getting caught – and I never saw Alvin more depressed, except once when young Alvin was in the hospital, had encephalitis, we thought we might lose him. But I don't want to talk about that.

'Anyway, I made coffee for him and took it to the bedroom, where he was supposed to be getting dressed. But he wasn't. He was sitting on the edge of our bed holding his head, as if he had a headache. Hadn't put on even a sock. So I said, "What do you want to do, get pneumonia?" And he looked at me and said, "Marie, listen, it's got to be these guys, has to, that's the only logical solution." Alvin's funny. Like the first time he ran for Finney County Sheriff. Election Night, when practically every vote had been counted and it was plain as plain he'd won, he said – I could have strangled him – said over and over, "Well, we won't know till the last return."

'I told him, "Now, Alvin, don't start that. Of course they did it." He said, "Where's our proof? We can't prove either of them ever set foot inside the Clutter house!" But that seemed to me exactly what he could prove: footprints – weren't footprints the one thing those animals left behind? Alvin said, "Yes, and a big lot of good they are – unless those boys still happen to be wearing the boots that made them. Just footprints by themselves aren't worth a Dixie dollar." I said, "All right, honey, drink your coffee and I'll help you pack." Sometimes you can't reason with Alvin. The way he kept on, he had me almost convinced Hickock and Smith were innocent, and if they weren't innocent they would never confess, and if they didn't confess they could never be convicted – the evidence was too circumstantial. What bothered him most, though – he was afraid that the story would leak, that the men would learn the truth before the K.B.I. could question them. As it was, they thought they'd been picked up for parole violation. Passing bad cheques. And Alvin felt it was very important they keep thinking that. He said, "The name Clutter has to hit them like a hammer, a blow they never knew was coming."

'Paul – I'd sent him out to the washline for some of Alvin's socks – Paul came back and stood around watching me pack. He wanted to know where Alvin was going. Alvin lifted him up in his arms. He said, "Can you keep a secret, Pauly?" Not that he needed to ask. Both boys knew they mustn't talk about Alvin's work – the bits and pieces they hear around the house. So he said, "Pauly, you remember those two fellows we've been looking for? Well, now we know where they are, and Daddy's going to go get them and bring them here to Garden City." But Paul begged him, "Don't do that, Daddy, don't bring them here." He was frightened – any nine-year-old might've been. Alvin kissed him. He said, "Now that's O.K., Pauly, we won't let them hurt anybody. They're not going to hurt anybody ever again." '

At five that afternoon, some twenty minutes after the stolen Chevrolet rolled off the Nevada desert into Las Vegas, the long ride came to an end. But not before Perry had visited the Las Vegas post office, where he claimed a package addressed to himself in care of General Delivery – the large cardboard box he had mailed from Mexico, and had insured for a hundred dollars, a sum exceeding to an impertinent extent the value of the contents, which were suntans and denim pants, worn shirts, underwear, and two pairs of steel-buckled boots. Waiting for Perry outside the post office, Dick was in excellent spirits; he had reached a decision that he was certain would eradicate his current difficulties and start him on a new road, with a new rainbow in view. The decision involved impersonating an Air Force officer. It was a project that had long fascinated him, and Las Vegas was the ideal place to try it out. He'd already selected the officer's rank and name, the latter borrowed from a former acquaintance, the then warden of Kansas State Penitentiary: Tracy Hand. As Captain Tracy Hand, smartly clothed in a made-to-order uniform, Dick intended to 'crawl the strip', Las Vegas's street of never-closed casinos. Small-time, big-time, the Sands, the Stardust – he meant to hit them all, distributing *en route* 'a bundle of confetti'. By writing worthless cheques right around the clock, he expected to haul in three, maybe four thousand dollars within a twenty-four-hour period. That was half the plot; the second half was: Good-bye, Perry. Dick was sick of him – his harmonica, his aches and ills, his superstitions, the weepy, womanly eyes, the nagging, whispering voice. Suspicious, self-righteous, spiteful, he was like a wife that must be got rid of. And there was but one way to do it: Say nothing – just go.

Absorbed in his plans, Dick did not notice a patrol car pass him, slow down, reconnoitre. Nor did Perry, descending the post-office steps with the Mexican box balanced on a shoulder, observe the prowling car and the policemen in it.

Officers Ocie Pigford and Francis Macauley carried in their heads pages of memorized data, including a description of a black-and-white 1956 Chevrolet bearing Kansas licence plate No. Jo 16212. Neither Perry nor Dick was aware of the police vehicle trailing them as they pulled away from the post office, and with Dick driving and Perry directing, they travelled five blocks north, turned left, then right, drove a quarter mile more, and stopped in front of a dying palm tree and a weather-wrecked sign from which all calligraphy had faded except the word 'OOM'.

'This it?' Dick asked.

Perry, as the patrol car drew alongside, nodded.

The Detective Division of the Las Vegas City Jail contains two interrogation rooms – fluorescent-lighted chambers, measuring ten by twelve, with walls and ceilings of celotex. In each room, in addition to an electric fan, a metal table, and folding metal chairs, there are camouflaged microphones, concealed tape recorders, and, set into the door, a mirrored one-way observation window. On Saturday, the second day of 1960, both rooms were booked for 2 p.m. – the hour that four detectives from Kansas had selected for their first confrontation of Hickock and Smith.

Shortly before the appointed moment, the quartet of K.B.I. agents – Harold Nye, Roy Church, Alvin Dewey, and Clarence Duntz – gathered in a corridor outside the interrogation rooms. Nye was running a temperature. 'Part flu. But mostly sheer excitement,' he subsequently informed a journalist. 'By then I'd already been waiting in Las Vegas two days – took the next plane out after news of the arrest reached our headquarters in Topeka. The rest of the team, Al and Roy and Clarence, came on by car – had a lousy trip, too. Lousy weather. Spent New Year's Eve snowed up in a motel in Albuquerque. Boy, when they finally hit Vegas, they needed good whisky and good news. I was ready with both. Our young men had signed waivers of extradition. Better yet: We had the boots, both pairs, and the soles – the Cat's Paw and the diamond pattern – matched perfectly life-size photographs of the footprints found in the Clutter house. The boots were in a box of stuff the boys picked up at the post office just before the curtain fell. Like I told Al Dewey, suppose the squeeze had come five minutes sooner!

'Even so, our case was very shaky – nothing that couldn't be pulled apart. But I remember, while we were waiting in the corridor – I remember being feverish and nervous as hell, but *confident*. We all were; we felt we were on the edge of the truth. My job, mine and Church's, was to pressure it out of Hickock. Smith belonged to Al and Old Man Duntz. At that time I hadn't seen the suspects – just examined their possessions and arranged the extradition waivers. I'd never laid eyes on Hickock until he was brought down to the interrogation room. I'd imagined a bigger guy. Brawnier. Not some skinny kid. He was twenty-eight, but he looked like a kid. Hungry – right down to the bone. He was wearing a blue shirt and suntans and white socks and black shoes. We shook hands; his hand was drier than mine. Clean, polite, nice voice, good diction, a pretty decent-looking fellow, with a very disarming smile – and in the beginning he smiled quite a lot.

'I said, "Mr Hickock, my name is Harold Nye, and this other gentleman is Mr Roy Church. We're Special Agents of the Kansas Bureau of Investigation, and we've come here to discuss your parole violation. Of course, you're under no obligation to answer our questions, and anything you say may be used against you in evidence. You're entitled to a lawyer at all times. We'll use no force, no threats, and we'll make you no promises." He was calm as could be.'

'I know the form,' Dick said. 'I've been questioned before.'
'Now, Mr Hickock –'
'Dick.'
'Dick, we want to talk to you about your activities since your parole. To our knowledge, you've gone on at least two big cheque sprees in the Kansas City area.'
'Uh-huh. Hung out quite a few.'
'Could you give us a list?'
The prisoner, evidently proud of his one authentic gift, a brilliant memory, recited the names and addresses of twenty Kansas City stores, cafés, and garages, and recalled, accurately, the 'purchase' made at each and the amount of the cheque passed.
'I'm curious, Dick. Why do these people accept your cheques? I'd like to know the secret.'

'The secret is: People are dumb.'

Roy Church said, 'Fine, Dick. Very funny. But just for the moment let's forget these cheques.' Though he sounds as if his throat were lined with hog bristle, and has hands so hardened that he can punch stone walls (his favourite stunt, in fact), persons have been known to mistake Church for a kindly little man, somebody's bald-headed, pink-cheeked uncle. 'Dick,' he said, 'suppose you tell us something about your family background.'

The prisoner reminisced. Once, when he was nine or ten, his father had fallen ill. 'It was rabbit fever,' and the illness lasted many months, during which the family had depended upon church assistance and the charity of neighbours – 'otherwise we would've starved'. That episode apart, his childhood had been O.K. 'We never had much money, but we were never really down-and-out,' Hickock said. 'We always had clean clothes and something to eat. My dad was strict, though. He wasn't happy unless he had me doing chores. But we got along O.K. – no serious arguments. My parents never argued, either. I can't recall a single quarrel. She's wonderful, my mother. Dad's a good guy, too. I'd say they did the best for me they could.' School? Well, he felt he might have been more than an average student if he had contributed to books a fraction of the time he'd 'wasted' on sports. 'Baseball. Football. I made all the teams. After high school I could have gone to college on a football scholarship. I wanted to study engineering, but even with a scholarship, deals like that cost plenty. I don't know, it seemed safer to get a job.'

Before his twenty-first birthday Hickock had worked as a railway trackman, an ambulance driver, a car painter, and a garage mechanic; he'd also married a girl sixteen years old. 'Carol. Her father was a minister. He was dead against me. Said I was a full-time nobody. He made all the trouble he could. But I was nuts about Carol. Still am. There's a real princess. Only – see, we had three kids. Boys. And we were too young to have three kids. Maybe if we hadn't got so deep into debt. If I could've earned extra money. I tried.'

He tried gambling, and started forging cheques and experimenting with other forms of theft. In 1958 he was convicted of house burglary in a Johnson County court and sentenced to five years in Kansas State Penitentiary. But by then Carol had departed and he'd taken as a bride another girl aged sixteen. 'Mean as hell. Her and her whole family. She divorced me while I was inside. I'm not complaining. Last August, when I left The Walls, I figured I had every chance to start new. I got a job in Olathe, lived with my family, and stayed home nights. I was doing swell –'

'Until November twentieth,' said Nye, and Hickock seemed not to understand him. 'The day you stopped doing swell and started hanging paper. Why?'

Hickock sighed, and said, 'That would make a book.' Then, smoking a cigarette borrowed from Nye and lighted by the courteous Church, he said, 'Perry – my buddy Perry Smith – was paroled in the spring. Later on, when I came out, he sent me a letter. Postmarked Idaho. He wrote reminding me of this deal we used to talk over. About Mexico. The idea was we would go to Acapulco, one of them places, buy a fishing boat, and run it ourselves – take tourists deep-sea fishing.'

Nye said, 'This boat. How did you plan to pay for it?'

'I'm coming to that,' Hickock said. 'See, Perry wrote me he had a sister living in Fort Scott. And she was holding some heavy change for him. Several thousand dollars. Money his dad owed him from the sale of some property up in Alaska. He said he was coming to Kansas to get the dough.'

'And the two of you would use it to buy a boat.'

'Correct.'

'But it didn't work out that way.'

'What happened was, Perry showed up maybe a month later. I met him at the bus station in Kansas City –'

'When?' said Church. 'The day of the week.'

'A Thursday.'

'And when did you go to Fort Scott?'

'Saturday.'

'November fourteenth.'

Hickock's eyes flashed with surprise. One could see that he was asking himself why Church should be so certain of the date; and hurriedly – for it was too soon to stir suspicions – the detective said, 'What time did you leave for Fort Scott?'

'That afternoon. We did some work on my car, and had a bowl of chili at the West Side Café. It must have been around three.'

'Around three. Was Perry Smith's sister expecting you?'

'No. Because, see, Perry lost her address. And she didn't have a telephone.'

'Then how did you expect to find her?'

'By inquiring at the post office.'

'Did you?'

'Perry did. They said she'd moved away. To Oregon, they thought. But she hadn't left any forwarding address.'

'Must have been quite a blow. After you'd been counting on a big piece of money like that.'

Hickock agreed. 'Because – well, we'd definitely decided to go to Mexico. Otherwise, I never would've cashed them cheques. But I hoped ... Now listen to me; I'm telling the truth. I thought once we got to Mexico and began making money, then I'd be able to pay them off. The cheques.'

Nye took over. 'One minute, Dick.' Nye is a short, short-tempered man who has difficulty moderating his aggressive vigour, his talent for language both sharp and outspoken. 'I'd like to hear a little more about the trip to Fort Scott,' he said, soft-pedalling. 'When you found Smith's sister no longer there, what did you do then?'

'Walked around. Had a beer. Drove back.'

'You mean you went home?'

'No. To Kansas City. We stopped at the Zesto Drive-In. Ate hamburgers. We tried Cherry Row.'

Neither Nye nor Church was familiar with Cherry Row. Hickock said, 'You kiddin'? Every cop in Kansas knows it.' When the detectives again pleaded ignorance, he explained that it was a stretch of park where one encountered 'hustlers mostly', adding, 'but plenty of amateurs, too. Nurses. Secretaries. I've had a lot of luck there.'

'And this particular evening. Have any luck?'

'The bad kind. We ended up with a pair of rollers.'

'Named?'

'Mildred. The other one, Perry's girl, I think she was called Joan.'

'Describe them.'

'Maybe they were sisters. Both blonde. Plump. I'm not too clear about it. See, we'd bought a bottle of ready-mix Orange Blossoms – that's orange pop and vodka – and I was getting stiff. We gave the girls a few drinks and drove them out to Fun Haven. I imagine you gentlemen never heard of Fun Haven?'

They hadn't.

Hickock grinned and shrugged. 'It's on the Blue Ridge Road. Eight miles south of Kansas City. A combination night-club-motel. You pay ten bucks for the key to a cabin.'

Continuing, he described the cabin in which he claimed that the foursome had stayed the night: twin beds, an old Coca-Cola calendar, a radio that wouldn't play unless the customer deposited a quarter.

His poise, his explicitness, the assured presentation of verifiable detail impressed Nye – though, of course, the boy was lying. Well, wasn't he? Whether because of flu and fever or an abrupt lessening in the warmth of his confidence, Nye exuded an icy sweat.

'Next morning we woke up to find they'd rolled us and beat it,' said Hickock. 'Didn't get much off me. But Perry lost his wallet, with forty or fifty dollars.'

'What did you do about it?'

'There wasn't nothing to do.'

'You could've notified the police.'

'Aw, come on. Quit it. *Notify* the police. For your information, a guy on parole's not allowed to booze. Or associate with another Old Grad –'

'All right, Dick. It's Sunday. The fifteenth of November. Tell us what you did that day from the moment you checked out of Fun Haven.'

'Well, we ate breakfast at a truck stop near Happy Hill. Then we drove to Olathe, and I dropped Perry off at the hotel where he was living. I'd say that was around eleven. Afterwards, I went home and had dinner with the family. Same as every Sunday. Watched TV – a basketball game, or maybe it was football. I was pretty tired.'

'When did you next see Perry Smith?'

'Monday. He came by where I worked. Bob Sand's Body Shop.'

'And what did you talk about? Mexico?'

'Well, we still liked the idea, even if we hadn't got hold of the money to do all we had in mind – put ourselves in business down there. But we wanted to go, and it seemed worth the risk.'

'Worth another stretch in Lansing?'

'That didn't figure. See, we never intended coming Stateside again.'

Nye, who had been jotting notes in a notebook, said, 'On the day following the cheque spree – that would be the twenty-first – you and your friend Smith disappeared. Now, Dick, please outline your movements between then and the time of your arrest here in Las Vegas. Just a rough idea.'

Hickock whistled and rolled his eyes. 'Wow!' he said, and then, summoning his talent for something very like total recall, he began an account of the long ride – the approximately ten thousand miles he and Smith had covered in the past six weeks. He talked for an hour and twenty-five minutes – from two-fifty to four-fifteen – and told, while Nye attempted to list them, of highways and hotels, motels, rivers, towns, and cities, a chorus of entwining names; Apache, El Paso, Corpus Christi, Santillo, San Luis Potosí, Acapulco, San Diego, Dallas, Omaha, Sweetwater, Stillwater, Tenville Junction, Tallahassee, Needles, Miami, Hotel Nuevo Waldorf, Somerset Hotel, Hotel Simone, Arrowhead Motel, Cherokee Motel, and many, many more. He gave them the name of the man in Mexico to whom he'd sold his own old 1949 Chevrolet, and confessed that he had stolen a newer model in Iowa. He described persons he and his partner had met: a Mexican widow, rich and sexy; Otto, a German 'millionaire'; a 'swish' pair of Negro prizefighters driving a 'swish' lavender Cadillac; the blind proprietor of a Florida rattlesnake farm; a dying old man and his grandson; and others. And when he had finished he sat with folded arms and a pleased smile, as though waiting to be commended for the humour, the clarity, and the candour of his traveller's tale.

But Nye, in pursuit of the narrative, raced his pen, and Church, lazily slamming a shut hand against an open palm, said nothing – until suddenly he said, 'I guess you know why we're here.'

Hickock's mouth straightened – his posture, too.

'I guess you realize we wouldn't have come all the way to Nevada just to chat with a couple of two-bit cheque chisellers.'

Nye had closed the notebook. He, too, stared at the prisoner, and observed that a cluster of veins had appeared in his left temple.

'Would we, Dick?'

'What?'

'Come this far to talk about a bunch of cheques.'

'I can't think of any other reason.'

Nye drew a dagger on the cover of his notebook. While doing so, he said, 'Tell me, Dick. Have you ever heard of the Clutter murder case?' Whereupon, he later wrote in a formal report of the interview, 'Suspect underwent an intense visible reaction. He turned grey. His eyes twitched.'

Hickock said, 'Whoa, now. Hold on here. I'm no goddam killer.'

'The question asked,' Church reminded him, 'was whether you'd *heard* of the Clutter murders.'

'I may have read something,' Hickock said.

'A vicious crime. Vicious. Cowardly.'

'And almost perfect,' Nye said. 'But you made two mistakes, Dick. One was, you left a witness. A living witness. Who'll testify in court. Who'll stand in the witness box and tell a jury how Richard Hickock and Perry Smith bound and gagged and slaughtered four helpless people.'

Hickock's face reddened with returning colour. 'Living witness! There can't be!'

T – H

'Because you thought you'd got rid of everyone?'

'I said whoa! There ain't anybody can connect me with any goddam murder. Cheques. A little petty thievery. But I'm no goddam killer.'

'Then why,' Nye asked hotly, 'have you been lying to us?'

'I've been telling you the goddam truth.'

'Now and then. Not always. For instance, what about Saturday afternoon, November fourteenth? You say you drove to Fort Scott.'

'Yes.'

'And when you got there you went to the post office.'

'Yes.'

'To obtain the address of Perry Smith's sister.'

'That's right.'

Nye rose. He walked around to the rear of Hickock's chair, and placing his hands on the back of the chair, leaned down as though to whisper in the prisoner's ear. 'Perry Smith has no sister living in Fort Scott,' he said. 'He never has had. And on Saturday afternoons the Fort Scott post office happens to be closed.' Then he said, 'Think it over, Dick. That's all for now. We'll talk to you later.'

After Hickock's dismissal, Nye and Church crossed the corridor, and looking through the one-way observation window set in the door of the interrogation room, watched the questioning of Perry Smith – a scene visible though not audible. Nye, who was seeing Smith for the first time, was fascinated by his feet – by the fact that his legs were so short that his feet, as small as a child's, couldn't quite make the floor. Smith's head – the stiff Indian hair, the Irish-Indian blending of dark skin and pert, impish features – reminded him of the suspect's pretty sister, the nice Mrs Johnson. But this chunky, misshapen child-man was not pretty; the pink end of his tongue darted forth, flickering like the tongue of a lizard. He was smoking a cigarette, and from the evenness of his exhalations Nye deduced that he was still a 'virgin' – that is, still uninformed about the real purpose of the interview.

Nye was right. For Dewey and Duntz, patient professionals, had gradually narrowed the prisoner's life story to the events of the last seven weeks, then reduced those to a concentrated recapitulation of the crucial week-end – Saturday noon to Sunday noon, 14 to 15 November. Now, having spent three hours preparing the way, they were not far from coming to the point.

Dewey said, 'Perry, let's review our position. Now, when you received parole, it was on condition that you never return to Kansas.'

'The Sunflower State. I cried my eyes out.'

'Feeling that way, why did you go back? You must have had some very strong reason.'

'I told you. To see my sister. To get the money she was holding for me.'

'Oh, yes. The sister you and Hickock tried to find in Fort Scott. Perry, how far is Fort Scott from Kansas City?'

Smith shook his head. He didn't know.

'Well, how long did it take you to drive there?'

No response.

'One hour? Two? Three? Four?'

The prisoner said he couldn't remember.

'Of course you can't. Because you've never in your life been to Fort Scott.'

Until then, neither of the detectives had challenged any part of Smith's statement. He shifted in his chair; with the tip of his tongue he wet his lips.

'The fact is, nothing you've told us is true. You never set foot in Fort Scott. You never picked up any two girls and never took them to any motel –'

'We did. No kidding.'

'What were their names?'

'I never asked.'

'You and Hickock spent the night with these women and never asked their names?'

'They were just prostitutes.'

'Tell us the name of the motel.'

'Ask Dick. He'll know. I never remember junk like that.'

Dewey addressed his colleague. 'Clarence, I think it's time we straightened Perry out.'

Duntz hunched forward. He is a heavyweight with a welterweight's spontaneous agility, but his eyes are hooded and lazy. He drawls; each word, formed reluctantly and framed in a cattle-country accent, lasts a while. 'Yes, sir,' he said. ' 'Bout time.'

'Listen good, Perry. Because Mr Duntz is going to tell you where you really were that Saturday night. Where you were and what you were doing.'

Duntz said, 'You were killing the Clutter family.'

Smith swallowed. He began to rub his knees.

'You were out in Holcomb, Kansas. In the home of Mr Herbert W. Clutter. And before you left that house you killed all the people in it.'

'Never. I never.'

'Never what?'

'Knew anybody by that name. Clutter.'

Dewey called him a liar, and then, conjuring a card that in prior consultation the four detectives had agreed to play face down, told him, 'We have a living witness, Perry. Somebody you boys overlooked.'

A full minute elapsed, and Dewey exulted in Smith's silence, for an innocent man would ask who was this witness, and who were these Clutters, and why did they think he'd murdered them – would, at any rate, say *something*. But Smith sat quiet, squeezing his knees.

'Well, Perry?'

'You got an aspirin? They took away my aspirin.'

'Feeling bad?'

'My legs do.'

It was five-thirty. Dewey, intentionally abrupt, terminated the interview. 'We'll take this up again tomorrow,' he said. 'By the way, do you know what tomorrow is? Nancy Clutter's birthday. She would have been seventeen.'

'She would have been seventeen.' Perry, sleepless in the dawn hours, wondered (he later recalled) if it was true that today was the girl's birthday, and decided no, that it was just another way of getting under his skin, like that phony business about a witness – 'a living witness'. There couldn't be. Or did they mean – If only he could talk to Dick. But he and Dick were being kept apart; Dick was locked in a cell on another floor. 'Listen good, Perry. Because Mr Duntz is going to tell you where you really were ...' Midway in the questioning, after he'd begun to notice the number of allusions to a particular November week-end, he'd nerved himself for what he knew was coming, yet when it did, when the big cowboy with the sleepy voice said, 'You were killing the Clutter family' – well, he'd damn near died, that's all. He must have lost ten pounds in two seconds. Thank God he hadn't let them see it. Or hoped he hadn't. And Dick? Presumably they'd pulled the same stunt on him. Dick was smart, a convincing performer, but his 'guts' were unreliable, he panicked too easily. Even so, and however much they pressured him, Perry was sure Dick would hold out. Unless he wanted to hang. 'And before you left that house you killed all the people in it.' It wouldn't amaze him if every Old Grad in Kansas had heard that line. They must have questioned hundreds of men, and no doubt accused dozens; he and Dick were merely two more. On the *other* hand – well, *would* Kansas send four Special Agents a thousand miles to pick up a small-time pair of parole violators? Maybe somehow they *had* stumbled on something, somebody – 'a living witness'. But that was impossible. Except – He'd give an arm, a leg to talk to Dick for just five minutes.

And Dick, awake in a cell on the floor below, was (he later recalled) equally eager to converse with Perry – find out what the punk had told them. Christ, you couldn't trust him to remember even the outline of the Fun Haven alibi – though they had discussed it often enough. And when those bastards threatened him with a witness! Ten to one the little spook had thought they meant an *eye*witness. Whereas he, Dick, had known at once who the so-called witness must be: Floyd Wells, his old friend and former cell-mate. While serving the last of his sentence, Dick had plotted to knife Floyd – stab him through the heart with a hand-made 'shiv' – and what a fool he was not to have done it. Except for Perry, Floyd Wells was the one human being who could link the names Hickock and Clutter. Floyd, with his sloping shoulders and inclining chin – Dick had thought he'd be too afraid. The sonofabitch was probably expecting some fancy reward – a parole or money, or both. But hell would freeze before he got it. Because a convict's tattle wasn't proof. Proof is footprints, fingerprints, witnesses, a confession. Hell, if all those cowboys had to go on was some story Floyd Wells had told, then there wasn't a lot to worry about. Come right down to it, Floyd wasn't half as dangerous as Perry. Perry, if he lost his nerve and let fly, could put them both in The Corner. And suddenly he saw the truth. It was *Perry* he ought to have silenced. On a mountain road in Mexico. Or while walking across the Mojave. Why had it never occurred to him until now? For now, now was much too late.

Ultimately, at five minutes past three that afternoon, Smith admitted the falsity of the Fort Scott tale. 'That was only something Dick told his family. So he could stay out overnight. Do some drinking. See, Dick's dad watched him pretty close – afraid he'd break parole. So we made up an excuse about my sister. It was just to pacify Mr Hickock.' Otherwise, he repeated the same story again and again, and Duntz and Dewey, regardless of how often they corrected him and accused him of lying, could not make him change it – except to add fresh details. The names of the prostitutes, he recalled today, were Mildred and Jane (or Joan). 'They rolled us,' he now remembered. 'Walked off with all our dough while we were asleep.' And though even Duntz had forfeited his composure – had shed, along with tie and coat, his enigmatic drowsy dignity – the suspect seemed content and serene; he refused to budge. He'd never heard of the Clutters or Holcomb, or even Garden City.

Across the hall, in the smoke-choked room where Hickock was undergoing his second interrogation, Church and Nye were methodically applying a more roundabout strategy. Not once during this interview, now almost three hours old, had either of them mentioned murder – an omission that kept the prisoner edgy, expectant. They talked of everything else: Hickock's religious philosophy ('I know about hell. I been there. Maybe there's a heaven, too. Lots of rich people think so'); his sexual history ('I've always behaved like a one-hundred-per-cent normal'); and, once more, the history of his recent cross-country hegira ('Why we kept going like that, the only reason was we were looking for jobs. Couldn't find anything decent, though. I worked one day digging a ditch ...'). But things unspoken were the centre of interest – the cause, the detectives were convinced, of Hickock's escalating distress. Presently, he shut his eyes and touched the lids with trembling fingertips. And Church said, 'Something wrong?'

'A headache. I get real bastards.'

Then Nye said, 'Look at me, Dick.' Hickock obeyed, with an expression that the detective interpreted as a pleading with him to speak, to accuse, and let the prisoner escape into the sanctuary of steadfast denial. 'When we discussed the matter yesterday, you may recall my saying that the Clutter murders were almost a perfect crime. The killers made only two mistakes. The first one was they left a witness. The second – well, I'll show you.' Rising, he retrieved from a corner a box and a briefcase, both of which he'd brought into the room at the start of the interview. Out of the briefcase came a large photograph. 'This,' he said, leaving it on the table, 'is a one-to-one reproduction of certain footprints found near Mr Clutter's body. And here' – he opened the box – 'are the boots that made them. Your boots, Dick.' Hickock looked, and looked away. He rested his elbows on his knees and cradled his head in his hands. 'Smith,' said Nye, 'was even more careless. We have his boots, too, and they exactly fit another set of prints. Bloody ones.'

Church closed in. 'Here's what's going to happen to you, Hickock,' he said. 'You'll be taken back to Kansas. You'll be charged on four counts of first-degree murder. Count One: That on or about the fifteenth day of November 1959, one Richard Eugene Hickock did unlawfully, feloniously, wilfully and with deliberation and premeditation, and while being engaged in the perpetration of a felony, kill and take the life of Herbert W. Clutter. Count Two: That on or about the fifteenth day of November 1959, the same Richard Eugene Hickock did unlawfully –'

Hickock said, 'Perry Smith killed the Clutters.' He lifted his head, and slowly straightened up in the chair, like a fighter staggering to his feet. 'It was Perry. I couldn't stop him. He killed them all.'

Postmistress Clare, enjoying a coffee break at Hartman's Café, complained of the low volume of the café's radio. 'Turn it up,' she demanded.

The radio was tuned to Garden City's Station KIUL. She heard the words '. . . after sobbing out his dramatic confession, Hickock emerged from the interrogation room and fainted in a hallway. K.B.I. agents caught him as he fell to the floor. The agents quoted Hickock as saying he and Smith invaded the Clutter home expecting to find a safe containing at least ten thousand dollars. But there was no safe, so they tied the family up and shot them one by one. Smith has neither confirmed nor denied taking part in the crime. When told that Hickock had signed a confession, Smith said, "I'd like to see my buddy's statement." But the request was rejected. Officers have declined to reveal whether it was Hickock or Smith who actually shot the members of the family. They emphasized that the statement was only Hickock's version. K.B.I. personnel, returning the two men to Kansas, have already left Las Vegas by car. It is expected the party will arrive in Garden City late Wednesday. Meanwhile, County Attorney Duane West . . .'

'One by one,' said Mrs Hartman. 'Just imagine. I don't wonder the varmint fainted.'

Others in the café – Mrs Clare and Mabel Helm and a husky young farmer who had stopped to buy a plug of Brown Mule chewing tobacco – muttered and mumbled. Mrs Helm dabbed at her eyes with a paper napkin. 'I won't listen,' she said. 'I mustn't. I won't.'

'. . . news of a break in the case has met with little reaction in the town of Holcomb, a half mile from the Clutter home.

Generally, townspeople in the community of two hundred and seventy expressed relief . . .'

The young farmer hooted. 'Relief! Last night, after we heard it on the TV, know what my wife did? Bawled like a baby.'

'Shush,' said Mrs Clare. 'That's me.'

'. . . and Holcomb's postmistress, Mrs Myrtle Clare, said the residents are glad the case has been solved, but some of them still feel others may be involved. She said plenty of folks are still keeping their doors locked and their guns ready . . .'

Mrs Hartman laughed. 'Oh, *Myrt!*' she said. 'Who'd you tell that to?'

'A reporter from the *Telegram*.'

The men of her acquaintance, many of them, treat Mrs Clare as though she were another man. The farmer slapped her on the back and said, 'Gosh, Myrt. Gee, fella. You don't still think one of us – anybody round here – had something to do with it?'

But that, of course, was what Mrs Clare did think, and though she was usually alone in her opinions, this time she was not without company, for the majority of Holcomb's population, having lived for seven weeks amid unwholesome rumours, general mistrust, and suspicion, appeared to feel disappointed at being told that the murderer was not someone among themselves. Indeed, a sizeable faction refused to accept the fact that two unknown men, two thieving strangers, were solely responsible. As Mrs Clare now remarked, 'Maybe they did it, these fellows. But there's more to it than that. Wait. Some day they'll get to the bottom, and when they do they'll find the one behind it. The one wanted Clutter out of the way. The *brains*.'

Mrs Hartman sighed. She hoped Myrt was wrong. And Mrs Helm said, 'What *I* hope is, I hope they keep 'em locked up good. I won't feel easy knowing they're in our vicinity.'

'Oh, I don't think you got to worry, ma'am,' said the young farmer. 'Right now those boys are a lot more scared of us than we are of them.'

On an Arizona highway, a two-car caravan is flashing across sage-brush country – the mesa country of hawks and rattlesnakes and towering red rocks. Dewey is driving the lead car, Perry Smith sits beside him, and Duntz is sitting in the back seat. Smith is handcuffed, and the handcuffs are attached to a security belt by a short length of chain – an arrangement so restricting his movements that he cannot smoke unaided. When he wants a cigarette, Dewey must light it for him and place it between his lips, a task that the detective finds 'repellent', for it seems such an intimate action – the kind of thing he'd done while he was courting his wife.

On the whole, the prisoner ignores his guardians and their sporadic attempts to goad him by repeating parts of Hickock's hour-long tape-recorded confession: 'He says he tried to stop you, Perry. But says he couldn't. Says he was scared you'd shoot him too', and 'Yes, sir, Perry. It's all your fault. Hickock himself, he says he wouldn't harm the fleas on a dog.' None of this – outwardly, at any rate – agitates Smith. He continues to contemplate the scenery, to read Burma-Shave doggerel, and to count the carcasses of shot-gunned coyotes festooning ranch fences.

Dewey, not anticipating any exceptional response, says, 'Hickock tells us you're a natural-born killer. Says it doesn't bother you a bit. Says one time out there in Las Vegas you went after a coloured man with a bicycle chain. Whipped him to death. For fun.'

To Dewey's surprise, the prisoner gasps. He twists around in his seat until he can see, through the rear window, the motorcade's second car, see inside it: 'The tough boy!' Turning back, he stares at the dark streak of desert highway. 'I thought it was a stunt. I didn't believe you. That Dick let fly. The tough boy! Oh, a real brass boy. Wouldn't harm the fleas on a dog. Just run over the dog.' He spits. 'I never killed any nigger.' Duntz agrees with him; having studied the files on unsolved Las Vegas homicides, he knows Smith to be innocent of this particular deed. 'I never killed any niggers. But *he* thought so. I always knew if we ever got caught, if Dick ever really let fly, dropped his guts all over the goddam floor – I knew he'd tell about the nigger.' He spits again. 'So Dick was afraid of me? That's amusing. I'm very amused. What he don't know is, I almost did shoot him.'

Dewey lights two cigarettes, one for himself, one for the prisoner. 'Tell us about it, Perry.'

Smith smokes with closed eyes, and explains, 'I'm thinking. I want to remember this just the way it was.' He pauses for quite a while. 'Well, it all started with a letter I got while I was out in Buhl, Idaho. That was September or October. The letter was from Dick, and he said he was on to a cinch. The perfect score. I didn't answer him, but he wrote again, urging me to come back to Kansas and go partners with him. He never said what kind of score it was. Just that it was a "sure-fire cinch". Now, as it happened, I had another reason for wanting to be in Kansas around about that time. A personal matter I'd just as soon keep to myself – it's got nothing to do with this deal. Only that otherwise I wouldn't have gone back there. But I did. And Dick met me at the bus station in Kansas City. We drove out to the farm, his parents' place. But they didn't want me there. I'm very sensitive; I usually know what people are feeling.

'Like you.' He means Dewey, but does not look at him. 'You hate handing me a butt. That's your business. I don't blame you. Any more than I blamed Dick's mother. The fact is, she's a very sweet person. But she knew what I was – a friend from The Walls – and she didn't want me in her house. Christ, I was glad to get out, go to a hotel. Dick took me to a hotel in Olathe. We bought some beer and carried it up to the room, and that's when Dick outlined what he had in mind. He said after I'd left Lansing he celled with someone who'd once worked for a wealthy wheat grower out in western Kansas. Mr Clutter. Dick drew me a diagram of the Clutter house. He knew where everything was – doors, halls, bedrooms. He said one of the ground-floor rooms was used as an office, and in the office there was a safe – a wall safe. He said Mr Clutter needed it because he always kept on hand large sums of cash. Never less than ten thousand dollars. The plan was to rob the safe, and if we were seen –

well, whoever saw us would have to go. Dick must have said it a million times: "No witnesses." '

Dewey says, 'How many of these witnesses did he think there might be? I mean, how many people did he expect to find in the Clutter house?'

'That's what I wanted to know. But he wasn't sure. At least four. Probably six. And it was possible the family might have guests. He thought we ought to be ready to handle up to a dozen.'

Dewey groans, Duntz whistles, and Smith, smiling wanly, adds, 'Me, too. Seemed to me that was a little off. Twelve people. But Dick said it was a cinch. He said, "We're gonna go in there and splatter those walls with hair." The mood I was in, I let myself be carried along. But also – I'll be honest – I had faith in Dick; he struck me as being very practical, the masculine type, and I wanted the money as much as he did. I wanted to get it and go to Mexico. But I hoped we could do it without violence. Seemed to me we could if we wore masks. We argued about it. On the way out there, out to Holcomb, I wanted to stop and buy some black silk stockings to wear over our heads. But Dick felt that even with a stocking he could still be identified. Because of his bad eye. All the same, when we got to Emporia – '

Duntz says, 'Hold on, Perry. You're jumping ahead. Go back to Olathe. What time did you leave there?'

'One. One-thirty. We left just after lunch and drove to Emporia. Where we bought some rubber gloves and a roll of cord. The knife and shotgun, the shells – Dick had brought all that from home. But he didn't want to look for black stockings. It got to be quite an argument. Somewhere on the outskirts of Emporia, we passed a Catholic hospital, and I persuaded him to stop and go inside and try and buy some black stockings from the nuns. I knew nuns wear them. But he only made believe. Came out and said they wouldn't sell him any. I was sure he hadn't even asked, and he confessed it; he said it was a puky idea – the nuns would've thought he was crazy. So we didn't stop again till Great Bend. That's where we bought the tape. Had dinner there, a big dinner. It put me to sleep. When I woke up, we were just coming into Garden City. Seemed like a real dead-dog town. We stopped for gas at a filling station—'

Dewey asks if he remembers which one.

'Believe it was a Phillips 66.'

'What time was this?'

'Around midnight. Dick said it was seven miles more to Holcomb. All the rest of the way, he kept talking to himself, saying this ought to be here and that ought to be there – according to the instructions he'd memorized. I hardly realized it when we went through Holcomb, it was such a little settlement. We crossed a railroad track. Suddenly Dick said, "This is it, this has to be it." It was the entrance to a private road, lined with trees. We slowed down and turned off the lights. Didn't need them. Account of the moon. There wasn't nothing else up there – not a cloud, nothing. Just that full moon. It was like broad day, and when we started up the road, Dick said, "Look at this spread! The barns! That house! Don't tell me this guy ain't loaded." But I didn't like the setup, the atmosphere; it was sort of *too* impressive. We parked in the shadows of a tree. While we were sitting there, a light came on – not in the main house but a house maybe a hundred yards to the left. Dick said it was the hired man's house; he knew because of the diagram. But he said it was a damn sight nearer the Clutter house than it was supposed to be. Then the light went off. Mr Dewey – the witness you mentioned. Is that who you meant – the hired man?'

'No. He never heard a sound. But his wife was nursing a sick baby. He said they were up and down the whole night.'

'A sick baby. Well, I wondered. While we were still sitting there, it happened again – a light flashed on and off. And that really put bubbles in my blood. I told Dick to count me out. If he was determined to go ahead with it, he'd have to do it alone. He started the car, we were leaving, and I thought, Bless Jesus. I've always trusted my intuitions; they've saved my life more than once. But half-way down the road Dick stopped. He was sore as hell. I could see he was thinking, Here I've set up this big score, here we've come all this way, and now this punk wants to chicken out. He said, "Maybe you think I ain't got the guts to do it alone. But, by God, I'll show you who's got guts." There was some liquor in the car. We each had a drink, and I told him, "O.K., Dick. I'm with you." So we turned back. Parked where we had before. In the shadows of a tree. Dick put on gloves; I'd already put on mine. He carried the knife and a flashlight. I had the gun. The house looked tremendous in the moonlight. Looked empty. I remember hoping there was nobody home –'

Dewey says, 'But you saw a dog?'

'No.'

'The family had an old gun-shy dog. We couldn't understand why he didn't bark. Unless he'd seen a gun and bolted.'

'Well, I didn't see anything or nobody. That's why I never believed it. About an eyewitness.'

'Not *eye*witness. Witness. Someone whose testimony associates you and Hickcock with this case.'

'Oh, Uh-huh. Uh-huh. Him. And Dick always said he'd be too scared. Ha!'

Duntz, not to be diverted, reminds him, 'Hickock had the knife. You had the gun. How did you get into the house?'

'The door was unlocked. A side door. It took us into Mr Clutter's office. Then we waited in the dark. Listening. But the only sound was the wind. There was quite a little wind outside. It made the trees move, and you could hear the leaves. The one window was curtained with Venetian blinds, but moonlight was coming through. I closed the blinds, and Dick turned on his flashlight. We saw the desk. The safe was supposed to be in the wall directly behind the desk, but we couldn't find it. It was a panelled wall, and there were books and framed maps, and I noticed, on a shelf, a terrific pair of binoculars. I decided I was going to take them with me when we left there.'

'Did you?' asks Dewey, for the binoculars had not been missed.

Smith nods. 'We sold them in Mexico.'

'Sorry. Go on.'

'Well, when we couldn't find the safe, Dick doused the

flashlight and we moved in darkness out of the office and across a parlour, a living-room. Dick whispered to me couldn't I walk quieter. But he was just as bad. Every step we took made a racket. We came to a hall and a door, and Dick, remembering the diagram, said it was a bedroom. He shined the flashlight and opened the door. A man said, "Honey?". He'd been asleep, and he blinked and said, "Is that you, honey?" Dick asked him, "Are you Mr Clutter?" He was wide-awake now; he sat up and said, "Who is it? What do you want?" Dick told him, very polite, like we were a couple of door-to-door salesmen, "We want to talk to you, sir. In your office, please." And Mr Clutter, barefoot, just wearing pyjamas, he went with us to the office and we turned on the office lights.

'Up till then he hadn't been able to see us very good. I think what he saw hit him hard. Dick says, "Now, sir, all we want you to do it show us where you keep that safe." But Mr Clutter says, "What safe?" He says he don't have any safe. I knew right then it was true. He had that kind of face. You just knew whatever he told you was pretty much the truth. But Dick shouted at him, "Don't lie to me, you sonofabitch! I know goddam well you got a safe!" My feeling was nobody had ever spoken to Mr Clutter like that. But he looked Dick straight in the eye and told him, being very mild about it – said, well, he was sorry but he just didn't have any safe. Dick tapped him on the chest with the knife, says, "Show us where that safe is or you're gonna be a good bit sorrier." But Mr Clutter – oh, you could see he was scared, but his voice stayed mild and steady – he went on denying he had a safe.

'Some time along in there, I fixed the telephone. The one in the office. I ripped out the wires. And I asked Mr Clutter if there were any other telephones in the house. He said yes, there was one in the kitchen. So I took the flashlight and went to the kitchen – it was quite a distance from the office. When I found the telephone, I removed the receiver and cut the line with a pair of pliers. Then, heading back, I heard a noise. A creaking overhead. I stopped at the foot of the stairs leading to the second floor. It was dark, and I didn't dare use the flashlight. But I could tell there was someone there. At the top of the stairs, silhouetted against a window. A figure. Then it moved away.'

Dewey imagines it must have been Nancy. He'd often theorized, on the basis of the gold wristwatch found tucked in the toe of a shoe in her closet, that Nancy had awakened, heard persons in the house, thought they might be thieves, and prudently hidden the watch, her most valuable property.

'For all I knew, maybe it was somebody with a gun. But Dick wouldn't even listen to me. He was so busy playing tough boy. Bossing Mr Clutter around. Now he'd brought him back to the bedroom. He was counting the money in Mr Clutter's billfold. There was about thirty dollars. He threw the billfold on the bed and told him, "You've got more money in this house than that. A rich man like you. Living on a spread like this." Mr Clutter said that was all the cash he had, and explained he always did business by cheque. He offered to write us a cheque. Dick just blew up – "What kind of Mongolians do you think we are?" – and I thought Dick was ready to smash him, so I said, "Dick. Listen to me. There's somebody awake upstairs." Mr Clutter told us the only people upstairs were his wife and a son and daughter. Dick wanted to know if the wife had any money, and Mr Clutter said if she did, it would be very little, a few dollars, and he asked us – really kind of broke down – please not to bother her, because she was an invalid, she'd been very ill for a long time. But Dick insisted on going upstairs. He made Mr Clutter lead the way.

'At the foot of the stairs, Mr Clutter switched on lights that lighted the hall above, and as we were going up, he said, "I don't know why you boys want to do this. I've never done you any harm. I never saw you before." That's when Dick told him, "Shut up! When we want you to talk, we'll tell you." Wasn't anybody in the upstairs hall, and all the doors were shut. Mr Clutter pointed out the rooms where the boy and girl were supposed to be sleeping, then opened his wife's door. He lighted a lamp beside the bed and told her, "It's all right, sweetheart. Don't be afraid. These men, they just want some money." She was a thin, frail sort of woman in a long white nightgown. The minute she opened her eyes, she started to cry. She says, talking to her husband, "Sweetheart, I don't have any money." He was holding her hand, patting it. He said, "Now, don't cry, honey. It's nothing to be afraid of. It's just I gave these men all the money I had, but they want some more. They believe we have a safe somewhere in the house. I told them we don't." Dick raised his hand, like he was going to crack him across the mouth. Says, "Didn't I tell you to shut up?" Mrs Clutter said, "But my husband's telling you the God's truth. There isn't any safe." And Dick answered back, "I know goddam well you got a safe. And I'll find it before I leave here. Needn't worry that I won't." Then he asked her where she kept her purse. The purse was in a bureau drawer. Dick turned it inside out. Found just some change and a dollar or two. I motioned to him to come into the hall. I wanted to discuss the situation. So we stepped outside, and I said –'

Duntz interrupts him to ask if Mr and Mrs Clutter could overhear the conversation.

'No. We were just outside the door, where we could keep an eye on them. But we were whispering. I told Dick, "These people are telling the truth. The one who lied is your friend Floyd Wells. There isn't any safe, so let's get the hell out of here." But Dick was too ashamed to face it. He said he wouldn't believe it till we searched the whole house. He said the thing to do was tie them all up, then take our time looking around. You couldn't argue with him, he was so excited. The glory of having everybody at his mercy, that's what excited him. Well, there was a bathroom next door to Mrs Clutter's room. The idea was to lock the parents in the bathroom, and wake the kids and put them there, then bring them out one by one and tie them up in different parts of the house. And then, says Dick, after we've found the safe, we'll cut their throats. Can't shoot them, he says – that would make too much noise.'

Perry frowns, rubs his knees with his manacled hands. 'Let me think a minute. Because along in here things begin to get a little complicated. I remember. Yes. Yes, I took a chair out of the hall and stuck it in the bathroom. So Mrs Clutter could sit down. Seeing she was said to be an invalid. When we locked them up, Mrs Clutter was crying and telling us, "Please don't hurt anybody. Please don't hurt my children." And her husband had his arms around her, saying, like, "Sweetheart, these fellows don't mean to hurt anybody. All they want is some money."

'We went to the boy's room. He was awake. Lying there like he was too scared to move. Dick told him to get up, but he didn't move, or move fast enough, so Dick punched him, pulled him out of bed, and I said, "You don't have to hit him, Dick." And I told the boy – he was only wearing a T-shirt – to put on his pants. He put on a pair of blue jeans, and we'd just locked him in the bathroom when the girl appeared – came out of her room. She was all dressed, like she been awake some while. I mean, she had on socks and slippers, and a kimono, and her hair was wrapped in a bandanna. She was trying to smile. She said, "Good grief, what is this? Some kind of joke?" I don't guess she thought it was much of a joke, though. Not after Dick opened the bathroom door and shoved her in ...'

Dewey envisions them: the captive family, meek and frightened but without any premonition of their destiny. Herb *couldn't* have suspected, or he would have fought. He was a gentle man but strong and no coward. Herb, his friend Alvin Dewey felt certain, would have fought to the death defending Bonnie's life and the lives of his children.

'Dick stood guard outside the bathroom door while I reconnoitred. I frisked the girl's room, and I found a little purse – like a doll's purse. Inside it was a silver dollar. I dropped it somehow, and it rolled across the floor. Rolled under a chair. I had to get down on my knees. And just then it was like I was outside myself. Watching myself in some nutty movie. It made me sick. I was just disgusted. Dick, and all his talk about a rich man's safe, and here I am crawling on my belly to steal a child's silver dollar. One dollar. And I'm crawling on my belly to get it.'

Perry squeezes his knees, asks the detectives for aspirin,

thanks Duntz for giving him one, chews it, and resumes talking. 'But that's what you do. You get what you can. I frisked the boy's room, too. Not a dime. But there was a little portable radio, and I decided to take it. Then I remembered the binoculars I'd seen in Mr Clutter's office. I went downstairs to get them. I carried the binoculars and the radio out to the car. It was cold, and the wind and the cold felt good. The moon was so bright you could see for miles. And I thought, Why don't I walk off? Walk to the highway, hitch a ride. I sure Jesus didn't want to go back in that house. And yet – How can I explain this? It was like I wasn't part of it. More as though I was reading a story. And I had to know what was going to happen. The end. So I went back upstairs. And now, let's see – uh-huh, that's when we tied them up. Mr Clutter first. We called him out of the bathroom, and I tied his hands together. Then I marched him all the way down to the basement–'

Dewey says, 'Alone and unarmed?'

'I had the knife.'

Dewey says, 'But Hickock stayed guard upstairs?'

'To keep them quiet. Anyway, I didn't need help. I've worked with rope all my life.'

Dewey says, 'Were you using the flashlight or did you turn on the basement lights?'

'The lights. The basement was divided into two sections. One part seemed to be a playroom. Took him to the other section, the furnace room. I saw a big cardboard box leaning against the wall. A mattress box. Well, I didn't feel I ought to ask him to stretch out on the cold floor, so I dragged the mattress box over, flattened it, and told him to lie down.'

The driver, via the rear-view mirror, glances at his colleague, attracts his eye, and Duntz slightly nods, as if in tribute. All along Dewey had argued that the mattress box had been placed on the floor for the *comfort* of Mr Clutter, and taking heed of similar hints, other fragmentary indications of ironic, erratic compassion, the detective had conjectured that at least one of the killers was not altogether uncharitable.

'I tied his feet, then tied his hands to his feet. I asked him was it too tight, and he said no, but said would we please leave his wife alone. There was no need to tie her up – she wasn't going to holler or try to run out of the house. He said she'd been sick for years and years, and she was just beginning to get a little better, but an incident like this might cause her to have a setback. I know it's nothing to laugh over, only I couldn't help it – him talking about a "setback".

'Next thing, I brought the boy down. First I put him in the room with his dad. Tied his hands to an overhead steampipe. Then I figured that wasn't very safe. He might somehow get loose and undo the old man, or vice versa. So I cut him down and took him to the playroom, where there was a comfortable-looking couch. I roped his feet to the foot of the couch, roped his hands, then carried the rope up and made a loop around his neck, so if he struggled he'd choke himself. Once, while I was working, I put the knife down on this – well, it was a freshly varnished cedar chest; the whole cellar smelled of varnish – and he asked me not to put my knife there. The chest was a wedding present he'd built for somebody. A sister, I believe he said. Just as I was leaving, he had a coughing fit, so I stuffed a pillow under his head. Then I turned off the lights –'

Dewey says, 'But you hadn't taped their mouths?'

'No. The taping came later, after I'd tied both the women in their bedrooms. Mrs Clutter was still crying, at the same time she was asking me about Dick. She didn't trust him, but said she felt I was a decent young man. I'm *sure* you are, she says, and made me promise I wouldn't let Dick hurt anybody. I think what she really had in mind was her daughter. I was worried about that myself. I suspected Dick was plotting something, something I wouldn't stand for. When I finished tying Mrs Clutter, sure enough, I found he'd taken the girl to her bedroom. She was in the bed, and he was sitting on the edge of it talking to her. I stopped that; I told him to go look for the safe while I tied her up. After he'd gone, I roped her feet together and tied her hands behind her back. Then I pulled up the covers, tucked her in till just her head showed. There was a little easy chair near the bed, and I thought I'd rest a minute; my legs were on fire – all that climbing and kneeling. I asked Nancy if she had a boy friend. She said yes, she did. She was trying hard to act casual and friendly. I really liked her. She was really nice. A very pretty girl, and not spoiled or anything. She told me quite a lot about herself. About school, and how she was going to go to university to study music and art. Horses. Said next to dancing what she liked best was to gallop a horse, so I mentioned my mother had been a champion rodeo rider.

'And we talked about Dick; I was curious, see, what he'd been saying to her. Seems she'd asked him why he did things like this. Rob people. And, wow, did he toss her a tearjerker – said he'd been raised an orphan in an orphanage, and how nobody had ever loved him, and his only relative was a sister who lived with men without marrying them. All the time we were talking, we could hear the lunatic roaming around below, looking for the safe. Looking behind pictures. Tapping the walls. Tap tap tap. Like some nutty woodpecker. When he came back, just to be a real bastard I asked had he found it. Course he hadn't, but he said he'd come across another purse in the kitchen. With seven dollars.'

Duntz says, 'How long now had you been in the house?'

'Maybe an hour.'

Duntz says, 'And when did you do the taping?'

'Right then. Started with Mrs Clutter. I made Dick help me – because I didn't want to leave him alone with the girl. I cut the tape in long strips, and Dick wrapped them around Mrs Clutter's head like you'd wrap a mummy. He asked her, "How come you keep on crying? Nobody's hurting you", and he turned off the bedside lamp and said, "Good night, Mrs Clutter. Go to sleep." Then he says to me, as we're heading along the hall towards Nancy's room, "I'm gonna bust that little girl." And I said, "Uh-huh. But you'll have to kill me first." He looked like he didn't believe he'd heard right. He says, "What do you care? Hell, you can bust her, too." Now, that's something I despise. Anybody that can't control themselves sexually, Christ, I hate that kind of stuff. I told him straight. "Leave her alone. Else you've got a buzzsaw to fight." That really burned him, but he realized it wasn't the time to have a flat-out free-for-all. So he says, "O.K., honey. If that's the way you feel." The end of it was we never even taped her. We switched off the hall light and went down to the basement.'

Perry hesitates. He has a question but phrases it as a statement: 'I'll bet he never said anything about wanting to rape the girl.'

Dewey admits it, but he adds that except for an apparently somewhat expurgated version of his own conduct, Hickock's story supports Smith's. The details vary, the dialogue is not identical, but in substance the two accounts – thus far, at least – corroborate one another.

'Maybe. But I knew he hadn't told about the girl. I'd have bet my shirt.'

Duntz says, 'Perry, I've been keeping track of the lights. The way I calculate it, when you turned off the upstairs light, that left the house completely dark.'

'Did. And we never used the lights again. Except the flashlight. Dick carried the flashlight when we went to tape Mr Clutter and the boy. Just before I taped him, Mr Clutter asked me – and these were his last words – wanted to know how his wife was, if she was all right, and I said she was fine, she was ready to go to sleep, and I told him it wasn't long till morning, and how in the morning somebody would find them, and then all of it, me and Dick and all, would seem like something they dreamed. I wasn't kidding him. I didn't want to harm the man. I thought he was a very nice gentleman. Soft-spoken. I thought so right up to the moment I cut his throat.

'Wait. I'm not telling it the way it was.' Perry scowls. He rubs his legs; the handcuffs rattle. 'After, see, after we'd taped them, Dick and I went off in a corner. To talk it over. Remember, now, there were hard feelings between us. Just then it made my stomach turn to think I'd ever admired him, lapped up all that brag. I said, "Well, Dick. Any qualms?" He didn't answer me. I said, "Leave them alive, and this won't be any small rap. Ten years the very least."

He still didn't say anything. He was holding the knife. I asked him for it, and he gave it to me, and I said, "All right, Dick. Here goes." But I didn't mean it. I meant to call his bluff, make him argue me out of it, make him admit he was a phony and a coward. See, it was something between me and Dick. I knelt down beside Mr Clutter, and the pain of kneeling – I thought of that goddam dollar. Silver dollar. The shame. Disgust. And *they'd* told me never to come back to Kansas. But I didn't realize what I'd done till I heard the sound. Like somebody drowning. Screaming under water. I handed the knife to Dick. I said, "Finish him. You'll feel better." Dick tried – or pretended to. But the man had the strength of ten men – he was half out of his ropes, his hands were free. Dick panicked. Dick wanted to get the hell out of there. But I wouldn't let him go. The man would have died anyway, I know that, but I couldn't leave him like he was. I told Dick to hold the flashlight, focus it. Then I aimed the gun. The room just exploded. Went blue. Just blazed up. Jesus, I'll never understand why they didn't hear the noise twenty miles around.'

Dewey's ears ring with it – a ringing that almost deafens him to the whispery rush of Smith's soft voice. But the voice plunges on, ejecting a fusillade of sounds and images: Hickock hunting the discharged shell; hurrying, hurrying, and Kenyon's head in a circle of light, the murmur of muffled pleadings, then Hickock again scrambling after a used cartridge; Nancy's room, Nancy listening to boots on hardwood stairs, the creak of the steps as they climb towards her, Nancy's eyes, Nancy watching the flashlight's shine seek the target ('She said, "Oh, no! Oh, please. No! No! No! No! Don't! Oh, please don't! Please!" I gave the gun to Dick. I told him I'd done all I could do. He took aim, and she turned her face to the wall'); the dark hall, the assassins hastening towards the final door. Perhaps, having heard all she had, Bonnie welcomed their swift approach.

'That last shell was a bitch to locate. Dick wiggled under the bed to get it. Then we closed Mrs Clutter's door and went downstairs to the office. We waited there, like we had when we first came. Looked through the blinds to see if the hired man was poking around, or anybody else who might have heard the gunfire. But it was just the same – not a sound. Just the wind – and Dick panting like wolves were after him. Right there, in those few seconds before we ran out to the car and drove away, that's when I decided I'd better shoot Dick. He'd said over and over, he'd drummed it into me: *No witnesses.* And I thought, *He's* a witness. I don't know what stopped me. God knows I should've done it. Shot him dead. Got in the car and kept on going till I lost myself in Mexico.'

A hush. For ten miles and more, the three men ride without speaking.

Sorrow and profound fatigue are at the heart of Dewey's silence. It had been his ambition to learn 'exactly what happened in that house that night'. Twice now he'd been told, and the two versions were very much alike, the only serious discrepancy being that Hickock attributed all four deaths to Smith, while Smith contended that Hickock had killed the two women. But the confessions, though they answered questions of how and why, failed to satisfy his sense of meaningful design. The crime was a psychological accident, virtually an impersonal act; the victims might as well have been killed by lightning. Except for one thing: they had experienced prolonged terror, they had suffered. And Dewey could not forget their sufferings. Nonetheless, he found it possible to look at the man beside him without anger – with, rather, a measure of sympathy – for Perry Smith's life had been no bed of roses but pitiful, an ugly and lonely progress towards one mirage and then another. Dewey's sympathy, however, was not deep enough to accommodate either forgiveness or mercy. He hoped to see Perry and his partner hanged – hanged back to back.

Duntz asked Smith, 'Added up, how much money did you get from the Clutters?'

'Between forty and fifty dollars.'

Among Garden City's animals are two grey tomcats who are always together – thin, dirty strays with strange and clever habits. The chief ceremony of their day is performed at twilight. First they trot the length of Main Street, stopping to scrutinize the engine grilles of parked automobiles, particularly those stationed in front of the two hotels, the Windsor and Warren, for these cars, usually the property of travellers from afar, often yield what the bony, methodical creatures are hunting: slaughtered birds – crows, chickadees, and sparrows foolhardy enough to have flown into the path of oncoming motorists. Using their paws as though they are surgical instruments, the cats extract from the grilles every feathery particle. Having cruised Main Street, they invariably turn the corner at Main and Grant, then lope along towards Courthouse Square, another of their hunting grounds – and a highly promising one on the afternoon of Wednesday, 6 January, for the area swarmed with Finney County vehicles that had brought to town part of the crowd populating the square.

The crowd started forming at four o'clock, the hour that the county attorney had given as the probable arrival time of Hickock and Smith. Since the announcement of Hickock's confession on Sunday evening, newsmen of every style had assembled in Garden City: representatives of the major wire services, photographers, newsreel and television cameramen, reporters from Missouri, Nebraska, Oklahoma, Texas, and, of course, all the principal Kansas papers – twenty or twenty-five men altogether. Many of them had been waiting three days without much to do except interview the service-station attendant James Spor, who, after seeing published photographs of the accused killers, had identified them as customers to whom he'd sold three dollars and six cents' worth of gas the night of the Holcomb tragedy.

It was the return of Hickock and Smith that these professional spectators were on hand to record, and Captain Gerald Murray, of the Highway Patrol, had reserved for them ample space on the sidewalk fronting the courthouse steps – the steps the prisoners must mount on their way to the county jail, an institution that occupies the top floor of the four-storey limestone structure. One reporter, Richard Parr, of the Kansas City *Star*, had obtained a copy of

Monday's Las Vegas *Sun*. The paper's headline raised rounds of laughter: FEAR LYNCH MOB AWAITING RETURN OF KILLER SUSPECTS. Captain Murray remarked, 'Don't look much like a necktie party to me.'

Indeed, the congregation in the square might have been expecting a parade, or attending a political rally. High-school students, among them former classmates of Nancy and Kenyon Clutter, chanted cheerleader rhymes, bubbled bubble gum, gobbled hot dogs and soda pop. Mothers soothed wailing babies. Men strode about with young children perched on their shoulders. The Boy Scouts were present – an entire troop. And the middle-aged member-ship of a woman's bridge club arrived *en masse*. Mr J. P. (Jap) Adams, head of the local Veterans Commission office, appeared, attired in a tweed garment so oddly tailored that a friend yelled, 'Hey, Jap! What ya doin' wearin' ladies clothes?' – for Mr Adams, in his haste to reach the scene, had unwittingly donned his secretary's coat. A roving radio reporter interviewed sundry other townsfolk, asking them what, in their opinion, the proper retribution would be for 'the doers of such a dastardly deed', and while most of his subjects said gosh or gee whiz, one student replied, 'I think they ought to be locked in the same cell for the rest of their lives. Never allowed any visitors. Just sit there staring at each other till the day they die.' And a tough, strutty little man said, 'I believe in capital punishment. It's like the Bible says – an eye for an eye. And even so we're two pair short!'

As long as the sun lasted, the day had been dry and warm – October weather in January. But when the sun descended, when the shadows of the square's giant shade trees met and combined, the coldness as well as darkness numbed the crowd. Numbed and pruned it; by six o'clock, fewer than three hundred persons remained. Newsmen, cursing the undue delay, stamped their feet and slapped frozen ears with ungloved, freezing hands. Suddenly, a murmuring arose on the south side of the square. The cars were coming.

Although none of the journalists anticipated violence,

several had predicted shouted abuse. But when the crowd caught sight of the murderers, with their escort of blue-coated highway patrolmen, it fell silent, as though amazed to find them humanly shaped. The handcuffed men, white-faced and blinking blindly, glistened in the glare of flash-bulbs and floodlights. The cameraman, pursuing the prisoners and the police into the courthouse and up three flights of stairs, photographed the door of the county jail slamming shut.

No one lingered, neither the press corps nor any of the townspeople. Warm rooms and warm suppers beckoned them, and as they hurried away, leaving the cold square to the two grey cats, the miraculous autumn departed too; the year's first snow began to fall.

4

The Corner

INSTITUTIONAL dourness and cheerful domesticity coexist on the fourth floor of the Finney County Courthouse. The presence of the county jail supplies the first quality, while the so-called Sheriff's Residence, a pleasant apartment separated from the jail proper by steel doors and a short corridor, accounts for the second.

In January 1960, the Sheriff's Residence was not in fact occupied by the sheriff, Earl Robinson, but by the under-sheriff and his wife, Wendle and Josephine ('Josie') Meier. The Meiers, who had been married more than twenty years, were very much alike: tall people with weight and strength to spare, with wide hands, square and calm and kindly faces – the last being most true of Mrs Meier, a direct and practical woman who nevertheless seems illuminated by a mystical serenity. As the undersheriff's helpmate her hours are long; between five in the morning, when she begins the day by reading a chapter in the Bible, and 10 p.m. her bedtime, she cooks and sews for the prisoners, darns, does their laundry, takes splendid care of her hus-band, and looks after their five-room apartment, with its *gemütlich* mélange of plump hassocks and squashy chairs and cream-coloured lace window curtains. The Meiers have a daughter, an only child, who is married and lives in Kan-sas City, so the couple live alone – or, as Mrs Meier more correctly puts it: 'Alone except for whoever happens to be in the ladies' cell.'

The jail contains six cells; the sixth, the one reserved for female prisoners, is actually an isolated unit situated inside the Sheriff's Residence – indeed, it adjoins the Meiers' kitchen. 'But,' says Josie Meier, 'that don't worry me. I enjoy the company. Having somebody to talk to while I'm doing my kitchen work. Most of these women, you got to feel sorry for them. Just met up with Old Man Trouble is all. Course

Hickock and Smith was a different matter. Far as I know, Perry Smith was the first man ever stayed in the ladies' cell. The reason was, the sheriff wanted to keep him and Hickock separated from each other until after their trial. The afternoon they brought them in, I made six apple pies and baked some bread and all the while kept track of the goings-on down there on the Square. My kitchen window overlooks the Square; you couldn't want a better view. I'm no judge of crowds, but I'd guess there were several hundred people waiting to see the boys that killed the Clutter family. I never met any of the Clutters myself, but from everything I've ever heard about them they must have been very fine people. What happened to them is hard to forgive, and I know Wendle was worried how the crowd might act when they caught sight of Hickock and Smith. He was afraid somebody might try to get at them. So I kind of had my heart in my mouth when I saw the cars arrive, saw the reporters, all the newspaper fellows running and pushing; but by then it was dark, after six, and bitter cold – more than half the crowd had given up and gone home. The ones that stayed, they didn't say boo. Only stared.

'Later, when they brought the boys upstairs, the first one I saw was Hickock. He had on light summer pants and just an old cloth shirt. Surprised he didn't catch pneumonia, considering how cold it was. But he looked sick all right. White as a ghost. Well, it must be a terrible experience – to be stared at by a horde of strangers, to have to walk among them knowing who you are and what you did. Then they brought up Smith. I had some supper ready to serve them in their cells, hot soup and coffee and some sandwiches and pie. Ordinarily, we feed just twice a day. Breakfast at seven-thirty, and at four-thirty we serve the main meal. But I didn't want those fellows going to bed on an empty stomach; seemed to me they must be feeling bad enough without that. But when I took Smith his supper, carried it in on a tray, he said he wasn't hungry. He was looking out the window of the ladies' cell. Standing with his back to me. That window has the same view as my kitchen window: trees and the Square and the tops of houses. I told him,

"Just taste the soup, it's vegetable, and not out of a can. I made it myself. The pie, too." In about an hour I went back for the tray and he hadn't touched a crumb. He was still at the window. Like he hadn't moved. It was snowing, and I remember saying it was the first snow of the year, and how we'd had such a beautiful long autumn right till then. And now the snow had come. And then I asked him if he had any special dish he liked; if he did I'd try and fix it for him the next day. He turned round and looked at me. Suspicious, like I might be mocking him. Then he said something about a movie – he had such a quiet way of speaking, almost a whisper. Wanted to know if I had seen a movie. I forget the name, anyway I hadn't seen it: never have been much for picture shows. He said this show took place in Biblical times, and there was a scene where a man was flung off a balcony, thrown to a mob of men and women, who tore him to pieces. And he said that was what came to mind when he saw the crowd on the Square. The man being torn apart. And the idea that maybe that was what they might do to him. Said it scared him so bad his stomach still hurt. Which was why he couldn't eat. Course he was wrong, and I told him so – nobody was going to harm him, regardless of what he'd done; folks around here aren't like that.

'We talked some, he was very shy, but after a while he said, "One thing I really like is Spanish rice." So I promised to make him some, and he smiled kind of, and I decided – well, he wasn't the worst young man I ever saw. That night, after I'd gone to bed, I said as much to my husband. But Wendle snorted. Wendle was one of the first on the scene after the crime was discovered. He said he wished I'd been out at the Clutter place when they found the bodies. Then I could've judged for myself just how *gentle* Mr Smith was. Him and his friend Hickock. He said they'd cut out your heart and never bat an eye. There was no denying it – not with four people dead. And I lay awake wondering if either one was bothered by it – the thought of those four graves.'

A month passed, and another, and it snowed some part of

almost every day. Snow whitened the wheat-tawny countryside, heaped the streets of the town, hushed them.

The topmost branches of a snow-laden elm brushed against the window of the ladies' cell. Squirrels lived in the tree, and after weeks of tempting them with leftover breakfast scraps, Perry lured one off a branch on to the window sill and through the bars. It was a male squirrel with auburn fur. He named it Red, and Red soon settled down, apparently content to share his friend's captivity. Perry taught him several tricks: to play with a paper ball, to beg, to perch on Perry's shoulder. All this helped to pass time, but still there were many long hours the prisoner had to lose. He was not allowed to read newspapers, and he was bored by the magazines Mrs Meier lent him: old issues of *Good Housekeeping* and *McCall's*. But he found things to do: file his fingernails with an emery board, buff them to a silky pink sheen; comb and comb his lotion-soaked and scented hair; brush his teeth three and four times a day; shave and shower almost as often. And he kept the cell, which contained a toilet, a shower stall, a cot, a chair, a table, as neat as his person. He was proud of a compliment Mrs Meier had paid him. 'Look!' she had said, pointing at his bunk. 'Look at that blanket! You could bounce dimes.' But it was at the table that he spent most of his waking life; he ate his meals there, it was where he sat when he sketched portraits of Red, drew flowers, and the face of Jesus, and the faces and torsos of imaginary women; and it was where, on cheap sheets of ruled paper, he made diary-like notes of day-to-day occurrences.

Thursday 7 January. Dewey here. Brought carton cigarettes. Also typed copies of Statement for my signature. I declined.

The 'Statement', a seventy-eight-page document which he had dictated to the Finney County court stenographer, recounted admissions already made to Alvin Dewey and Clarence Duntz. Dewey, speaking of his encounter with Perry Smith on this particular day, remembered that he had been very surprised when Perry refused to sign the statement. 'It wasn't important: I could always testify in court as to the oral confession he'd made to Duntz and myself. And of course Hickock had given us a signed confession while we were still in Las Vegas – the one in which he accused Smith of having committed all four murders. But I was curious. I asked Perry why he'd changed his mind. And he said, "Everything in my statement is accurate except for two details. If you'll let me correct those items then I'll sign it." Well, I could guess the items he meant. Because the only serious difference between his story and Hickock's was that he denied having executed the Clutters singlehanded. Until now he'd sworn Hickock killed Nancy and her mother.

'And I was right! – that's just what he wanted to do: admit that Hickock had been telling the truth, and that it was he, Perry Smith, who had shot and killed the whole family. He said he'd lied about it because, in his words, "I wanted to fix Dick for being such a coward. Dropping his guts all over the goddam floor." And the reason he'd decided to set the record straight wasn't that he suddenly felt any kinder towards Hickock. According to him he was doing it out of consideration for Hickock's parents – said he was sorry for Dick's mother. Said, "She's a real sweet person. It might be some comfort to her to know Dick never pulled the trigger, none of it would have happened without him, in a way it was mostly his fault, but the fact remains I'm the one who killed them." But I wasn't certain I believed it. Not to the extent of letting him alter his statement. As I say, we weren't dependent on a formal confession from Smith to prove any part of our case. With or without it, we had enough to hang them ten times over.'

Among the elements contributing to Dewey's confidence was the recovery of the radio and pair of binoculars the murderers had stolen from the Clutter house and subsequently disposed of in Mexico City (where, having flown there for the purpose, K.B.I. Agent Harold Nye traced them to a pawnshop). Moreover, Smith, while dictating his statement, had revealed the whereabouts of other potent evidence. 'We hit the highway and drove east,' he'd said, in the process of describing what he and Hickock had done after fleeing the murder scene. 'Drove like hell, Dick driving. I think we both felt very high. I did. Very high, and very relieved at the same time. Couldn't stop laughing, neither one of us; suddenly it all seemed very funny – I don't know why, it just did. But the gun was dripping blood, and my clothes were stained; there was even blood in my hair. So we turned off on to a country road, and drove maybe eight miles till we were way out on the prairie. You could hear coyotes. We smoked a cigarette, and Dick went on making jokes about what had happened back there. I got out of the car, and siphoned some water out of the water tank and washed the blood off the gun barrel. Then I scraped a hole in the ground with Dick's hunting knife, the one I used on Mr Clutter, and buried in it the empty shells and all the leftover nylon cord and adhesive tape. After that we drove till we came to U.S. 83, and headed east towards Kansas City and Olathe. Around dawn Dick stopped at one of those picnic places: what they call rest areas – where they had open fireplaces. We built a fire and burned stuff. The gloves we'd worn, and my shirt. Dick said he wished we had an ox to roast; he said he'd never been so hungry. It was almost noon when we got to Olathe. Dick dropped me at my hotel, and went on home to have Sunday dinner with his family. Yes, he took the knife with him. The gun, too.'

K.B.I. agents, dispatched to Hickock's home, found the knife inside a fishing-tackle box and the shotgun still casually propped against a kitchen wall. (Hickock's father, who refused to believe his 'boy' could have taken part in such a 'horrible crime', insisted the gun hadn't been out of the house since the first week in November, and therefore could not be the death weapon.) As for the empty cartridge shells, the cord and tape, these were retrieved with the aid of Virgil Pietz, a county-highway employee, who, working with a road-grader in the area pinpointed by Perry Smith, shaved away the earth inch by inch until the buried articles were uncovered. Thus the last loose strings were tied; the K.B.I. had now assembled an unshakeable case, for tests established that the shells had been discharged by Hickock's shotgun, and the remnants of cord and tape were of a piece with the materials used to bind and silence the victims.

Monday 11 January. Have a lawyer. Mr Fleming. Old man with red tie.

Informed by the defendants that they were without funds to hire legal counsel, the court, in the person of Judge Roland H. Tate, appointed as their representatives two local lawyers, Mr Arthur Fleming and Mr Harrison Smith. Fleming, seventy-one, a former mayor of Garden City, a short man who enlivens an unsensational appearance with rather conspicuous neckwear, resisted the assignment. 'I do not desire to serve,' he told the judge. 'But if the court sees fit to appoint me, then of course I have no choice.' Hickock's attorney, Harrison Smith, forty-five, six feet tall, a golfer, an Elk of exalted degree, accepted the task with resigned grace: 'Someone has to do it. And I'll do my best. Though I doubt that'll make me too popular around here.'

Friday 15 January. Mrs Meier playing radio in her kitchen and I heard man say the county attorney will seek Death Penalty. 'The rich never hang. Only the poor and friendless.'

In making his announcement, the county attorney, Duane West, an ambitious, portly young man of twenty-eight who looks forty and sometimes fifty, told newsmen, 'If the case goes before a jury, I will request the jury, upon finding them guilty, to sentence them to the death penalty. If the defendants waive right to jury trial and enter a plea of guilty before the judge, I will request the judge to set the death penalty. This was a matter I knew I would be called upon to decide, and my decision has not been arrived at lightly. I feel that due to the violence of the crime and the apparent utter lack of mercy shown the victims, the only way the public can be absolutely protected is to have the death penalty set against these defendants. This is especially true since in Kansas there is no such thing as life imprisonment without possibility of parole. Persons sentenced to life imprisonment actually serve, on the average, less than fifteen years.'

Wednesday 20 January. Asked to take lie-detector in regards to this Walker deal.

A case like the Clutter case, crimes of that magnitude, arouse the interest of lawmen everywhere, particularly those investigators burdened with unsolved but similar crimes, for it is always possible that the solution to one mystery will solve another. Among the many officers intrigued by events in Garden City was the sheriff of Sarasota County, Florida, which includes Osprey, a fishing settlement not far from Tampa, and the scene, slightly more than a month after the Clutter tragedy, of the quadruple slaying on an isolated cattle ranch which Smith had read about in a Miami newspaper on Christmas Day. The victims were again four members of a family: a young couple, Mr and Mrs Clifford Walker, and their two children, a boy and a girl, all of whom had been shot in the head with a rifle. Since the Clutter murderers had spent the night of December 19, the date of the murders, in a Tallahassee hotel, Osprey's sheriff, who had no other leads whatever, was understandably anxious to have the two men questioned and a polygraph examination administered. Hickock consented to take the test and so did Smith, who told Kansas authorities, 'I remarked at the time, I said to Dick, I'll bet whoever did this must be somebody that read about what happened out here in Kansas. A nut.' The results of the test, to the dismay of Osprey's sheriff as well as Alvin Dewey, who does not believe in exceptional coincidences, were decisively negative. The murderer of the Walker family remains unknown.

Sunday 31 January. Dick's dad here to visit Dick. Said hello when I saw him go past [the cell door] *but he kept going. Could be he never heard me. Understand from Mrs M* [Meier] *that Mrs H* [Hickock] *didn't come because she felt too bad to. Snowing like a bitch. Dreamed last night I was up in Alaska with Dad – woke up in a puddle of cold urine! ! !*

Mr Hickock spent three hours with his son. Afterwards he walked through the snow to the Garden City depot, a work-worn old man, stooped and thinned-down by the cancer that would kill him a few months hence. At the station, while waiting for a homeward-bound train, he spoke to a reporter: 'I seen Dick, uh-huh. We had a long talk. And I can guarantee you it's not like people say. Or what's put in the papers. Those boys didn't go to that house planning to do violence. My boy didn't. He may have some bad sides, but he's nowhere near bad as that. Smitty's the one. Dick told me he didn't even know it when Smitty attacked the man [Mr Clutter], cut his throat. Dick wasn't even in the same room. He only run in when he heard them struggling. Dick was carrying his shotgun, and how he described it was: "Smitty took my shotgun and just blew that man's head off." And he says, "Dad, I ought to have grabbed back the gun and shot Smitty dead. Killed him 'fore he killed the rest of that family. If I'd done it I'd be better off than I am now." I guess he would, too. How it is, the way folks feel, he don't stand no chance. They'll hang them both. And,' he added, fatigue and defeat glazing his eyes, 'having your boy hang, knowing he will, nothing worse can happen to a man.'

Neither Perry Smith's father nor sister wrote him or came to see him. Tex John Smith was presumed to be prospecting for gold somewhere in Alaska – though lawmen, despite great effort, had been unable to locate him. The sister had told investigators that she was afraid of her brother, and requested that they please not let him know her present address. (When informed of this, Smith smiled slightly and said, 'I wish she'd been in that house that night. What a sweet scene!')

Except for the squirrel, except for the Meiers and an occasional consultation with his lawyer, Mr Fleming, Perry was very much alone. He missed Dick. *Many thoughts of Dick,* he wrote one day in his makeshift diary. Since their arrest they had not been allowed to communicate, and that, freedom apart, was what he most desired – to talk to Dick, be with him again. Dick was not the 'hardrock' he'd once thought him: 'pragmatic', 'virile', 'a real brass boy'; he'd proven himself to be 'pretty weak and shallow', 'a coward'. Still, of everyone in all the world, this was the person to whom he was closest at that moment, for they at least were of the same species, brothers in the breed of Cain; separated from him, Perry felt 'all by myself. Like somebody covered with sores. Somebody only a big nut would have anything to do with.'

But then one mid-February morning Perry received a letter. It was postmarked Reading, Mass., and it read:

Dear Perry, I was sorry to hear about the trouble you are in and I decided to write and let you know that I remember you and would like to help you in any way that I can. In case you don't remember my name, Don Cullivan, I've enclosed a picture taken at about the time we met. When I first read about you in the news recently I was startled and then I began to think back to those days when I knew you. While we were never close personal friends I can remember you a lot more clearly than most fellows I met in the Army. It must have been about the fall of 1951 when you were assigned to the 761st Engineer Light Equipment Company at Fort Lewis, Washington. You were short (I'm not much taller), solidly built, dark with a heavy shock of black hair and a grin on your face almost all the time. Since you had lived in Alaska quite a few of the fellows used to call you 'Eskimo'. One of my first recollections of you was at a Company inspection in which all the footlockers were open for inspection. As I recall it all the footlockers were in order, even yours, except that the inside cover of your footlocker was plastered with pictures of pin-up girls. The rest of us were sure you were in for trouble. But the inspecting officer took it in stride and when it was all over and he let it pass I think we all felt you were a nervy guy. I remember that you were a fairly good pool player and I can picture you quite clearly in the Company day room at the pool table. You were one of the best truck drivers in the outfit. Remember the Army field problems we went out on? On one trip that took place in the winter I remember that we each were assigned to a truck for the duration of the problem. In our outfit, Army trucks had no heaters and it used to get pretty cold in those cabs. I remember you cutting a hole in the floor-boards of your truck in order to let the heat from the engine come into the cab. The reason I remember this so well is the impression it made on me because 'mutilation' of Army property was a crime for which you could get severely punished. Of course I was pretty green in the Army and probably afraid to stretch the rules even a little bit, but I can remember you grinning about it (and keeping warm) while I worried about it (and froze). I recall that you bought a motorcycle, and vaguely remember you had some trouble with it – chased by the police? – crackup? Whatever it was, it was the first time I realized the wild streak in you. Some of my recollections may be wrong; this was over eight years ago and I only knew you for a period of about eight months. From what I remember, though, I got along with you very well and rather liked you. You always seemed cheerful and cocky, you were good at your Army work and I can't remember that you did much griping. Of course you were apparently quite wild but I never knew too much about that. But now you are in real trouble. I try to imagine what you are like now. What you think about. When first I read about you I was stunned. I really was. But then I put the paper down and turned to something else. But the thought of you returned. I wasn't satisfied just to forget. I am, or try to be, fairly religious [Catholic]. I wasn't always. I used to just drift along with little thought about the only important thing there is. I never considered death or the possibility of a life hereafter. I was too much alive: car, college, dating, etc. But my kid brother died of leukemia when he was just 17 years old. He knew he was dying and afterwards I used to wonder what he thought about. And now I think of you, and wonder what you think about. I didn't know what to say to my brother in the last weeks before he died. But I know what I'd say now. And this is why I am writing you: because God made you as well as me and He loves you just as He loves me, and for the little we know of God's will what has happened to you could have happened to me. Your friend, Don Cullivan.

The name meant nothing, but Perry at once recognized the face in the photograph of a young soldier with crew-cut hair and round, very earnest eyes. He read the letter many times; though he found the religious allusions unpersuasive ('I've tried to believe, but I don't, I can't, and there's no use pretending'), he was thrilled by it. Here was someone offering help, a sane and respectable man who had once known and liked him, a man who signed himself *friend*. Gratefully, in great haste, he started a reply: 'Dear Don, Hell yes I remember Don Cullivan . . .'

Hickock's cell had no window; he faced a wide corridor and the façades of other cells. But he was not isolated, there were people to talk to, a plentiful turnover of drunkards, forgers, wife-beaters and Mexican vagrants; and Dick, with his light-hearted 'con-man' patter, his sex anecdotes and gamy jokes, was popular with the inmates (though there was one who had no use for him whatever – an old man who hissed at him: 'Killer! Killer!' and who once drenched him with a bucketful of dirty scrubwater).

Outwardly, Hickock seemed to one and all an unusually untroubled young man. When he was not socializing or sleeping, he lay on his cot smoking or chewing gum and reading sports magazines or paperback thrillers. Often he simply lay there whistling old favourites ('You Must Have Been a Beautiful Baby', 'Shuffle Off to Buffalo'), and staring at an unshaded light bulb that burned day and night in the ceiling of the cell. He hated the light bulb's monotonous surveillance; it disturbed his sleep and, more explicitly, endangered the success of a private project – escape. For the prisoner was not as unconcerned as he appeared to be, or as resigned; he intended taking every step possible to avoid 'a ride on the Big Swing'. Convinced that such a ceremony would be the outcome of any trial – certainly any trial held in the State of Kansas – he had decided to 'bust jail. Grab a car and raise dust'. But first he must have a weapon; and over a period of weeks he'd been making one: a 'shiv', an instrument very like an icepick – something that would fit with lethal niceness between the shoulder-blades of Undersheriff Meier. The weapon's components, a piece of wood and a length of hard wire, were originally part of a toilet brush he'd confiscated, dismantled and hidden under his mattress. Late at night, when the only noises were snores and coughs and the mournful whistle-wailings of Santa Fe trains rumbling through the darkened town, he honed the wire against the cell's concrete floor. And while he worked he schemed.

Once, the first winter after he had finished high school, Hickock had hitchhiked across Kansas and Colorado: 'This was when I was looking for a job. Well, I was riding in a truck, and the driver, me and him got into a little argument, no reason exactly, but he beat up on me. Shoved me out. Just left me there. High the hell up in the Rockies. It was sleeting like, and I walked miles, my nose bleeding like fifteen pigs. Then I come to a bunch of cabins on a wooded slope. Summer cabins, all locked up and empty that time of year. And I broke into one of them. There was firewood and canned goods, even some whisky. I laid up there over a week, and it was one of the best times I ever knew. Despite the fact my nose hurt so and my eyes were green and yellow. And when the snow stopped the sun came out. You never saw such skies. Like Mexico. If Mexico was in a cold climate. I hunted through the other cabins and found some smoked hams and a radio and a rifle. It was great. Out all day with a gun. With the sun in my face. Boy, I felt good. I felt like Tarzan. And every night I ate beans and fried ham and rolled up in a blanket by the fire and fell asleep listening to music on the radio. Nobody came near the place. I bet I could've stayed till spring.' If the escape succeeded, that was the course Dick had determined upon – to head for the Colorado mountains, and find there a cabin where he could hide until spring (alone, of course; Perry's future did not concern him). The prospect of so idyllic an interim added to the inspired stealth with which he whetted his wire, filed it to a limber stiletto fineness.

Thursday 10 March. Sheriff had a shake-out. Searched through all the cells and found a shiv tucked under D's mattress. Wonder what he had in mind (smile).

Not that Perry really considered it a smiling matter, for Dick, flourishing a dangerous weapon, could have played a decisive role in plans he himself was forming. As the weeks went by he had become familiar with life on Courthouse Square, its habitués and their habits. The cats, for example: the two thin grey toms who appeared with every twilight and prowled the Square, stopping to examine the cars parked around its periphery – behaviour puzzling to him until Mrs Meier explained that the cats were hunting for dead birds caught in the vehicles' engine grilles. Thereafter it pained him to watch their manoeuvres: 'Because most of my life I've done what they're doing. The equivalent.'

And there was one man of whom Perry had grown especially aware, a robust, upright gentleman with hair like a grey-and-silver skullcap; his face, filled out, firm-jawed, was somewhat cantankerous in repose, the mouth down-curved, the eyes downcast as though in mirthless reverie – a picture of unsparing sternness. And yet this was at least a partially inaccurate impression, for now and again the prisoner glimpsed him as he paused to talk to other men, joke with them and laugh, and then he seemed carefree, jovial, generous: 'The kind of person who might see the human side' – an important attribute, for the man was Roland H. Tate, Judge of the 32nd Judicial District, the jurist who would preside at the trial of the State of Kansas versus Smith and Hickock. Tate, as Perry soon learned, was an old and awesome name in western Kansas. The judge was rich, he raised horses, he owned much land, and his wife was said to be very beautiful. He was the father of two sons, but the younger had died, a tragedy that greatly affected the parents and led them to adopt a small boy who had appeared in court as an abandoned, homeless child. 'He sounds softhearted to me,' Perry once said to Mrs Meier. 'Maybe he'll give us a break.'

But that was not what Perry really believed; he believed what he'd written Don Cullivan, with whom he now corresponded regularly: his crime was 'unforgivable', and he fully expected to 'climb those thirteen steps'. However, he was not altogether without hope, for he too had plotted an escape. It depended upon a pair of young men that he had often observed observing him. One was red-haired, the other dark. Sometimes, standing in the Square under the tree that touched the cell window, they smiled and signalled to him – or so he imagined. Nothing was ever said, and always, after perhaps a minute, they drifted away. But the prisoner had convinced himself that the young men, possibly motivated by a desire for adventure, meant to help him escape. Accordingly he drew a map of the Square, indicating the points at which a 'getaway car' could most advantageously be stationed. Beneath the map he wrote: *I need a Hacksaw Blade 5 inch. Nothing else. But do you realize the consequences if you get caught (nod your head if you do)? It could mean a long stretch in prison. Or you might get killed. All for someone you don't know. YOU BETTER THINK IT OVER! Seriously! Besides, how do I know I can trust you? How do I know it isn't a trick to get me out there and gun me down? What about Hickock? All preparations must include him.*

Perry kept this document on his desk, wadded and ready to drop out the window the next time the young men appeared. But they never did; he never saw them again. Eventually, he wondered if perhaps he had invented them (a notion that he 'might not be normal, maybe insane' had troubled him 'even when I was little, and my sisters laughed because I liked moonlight. To hide in the shadows and watch the moon'). Phantoms or not, he ceased to think of the young men. Another method of escape, suicide, replaced them in his musings; and despite the jailer's precautions (no mirror, no belt or tie or shoelaces), he had devised a way to do it. For he also was furnished with a ceiling bulb that burned eternally, but, unlike Hickock, he had in his cell a broom, and by pressing the broombrush against the bulb he could unscrew it. One night he dreamed that he'd unscrewed the bulb, broken it, and with the broken glass cut his wrists and ankles. 'I felt all breath and light leaving me,' he said, in a subsequent description of his sensations. 'The walls of the cell fell away, the sky came down, I saw the big yellow bird.'

Throughout his life – as a child, poor and meanly treated, as a foot-loose youth, as an imprisoned man – the yellow bird, huge and parrot-faced, had soared across Perry's dreams, an avenging angel who savaged his enemies or, as now, rescued him in moments of mortal danger:

'She lifted me, I could have been light as a mouse, we went up, up, I could see the Square below, men running, yelling, the sheriff shooting at us, everybody sore as hell because I was free, I was flying, I was better than any of *them*.'

The trial was scheduled to start on 22 March, 1960. In the weeks preceding that date the defence attorneys frequently consulted the defendants. The advisability of requesting a change of venue was discussed, but as the elderly Mr Fleming warned his client, 'It wouldn't matter where in Kansas the trial was held. Sentiment's the same all over the state. We're probably better off in Garden City. This is a religious community. Eleven thousand population and twenty-two churches. And most of the ministers are opposed to capital punishment, say it's immoral, unchristian; even the Reverend Cowan, the Clutters' own minister and a close friend of the family, he's been preaching against the death penalty in this very case. Remember, all we can hope is to save your lives. I think we stand as good a chance here as anywhere.'

Soon after the original arraignment of Smith and Hickock, their advocates appeared before Judge Tate to argue a motion urging comprehensive psychiatric examinations for the accused. Specifically, the court was asked to permit the state hospital in Larned, Kansas, a mental institution with maximum-security facilities, to take custody of the prisoners for the purpose of ascertaining whether either or both were 'insane, imbeciles or idiots, unable to comprehend their position and aid in their defence'.

Larned is a hundred miles east of Garden City; Hickock's attorney, Harrison Smith, informed the court that he had driven there the previous day and conferred with several of the hospital's staff: 'We have no qualified psychiatrists in our own community. In fact, Larned is the only place within a radius of two hundred and twenty-five miles where you'll find such men – doctors trained to make serious psychiatric evaluations. That takes time. Four to eight weeks. But the personnel with whom I discussed the matter said they were willing to start work at once; and, of course, being a state institution it won't cost the county a nickel.'

This plan was opposed by the special assistant prosecut-
ing attorney, Logan Green, who, certain that 'temporary
insanity' was the defence his antagonists would attempt to
sustain in the forthcoming trial, feared that the ultimate
outcome of the proposal would be, as he predicted in private conversation, the appearance on the witness stand of
a 'pack of head-healers' sympathetic to the defendants
('Those fellows, they're always crying over the killers. Never
a thought for the victims'). Short, pugnacious, a Kentuck-
ian by birth, Green began by pointing out to the court that
Kansas law, in regard to sanity, adheres to the M'Naughten
Rule, the ancient British importation which contends that
if the accused knew the nature of his act, and knew it was
wrong, then he is mentally competent and responsible for
his actions. Furthermore, said Green, there was nothing in
the Kansas statutes indicating that the physicians chosen
to determine a defendant's mental condition must be of any
particular qualification: 'Just plain doctors. Medical doctors in general practice. That's all the law requires. We
have sanity hearings in this county every year for the purpose of committing people to the institution. We never call
anybody in from Larned or psychiatric institutions of any
kind. Our own local physicians attend to the matter. It's no
great job to find whether a man is insane or an idiot or an
imbecile ... It is entirely unnecessary, a waste of time to
send the defendants to Larned.'

In rebuttal, Counsel Smith suggested that the present
situation was 'far graver than a simple sanity hearing in
probate court. Two lives are at stake. Whatever their crime,
these men are entitled to examination by persons of train-
ing and experience. Psychiatry,' he added, pleading with
the judge quite directly, 'has matured rapidly in the past
twenty years. The Federal courts are beginning to keep in
tune with this science as related to people charged with
criminal offences. It just seems to me we have a golden opportunity to face up to the new concepts in this field.'

It was an opportunity the judge preferred to reject, for as
a fellow jurist once remarked, 'Tate is what you might

call a lawbook lawyer, he never experiments, he goes
strictly by the text'; but the same critic also said of him, 'If
I were innocent, he's the first man I'd want on the bench;
if I was guilty, the last.' Judge Tate did not entirely deny
the motion; rather, he did exactly all the law demanded
by appointing a commission of three Garden City doctors
and directing them to pronounce a verdict upon the mental capacities of the prisoners. (In due course the medical
trio met the accused and, after an hour or so of conversa-
tional prying, announced that neither man suffered from
any mental disorder. When told of their diagnosis, Perry
Smith said, 'How would they know? They just wanted to
be entertained. Hear all the morbid details from the killer's
own terrible lips. Oh, their eyes were shining.' Hickock's
attorney was also angry; once more he travelled to Larned
State Hospital, where he appealed for the unpaid services
of a psychiatrist willing to go to Garden City and interview
the defendants. The one man who volunteered, Dr W.
Mitchell Jones, was exceptionally competent; not yet thirty,
a sophisticated specialist in criminal psychology and the
criminally insane who had worked and studied in Europe
and the United States, he agreed to examine Smith and
Hickock, and, should his findings warrant it, testify in
their behalf.)

On the morning of March 14 counsels for the defence
again stood before Judge Tate, there on this occasion to
plead for a postponement of the trial, which was then eight
days distant. Two reasons were given, the first was that a
'most material witness', Hickock's father, was at present too
ill to testify. The second was a subtler matter. During the
past week a boldly lettered notice had begun to appear in
the town's shop windows, and in banks, restaurants, and
at the railroad station; and it read: H. W. CLUTTER ESTATE
AUCTION SALE* 21 MARCH 1960*. AT THE CLUTTER
HOMESTEAD. 'Now,' said Harrison Smith, addressing the
bench, 'I realize it is almost impossible to prove prejudice.
But this sale, an auction of the victim's estate, occurs one
week from today – in other words, the very day before the
trial begins. Whether that's prejudical to the defendants I'm

not able to state. But these signs, coupled with newspaper advertisements, and advertisements on the radio, will be a
constant reminder to every citizen in the community,
among whom one hundred and fifty have been called as
prospective jurors.'

Judge Tate was not impressed. He denied the motion
without comment.

Earlier in the year Mr Clutter's Japanese neighbour,
Hideo Ashida, had auctioned his farming equipment and
moved to Nebraska. The Ashida sale, which was considered a success, attracted not quite a hundred customers.
Slightly more than five thousand people attended the Clutter auction. Holcomb's citizenry expected an unusual turn-
out – the Ladies' Circle of the Holcomb Community Church
had converted one of the Clutter barns into a cafeteria
stocked with two hundred homemade pies, two hundred
and fifty pounds of hamburger meat, and sixty pounds of
sliced ham – but no one was prepared for the largest auction crowd in the history of western Kansas. Cars con-
verged on Holcomb from half the counties in the state, and
from Oklahoma, Colorado, Texas, Nebraska. They came
bumper to bumper down the lane leading to River Valley
Farm.

It was the first time the public had been permitted to
visit the Clutter place since the discovery of the murders,
a circumstance which explained the presence of perhaps a
third of the immense congregation – those who had come
out of curiosity. And of course the weather was an aid to
attendance, for by mid-March winter's high snows have
dissolved, and the earth beneath, thoroughly thawed, has
emerged as acre upon acre of ankle-deep mud; there is not
much a farmer can do until the ground hardens. 'Land's so
wet and nasty,' said Mrs Bill Ramsey, the wife of a farmer.
'Can't work nohow. We figured we might as well drive on
out to the sale.' Actually, it was a beautiful day. Spring.
Though mud abounded underfoot, the sun, so long
shrouded by snow and cloud, seemed an object freshly
made, and the trees – Mr Clutter's orchard of pear and

apple trees, the elms shading the lane – were lightly veiled in a haze of virginal green. The fine lawn surrounding the Clutter house was also newly green, and trespassers upon it, women anxious to have a closer look at the uninhabited home, crept across the grass and peered through the windows as though hopeful but fearful of discerning, in the gloom beyond the pleasant flower-print curtains, grim apparitions.

Shouting, the auctioneer praised his wares – tractors, trucks, wheelbarrows, nail kegs and sledgehammers and unused lumber, milk buckets, branding irons, horses, horseshoes, everything needed to run a ranch from rope and harness to sheep dip and tin washtubs – it was the prospect of buying this merchandise at bargain prices that had lured most of the crowd. But the hands of bidders flickered shyly – work-roughened hands timid of parting with hardearned cash; yet nothing went unsold, there was even someone keen to acquire a bunch of rusty keys, and a youthful cowboy sporting pale-yellow boots bought Kenyon Clutter's 'Coyote wagon', the dilapidated vehicle the dead boy had used to harass coyotes, chase them on moonlit nights.

The stagehands, the men who hauled the smaller items on and off the auctioneer's podium, were Paul Helm, Vic Irsik, and Alfred Stoecklein, each of them an old, stillfaithful employee of the late Herbert W. Clutter. Assisting at the disposal of his possessions was their final service, for today was their last day at River Valley Farm; the property had been leased to an Oklahoma rancher, and henceforward strangers would live and work there. As the auction progressed, and Mr Clutter's worldly domain dwindled, gradually vanished, Paul Helm, remembering the burial of the murdered family, said, 'It's like a second funeral.'

The last thing to go was the contents of the livestock corral, mostly horses, including Nancy's horse, big, fat Babe, who was much beyond her prime. It was late afternoon, school was out, and several schoolmates of Nancy's were among the spectators when bidding on the horse began; Susan Kidwell was there. Sue, who had adopted another of Nancy's orphaned pets, a cat, wished she could give Babe a home, for she loved the old horse and knew how much Nancy had loved her. The two girls had often gone riding together aboard Babe's wide back, jogged through the wheat fields on hot summer evenings down to the river and into the water, the mare wading against the current until, as Sue once described it, 'the three of us were cool as fish'. But Sue had no place to keep a horse.

'I hear fifty ... sixty-five ... seventy ...': the bidding was laggardly, nobody seemed really to want Babe, and the man who got her, a Mennonite farmer who said he might use her for ploughing, paid seventy-five dollars. As he led her out of the corral, Sue Kidwell ran forward, she raised her hand as though to wave good-bye, but instead clasped it over her mouth.

The Garden City *Telegram*, on the eve of the trial's start, printed the following editorial: 'Some may think the eyes of the entire nation are on Garden City during this sensational murder trial. But they are not. Even a hundred miles west of here in Colorado few persons are even acquainted with the case – other than just remembering some members of a prominent family were slain. This is a sad commentary on the state of crime in our nation. Since the four members of the Clutter family were killed last fall, several other such multiple murders have occurred in various parts of the country. Just during the few days leading up to this trial at least three mass murder cases broke into the headlines. As a result, this crime and trial are just one of many such cases people have read about and forgotten. . . .'

Although the eyes of the nation were not upon them, the demeanour of the event's main participants from the court recorder to the judge himself, was markedly self-aware on the morning of the court's first convening. All four of the lawyers sported new suits; the new shoes of the big-footed county attorney creaked and squealed with every step. Hickocks, too, was sharply dressed in clothes provided by his parents: trim blue-serge trousers, a white shirt, a narrow dark-blue tie. Only Perry Smith, who owned neither jacket nor tie, seemed sartorially misplaced.

Wearing an open-necked shirt (borrowed from Mr Meier) and blue jeans rolled up at the cuffs, he looked as lonely and inappropriate as a seagull in a wheat field.

The courtroom, an unpretentious chamber situated on the third floor of the Finney County Courthouse, has dull white walls and furnishings of darkly varnished wood. The spectators benches can seat perhaps one hundred and sixty persons. On Tuesday morning, 22 March, the benches were occupied exclusively by the all-male venire of Finney County residents from which a jury was to be selected. Not many of the summoned citizenry seemed anxious to serve (one potential juror, in conversation with another, said, 'They can't use me. I can't hear well enough.' To which his friend, after a bit of sly reflection, replied, 'Come to think of it, my hearing's not too good either'), and it was generally thought that the choosing of the jury would take several days. As it turned out, the process was completed within four hours; moreover, the jury, including two alternative members, was extracted from the first forty-four candidates. Seven were rejected on pre-emptory challenge by the defence, and three were excused at the request of the prosecution; another twenty won dismissal either because they opposed capital punishment or because they admitted to having already formed a firm opinion regarding the guilt of the defendants.

The fourteen men ultimately elected consisted of half a dozen farmers, a pharmacist, a nursery manager, an airport employee, a well driller, two salesmen, a machinist, and the manager of Ray's Bowling Alley. They were all family men (several had five children or more), and were seriously affiliated with one or another of the local churches. During the *voir dire* examination, four of them told the court that they had been personally, though not intimately, acquainted with Mr Clutter; but upon further questioning, each said he did not feel this circumstance would hinder his ability to reach an impartial verdict. The airport employee, a middle-aged man named N. L. Dunnan, said, when asked his opinion of capital punishment, 'Ordinarily I'm against it. But in this case, no' – a declaration which, to some who heard it, seemed clearly indicative of prejudice. Dunnan was nevertheless accepted as a juror.

The defendants were inattentive observers of the *voir dire* proceedings. The previous day, Dr Jones, the psychiatrist who had volunteered to examine them, had interviewed them separately for approximately two hours: at the end of the interviews, he had suggested that they each write for him an autobiographical statement, and it was the act of composing these statements that occupied the accused throughout the hours spent assembling a jury. Seated at opposite ends of their counsel's table, Hickock worked with a pen and Smith with a pencil.

Smith wrote:

I was born Perry Edward Smith 27 Oct. 1928 in Huntington, Elko County, Nevada, which is situated way out in the boon docks, so to speak. I recall that in 1929 our family had ventured to Juneau, Alaska. In my family were my brother Tex Jr. (he later changed his name to James because of the ridicule of the name 'Tex' & also I believe he hated my father in his early years – my mother's doing). My sister Fern (She also changed her name – to Joy). My sister Barbaara. And myself. . . . In Juneau, my father was making bootleg hooch. I believe it was during this period my mother became acquainted with alcohol. Mom & Dad began having quarrels. I remember my mother was 'entertaining' some sailors while my father was away. When he came home a fight ensued, and my father, after a violent struggle, threw the sailors out & proceeded to beat my mother. I was frightfully scared, in fact all us children were terrified. Crying. I was scared because I thought my father was going to hurt me, also because he was beating my mother. I really didn't understand why he was beating her but I felt she must have done something dreadfully wrong. . . . The next thing I can vaguely recall is living in Fort Bragg, Calif. My brother had been presented a B.B. gun. He had shot a hummingbird, and after he had shot it he was sorry. I asked him to let me shoot the B.B. gun. He pushed me away, telling me I was too small. It made me so mad I started to cry. After I finished crying, my anger mounted again, and during the evening when I grabbed it & held it to my brother's ear & hollered B A N G ! My father (or mother) beat me and made me apologize. My brother used to shoot at a big white horse ridden by a neighbour who went by our place on his way to town. The neighbour caught my brother and I hiding in the bushes and took us to Dad & we got a beating & brother had his B.B. gun taken away & I was *glad* he had his gun taken away! ... This is about all I remember when we lived in Fort Bragg (Oh! We kids used to jump from a hay-loft, holding an umbrella, on to a pile of hay on the ground). ... My next recollection is several years later when we were living in Calif.? Nevada? I recall a very odious episode between my mother and a Negro. We children slept on a porch in the summertime. One of our beds was directly under my mother and father's room. Everyone of us kids had taken a good look through the partly open curtain and seen what was going on. Dad had hired a Negro (Sam) to do odd jobs around the farm, or ranch, while he was working somewhere down the road. He used to come home late in the evening in his Model A truck. I do not recall the chain of events but assumed Dad had known or suspected what was happening. It ended in a seperation between Mom & Dad & Mom took us kids to San Francisco. She run off with Dad's truck & all of the many souvenirs he brought from Alaska. I believe this was in 1935 (?). ... In Frisco I was continuously in trouble. I had started to run around with a gang, all of which were older than myself. My mother was always drunk, never in a fit condition to properly provide and care for us. I run as free & wild as a coyote. There was no rule or discipline, or anyone to show me right from wrong. I came & went as I pleased – until my first encounter with Trouble. I was in & out of Detention Homes many many times for running away from home & stealing. I remember one place I was sent to. I had weak kidneys & wet the bed every night. This was very humiliating to me, but I couldn't control myself. I was very severly beaten by the cottage mistress, who had called me names and made fun of me in front of all the boys. She used to come around at all hours of the night to see if I wet the bed. She would throw back the covers & and furiously beat me with a large black leather belt – pull me out of bed by my hair & drag me to the bathroom & throw me in the tub & turn the cold water on & tell me to wash myself and the sheets. Every night was a nightmare. Later on she thought it was very funny to put some kind of ointment on my penis. This was almost unbearable. It burned something terrible. She was later discharged from her job. But this never changed my mind about her & what I wished I could have done to her & all the people who made fun of me.'

Then, because Dr Jones had told him he must have the statement that very afternoon, Smith skipped forward to early adolescence and the years he and his father had lived together, the two of them wandering all over the West and Far West, prospecting, trapping, doing odd jobs:

I loved my father but there were times when this love and affection I had for him drained from my heart like wasted water. Whenever he would not try to understand my problems. Give me a little consideration & voice & responsibility. I had to get away from him. When I was sixteen I joined the Merchant Marine. In 1948 I joined the army – the recruiting officer gave me a break and upped my test. From this time on I started to realize the importance of an education. This only added to the hatred and bitterness I held for others. I began to get into fights. I threw a Japanese policeman off a bridge into the water. I was court-martialed for demolishing a Japanese cafe. I was court-martialed again in Kyoto, Japan, for stealing a Japanese taxicab. I was in the army almost four years. I had many violent outbursts of anger while I served time in Japan & Korea. I was in Korea 15 months, was rotated and sent back to the states – and was given special recognition as being the first Korean Vet to come back to the territory of Alaska. Big write up, picture in paper, paid trip to Alaska by air, all the trimmings. ... I finished my army service in Ft. Lewis, Washington.

Smith's pencil sped almost indecipherably as he hurried towards more recent history: the motorcycle accident that had crippled him, the burglary in Phillipsburg, Kansas, that had led to his first prison sentence:

... I was sentenced to 5 to 10 years for grand larceny, burglary and jailbreak. I felt I was very unjustly dealt with. I became very bitter while I was in prison. Upon my release I was supposed to go to Alaska with my father – I didn't go – I worked for a while in Nevada and Idaho – went to Las Vegas and continued to Kansas where got into the situation I'm in now. No time for more.

He signed his name, and added a postscript:

Would like to speak to you again. There's much I haven't said that may interest you. I have always felt a remarkable exhiliration being among people with a purpose and sense of dedication to carry out that purpose. I felt this about you in your presence.

Hickock did not write with his companion's intensity. He often stopped to listen to the questioning of a prospective juror, or to stare at the faces around him – particularly, and with plain displeasure, the muscular face of the county attorney, Duane West, who was his own age, twenty-eight. But his statement, written in a stylized script that looked like slanting rain, was finished before the court adjourned for the day:

I will try to tell you all I can about myself, though most of my early life is vague to me – up until about my tenth birthday. My school years went quite the same as most other boys my own age. I had my share of fights, girls, and other things that go with a growing boy. My home life was also normal, but as I told you before, I was hardly ever allowed to leave my yard and visit with playmates. My father was always strict about us boys [his brother and him] in that line. Also I had to help my dad quite a lot around the house. ... I can only remember my mother and dad having one argument that amounted to anything. What it was about, I don't know. ... My dad bought me a bicycle once, and I believe that I was the proudest boy in town. It was a girl's bike and he changed it over to a boy's. He painted it all up and it looked like new. But I had a lot of toys when I was little, a lot for the financial condition that my folks were in. We were always what you would call semi-poor. Never down and out, but several times on the verge of it. My dad was a hard worker and did his best to provide for us. My mother also was always a hard worker. Her house was always neat, and we had clean clothes aplenty. I remember my dad used to wear those old fashioned flat crown caps, and he would make me wear them too, and I didn't like them. ... In high-school I did real well, made above average grades the first year or two. But then started falling off a little. I had a girl friend. She was a nice girl, and I never once tried to touch her anyway but just kissing. It was a real clean courtship. ... While in school I participated in all the sports, and received 9 letters in all. Basketball, football, track and baseball. My senior year was best. I never had any steady girl, just played the field. That was when I had my first relationship with a girl. Of course I told the boys that I'd had a lot of girls. ... I got offers from two colleges to play ball, but never attended any of them. After I graduated from school I went to work for the Santa Fe railroad, and stayed until the following winter when I got laid off. The following spring I got a job with the Roark Motor Company. I had been working there about four months when I had an automobile wreck with a company car. I was in the hospital several days with extensive head injuries. While I was in the condition I was in I couldn't find another job, so I was unemployed most of the winter. Meantime, I had met a girl and fallen in love. Her dad was a Baptist preacher and resented me going with her. In July we were married. All hell broke loose from her dad until he learned she was pregnant. But still he never wished me good luck and that has always gone against the grain. After we were married, I worked at a service-station near Kansas·City. I worked from 8 at night till 8 in the morning. Sometimes my wife stayed with me all night – she was afraid I couldn't keep awake, so she came to help me. Then I got an offer to work at Perry Pontiac, which I gladly accepted. It was very satisfactory, though I didn't make a lot of money – $75 a week. I got along good with the other men, and was well liked by my boss. I worked there five years. . . . During my employment there was the beginning of some of the lowest things I have ever done.

Here Hickock revealed his pedophiliac tendencies, and after describing several sample experiences, wrote:

I know it is wrong. But at the time I never give any thought to whether it is right or wrong. The same with stealing. It seems to be an impulse. One thing I never told you about the Clutter deal is this. Before I ever went to their house I knew there would be a girl there. I think the main reason I went there was not to rob them but to rape the girl. Because I thought a lot about it. That is one reason why I never wanted to turn back when we started to. Even when I saw there was no safe. I did make some advances towards the Clutter girl when I was there. But Perry never gave me a chance. I hope no one finds this out but you, as I haven't even told my lawyer. There were other things I should have told you, but I'm afraid of my people finding them out. Because I am more ashamed of them (these things I did) than hanging. . . . I have had sickness. I think caused from the car wreck I had. Spells of passing out, and sometimes I would hemhorrage at the nose and left ear. I had one at some people's house by the name of Crist – they live south of my parents. Not long ago I had a piece of glass work out of my head. It came out the corner of my eye. My dad helped me to get it out. .... I figure I should tell you the things that led to my divorce, and things that caused me to go to prison. It started the early part of 1957. My wife and I were living in an apartment in Kansas City. I had quit my job at the automobile company, and went into the garage business for myself. I was renting the garage from a woman who had a daughter-in-law named Margaret. I met this girl one day while I was at work, and we went to have a cup of coffee. Her husband was away in the Marine Corps. To make a long story short, I started going out with her. My wife sued for divorce. I began thinking I never really loved my wife. Because if I had, I wouldn't have done all the things I'd done. So I never fought the divorce. I started drinking, and was drunk for almost a month. I neglected my business, spent more money than I earned, wrote bad cheques, and in the end became a thief. For this last I was sent to the penitentiary. .... My lawyer said I should be truthful with you as you can help me. And I need help, as you know.

The next day, Wednesday, was the proper start of the trial; it was also the first time ordinary spectators were admitted into the courtroom, an area too small to accommodate more than a modest percentage of those who applied at the door. The best seats had been reserved for twenty members of the press, and for such special personages as Hickock's parents and Donald Cullivan (who, at the request of Perry Smith's lawyer, had travelled from Massachusetts to appear as a character witness in behalf of his former Army friend). It had been rumoured that the two surviving Clutter daughters would be present; they were not, nor did they attend any subsequent session. The family was represented by Mr Clutter's younger brother, Arthur, who had driven a hundred miles to be there. He told newsmen: 'I just want to get a good look at them [Smith and Hickock]. I just want to see what kind of animals they are. The way I feel, I could tear them apart.' He took a seat directly behind the defendants, and fixed them with a gaze of unique persistence, as though he planned to paint their portraits from memory. Presently, and it was as if Arthur Clutter had willed him to do it, Perry Smith turned and looked at him – and recognized a face very like the face of the man he had killed: the same mild eyes, narrow lips, firm chin. Perry, who was chewing gum, stopped chewing; he lowered his eyes, a minute elapsed, then slowly his jaws began to move again. Except for this moment, Smith, and Hickock too, affected a courtroom attitude that was simultaneously uninterested and disinterested; they chewed gum and tapped their feet with languid impatience as the state summoned its first witness.

Nancy Ewalt. And after Nancy, Susan Kidwell. The young girls described what they saw upon entering the Clutter house on Sunday, November 15: the quiet rooms, an empty purse on a kitchen floor, sunshine in a bedroom, and their schoolmate, Nancy Clutter, surrounded by her own blood. The defence waived cross-examination, a policy they pursued with the next three witnesses (Nancy Ewalt's father, Clarence, and Sheriff Earl Robinson, and the county coroner, Dr Robert Fenton), each of whom added to the narrative of events that sunny November morning: the discovery, finally, of all four victims, and accounts of how they looked, and, from Dr Fenton, a clinical diagnosis of why – 'Severe traumas to brain and vital cranial structures inflicted by a shotgun.'

Then Richard G. Rohleder took the stand.

Rohleder is Chief Investigator of the Garden City Police Department. His hobby is photography, and he is good at it. It was Rohleder who took the pictures that, when developed, revealed Hickock's dusty footprints in the Clutter cellar, prints the camera could discern, though not the human eye. And it was he who had photographed the corpses, those death-scene images Alvin Dewey had continuously pondered while the murders were still unsolved. The point of Rohleder's testimony was to establish the fact of his having made these pictures, which the prosecution proposed to put into evidence. But Hickock's attorney objected: 'The sole reason the pictures are being introduced is to prejudice and inflame the minds of the jurors.' Judge Tate overruled the objection and allowed the photographs into evidence, which meant they must be shown to the jury.

While this was being done, Hickock's father, addressing

a journalist seated near him, said, 'The judge up there! I never seen a man so prejudiced. Just no sense having a trial. Not with him in charge. Why, that man was a pall-bearer at the funeral!' (Actually, Tate was but slightly acquainted with the victims, and was not present at their funeral in any capacity.) But Mr Hickock's was the only voice raised in an exceedingly silent courtroom. Altogether, there were seventeen prints, and as they were passed from hand to hand, the jurors' expressions reflected the impact the pictures made: one man's cheeks reddened, as if he had been slapped, and a few, after the first distressing glance, obviously had no heart for the task; it was as though the photographs had prised open their mind's eye, and forced them to at last really *see* the true and pitiful thing that had happened to a neighbour and his wife and children. It amazed them, it made them angry, and several of them – the pharmacist, the manager of the bowling alley – stared at the defendants with total contempt.

The elder Mr Hickock, wearily wagging his head, again and again murmured, 'No sense. Just no sense having a trial.'

As the day's final witness, the prosecution had promised to produce a 'mystery man'. It was the man who had supplied the information that led to the arrest of the accused: Floyd Wells, Hickock's former cellmate. Because he was still serving a sentence at Kansas State Penitentiary, and therefore was in danger of retaliation from other inmates, Wells had never been publicly identified as the informer. Now, in order that he might safely testify at the trial, he had been removed from the prison and lodged in a small jail in an adjacent county. Nevertheless, Wells' passage across the courtroom towards the witness stand was oddly stealthy – as though he expected to encounter an assassin along the way – and, as he walked past Hickock, Hickock's lips writhed as he whispered a few atrocious words. Wells pretended not to notice; but like a horse that has heard the hum of a rattlesnake, he shied away from the betrayed man's venomous vicinity. Taking the stand, he stared straight ahead, a somewhat chinless little farmboyish fellow wearing a very decent dark-blue suit which the State of Kansas had bought for the occasion – the state being concerned that its most important witness should look respectable, and consequently trustworthy.

Wells' testimony, perfected by pre-trial rehearsal, was as tidy as his appearance. Encouraged by the sympathetic promptings of Logan Green, the witness acknowledged that he had once, for approximately a year, worked as a hired hand at River Valley Farm; he went on to say that some ten years later, following his conviction on a burglary charge, he had become friendly with another imprisoned burglar, Richard Hickock, and had described to him the Clutter farm and family.

'Now,' Green asked, 'during your conversations with Mr Hickock what was said about Mr Clutter by either of you?'

'Well, we talked quite a bit about Mr Clutter. Hickock said he was about to be paroled, and he was going to go West looking for a job; he might stop to see Mr Clutter to get a job. I was telling him how wealthy Mr Clutter was.'

'Did that seem to interest Mr Hickock?'

'Well, he wanted to know if Mr Clutter had a safe around there.'

'Mr Wells, did you think at the time there was a safe in the Clutter house?'

'Well, it has been so long since I worked out there. I thought there was a safe. I knew there was a cabinet of some kind. ... The next thing I knew he [Hickock] was talking about robbing Mr Clutter.'

'Did he tell you anything about how he was going to commit the robbery?'

'He told me if he done anything like that he wouldn't leave no witnesses.'

'Did he actually say what he was going to do with the witnesses?'

'Yes. He told me he would probably tie them up and then rob them and then kill them.'

Having established premeditation of great degree, Green left the witness to the ministrations of the defence. Old Mr Fleming, a classic country lawyer more happily at home with land deeds than ill deeds, opened the cross-examination. The intent of his queries, as he soon established, was to introduce a subject the prosecution had emphatically avoided: the question of Wells' own role in the murder plot, and his own moral liability.

'You didn't,' Fleming said, hastening to the heart of the matter, 'say anything at all to Mr Hickock to discourage him from coming out here to rob and kill the Clutter family?'

'No. Anybody tells you anything about that up there [Kansas State Penitentiary], you don't pay any attention to it because you think they are just talking anyway.'

'You mean you talked that way and didn't *mean* anything? Didn't you mean to convey to him [Hickock] the idea that Mr Clutter had a safe? You wanted Mr Hickock to believe that, did you not?'

In his quiet way, Fleming was giving the witness a rough time; Wells plucked at his tie, as though the knot was suddenly too tight.

'And you meant for Mr Hickock to believe that Mr Clutter had a lot of money, didn't you?'

'I told him Mr Clutter had a lot of money, yes.'

Fleming once more elicited an account of how Hickock had fully informed Wells of his violent plans for the Clutter family. Then, as though veiled in a private grief, the lawyer wistfully said, 'And even after all of that you did nothing to discourage him?'

'I didn't believe he'd do it.'

'You didn't believe him. Then why, when you heard about the thing that happened out here, why did you think he was the one that was guilty?'

Wells cockily replied, 'Because it was done just like he said he was going to do!'

Harrison Smith, the younger half of the defence team, took charge. Assuming an aggressive, sneering manner that seemed forced, for really he is a mild and lenient man, Smith asked the witness if he had a nickname.

'No. I just go by "Floyd".'

The lawyer snorted. 'Don't they call you "Squealer" now? Or do they call you "Snitch"?'

'I just go by "Floyd",' Wells repeated, rather hangdog.

'How many times have you been in jail?'

'About three times.'

'Some of those times for lying, were they?'

Denying it, the witness said that once he'd gone to jail for driving without an operator's licence, that burglary was the reason for his second incarceration, and the third, a ninety-day hitch in an Army stockade, had been the outcome of something that happened while he was a soldier: 'We was on a train trip guard. We got a little intoxicated on the train, done a little extra shooting at some windows and lights.'

Everyone laughed; everyone except the defendants (Hickock spat on the floor) and Harrison Smith, who now asked Wells why, after learning of the Holcomb tragedy, he had tarried several weeks before telling the authorities what he knew. 'Weren't you,' he said, 'waiting for something to come out? Maybe like a reward?'

'No.'

'You didn't hear anything about a reward?' The lawyer was referring to the reward of one thousand dollars that had been offered by the Hutchinson *News,* for information resulting in the arrest and conviction of the Clutter murderers.

'I seen it in the paper.'

'That was before you went to the authorities, wasn't it?' And when the witness admitted that this was true, Smith triumphantly continued by asking, 'What kind of immunity did the county attorney offer you for coming up here today and testifying?'

But Logan Green protested: 'We object to the form of the question, Your Honour. There's been no testimony about immunity to anybody.' The objection was sustained, and the witness dismissed; as he left the stand, Hickock announced to everyone within earshot, 'Sonofabitch. Anybody ought to hang, he ought to hang. Look at him. Gonna walk out of here and get that money and go scot-free.'

This prediction proved correct, for not long afterwards Wells collected both the reward and a parole. But his good fortune was short-lived. He was soon in trouble again, and, over the years, has experienced many vicissitudes. At present he is a resident of the Mississippi State Prison in Parchman, Mississippi, where he is serving a thirty-year sentence for armed robbery.

By Friday, when the court recessed for the weekend, the state had completed its case, which included the appearance of four Special Agents of the Federal Bureau of Investigation in Washington, D.C. These men, laboratory technicians skilled in various categories of scientific crime detection, had studied the physical evidence connecting the accused to the murders (blood samples, footprints, cartridge shells, rope and tape), and each of them certified the validity of the exhibits. Finally, the four K.B.I. agents provided accounts of interviews with the prisoners, and of the confessions eventually made by them. In cross-examining the K.B.I. personnel, the defence attorneys, a beleaguered pair, argued that the admissions of guilt had been obtained by improper means – brutal interrogation in sweltering, brightly lighted, closet-like rooms. The allegation, which was untrue, irritated the detectives into expounding very convincing denials. (Later, in reply to a reporter who asked him why he had dogged this artificial scent at such length, Hickock's lawyer snapped, 'What am I supposed to do? Hell, I'm playing without any cards. But I can't just sit here like a dummy. I've got to sound off once in a while.')

The prosecution's most damaging witness proved to be Alvin Dewey; his testimony, the first public rendering of the events detailed in Perry Smith's confession, earned large headlines (UNVEIL MUTE MURDER HORROR – Cold, Chilling Facts Told), and shocked his listeners – none more so than Richard Hickock, who came to a startled and chagrined attention when, in the course of Dewey's commentary, the agent said, 'There is one incident Smith related to me that I haven't as yet mentioned. And that was that after the Clutter family was tied up, Hickock said to him how well built he thought Nancy Clutter was, and that he was going to rape her. Smith said he told Hickock there wasn't going to be anything like that go on. Smith told me he had no respect for anyone who couldn't control their sexual desires, and that he would have fought Hickock before allowing him to rape the Clutter girl.' Heretofore, Hickock had not known that his partner had informed the police of the proposed assault; nor was he aware that, in a friendlier spirit, Perry had altered his original story to claim that he alone had shot the four victims – a fact revealed by Dewey as he neared the end of his testimony: 'Perry Smith told me he wished to change two things in the statement he had given us. He said everything else in that statement was true and correct. Except these two things. And that was that he wanted to say he killed Mrs Clutter and Nancy Clutter – not Hickock. He told me that Hickock ... didn't want to die with his mother thinking he had killed any members of the Clutter family. And he said the Hickocks were good people. So why not have it that way.'

Hearing this, Mrs Hickock wept. Throughout the trial she had sat quietly beside her husband, her hands worrying a rumpled handkerchief. As often as she could she caught her son's eye, nodded at him and simulated a smile which, though flimsily constructed, affirmed her loyalty. But clearly the woman's control was exhausted; she began to cry. A few spectators glanced at her, and glanced away, embarrassed; the rest seemed oblivious of the raw dirge counterpointing Dewey's continuing recitation; even her husband, perhaps because he believed it unmanly to take notice, remained aloof. At last a woman reporter, the only one present, led Mrs Hickock out of the courtroom and into the privacy of a ladies' room.

Once her anguish had subsided, Mrs Hickock expressed a need to confide. 'There's nobody much I can talk to,' she told her companion. 'I don't mean people haven't been kind, neighbours and all. And strangers, too – strangers have wrote letters to say they know how hard it must be and how sorry they are. Nobody's said a mean word, either to Walter or me. Not even here, where you might expect it. Everybody here has gone out of their way to be friendly.

The waitress over at the place where we take our meals, she puts ice-cream on the pie and don't charge for it. I tell her don't, I can't eat it. Used to be I could eat anything didn't eat me first. But she puts it on. To be nice. Sheila, that's her, she says it's not our fault what happened. But it seems to me like people are looking at me and thinking, Well, she must be to blame somehow. The way I raised Dick. Maybe I did do something wrong. Only I don't know what it could have been; I get headaches trying to remember. We're plain people, just country people, getting along the same as every-body else. We had some good times at our house. I taught Dick the foxtrot. Dancing, I was always crazy about it, it was my whole life when I was a girl; and there was a boy, gosh, he could dance like Christmas – we won a silver cup waltzing together. For a long time we planned to run away and go on the stage. Vaudeville. It was just a dream. Chil-dren dreaming. He left town, and one day I married Walter, and Walter Hickock couldn't do step one. He said if I wanted a hoofer I should've married a horse. Nobody ever danced with me again until I learned Dick, and he didn't take to it exactly, but he was sweet, Dick was the best-natured little kid.'

Mrs. Hickock removed the spectacles she was wearing, polished the smeared lenses and resettled them on her pudgy, agreeable face. 'There's lots more to Dick than what you hear back there in the courtroom. The lawyers jabber-ing how terrible he is – no good at all. I can't make any excuses for what he did, his part in it. I'm not forgetting that family; I pray for them every night. But I pray for Dick, too. And this boy Perry. It was wrong of me to hate him; I've got nothing but pity for him now. And you know – I believe Mrs Clutter would feel pity, too. Being the kind of woman they say she was.'

Court had adjourned; the noises of the departing audi-ence clattered in the corridor beyond the lavatory door. Mrs Hickock said she must go and meet her husband. 'He's dying. I don't think he minds any more.'

Many observers of the trial scene were baffled by the

visitor from Boston, Donald Cullivan. They could not quite
understand why this staid young Catholic, a successful engineer who had taken his degree at Harvard, a husband
and the father of three children, should choose to befriend
an uneducated, homicidal half-breed whom he knew but
slightly and had not seen for nine years. Cullivan himself
said, 'My wife doesn't understand it either. Coming out here
was something I couldn't afford to do – it meant using a
week of my vacation, and money we really need for other
things. On the other hand, it was something I couldn't
afford not to do. Perry's lawyer wrote me asking if I would
be a character witness; the moment I read the letter I knew
I had to do it. Because I'd offered this man my friendship.
And because – well, I believe in the life everlasting. All
souls can be saved for God.'

The salvation of a soul, namely Perry Smith's, was an enterprise the deeply Catholic undersheriff and his wife were
eager to assist – although Mrs Meier had been rebuffed by
Perry when she had suggested a consultation with Father
Goubeaux, a local priest. (Perry said, 'Priests and nuns have
had their chance with me. I'm still wearing the scars to prove
it.') And so, during the weekend recess, the Meiers invited
Cullivan to eat Sunday dinner with the prisoner in his
cell.

The opportunity to entertain his friend, play host as it
were, delighted Perry, and the planning of the menu – wild
goose, stuffed and roasted, with gravy and creamed potatoes
and string beans, aspic salad, hot biscuits, cold milk, freshly
baked cherry tarts, cheese, and coffee – seemed to concern
him more than the outcome of the trial (which, to be sure,
he did not consider a suspenseful matter: 'Those prairiebillys, they'll vote to hang fast as pigs eat slop. Look at their
eyes. I'll be damned if I'm the only killer in the courtroom.')
All Sunday morning he prepared to receive his guest. The
day was warm, a little windy, and leaf shadows, supple
emanations from the tree boughs that brushed the cell's
barred window, tantalized Perry's tamed squirrel. Big Red
chased the swaying patterns while his master swept and
dusted, scrubbed the floor and scoured the toilet and cleared

the desk of literary accumulations. The desk was to be the dining-table, and once Perry had finished setting it, it looked most inviting, for Mrs Meier had donated a linen tablecloth, starched napkins, and her best china and silver.

Cullivan was impressed – he whistled when the feast, arriving on trays, was placed upon the table – and before sitting down, he asked the host if he might offer a blessing. The host, head unbowed, cracked his knuckles as Cullivan, with bowed head and palms together, intoned, 'Bless us, O Lord, and these thy gifts which we are about to receive from thy bounty, through the mercy of Christ, our Lord. Amen.' Perry murmuringly remarked that in his opinion any credit due belonged to Mrs Meier. 'She did all the work. Well,' he said, heaping his guest's plate, 'it's good to see you, Don. You look just the same. Haven't changed a bit.'

Cullivan, in appearance a cautious bank clerk with depleted hair and a face rather difficult to recall, agreed that outwardly he hadn't changed much. But his interior self, the invisible man, was another matter: 'I was coasting along. Not knowing God is the only reality. Once you realize that, then everything falls into place. Life has meaning – and so does death. Boy, do you always eat like this?'

Perry laughed. 'She's really a terrific cook, Mrs Meier. You ought to taste her Spanish rice. I've gained fifteen pounds since I got here. Course I was on the thin side. I'd lost a lot of weight while Dick and me were out on the road riding all to hell and gone – hardly ever eating a square meal, hungry as hell most of the time. Mostly, we lived like animals. Dick was always stealing canned stuff out of grocery stores. Baked beans and canned spaghetti. We'd open it up in the car and gobble it cold. Animals. Dick loves to steal. It's an emotional thing with him – a sickness. I'm a thief too, but only if I don't have the money to pay. Dick, if he was carrying a hundred dollars in his pocket, he'd steal a stick of chewing-gum.'

Later, over cigarettes and coffee, Perry returned to the subject of thievery. 'My friend Willie-Jay used to talk about it. He used to say that all crimes were only "varieties of theft". Murder included. When you kill a man you steal his life. I guess that makes me a pretty big thief. See, Don – I did kill them. Down there in court, old Dewey made it sound like I was prevaricating – on account of Dick's mother. Well, I wasn't. Dick helped me, he held the flashlight and picked up the shells. And it was his idea, too. But Dick didn't shoot them, he never could've – though he's damn quick when it comes to running down an old dog. I wonder why I did it.' He scowled, as though the problem was new to him, a newly unearthed stone of surprising, unclassified colour. 'I don't know why,' he said, as if holding it to the light, and angling it now here, now there. 'I was sore at Dick. The tough brass boy. But it wasn't Dick. Or the fear of being identified. I was willing to take that gamble. And it wasn't because of anything the Clutters did. They never hurt me. Like other people. Like people have all my life. Maybe it's just that the Clutters were the ones who had to pay for it.'

Cullivan probed, trying to gauge the depth of what he assumed would be Perry's contrition. Surely he must be experiencing a remorse sufficiently profound to summon a desire for God's mercy and forgiveness? Perry said, 'Am I sorry? If that's what you mean – I'm not. I don't feel anything about it. I wish I did. But nothing about it bothers me a bit. Half an hour after it happened, Dick was making jokes and I was laughing at them. Maybe we're not human. I'm human enough to feel sorry for myself. Sorry I can't walk out of here when you walk out. But that's all.' Cullivan could scarcely credit so detached an attitude; Perry was confused, mistaken, it was not possible for any man to be that devoid of conscience or compassion. Perry said, 'Why? Soldiers don't lose much sleep. They murder, and get medals for doing it. The good people of Kansas want to murder me – and some hangman will be glad to get the work. It's easy to kill – a lot easier than passing a bad cheque. Just remember: I only knew the Clutters maybe an hour. If I'd really known them, I guess I'd feel different. I don't think I could live with myself. But the way it was, it was like picking off targets in a shooting gallery.'

Cullivan was silent, and his silence upset Perry, who

seemed to interpret it as implying disapproval. 'Hell, Don, don't make me act the hypocrite with *you*. Throw a load of bull – how sorry I am, how all I want to do now is crawl on my knees and pray. That stuff don't ring with me. I can't accept overnight what I've always denied. The truth is, you've done more for me than any what you call God ever has. Or ever will. By writing to me, by signing yourself "friend". When I had no friends. Except Joe James.' Joe James, he explained to Cullivan, was a young Indian logger with whom he had once lived in a forest near Bellingham, Washington. 'That's a long way from Garden City. A good two thousand miles. I sent word to Joe about the trouble I'm in. Joe's a poor guy, he's got seven kids to feed, but he promised to come here if he had to walk. He hasn't shown up yet, and maybe he won't, only I think he will. Joe always liked me. Do you, Don?'

'Yes, I like you.'

Cullivan's softly emphatic answer pleased and rather flustered Perry. He smiled and said, 'Then you must be some kind of nut.' Suddenly rising, he crossed the cell and picked up a broom. 'I don't know why I should die among strangers. Let a bunch of prairiebillys stand around and watch me strangle. Shit. I ought to kill myself first.' He lifted the broom and pressed the bristles against the light bulb that burned in the ceiling. 'Just unscrew the bulb and smash it and cut my wrists. That's what I ought to do. While you're still here. Somebody who cares about me a little bit.'

The trial resumed on Monday morning at ten o'clock. Ninety minutes later the court adjourned, the case for the defence having been completed in that brief time. The defendants declined to testify in their own behalf, and therefore the question of whether Hickock or Smith had been actual executioner of the Clutter family did not arise.

Of the five witnesses who did appear, the first was the hollow-eyed Mr Hickock. Though he spoke with a dignified and mournful clarity, he had but one contribution to make that was relevant to a claim of temporary insanity.

His son, he said, had suffered head injuries in a car accident in July, 1950. Prior to the accident, Dick had been a 'happy-go-lucky boy', had done well in school, been popular with his classmates and considerate of his parents – 'No trouble to anybody.'

Harrison Smith, gently guiding the witness, said, 'I will ask you if, after July, 1950, you observed any change in the personality and habits and actions of your son, Richard?'

'He just didn't act like the same boy.'

'What were the changes you observed?'

Mr Hickock, between pensive hesitations, listed several: Dick was sulky and restless, he ran around with older men, drank and gambled. 'He just wasn't the same boy.'

The last assertion was promptly challenged by Logan Green, who undertook the cross-examination. 'Mr Hickock, you say you never had any trouble with your son until *after* 1950?'

'. . . I think he got arrested in 1949.'

A citric smile bent Green's tiny lips. 'Remember what he was arrested for?'

'He was accused of breaking into a drugstore.'

'Accused? Didn't he admit that he broke into the store?'

'That's right, he did.'

'And that was in 1949. Yet now you tell us your son had a change in his attitude and conduct after 1950?'

'I would say so, yes.'

'You mean that after 1950 he became a *good* boy?'

Hard coughs agitated the old man; he spat into a handkerchief. 'No,' he said, studying the discharge. 'I wouldn't say that.'

'Then what was the change that took place?'

'Well, that would be pretty hard to explain. He just didn't act like the same boy.'

'You mean he *lost* his criminal tendencies?'

The lawyer's sally induced guffaws, a courtroom flare-up that Judge Tate's dour gaze soon extinguished. Mr Hickock, presently set free, was replaced on the stand by Dr W. Mitchell Jones.

Dr Jones identified himself to the court as a 'physician

specializing in the field of psychiatry', and in support of his qualifications added that he had attended perhaps fifteen hundred patients since 1956, the year he had entered a psychiatric residency at Topeka State Hospital in Topeka, Kansas. For the past two years he had served on the staff of Larned State Hospital, where he was in charge of the Dillon Building, a section reserved for the criminally insane.

Harrison Smith asked the witness, 'Approximately how many murderers have you dealt with?'

'About twenty-five.'

'Doctor, I would like to ask you if you know my client, Richard Eugene Hickock?'

'I do.'

'Have you had occasion to examine him professionally?'

'Yes, sir ... I made a psychiatric evaluation of Mr Hickock.'

'Based upon your examination, do you have an opinion as to whether or not Richard Eugene Hickock knew right from wrong at the time of the commission of the crime?'

The witness, a stout man of twenty-eight with a moon-shaped but intelligent, subtly delicate face, took a deep breath, as though to equip himself for a prolonged reply – which the judge then cautioned him he must not make: 'You may answer the question yes or no, Doctor. Limit your answer to yes or no.'

'Yes.'

'And what is your opinion?'

'I think that within the usual definitions Mr Hickock did know right from wrong.'

Confined as he was by the M'Naughten Rule ('the usual definitions'), a formula quite colour-blind to any permutations between black and white, Dr Jones was impotent to answer otherwise. But of course the response was a letdown for Hickock's attorney, who hopelessly asked, 'Can you qualify that answer?'

It was hopeless because though Dr Jones agreed to elaborate, the plaintiffs were entitled to object – and did, citing the fact that Kansas law allowed nothing more than a yes or no reply to the pertinent question. The objection was upheld, and the witness dismissed. However, had Dr Jones been allowed to speak further, here is what he would have testified: 'Richard Hickock is above average in intelligence, grasps new ideas easily and has a wide fund of information. He is alert to what is happening around him, and he shows no sign of mental confusion or disorientation. His thinking is well organized and logical and he seems to be in good contact with reality. Although I did not find the usual signs of organic brain damage – memory loss, concrete concept formation, intellectual deterioration – this cannot be completely ruled out. He had a serious head injury with concussion and several hours of unconsciousness in 1950 – this was verified by me by checking hospital records. He says he has had blackout spells, periods of amnesia, and headaches ever since that time, and a major portion of his antisocial behaviour has occurred since that time. He has never had the medical test which would definitely prove or disprove the existence of residual brain damage. Definitive medical tests are indicated before a complete evaluation can be said to exist. ... Hickock does show signs of emotional abnormality. That he knew what he was doing and still went ahead with it is possibly the most clear-cut demonstration of this fact. He is a person who is impulsive in action, likely to do things without thought of consequences or future discomfort to himself or to others. He does not seem to be capable of learning from experience, and he shows an unusual pattern of intermittent periods of productive activity followed by patently irresponsible actions. He cannot tolerate feelings of frustration as a more normal person can, and he is poorly able to rid himself of those feelings except through antisocial activity. ... His self-esteem is very low, and he secretly feels inferior to others and sexually inadequate. These feelings seem to be over-compensated for by dreams of being rich and powerful, a tendency to brag about his exploits, spending sprees when he has money, and dissatisfaction with only the normal slow advancement he could expect from his job. ... He is uncomfortable in his relationships to other people, and has a pathological inability to form and hold enduring personal attachments. Although he professes usual moral standards he seems obviously uninfluenced by them in his actions. In summary, he shows fairly typical characteristics of what would psychiatrically be called a severe character disorder. It is important that steps be taken to rule out the possibility of organic brain damage, since, if present, it might have substantially influenced his behaviour during the past several years and at the time of the crime.'

Apart from a formal plea to the jury, which would not take place until the morrow, the psychiatrist's testimony terminated Hickock's planned defence. Next it was the turn of Arthur Fleming, Smith's elderly counsellor. He presented four witnesses: the Reverend James E. Post, the Protestant chaplain at Kansas State Penitentiary; Perry's Indian friend Joe James, who after all had arrived by bus that morning, having travelled a day and two nights from his wilderness home in the Far Northwest; Donald Cullivan; and, once again, Dr Jones. Except for the latter, these men were offered as 'character witnesses' – persons expected to attribute to the accused a few human virtues. They did not fare very well, though each of them negotiated some skimpily favourable remark before the protesting prosecution, which contended that personal comments of this nature were 'incompetent, irrelevant, immaterial', hushed and banished them.

For example, Joe James, dark-haired, even darker-skinned than Perry, a lithe figure who with his faded huntsman's shirt and moccasined feet looked as though he had that instant mysteriously emerged from woodland shadows, told the court that the defendant had lived with him off and on for over two years. 'Perry was a likeable kid, well liked around the neighbourhood – he never done one thing out of the way to my knowledge.' The state stopped him there; and stopped Cullivan, too, when he said, 'During the time I knew him in the Army, Perry was a very likeable fellow.'

The Reverend Post survived somewhat longer, for he

made no direct attempt to compliment the prisoner, but
described sympathetically an encounter with him at Lansing. 'I first met Perry Smith when he came to my office in
the prison chapel with a picture he had painted – a head-
and-shoulders portrait of Jesus Christ done in pastel crayon.
He wanted to give it to me for use in the chapel. It's been
hanging on the walls of my office ever since.'

Fleming said, 'Do you have a photograph of that painting?' The minister had an envelope full; but when he produced them, ostensibly for distribution among the jurors,
an exasperated Logan Green leaped to his feet: 'If Your
Honour please, this is going too *far* ...' His Honour saw
that it went no further.

Dr Jones was now recalled, and following the prelimin-
aries that had accompanied his original appearance, Fleming put to him the crucial query: 'From your conversations
and examination of Perry Edward Smith, do you have an
opinion as to whether he knew right from wrong at the
time of the offence involved in this action?' And once
more the court admonished the witness: 'Answer yes or
no, do you have an opinion?'

'No.'

Amid surprised mutters, Fleming, surprised himself,
said, 'You may state to the jury why you have no
opinion.'

Green objected: 'The man has no opinion, and that's
it.' Which it was, legally speaking.

But had Dr Jones been permitted to discourse on the
cause of his indecision, he would have testified: 'Perry
Smith shows definite signs of severe mental illness. His
childhood, related to me and verified by portions of the
prison records, was marked by brutality and lack of concern
on the part of both parents. He seems to have grown up
without direction, without love, and without ever having
absorbed any fixed sense of moral values. ... He is
oriented, hyper-alert to things going on about him, and
shows no sign of confusion. He is above average in intelligence, and has a good range of information considering
his poor educational background. ... Two features in his

personality make-up stand out as particularly pathological. The first is his "paranoid" orientation towards the world. He is suspicious and distrustful of others, tends to feel that others discriminate against him, and feels that others are unfair to him and do not understand him. He is overly sensitive to criticisms that others make of him, and cannot tolerate being made fun of. He is quick to sense slight or insult in things others say, and frequently may misinterpret well-meant communications. He feels he has great need of friendship and understanding, but he is reluctant to confide in others, and when he does, expects to be misunderstood or even betrayed. In evaluating the intentions and feelings of others, his ability to separate the real situation from his own mental projections is very poor. He not infrequently groups all people together as being hypocritical, hostile, and deserving of whatever he is able to do to them. Akin to this first trait is the second, an ever-present, poorly controlled rage – easily triggered by any feeling of being tricked, slighted, or labelled inferior by others. For the most part, his rages in the past have been directed at authority figures – father, brother, Army sergeant, state parole officer – and have led to violent assaultive behaviour on several occasions. Both he and his acquaintances have been aware of these rages, which he says "mount up" in him, and of the poor control he has over them. When turned towards himself his anger has precipitated ideas of suicide. The inappropriate force of his anger and lack of ability to control or channel it reflect a primary weakness of personality structure. . . . In addition to these traits, the subject shows mild early signs of a disorder of his thought processes. He has poor ability to organize his thinking, he seems unable to scan or summarize his thought, becoming involved and sometimes lost in detail, and some of his thinking reflects a "magical" quality, a disregard of reality. . . . He has had few close emotional relationships with other people, and these have not been able to stand small crises. He has little feeling for others outside a very small circle of friends, and attaches little real value to human life. This emotional detachment and blandness in certain areas is other evidence of his mental abnormality. More extensive evaluation would be necessary to make an exact psychiatric diagnosis, but his present personality structure is very nearly that of a paranoid schizophrenic reaction.'

It is significant that a widely respected veteran in the field of forensic psychiatry, Dr Joseph Satten of the Menninger Clinic in Topeka, Kansas, consulted with Dr Jones and endorsed his evaluations of Hickock and Smith. Dr Satten, who afterwards gave the case close attention, suggests that though the crime would not have occurred except for a certain frictional interplay between the perpetrators, it was essentially the act of Perry Smith who, he feels, represents a type of murderer described by him in an article: 'Murder Without Apparent Motive – A Study in Personality Disorganization.'

The article, printed in *The American Journal of Psychiatry* (July 1960), and written in collaboration with three colleagues, Karl Menninger, Irwin Rosen, and Martin Mayman, states its aim at the outset: 'In attempting to assess the criminal responsibility of murderers, the law tries to divide them (as it does all offenders) into two groups, the "sane" and the "insane". The "sane" murderer is thought of as acting upon rational motives that can be understood, though condemned, and the "insane" one as being driven by irrational senseless motives. When rational motives are conspicuous (for example, when a man kills for personal gain) or when the irrational motives are accompanied by delusions or hallucinations (for example, a paranoid patient who kills his fantasied persecutor), the situation presents little problem to the psychiatrist. But murderers who seem rational, coherent, and controlled, and yet whose homicidal acts have a bizarre, apparently senseless quality, pose a difficult problem, if courtroom disagreements and contradictory reports about the same offender are an index. It is our thesis that the psychopathology of such murderers forms at least one specific syndrome which we shall describe. In general, these individuals are predisposed to severe lapses in ego-control which makes possible the open expression of primitive violence, born out of previous, and now unconscious, traumatic experiences.'

The authors, as part of an appeals process, had examined four men convicted of seemingly unmotivated murders. All had been examined prior to their trials, and found to be 'without psychosis' and 'sane'. Three of the men were under death sentence, and the fourth was serving a long prison sentence. In each of these cases, further psychiatric investigation had been requested because someone – either the lawyer, a relative, or a friend – was dissatisfied with the psychiatric explanations previously given, and in effect had asked, 'How can a person as sane as this man seems to be commit an act as crazy as the one he was convicted of?' After describing the four criminals and their crimes (a Negro soldier who mutilated and dismembered a prostitute, a labourer who strangled a fourteen-year-old boy when the boy rejected his sexual advances, an Army corporal who bludgeoned to death another young boy because he imagined the victim was making fun of him, and a hospital employee who drowned a girl of nine by holding her head under water), the authors surveyed the areas of similarity. The men themselves, they wrote, were puzzled as to why they killed their victims, who were relatively unknown to them, and in each instance the murderer appears to have lapsed into a dreamlike dissociative trance from which he awakened to 'suddenly discover' himself assaulting his victim. 'The most uniform, and perhaps the most significant, historical finding was a long-standing, sometimes lifelong, history of erratic control over aggressive impulses. For example, three of the men, throughout their lives, had been frequently involved in fights which were not ordinary altercations, and which would have become homicidal assaults if not stopped by others.'

Here, in excerpt, are a number of other observations contained in the study: 'Despite the violence in their lives, all of the men had ego-images of themselves as physically inferior, weak, and inadequate. The histories revealed in each a severe degree of sexual inhibition. To all of them, adult women were threatening creatures, and in two cases there was overt sexual perversion. All of them, too, had been concerned throughout their early years about being considered "sissies", physically undersized or sickly. . . . In all four cases, there was historical evidence of altered states of consciousness, frequently in connexion with the outbursts of violence. Two of the men reported severe dissociative trancelike states during which violent and bizarre behaviour was seen, while the other two reported less severe, and perhaps less well-organized, amnesiac episodes. During moments of actual violence, they often felt separated or isolated from themselves, as if they were watching someone else. . . . Also seen in the historical background of all the cases was the occurrence of extreme parental violence during childhood. . . . One man said he was "whipped every time I turned around". . . . Another of the men had many violent beatings in order to "break" him of his stammering and "fits", as well as to correct him for his allegedly "bad" behaviour. . . . The history relating to *extreme* violence, whether fantasied, observed in reality, or actually experienced by the child, fits in with the psychoanalytic hypothesis that the child's exposure to overwhelming stimuli, before he can master them, is closely linked to early defects in ego formation and later severe disturbances in impulse control. In all of these cases, there was evidence of severe emotional deprivation in early life. This deprivation may have involved prolonged or recurrent absence of one or both parents, a chaotic family life in which the parents were unknown, or an outright rejection of the child by one or both parents with the child being raised by others. . . . Evidence of disturbances in affect organization was seen. Most typically the men displayed a tendency not to experience anger or rage in association with violent aggressive action. None reported feelings of rage in connexion with the murders, nor did they experience anger in any strong or pronounced way, although each of them was capable of enormous and brutal aggression. . . . Their relationships with others were of a shallow, cold nature, lending a quality of loneliness and isolation to these

men. People were scarcely real to them, in the sense of being warmly or positively (or even angrily) felt about. . . .
The three men under sentence of death had shallow emotions regarding their own fate and that of their victims.
Guilt, depression, and remorse were strikingly absent. . . .
Such individuals can be considered to be murder-prone in
the sense of either carrying a surcharge of aggressive energy
or having an unstable ego-defence system that periodically
allows the naked and archaic expression of such energy.
The murderous potential can become activated, especially
if some disequilibrium is already present, when the
victim-to-be is unconsciously perceived as a key figure in
some past traumatic configuration. The behaviour, or even
the mere presence, of this figure adds a stress to the unstable balance of forces that results in a sudden extreme
discharge of violence, similar to the explosion that takes
place when a percussion cap ignites a charge of dynamite.
. . . The hypothesis of unconscious motivation explains why
the murderers perceived innocuous and relatively unknown
victims as provocative and thereby suitable targets for aggression. But why murder? Most people, fortunately, do
not respond with murderous outbursts even under extreme
provocation. The cases described, on the other hand, were
predisposed to gross lapses in reality contact and extreme
weakness in impulse control during periods of heightened
tension and disorganization. At such times, a chance acquaintance or even a stranger was easily able to lose his
"real" meaning and assume an identity in the unconscious
traumatic configuration. The "old" conflict was reactivated
and aggression swiftly mounted to murderous proportions.
. . . When such senseless murders occur, they are seen to be
an end result of a period of increasing tension and disorganization in the murderer starting before the contact
with the victim who, by fitting into the unconscious con-
flicts of the murderer, unwittingly serves to set into motion
his homicidal potential.'

Because of the many parallels between the background
and personality of Perry Smith and the subjects of his
study, Dr Satten feels secure in assigning him to a position

among their ranks. Moreover, the circumstances of the crime seem to him to fit exactly the concept of 'murder without apparent motive'. Obviously, three of the murders Smith committed *were* logically motivated – Nancy, Kenyon, and their mother had to be killed because Mr Clutter had been killed. But it is Dr Satten's contention that only the first murder matters psychologically, and that when Smith attacked Mr Clutter he was under a mental eclipse, deep inside a schizophrenic darkness, for it was not entirely a flesh-and-blood man he 'suddenly discovered' himself destroying, but 'a key figure in some traumatic configuration': his father? the orphanage nuns who had derided and beaten him? the hated Army sergeant? the parole officer who had ordered him to 'stay out of Kansas'? One of them, or all of them.

In his confession, Smith said, 'I didn't want to harm the man. I thought he was a very nice gentleman. Soft-spoken. I thought so right up to the moment I cut his throat.' While talking to Donald Cullivan, Smith said, 'They [the Clutters] never hurt me. Like other people. Like people have all my life. Maybe it's just that the Clutters were the ones who had to pay for it.'

So it would appear that by independent paths, both the professional and the amateur analyst reached conclusions not dissimilar.

The aristocracy of Finney County had snubbed the trial. 'It doesn't do,' announced the wife of one rich rancher, 'to seem curious about that sort of thing.' Nevertheless, the trial's last session found a fair segment of the local Establishment seated alongside the plainer citizenry. Their presence was a courteous gesture towards Judge Tate and Logan Green, esteemed members of their own order. Also, a large contingent of out-of-town lawyers, many of whom had journeyed great distances, filled several benches; specifically, they were on hand to hear Green's final address to the jury. Green, a suavely tough little septuagenarian, has an imposing reputation among his peers, who admire his stagecraft – a repertoire of actorish gifts that includes a sense of timing acute as a night-club comedian's. An expert criminal lawyer, his usual role is that of defender, but in this instance the state had retained him as a special assistant to Duane West, for it was felt that the young county attorney was too unseasoned to prosecute the case without experienced support.

But like most star turns, Green was the last act on the programme. Judge Tate's level-headed instructions to the jury preceded him, as did the county attorney's summation: 'Can there be a single doubt in your minds regarding the guilt of these defendants? No! Regardless of who pulled the trigger on Richard Eugene Hickock's shotgun, both men are equally guilty. There is only one way to assure that these men will never again roam the towns and cities of this land. We request the maximum penalty – death. This request is made not in vengeance, but in all humbleness. . . .'

Then the pleas of the defence attorneys had to be heard. Fleming's speech, described by one journalist as 'soft-sell', amounted to a mild churchly sermon: 'Man is not an animal. He has a body, and he has a soul that lives for ever. I don't believe man has the right to destroy that house, a temple, in which the soul dwells. . . .' Harrison Smith, though he too appealed to the jurors' presumed Christianity, took as his main theme the evils of capital punishment: 'It is a relic of human barbarism. The law tells us that the taking of human life is wrong, then goes ahead and sets the example. Which is almost as wicked as the crime it punished. The state has no right to inflict it. It isn't effective. It doesn't deter crime, but merely cheapens human life and gives rise to more murders. All we ask is mercy. Surely life imprisonment is small mercy to ask. . . .' Not everyone was attentive; one juror, as though poisoned by the numerous spring-fever yawns weighting the air, sat with drugged eyes and jaws so utterly ajar bees could have buzzed in and out.

Green woke them up. 'Gentlemen,' he said, speaking without notes, 'you have just heard two energetic pleas for mercy in behalf of the defendants. It seems to me fortunate that these admirable attorneys, Mr Fleming and Mr Smith, were not at the Clutter house that fateful night – very fortunate for them that they were not present to plead mercy for the doomed family. Because had they been there – well, come next morning we would have had more than four corpses to count.'

As a boy in his native Kentucky, Green was called Pinky, a nickname he owed to his freckled colouring; now, as he strutted before the jury, the stress of his assignment warmed his face and splotched it with patches of pink. 'I have no intention of engaging in theological debate. But I anticipated that defence counsel would use the Holy Bible as an argument against the death penalty. You have heard the Bible quoted. But *I* can read, too.' He slapped open a copy of the Old Testament. 'And here are a few things the Good Book has to say on the subject. In Exodus Twenty, Verse Thirteen, we have one of the Ten Commandments: "Thou shalt not kill." This refers to *unlawful* killing. Of course it does, because in the *next* chapter, Verse Twelve, the penalty for disobedience of that Commandment reads: "He that smiteth a man, so that he die, shall be surely put to death." Now, Mr Fleming would have you believe that all this was changed by the coming of Christ. Not so. For Christ says, "Think not that I am come to destroy the law, or the prophets: I am not come to destroy, but to fulfil." And finally –' Green fumbled, and seemed to accidentally shut the Bible, whereupon the visiting legal dignitaries grinned and nudged each other, for this was a venerable courtroom ploy – the lawyer who while reading from the Scriptures pretends to lose his place, and then remarks, as Green now did, 'Never mind. I think I can quote from memory. Genesis Nine, Verse Six: "Whoso sheddeth man's blood, by man shall his blood be shed."

'But,' Green went on, 'I see nothing to be gained by arguing the Bible. Our state provides that the punishment for murder in the first degree shall be imprisonment for life or death by hanging. That is the law. You, gentlemen, are here to enforce it. And if ever there was a case in which the maximum penalty was justified, this is it. These were strange, ferocious murders. Four of your fellow citizens were slaughtered like hogs in a pen. And for what reason? Not out of vengeance or hatred. But for money. *Money*. It was the cold and calculated weighing of so many ounces of silver against so many ounces of blood. And how cheaply those lives were bought! For forty dollars' worth of loot! Ten dollars a life!' He whirled, and pointed a finger that moved back and forth between Hickock and Smith. 'They went armed with a shotgun and a *dag*ger. They went to rob and kill –' His voice trembled, toppled, disappeared, as though strangled by the intensity of his own loathing for the debonair, gum-chewing defendants. Turning again to the jury, he hoarsely asked, 'What are you going to do? What are you going to do with these men that bind a man hand and foot and cut his throat and blow out his brains? Give them the *minimum* penalty? Yes, and that's only one of four counts. What about Kenyon Clutter, a young boy with his whole life before him, tied helplessly in sight of his father's death struggle. Or young Nancy Clutter, hearing the gunshots and knowing her time was next. Nancy, begging for her life: "Don't. Oh, please don't. Please. Please." What agony! What unspeakable torture! And there remains the mother, bound and gagged and having to listen as her husband, her beloved children died one by one. Listen until at last the killers, these defendants before you, entered her room, focused a flashlight in her eyes, and let the blast of a shotgun end the existence of an entire household.'

Pausing, Green gingerly touched a boil on the back of his neck, a mature inflammation that seemed, like its angry wearer, about to burst. 'So, gentlemen, what are you going to do? Give them the minimum? Send them back to the penitentiary, and take the chance of their escaping or being paroled? The next time they go slaughtering it may be *your* family. I say to you,' he solemnly said, staring at the panel in a manner that encompassed and challenged them all, 'some of our enormous crimes only happen because once upon a time a pack of chicken-hearted jurors refused to do their duty. Now, gentlemen, I leave it to you and your consciences.'

He sat down. West whispered to him, 'That was masterly, sir.'

But a few of Green's auditors were less enthusiastic; and after the jury retired to discuss the verdict one of them, a young reporter from Oklahoma, exchanged sharp words with another newsman, Richard Parr of the Kansas City *Star*. To the Oklahoman, Green's address had seemed 'rabble-rousing, brutal'.

'He was just telling the truth,' Parr said. 'The truth can be brutal. To coin a phrase.'

'But he didn't have to hit that hard. It's unfair.'

'What's unfair?'

'The whole trial. These guys don't stand a chance.'

'Fat chance they gave Nancy Clutter.'

'Perry Smith. My God. He's had such a rotten life – '

Parr said, 'Many a man can match sob stories with that little bastard. Me included. Maybe I drink too much, but I sure as hell never killed four people in cold blood.'

'Yeah, and how about hanging the bastard? That's pretty goddam cold-blooded too.'

The Reverend Post, overhearing the conversation, joined in. 'Well,' he said, passing around a snapshot reproduction of Perry Smith's portrait of Jesus, 'any man who could paint this picture can't be one hundred per cent bad. All the same it's hard to know what to do. Capital punishment is no answer: it doesn't give the sinner time enough to come to God. Sometimes I despair.' A jovial fellow with gold-filled teeth and silvery widow's peak, he jovially repeated, 'Sometimes I despair. Sometimes I think old Doc Savage had the right idea.' The Doc Savage to whom he referred was a fictional hero popular among adolescent readers of pulp magazines a generation ago. 'If you boys remember, Doc Savage was a kind of superman. He'd made himself proficient in every field – medicine, science, philosophy, art. There wasn't much old Doc didn't know or couldn't do. One of the projects was, he decided, to rid the world of criminals. First he bought a big island out in the ocean. Then he and his assistants – he had an army of trained assistants – kidnapped all the world's criminals and brought them to the island. And Doc Savage operated on their brains. He removed the part that holds wicked thoughts. And when they recovered they were all decent citizens. They *couldn't* commit crimes because that part of their brain was out. Now it strikes me that surgery of this nature might really be the answer to –'

A bell, the signal that the jury was returning, interrupted him. The jury's deliberations had lasted forty minutes. Many spectators, anticipating a swift decision, had never left their seats. Judge Tate, however, had to be fetched from his farm, where he had gone to feed his horses. A hurriedly donned black robe billowed about him when at last he arrived, but it was with impressive sedateness and dignity that he asked, 'Gentlemen of the jury, have you reached your verdicts?' Their foreman replied: 'We have, Your Honour.' The court bailiff carried the sealed verdicts to the bench.

Train whistles, the fanfare of an approaching Santa Fe express, penetrated the courtroom. Tate's bass voice interlaced with the locomotive's cries as he read: ' "Count One. We the jury find the defendant, Richard Eugene Hickock, guilty of murder in the first degree, and the punishment is death." ' Then, as though interested in their reaction, he looked down upon the prisoners, who stood before him handcuffed to guards; they stared back impassively until he resumed and read the seven counts that followed: three more convictions for Hickock, and four for Smith.

' – and the punishment is death'; each time he came to the sentence, Tate enunciated it with a dark-toned hollowness that seemed to echo the train's mournful, now fading call. Then he dismissed the jury ('You have performed a courageous service'), and the condemned men were led away. At the door, Smith said to Hickock, 'No chicken-hearted jurors, they!' They both laughed loudly, and a cameraman photographed them. The picture appeared in a Kansas paper above a caption entitled: 'The Last Laugh?'

A week later Mrs Meier was sitting in her parlour talking to a friend. 'Yes, it's turned quiet around here,' she said. 'I guess we ought to be grateful things have settled down. But I still feel bad about it. I never had much truck with Dick, but Perry and I got to know each other real well. That afternoon, after he heard the verdict and they brought him back up here – I shut myself in the kitchen to keep from having to see him. I sat by the kitchen window and watched the crowd leaving the courthouse. Mr Cullivan – he looked up and saw me and waved. The Hickocks. All going away. Just this morning I had a lovely letter from Mrs Hickock; she visited with me several times while the trial was going on, and I wished I could have helped her, only what can you say to someone in a situation like that? But after everybody had gone, and I'd started to wash some dishes – I heard him crying. I turned on the radio. Not to hear him. But I could. Crying like a child. He'd never broke down before, shown any sign of it. Well, I went to him. The door of his cell. He reached out his hand. He wanted me to hold his hand, and I did, I held his hand, and all he said was, "I'm embraced by shame." I wanted to send for Father Goubeaux – I said first thing tomorrow I'd make him Spanish rice – but he just held my hand tighter.

'And that night, of all nights, we had to leave him alone. Wendle and I almost never go out, but we had a long-standing engagement, and Wendle didn't think we ought to break it. But I'll always be sorry we left him alone. Next day I did fix the rice. He wouldn't touch it. Or hardly speak to me. He hated the whole world. But the morning the men came to take him to the penitentiary, he thanked me and gave me a picture of himself. A little Kodak made when he was sixteen years old. He said it was how he wanted me to remember him, like the boy in the picture.

'The bad part was saying good-bye. When you knew where he was going, and what would happen to him. That squirrel of his, he sure misses Perry. Keeps coming to the cell looking for him. I've tried to feed him, but he won't have anything to do with me. It was just Perry he liked.'

Prisons are important to the economy of Leavenworth County, Kansas. The two state penitentiaries, one for each sex, are situated there; so is Leavenworth, the largest Federal prison, and, at Fort Leavenworth, the country's principal military prison, the grim United States Army and Air Force Disciplinary Barracks. If all the inmates in these institutions were let free, they could populate a small city.

The oldest of the prisons is the Kansas State Penitentiary for Men, a turreted black-and-white palace that visually distinguishes an otherwise ordinary rural town, Lansing. Built during the Civil War, it received its first resident in 1864. Nowadays the convict population averages around two thousand; the present warden, Sherman H. Crouse, keeps a chart which lists the daily total according to race (for example, White 1405, Coloured 360, Mexicans 12, Indians 6). Whatever his race, each convict is a citizen of a stony village that exists within the prison's steep, machine-gun-guarded walls – twelve grey acres of cement streets and cell blocks and workshops.

In a south section of the prison compound there stands a curious little building: a dark two-storeyed building shaped like a coffin. This establishment, officially called the Segregation and Isolation Building, constitutes a prison inside a prison. Among the inmates, the lower floor is known as The Hole – the place to which difficult prisoners, the 'hardrock' troublemakers, are now and then banished. The upper storey is reached by climbing a circular iron staircase; at the top is Death Row.

The first time the Clutter murderers ascended the staircase was late one rainy April afternoon. Having arrived at Lansing after an eight-hour, four-hundred-mile car ride from Garden City, the newcomers had been stripped, showered, given close haircuts, and supplied with coarse denim uniforms and soft slippers (in most American prisons such slippers are a condemned man's customary footwear); then armed escorts marched them through a wet twilight to the coffin-shaped edifice, hustled them up the spiral stairs and into two of the twelve side-by-side cells that comprise Lansing's Death Row.

The cells are identical. They measure seven by ten feet, and are unfurnished except for a cot, a toilet, a basin, and an overhead light bulb that is never extinguished night or day. The cell windows are very narrow, and not only barred but covered with a wire mesh black as a widow's veil; thus the faces of those sentenced to hang can be but hazily discerned by passers-by. The doomed themselves can see out well enough; what they see is an empty dirt lot that serves in summer as a baseball diamond, beyond the lot a piece of prison wall, and above that, a piece of sky.

The wall is made of rough stone; pigeons nest inside its crevices. A rusty iron door, set into the part of the wall visible to the Row's occupants, rouses the pigeons whenever it is opened, puts them in a flap for the hinges creak so, scream. The door leads into a cavernous storage room, where on even the warmest day the air is moist and chilly. A number of things are kept there: stockpiles of metal used by the convicts to manufacture automobile licence plates, lumber, old machinery, baseball paraphernalia – and also an unpainted wooden gallows that smells faintly of pine. For this is the state's execution chamber; when a man is brought here to be hanged, the prisoners say he has 'gone to The Corner', or, alternatively, 'paid a visit to the warehouse'.

In accordance with the sentence of the court, Smith and Hickock were scheduled to visit the warehouse six weeks hence: at one minute after midnight on Friday, 13 May 1960.

Kansas abolished capital punishment in 1907; in 1935, due to a sudden prevalence in the Midwest of rampaging professional criminals (Alvin 'Old Creepy' Karpis, Charles 'Pretty Boy' Floyd, Clyde Barrow and his homicidal sweetheart, Bonnie Parker), the state legislators voted to restore it. However, it was not until 1944 that an executioner had a chance to employ his craft; over the next ten years he was given nine additional opportunities. But for six years, or since 1954, there had been no pay cheques for a hangman in Kansas (except at the Army and Air Force Disciplinary Barracks, which also has a gallows). The late George Docking, Governor of Kansas from 1957 through 1960, was re-

sponsible for this hiatus, for he was unreservedly opposed
to the death penalty ('I just don't like killing people').

Now, at that time – April, 1960 – there were in United
States prisons one hundred and ninety persons awaiting
civil execution; five, the Clutter killers included, were
among the lodgers at Lansing. Occasionally, important
visitors to the prison are invited to take what one high official calls 'a little peek at Death Row'. Those who accept are
assigned a guard who, as he leads the tourist along the
iron walkway fronting the death cells, is likely to identify
the condemned with what he must consider comic for-
mality. 'And this,' he said to a visitor in 1960, 'this is Mr
Perry Edward Smith. Now next door, that's Mr Smith's
buddy, Mr Richard Eugene Hickock. And over here we
have Mr Earl Wilson. And after Mr Wilson – meet Mr
Bobby Joe Spencer. And as for this last gentleman, I'm sure
you recognize the famous Mr Lowell Lee Andrews.'

Earl Wilson, a husky, hymn-singing Negro, had been
sentenced to die for the kidnapping, rape, and torture of
a young white woman; the victim, though she survived, was
left severely disabled. Bobby Joe Spencer, white, an effeminate youth, had confessed to murdering an elderly Kansas
City woman, the owner of a rooming house where he
lived. Prior to leaving office in January, 1961, Governor Docking, who had been defeated for re-election (in large measure because of his attitude towards capital punishment),
commuted the sentences of both these men to life imprisonment, which generally meant that they could apply
for parole in seven years. However, Bobby Joe Spencer
soon killed again: stabbed with a shiv another young convict, his rival for the affections of an older inmate (as one
prison officer said, 'Just two punks fighting over a jocker').
This deed earned Spencer a second life sentence. But the
public was not much aware of either Wilson or Spencer;
compared to Smith and Hickock, or the fifth man on the
Row, Lowell Lee Andrews, the press had rather slighted
them.

Two years earlier Lowell Lee Andrews, an enormous,
weak-eyed boy of eighteen who wore horn-rimmed glasses

and weighed almost three hundred pounds, had been a sophomore at the University of Kansas, an honour student majoring in biology. Though he was a solitary creature, withdrawn and seldom communicative, his acquaintances, both at the university and in his home town of Wolcott, Kansas, regarded him as exceptionally gentle and 'sweet-natured' (later one Kansas paper printed an article about him entitled: 'The Nicest Boy in Wolcott'). But inside the quiet young scholar there existed a second, unsuspected personality, one with stunted emotions and a distorted mind through which cold thoughts flowed in cruel directions. His family – his parents and a slightly older sister, Jennie Marie – would have been astounded had they known the daydreams Lowell Lee dreamed throughout the summer and autumn of 1958; the brilliant son, the adored brother, was planning to poison them all.

The elder Andrews was a prosperous farmer; he had not much money in the bank, but he owned land valued at approximately two hundred thousand dollars. A desire to inherit this estate was ostensibly the motivation behind Lowell Lee's plot to destroy his family. For the secret Lowell Lee, the one concealed inside the shy church-going biology student, fancied himself an ice-hearted master criminal: he wanted to wear gangsterish silk shirts and drive scarlet sports cars; he wanted to be recognized as no mere bespectacled, bookish, overweight, virginal school boy; and while he did not dislike any member of his family, at least not consciously, murdering them seemed the swiftest, most sensible way of implementing the fantasies that possessed him. Arsenic was the weapon he decided upon; after poisoning the victims, he meant to tuck them in their beds and burn down the house, in the hope that investigators would believe the deaths accidental. However, one detail perturbed him: suppose autopsies revealed the presence of arsenic? And suppose the purchase of the poison could be traced to him? Towards the end of the summer he evolved another plan. He spent three months polishing it. Finally, there came a near-zero November night when he was ready to act.

It was Thanksgiving week, and Lowell Lee was home for the holidays, as was Jennie Marie, an intelligent but rather plain girl who attended a college in Oklahoma. On the evening of November 28, somewhere around seven, Jennie Marie was sitting with her parents in the parlour watching television; Lowell Lee was locked in his bedroom reading the last chapter of *The Brothers Karamazov*. That task completed, he shaved, changed into his best suit, and proceeded to load both a semi-automatic .22-calibre rifle and a Luger .22-calibre revolver. He fitted the revolver into a hip holster, shouldered the rifle, and ambled down the hall to the parlour, which was dark except for the flickering television screen. He switched on a light, aimed the rifle, pulled the trigger, and hit his sister between the eyes, killing her instantly. He shot his mother three times, and his father twice. The mother, eyes gaping, arms outstretched, staggered towards him; she tried to speak, her mouth opened, closed, but Lowell Lee said: 'Shut up.' To be certain she obeyed him, he shot her three time more. Mr Andrews, however, was still alive; sobbing, whimpering, he thrashed along the floor towards the kitchen, but at the kitchen's threshold the son unholstered his revolver and discharged every chamber, then reloaded the weapon and emptied it again; altogether, his father absorbed seventeen bullets.

Andrews, according to statements credited to him, 'didn't feel anything about it. The time came, and I was doing what I had to do. That's all there was to it.' After the shootings he raised a window in his bedroom and removed the screen, then roamed the house rifling dresser drawers and scattering the contents: it was his intention to blame the crime on thieves. Later, driving his father's car, he travelled forty miles over snow-slippery roads to Lawrence, the town where the University of Kansas is located; *en route*, he parked on a bridge, dismantled his lethal artillery, and disposed of it by dropping the parts into the Kansas River. But of course the journey's true purpose was to arrange an alibi. First he stopped at the campus house where he roomed; he talked with the landlady, told her that he had come to pick up his typewriter, and that because of the bad weather the trip from Wolcott to Lawrence had taken two hours. Departing, he visited a movie theatre, where, uncharacteristically, he chatted with an usher and a candy vendor. At eleven, when the movie let out, he returned to Wolcott. The family's mongrel dog was waiting on the front porch; it was whining with hunger, so Lowell Lee, entering the house and stepping across his father's corpse, prepared a bowl of warm milk and mush; then, while the dog was lapping it up, he telephoned the sheriff's office and said, 'My name is Lowell Lee Andrews. I live at 6040 Wolcott Drive, and I want to report a robbery –'

Four officers of the Wyandotte County Sheriff's Patrol responded. One of the group, Patrolman Meyers, described the scene as follows: 'Well, it was one in the morning when we got there. All the lights in the house was on. And this big dark-haired boy, Lowell Lee, he was sitting on the porch petting his dog. Patting it on the head, Lieutenant Athey asked the boy what happened, and he pointed to the door, real casual, and said, "Look in there."' Having looked, the astonished officers summoned the county coroner, a gentleman who was also impressed by young Andrews' callous nonchalance, for when the coroner asked him what funeral arrangements he wished to have made, Andrews replied with a shrug, '*I* don't care what you do with them.'

Shortly, two senior detectives appeared and began to question the family's lone survivor. Though convinced he was lying, the detectives listened respectfully to the tale of how he had driven to Lawrence to fetch a typewriter, gone to a movie, and arrived home after midnight to find the bedrooms ransacked and his family slain. He stayed with the story, and might never have altered it if, subsequent to his arrest and removal to the county jail, the authorities had not obtained the aid of the Reverend Mr Virto C. Dameron.

The Reverend Dameron, a Dickensian personage, an unctuous and jolly brimstone-and-damnation orator, was minister of the Grandview Baptist Church in Kansas City,

Kansas, the church the Andrews family attended regularly. Awakened by an urgent call from the county coroner, Dameron presented himself at the jail around 3 a.m., whereupon detectives, who had been strenuously but abortively interrogating the suspect, withdrew to another room, leaving the minister to consult privately with his parishioner. It proved a fatal interview for the latter, who many months afterwards gave this account of it to a friend: 'Mr Dameron said, "Now, Lee, I've known you all your life. Since you were just a little tadpole. And I knew your daddy all his life, we grew up together, we were childhood friends. And that's why I'm here – not just because I'm your minister, but because I feel like you're a member of my own family. And because you need a friend that you can talk to and trust. And I feel terrible about this terrible event, and I'm every bit as anxious as you are to see the guilty party caught and punished."

'He wanted to know was I thirsty, and I was, so he got me a Coke, and after that he's going on about the Thanksgiving vacation and how do I like school, when all of a sudden he says, "Now, Lee, there seems to be some doubt among the people here regarding your innocence. I'm sure you'd be willing to take a lie detector and convince these men of your innocence so they can get busy and catch the guilty party." Then he said, "Lee, you didn't do this terrible thing, did you? If you did, now is the time to purge your soul." The next thing was, I thought what difference does it make, and I told him the truth, most everything about it. He kept wagging his head and rolling his eyes and rubbing his hands together, and he said it was a terrible thing, and I would have to answer to the Almighty, have to purge my soul by telling the officers what I'd told him, and would I?' Receiving an affirmative nod, the prisoner's spiritual adviser stepped into an adjacent room, which was crowded with expectant policemen, and elatedly issued an invitation: 'Come on in. The boy's ready to make a statement.'

The Andrews case became the basis for a legal and medical crusade. Prior to the trial, at which Andrews pleaded innocent by reason of insanity, the psychiatric staff of the

Menninger Clinic conducted an exhaustive examination of the accused; this produced a diagnosis of 'schizophrenia, simple type'. By 'simple', the diagnosticians meant that Andrews suffered no delusions, no false perceptions, no hallucinations, but the primary illness of separation of thinking from feeling. He understood the nature of his acts, and that they were prohibited, and that he was subject to punishment. 'But,' to quote Dr Joseph Satten, one of the examiners, 'Lowell Lee Andrews felt no emotions whatsoever. He considered himself the only important, only significant person in the world. And in his own seclusive world it seemed to him just as right to kill his mother as to kill an animal or a fly.'

In the opinion of Dr Satten and his colleagues, Andrews' crime amounted to such an undebatable example of diminished responsibility that the case offered an ideal chance to challenge the M'Naughten Rule in Kansas courts. The M'Naughten Rule, as has been previously stated, recognizes no form of insanity provided the defendant has the capacity to discriminate between right and wrong – legally, not morally. Much to the distress of psychiatrists and liberal jurists, the Rule prevails in the courts of the British Commonwealth and, in the United States, in the courts of the District of Columbia and all but half a dozen or so of the states, which abide by the more lenient, though to some minds impractical, Durham Rule, which is simply that an accused is not criminally responsible if his unlawful act is the product of mental disease or mental defect.

In short, what Andrews' defenders, a team composed of Menninger Clinic psychiatrists and two first-class attorneys, hoped to achieve was a victory of legal-landmark stature. The great essential was to persuade the court to substitute the Durham Rule for the M'Naughten Rule. If that happened, then Andrews, because of the abundant evidence concerning his schizophrenic condition, would certainly be sentenced not to the gallows, or even to prison, but to confinement in the State Hospital for the Criminally Insane.

However, the defence reckoned without the defendant's religious counsellor, the tireless Reverend Mr Dameron, who appeared at the trial as the chief witness for the prosecution, and who, in the over-wrought rococo style of a tent-show revivalist, told the court he had often warned his former Sunday School pupil of God's impending wrath: 'I says, there isn't anything in this world that is worth more than your soul, and you have acknowledged to me a number of times in our conversations that your faith is weak, that you have no faith in God. You know that all sin is against God and God is your final judge, and you have got to answer to Him. That is what I said to make him feel the terribleness of the thing he'd done, and that he had to answer to the Almighty for this crime.'

Apparently the Reverend Dameron was determined young Andrews should answer not only to the Almighty, but also to more temporal powers, for it was his testimony, added to the defendant's confession, that settled matters. The presiding judge upheld the M'Naughten Rule, and the jury gave the state the death penalty it demanded.

Friday, May 13, the first date set for the execution of Smith and Hickock, passed harmlessly, the Kansas Supreme Court having granted them a stay pending the outcome of appeals for a new trial filed by their lawyers. At that time the Andrews verdict was under review by the same court.

Perry's cell adjoined Dick's; though invisible to each other, they could easily converse, yet Perry seldom spoke to Dick, and it wasn't because of any declared animosity between them (after the exchange of a few tepid reproaches, their relationship had turned into one of mutual toleration: the acceptance of uncongenial but helpless Siamese twins); it was because Perry, cautious as always, secretive, suspicious, disliked having the guards and other inmates overhear his 'private business' – especially Andrews, or Andy, as he was called on the Row. Andrews' educated accent and the formal quality of his college-trained intelligence were anathema to Perry, who though he had not gone beyond third grade, imagined himself more learned than most of his acquaintances, and enjoyed correcting them, especially their grammar and pronunciation. But here suddenly was someone – 'just a kid!' – constantly correcting *him*. Was it any wonder he never opened his mouth? Better to keep your mouth shut than to risk one of the college kid's snotty lines, like: 'Don't say *dis*interested. When what you mean is *un*interested.' Andrews meant well, he was without malice, but Perry could have boiled him in oil – yet he never admitted it, never let anyone there guess why, after one of these humiliating incidents, he sat and sulked and ignored the meals that were delivered to him three times a day. At the beginning of June he stopped eating altogether – he told Dick, 'You can wait around for the rope. But not me' – and from that moment he refused to touch food or water, or say one word to anybody.

The fast lasted five days before the warden took it seriously. On the sixth day he ordered Smith transferred to the prison hospital, but the move did not lessen Perry's resolve; when attempts were made to force-feed him he fought back, tossed his head and clenched his jaws until they were rigid as horseshoes. Eventually, he had to be pinioned and fed intravenously or through a tube inserted in a nostril. Even so, over the next nine weeks his weight fell from 168 to 115 pounds, and the warden was warned that forced-feeding alone could not keep the patient alive indefinitely.

Dick, though impressed by Perry's will power, would not concede that his purpose was suicide; even when Perry was reported to be in a coma, he told Andrews, with whom he had become friendly, that his former confederate was faking. 'He just wants them to think he's crazy.'

Andrews, a compulsive eater (he had filled a scrapbook with illustrated edibles, everything from strawberry shortcake to roasted pig), said, 'Maybe he is crazy. Starving himself like that.'

'He just wants to get out of here. Play-acting. So they'll say he's crazy and put him in the crazy house.'

Dick afterwards grew fond of quoting Andrews' reply, for it seemed to him a fine specimen of the boy's 'funny thinking', his 'off on a cloud' complacency. 'Well,' Andrews allegedly said, 'it sure strikes me a hard way to do it. Starving yourself. Because sooner or later we'll all get out of here. Either walk out – or be carried out in a coffin. Myself, I don't care whether I walk or get carried. It's all the same in the end.'

Dick said, 'The trouble with you, Andy, you've got no respect for human life. Including your own.'

Andrews agreed. 'And,' he said, 'I'll tell you something else. If ever I do get out of here alive, I mean over the walls and clear out – well, maybe nobody will know where Andy went, but they'll sure hell know where Andy's been.'

All summer Perry undulated between half-awake stupors and sickly, sweat-drenched sleep. Voices roared through his head; one voice persistently asked him, 'Where is Jesus? Where?' And once he woke up shouting, 'The bird is Jesus! The bird is Jesus!' His favourite old theatrical fantasy, the one in which he thought of himself as 'Perry O'Parsons, The One-Man Symphony' returned in the guise of a recurrent dream. The dream's geographical centre was a Las Vegas night club where, wearing a white top hat and a white tuxedo, he strutted about a spotlighted stage playing in turn a harmonica, a guitar, a banjo, drums, sang 'You are My Sunshine', and tap-danced up a short flight of gold-painted prop steps; at the top, standing on a platform, he took a bow. There was no applause, none, and yet thousands of patrons packed the vast and gaudy room – a strange audience, mostly men and mostly Negroes. Staring at them, the perspiring entertainer at last understood their silence, for suddenly he knew that these were phantoms, the ghosts of the legally annihilated, the hanged, the gassed, the electrocuted – and in the same instant he realized that he was there to join them, that the gold-painted steps had led to a scaffold, that the platform on which he stood was opening beneath him. His top hat tumbled; urinating, defecating, Perry O'Parsons entered eternity.

One afternoon he escaped from a dream and wakened to find the warden standing beside his bed. The warden said, 'Sounds like you were having a little nightmare?' But Perry wouldn't answer him, and the warden who on several occasions had visited the hospital and tried to persuade the prisoner to cease his fast, said, 'I have something here. From your father. I thought you might want to see it.' Perry, his eyes glitteringly immense in a face now almost phosphorescently pale, studied the ceiling; and presently, after placing a picture postcard on the patient's bedside table, the rebuffed visitor departed.

That night Perry looked at the card. It was addressed to the warden, and postmarked Blue Lake, California; the message, written in a familiar stubby script, said: 'Dear Sir, I understand you have my boy Perry back in custody. Write to me please what did he do wrong and if I come there could I see him. Alls well with me and trust the same with you. Tex J. Smith.' Perry destroyed the card, but his mind preserved it, for the few crude words had resurrected him emotionally, revived love and hate, and reminded him that he was still what he had tried not to be – alive. 'And I just decided,' he later informed a friend, 'that I ought to stay that way. Anybody wanted my life wasn't going to get any more help from me. They'd have to fight for it.'

The next morning he asked for a glass of milk, the first sustenance he had volunteered to accept in fourteen weeks. Gradually, on a diet of eggnogs and orange juice, he regained weight; by October the prison physician, Dr Robert Moore, considered him strong enough to be returned to the Row. When he arrived there, Dick laughed and said, 'Welcome home, honey.'

Two years passed.

The departures of Wilson and Spencer left Smith and Hickock and Andrews alone with the Row's burning lights and veiled windows. The privileges granted ordinary prisoners were denied them; no radios or card games, not even an exercise period – indeed, they were never allowed out of their cells, except each Saturday when they were taken to a shower room, then given a once-weekly change of clothing; the only other occasions for momentary release were the far-between visits of lawyers or relatives. Mrs Hickock came once a month; her husband had died, she had lost the farm, and, as she told Dick, lived now with one relative, now another.

It seemed to Perry as though he existed 'deep underwater' – perhaps because the Row usually was as grey and quiet as ocean depths, soundless except for snores, coughs, the whisper of slippered feet, the feathery racket of the pigeons nesting in the prison walls. But not *always*. 'Sometimes,' Dick wrote in a letter to his mother, 'you can't hear yourself think. They throw men in the cells downstairs, what they call the hole, and plenty of them are fighting mad and crazy to boot. Curse and scream the whole time. It's intolerable, so everybody starts yelling shut up. I wish you'd send me earplugs. Only they wouldn't allow me to have them. No rest for the wicked, I guess.'

The little building had been standing for more than a century, and seasonal changes provoked different symptoms of its antiquity: winter cold saturated the stone-and-iron fixtures, and in summer, when temperatures often hurtled over the hundred mark, the old cells were malodorous cauldrons. 'So hot my skin stings,' Dick wrote in a letter dated July 5, 1961. 'I try not to move much. I just sit on the floor. My bed's too sweaty to lie down, and the smell makes me sick because of only the one bath a week and always wearing the same clothes. No ventilation whatever and the light bulbs make everything hotter. Bugs keep bumping on the walls.'

Unlike conventional prisoners, the condemned are not subjected to a work routine; they can do with their time what they like – sleep all day, as Perry frequently did ('I pretend I'm a tiny little baby that can't keep its eyes open'); or, as was Andrews' habit, read all night. Andrews averaged fifteen to twenty books a week; his taste encompassed both trash and *belles-lettres*, and he liked poetry, Robert Frost's particularly, but he also admired Whitman, Emily Dickinson, and the comic poems of Ogden Nash. Though the quenchless quality of his literary thirst had soon depleted the shelves of the prison library, the prison chaplain and others sympathetic to Andrews kept him supplied with parcels from the Kansas City public library.

T–L

Dick was rather a bookworm, too; but his interest was restricted to two themes – sex, as represented in the novels of Harold Robbins and Irving Wallace (Perry, after being lent one of these by Dick, returned it with an indignant note: 'Degenerate filth for filthy degenerated minds!') and law literature. He consumed hours each day leafing through law books, compiling research that he hoped would help reverse his conviction. Also, in pursuit of the same cause he fired off a cannonade of letters to such organizations as the American Civil Liberties Union and the Kansas State Bar Association – letters attacking his trial as a 'travesty of due process', and urging the recipients to aid him in his quest for a new trial. Perry was persuaded to draft similar pleas, but when Dick suggested that Andy follow their example by writing protests in his own behalf, Andrews replied, 'I'll worry about my neck and you worry about yours.' (Actually, Dick's neck was not the part of his anatomy that most immediately troubled him. 'My hair is coming out by the handfuls,' he confided in yet another letter to his mother. 'I'm frantic. Nobody in our family was baldheaded as I can recall, and it makes me frantic the idea of being an ugly old baldhead.')

The Row's two night guards, arriving at work on an autumn evening in 1961, had a piece of news. 'Well,' one of them announced, 'seems like you boys can expect company.' The import of the remark was clear to his audience: it meant that two young soldiers, who had been standing trial for the murder of a Kansas railroad worker, had received the ultimate sentence. 'Yessir,' the guard said, confirming this, 'they got the death penalty.' Dick said, 'Sure. It's very popular in Kansas. Juries hand it out like they were giving candy to kids.'

One of the soldiers, George Ronald York, was eighteen; his companion, James Douglas Latham, was a year older. They were both exceptionally personable, which perhaps explains why hordes of teen-aged girls had attended the trial. Though convicted of a single slaying, the pair had claimed seven victims in the course of a cross-country murder spree.

Ronnie York, blond and blue-eyed, had been born and raised in Florida, where his father was a well-known, well-paid deep-sea diver. The Yorks had a pleasantly comfortable home life, and Ronnie, overloved and overpraised by his parents and a worshipful younger sister, was the adored centre of it. Latham's background was at the opposite extreme, being every bit as bleak as Perry Smith's. Born in Texas, he was the youngest child of fertile, moneyless, embattled parents who, when finally they separated, left their progeny to fend for themselves, to scatter hither and thither, loose and unwanted as bundles of Panhandle tumbleweed. At seventeen, in need of a refuge, Latham enlisted in the Army; two years later, found guilty of an AWOL offence, he was imprisoned in the stockade at Fort Hood, Texas. It was there that he met Ronnie York, who was also under sentence for having gone AWOL. Though they were very unlike – even physically, York being tall and phlegmatic, whereas the Texan was a short young man with foxy brown eyes animating a compact, cute little face – they found they shared at least one firm opinion: the world was hateful, and everybody in it would be better off dead. 'It's a rotten world,' Latham said. 'There's no answer to it but meanness. That's all anybody understands – meanness. Burn down the man's barn – he'll understand that. Poison his dog. Kill him.' Ronnie said Latham was 'one hundred per cent correct,' adding, 'Anyway, anybody you kill, you're doing them a favour.'

The first persons they chose to so favour were two Georgia women, respectable housewives who had the misfortune to encounter York and Latham not long after the murderous pair escaped from the Fort Hood stockade, stole a pickup truck, and drove to Jacksonville, Florida, York's home town. The scene of the encounter was an Esso station on the dark outskirts of Jacksonville; the date was the night of 29 May 1961. Originally, the absconding soldiers had travelled to the Florida city with the intention of visiting York's family; once there, however, York decided it might be unwise to contact his parents; his father sometimes had quite a temper. He and Latham talked it over, and New Orleans was their new destination when they stopped at the Esso station to buy gas. Alongside them another car was imbibing fuel; it contained the two matronly victims-to-be, who after a day of shopping and pleasure in Jacksonville, were returning to their homes in a small town near the Florida-Georgia border. Alas, they had lost their way. York, from whom they asked directions, was most obliging: 'You just follow us. We'll put you on the right road.' But the road to which he led them was very wrong indeed: a narrow side-turning that petered off into swamp. Nevertheless the ladies followed along faithfully until the lead vehicle halted, and they saw, in the shine of their headlights, the helpful young men approaching them on foot, and saw, but too late, that each was armed with a black bullwhip. The whips were the property of the stolen truck's rightful custodian, a cattleman; it had been Latham's notion to use them as garrottes – which, after robbing the women, is what they did. In New Orleans the boys bought a pistol and carved two notches in the handle.

During the next ten days notches were added in Tullahoma, Tennessee, where they acquired a snappy red Dodge convertible by shooting the owner, a travelling salesman; and in an Illinois suburb of St Louis, where two more men were slain. The Kansas victim, who followed the preceding five, was a grandfather; his name was Otto Ziegler, he was sixty-two, a robust, friendly fellow, the sort not likely to pass distressed motorists without offering assistance. While spinning along a Kansas highway one fine June morning, Mr Ziegler spied a red convertible parked by the roadside, its hood up, and a couple of nice-looking youngsters fiddling with the motor. How was the good-hearted Mr Ziegler to know that nothing ailed the machine – that this was a ruse devised to rob and kill would-be Samaritans? His last words were, 'Anything I can do?' York, at a distance of twenty feet, sent a bullet crashing through the old man's skull, then turned to Latham and said, 'Pretty good shootin', huh?'

Their final victim was the most pathetic. It was a girl, only eighteen; she was employed as a maid in a Colorado motel where the rampaging pair spent a night, during which she let them make love to her. Then they told her they were on their way to California, and invited her to come along. 'Come on,' Latham urged her, 'maybe we'll all end up movie stars.' The girl and her hastily packed cardboard suitcase ended up as blood-soaked wreckage at the bottom of a ravine near Craig, Colorado; but not many hours after she had been shot and thrown there, her assassins were in fact performing before motion-picture cameras.

Descriptions of the red car's occupants, provided by witnesses who had noticed them loitering in the area where Otto Ziegler's body was discovered, had been circulated though the Midwest and Western states. Roadblocks were erected, and helicopters patrolled the highways; it was a roadblock in Utah that caught York and Latham. Later, at Police Headquarters in Salt Lake City, a local television company was allowed to film an interview with them. The result, if viewed without sound, would seem to concern two cheerful, milkfed athletes discussing hockey or baseball – anything but murder and the roles, boastfully confessed, they had played in the deaths of seven people. 'Why,' the interviewer asks, 'why did you do it?' And York, with a self-congratulatory grin, answers, 'We hate the world.'

All five of the states that vied for the right to prosecute York and Latham endorse judicial homicide: Florida (electrocution), Tennessee (electrocution), Illinois (electrocution), Kansas (hanging), and Colorado (lethal gas). But because it had the firmest evidence, Kansas was victorious.

The men on the Row first met their new companions 2 November 1961. A guard, escorting the arrivals to their cells, introduced them: 'Mr York, Mr Latham, I'd like you to know Mr Smith here. And Mr Hickock. And Mr Lowell Lee Andrews – "the nicest boy in Wolcott!" '

When the parade had passed, Hickock heard Andrews chuckling, and said, 'What's so funny about that sonofabitch?'

'Nothing,' Andrews said. 'But I was thinking: when you count my three and your four and their seven, that makes

fourteen of them and five of us. Now five into fourteen averages out – '

'*Four* into fourteen,' Hickock curtly corrected. 'There are
four killers up here and one railroaded man. I'm no goddam
killer. I never touched a hair on a human head.'

Hickock continued writing letters protesting his conviction, and one of these at last bore fruit. The recipient,
Everett Steerman, Chairman of the Legal Aid Committee
of the Kansas State Bar Association, was disturbed by the
allegations of the sender, who insisted that he and his co-
defendant had not had a fair trial. According to Hickock,
the 'hostile atmosphere' in Garden City had made it impossible to empanel an unbiased jury, and therefore a
change of venue should have been granted. As for the jurors
that were chosen, at least two had clearly indicated a pre-
sumption of guilt during the *voir dire* examination ('When
asked to state his opinion of capital punishment, one man
said that ordinarily he was against it, but in this case no');
unfortunately, the *voir dire* had not been recorded because Kansas law does not require it unless a specific demand is made. Many of the jurors, moreover, were 'well
acquainted with the deceased. So was the judge. Judge Tate
was an intimate friend of Mr Clutter.'

But the bulkiest of Hickock's mudpies was aimed at the
two defence attorneys, Arthur Fleming and Harrison
Smith, whose 'incompetence and inadequacy' were the
chief cause of the correspondent's present predicament,
for no real defence had been prepared or offered by them,
and this lack of effort, it was implied, had been deliberate
– an act of collusion between the defence and the prosecution.

These were grave assertions, reflecting upon the integrity
of two respected lawyers and a distinguished district judge,
but if even partially true, then the constitutional rights of
the defendants had been abused. Prompted by Mr Steerman, the Bar Association undertook a course of action
without precedent in Kansas legal history: it appointed a
young Wichita attorney, Russell Shultz, to investigate the

charges and, should evidence warrant it, challenge the validity of the conviction by bringing *habeas corpus* proceedings in the Kansas Supreme Court, which had recently upheld the verdict.

It would appear that Shultz's investigation was rather one-sided, since it consisted of little more than an interview with Smith and Hickock, from which the ambitious lawyer emerged with crusading phrases for the press: 'The question is this – do poor, plainly guilty defendants have a right to a complete defence? I do not believe that the State of Kansas would be either greatly or for long harmed by the death of these appellants. But I do not believe it could ever recover from the death of due process.'

Shultz filed his *habeas corpus* petition, and the Kansas Supreme Court commissioned one of its own retired justices, the Honourable Walter G. Thiele, to conduct a full-scale hearing. And so it came to pass that almost two years after the trial, the whole case reassembled in the courtroom at Garden City. The only important participants absent were the original defendants; in their stead, as it were, stood Judge Tate, old Mr Fleming, and Harrison Smith, whose careers were imperilled – not because of the appellant's allegations *per se*, but because of the apparent credit the Bar Association bestowed upon them.

The hearing, which at one point was transferred to Lansing, where Judge Thiele heard Smith and Hickock testify, took six days to complete; ultimately, every point was covered. Eight jurors swore they had never known any member of the slain family; four admitted some slight acquaintance with Mr Clutter, but each, including N. L. Dunnan, the airport operator who had made the controversial reply during the *voir dire*, testified that he had entered the jury-box with an unprejudiced mind. Shultz challenged Dunnan: 'Do you feel, sir, that you would have been willing to go to trial with a juror whose state of mind was the same as yours?' Dunnan said yes, he would; and Shultz then said, 'Do you recall being asked whether or not you were adverse to capital punishment?' Nodding, the witness answered, 'I told them under normal conditions I would probably be adverse to it. But with the magnitude of this crime I could probably vote in favour.'

Tangling with Tate was more difficult: Shultz soon realized he had a tiger by the tail. Responding to questions relevant to his supposed intimacy with Mr Clutter, the judge said, 'He [Clutter] was once a litigant in this court, a case over which I presided, a damage action involving an airplane falling on his property; he was suing for damages to – I believe some fruit trees. Other than that, I had no occasion to associate with him. *None whatever.* I saw him perhaps once or twice in the course of a year . . .' Shultz, floundering, switched the subject. 'Do you know, he asked, 'what the attitude of the people was in this community after the apprehension of these two men?' 'I believe I do,' the judge told him with scathing confidence. 'It is my opinion that the attitude towards them was that of anyone else charged with a criminal offence – that they should be tried as the law provides; that if they were guilty they should be convicted; that they should be given the same fair treatment as any other person. There was no prejudice against them because they were accused of crime.' 'You mean,' Shultz slyly said, 'you saw no reason for the court on its own motion to grant a change of venue?' Tate's lips curved downward, his eyes blazed. 'Mr Shultz,' he said, as though the name was a prolonged hiss, 'the court *cannot* on its *own* grant a change of venue. That would be contrary to Kansas law. I couldn't grant a change unless it was properly requested.'

But why had such a request not been made by the defendants' attorneys? Shultz now pursued this question with the attorneys themselves, for to discredit them and prove that they had not supplied their clients with the minimum protection was, from the Wichita lawyer's viewpoint, the hearing's principal objective. Fleming and Smith withstood the onslaught in good style, particularly Fleming, who, wearing a bold red tie and an abiding smile, endured Shultz with gentlemanly resignation. Explaining why he had not applied for a change of venue, he said, 'I felt that since the Reverend Cowan, the minister of the Methodist church, and a man of substance here, a man of high standing, as well as many other ministers here, had expressed themselves against capital punishment, that at least the leaven had been cast in the area, and there were likely more people here inclined to be lenient in the matter of the penalty than perhaps in other parts of the state. Then I believe it was a brother of Mrs Clutter's who made a statement that appeared in the press indicating he did not feel the defendants should be put to death.'

Shultz had a score of charges, but underlying them all was the implication that because of community pressure, Fleming and Smith had deliberately neglected their duties. Both men, Shultz maintained, had betrayed their clients by not consulting with them sufficiently (Mr Fleming replied, 'I worked on the case to the very best of my ability, giving it more time than I do most cases'); by waiving a preliminary hearing (Smith answered, 'But, sir, neither Mr Fleming nor I had been appointed counsel at the time of the waiver'); by making remarks to newsmen damaging to the defendants (Shultz to Smith: 'Are you aware that a reporter, Ron Kull of the Topeka *Daily Capital*, quoted you, on the second day of the trial, as saying there was no doubt of Mr Hickock's guilt, but that you were concerned only with obtaining life imprisonment rather than the death penalty?' Smith to Shultz: 'No, sir. If I was quoted as saying that it was incorrect'); and by failing to prepare a proper defence.

This last proposition was the one Shultz pedalled hardest; it is relevant, therefore, to reproduce an opinion of it written by three Federal judges as the result of a subsequent appeal to the United States Court of Appeals, Tenth Circuit: 'We think, however, that those viewing the situation in retrospect have lost sight of the problems which confronted Attorneys Smith and Fleming when they undertook the defence of these petitioners. When they accepted the appointments each petitioner had made a full confession, and they did not then contend, nor did they seriously contend at any time in the state courts, that these confessions were not voluntary. A radio taken from the Clutter

home and sold by the petitioners in Mexico City had been
recovered, and the attorneys knew of other evidence of
their guilt then in the possession of the prosecution. When
called upon to plead to the charges against them they stood
mute, and it was necessary for the court to enter a plea of not
guilty for them. There was no substantial evidence then, and
none has been produced since the trial, to substantiate a defence of insanity. The attempt to establish insanity as a
defence because of serious injuries in accidents years before,
and headaches and occasional fainting spells of Hickock,
was like grasping at the proverbial straw. The attorneys
were faced with a situation where outrageous crimes committed on innocent persons had been admitted. Under
these circumstances, they would have been justified in
advising that petitioners enter pleas of guilty and throw
themselves on the mercy of the court. Their only hope was
through some turn of fate the lives of these misguided individuals might be spared.'

In the report he submitted to the Kansas Supreme Court,
Judge Thiele found that the petitioners had received a
constitutionally fair trial; the court thereupon denied the
writ to abolish the verdict, and set a new date of execution
– 25 October 1962. As it happened, Lowell Lee Andrews,
whose case had twice travelled all the way to the United
States Supreme Court, was scheduled to hang one month
later.

The Clutter slayers, granted a reprieve by a Federal
judge, evaded their date. Andrews kept his.

In the disposition of capital cases in the United States, the
median elapsed time between sentence and execution is
approximately seventeen months. Recently, in Texas, an
armed robber was electrocuted one month after his conviction; but in Louisiana, at the present writing, two rapists
have been waiting for a record twelve years. The variance
depends a little on luck and a great deal on the extent of
litigation. The majority of the lawyers handling these cases
are court-appointed and work without recompense; but
more often than not the courts, in order to avoid future

appeals based on complaints of inadequate representation,
appoint men of first quality who defend with commendable
vigour. However, even an attorney of moderate talent can
postpone doomsday year after year, for the system of appeals that pervades American jurisprudence amounts to
a legalistic wheel of fortune, a game of chance, somewhat
fixed in the favour of the criminal, that the participants
play interminably, first in the state courts, then through the
Federal courts until the ultimate tribunal is reached – the
United States Supreme Court. But even defeat there does
not signify if petitioner's counsel can discover or invent
new grounds for appeal; usually they can, and so once more
the wheel turns, and turns until, perhaps some years later,
the prisoner arrives back at the nation's highest court, probably only to begin again the slow cruel contest. But at in-
tervals the wheel does pause to declare a winner – or,
though with increasing rarity, a loser: Andrews' lawyers
fought to the final moment, but their client went to the
gallows on Friday, 30 November 1962.

'That was a cold night,' Hickock said, talking to a
journalist with whom he corresponded and who was periodically allowed to visit him. 'Cold and wet. It had been raining like a bastard, and the baseball field was mud up to your
cojones. So when they took Andy out to the warehouse,
they had to walk him along the path. We were all at our
windows watching – Perry and me, Ronnie York, Jimmy
Latham. It was just after midnight, and the warehouse was
lit up like a Halloween pumpkin. The doors wide open. We
could see the witnesses, a lot of guards, the doctor and the
warden – every damn thing but the gallows. It was off at an
angle, but we could see its shadow. A shadow on the wall
like the shadow of a boxing ring.

'The chaplain and four guards had charge of Andy, and
when they got to the door they stopped a second. Andy was
looking at the gallows – you could sense he was. His arms
were tied in front of him. All of a sudden the chaplain
reached out and took off Andy's glasses. Which was kind of
pitiful, Andy without his glasses. They led him on inside,

and I wondered he could see to climb the steps. It was real quiet, just nothing but this dog barking way off. Some town dog. Then we heard it, the sound, and Jimmy Latham said, "What was that?"; and I *told* him what it was – the trap-door.

'Then it was real quiet again. Except that dog. Old Andy, he danced a long time. They must have had a real mess to clean up. Every few minutes the doctor came to the door and stepped outside, and stood there with this stethoscope in his hand. I wouldn't say he was enjoying his work – kept gasping, like he was gasping for breath, and he was crying, too. Jimmy said, "Get a load of that nance." I guess the reason he stepped outside was so the others wouldn't see he was crying. Then he'd go back and listen to hear if Andy's heart had stopped. Seems like it never would. The fact is, his heart kept beating for nineteen minutes.

'Andy was a funny kid,' Hickock said, smiling lopsidedly as he propped a cigarette between his lips. 'It was like I told him: he had no respect for human life, not even his own. Right before they hanged him, he sat down and ate two fried chickens. And that last afternoon he was smoking cigars and drinking Coke and writing poetry. When they came to get him, and we said our good-bye, I said, "I'll be seeing you soon, Andy. 'Cause I'm sure we're going to the same place. So scout around and see if you can't find a cool shady spot for us Down There." He laughed, and said he didn't believe in heaven or hell, just dust unto dust. And he said an aunt and uncle had been to see him, and told him they had a coffin waiting to carry him to some little cemetery in north Missouri. The same place where the three he disposed of were buried. They planned to put Andy right alongside them. He said when they told him that he could hardly keep a straight face. I said, "Well, you're lucky to have a grave. Most likely they'll give Perry and me to the vivisectionist." We joked on like that till it was time to go, and just as he was going he handed me a piece of paper with a poem on it. I don't know if he wrote it. Or copied it out of a book. My impression was he wrote it. If you're interested, I'll send it to you.'

He later did so, and Andrews' farewell message turned out to be the ninth stanza of Gray's 'Elegy Written in a Country Churchyard':

> 'The boasts of heraldry, the pomp of pow'r,
> And all that beauty, all that wealth e'er gave,
> Await alike the inevitable hour:
> The paths of glory lead but to the grave.'

'I really liked Andy. He was a nut – not a real nut, like they kept hollering; but, you know, just goofy. He was always talking about breaking out of here and making his living as a hired gun. He liked to imagine himself roaming around Chicago or Los Angeles with a machine-gun inside a violin case. Cooling guys. Said he'd charge a thousand bucks per stiff.'

Hickock laughed, presumably at the absurdity of his friend's ambitions, sighed, and shook his head. 'But for someone his age he was the smartest person I ever come across. A human library. When that boy read a book it stayed read. Course he didn't know a dumb-darn thing about *life*. Me, I'm an ignoramus except when it comes to what I know about life. I've walked along a lot of mean streets. I've seen a white man flogged. I've watched babies born. I've seen a girl, and her no more than fourteen, take on three guys at the same time and give them all their money's worth. Fell off a ship once five miles out to sea. Swam five miles with my life passing before me with every stroke. Once I shook hands with President Truman in the lobby of the Hotel Muhlebach. Harry S. Truman. When I was working for the hospital, driving an ambulance, I saw every side of life there is – things that would make a dog vomit. But *Andy*. He didn't know one dumb-damn-darn thing except what he'd read in books.

'He was innocent as a little child, some kid with a box of Cracker Jack. He'd never once been with a woman. Man or mule. He said so himself. Maybe that's what I liked about him most. How he wouldn't prevaricate. The rest of us on the Row, we're all a bunch of bull-artists. I'm one of the worst. Shoot, you've got to talk about something. Brag. Otherwise you're nobody, nothing, a potato vegetating in your seven-by-ten limbo. But Andy never would partake. He said what's the use telling a lot of stuff that never happened.

'Old Perry, though, *he* wasn't sorry to see the last of Andy. Andy was the one thing in the world Perry wants to be – educated. And Perry couldn't forgive him for it. You know how Perry's always using hundred-dollar words he doesn't half know the meaning of? Sounds like one of them college niggers? Boy, it burned his bottom to have Andy catch up on him and haul him to the kerb. Course Andy was just trying to give him what he wanted – an education. The truth is, can't anybody get along with Perry. He hasn't got a single friend on the premises. I mean, just who the hell does he think he is? Sneering at everybody. Calling people perverts and degenerates. Going on about what low I.Q.s they have. It's too bad we can't all be such sensitive souls like little Perry. Saints. Boy, but I know some hard-rocks who'd gladly go to The Corner if they could get him alone in the shower room for just one hot minute. The way he high-hats York and Latham! Ronnie says he sure wishes he knew where he could lay hold of a bullwhip. Says he'd like to squeeze Perry a little. I don't blame him. After all, we're all in the same fix, and they're pretty good boys.'

Hickock chuckled ruefully, shrugged, and said, 'You know what I mean. *Good* – considering. Ronnie York's mother has been here to visit him several times. One day, out in the waiting-room, she met my mother, and now they've come to be each other's number-one buddy. Mrs York wants my mother to come visit her home in Florida, maybe even live there. Jesus, I wish she would. Then she wouldn't have to go through this ordeal. Once a month riding the bus here to see me. Smiling, trying to find something to say, make me feel good. The poor lady. I don't know how she stands it. I wonder she isn't crazy.'

Hickock's uneven eyes turned towards a window in the visiting room; his face, puffy, pallid as a funeral lily, gleamed in the weak winter sunshine filtering through the bar-shrouded glass.

'The poor lady. She wrote the warden, and asked him if she could speak to Perry the next time she came here. She wanted to hear from Perry himself how he killed those people, how I never fired shot one. All I can hope is that some day we'll get a new trial, and Perry will testify and tell the truth. Only I doubt it. He's plain determined that if he goes I go. Back to back. It's not right. Many a man has killed and never seen the inside of a death cell. And I never killed *any*body. If you've got fifty thousand dollars to spend, you could bump off half of Kansas City and just laugh ha ha.' A sudden grin obliterated his woeful indignation. 'Uh-oh. There I go again. Old crybaby. You'd think I'd learn. But honest to God, I've done my damnedest to get along with Perry. Only he's so critical. Two-faced. So jealous of every little thing. Every letter I get, every visit. Nobody ever comes to see him except you,' he said, nodding at the journalist, who was as equally well acquainted with Smith as he was with Hickock. 'Or his lawyer. Remember when he was in the hospital? With that phony starvation routine? And his dad sent the postcard? Well, the warden wrote Perry's dad and said he was welcome to come here any time. But he never has showed up. I don't know. Sometimes you got to feel sorry for Perry. He must be one of the most alone people there ever was. But. Aw, the hell with him. It's mostly every bit his own fault.'

Hickock slipped another cigarette away from a package of Pall Malls, wrinkled his nose, and said, 'I've tried to quit smoking. Then I figure what difference does it make under the circumstances. With a little luck, maybe I'll get cancer and beat the state at its own game. For a while there I was smoking cigars. Andy's. The morning after they hanged him, I woke up and called to him, "Andy?" – the way I usually did. Then I remembered he was on his way to Missouri. With the aunt and uncle. I looked out in the corridor. His cell had been cleaned out, and all his junk was piled there. The mattress off his bunk, his slippers, and the scrapbook with all the food pictures – he called it his icebox. And this box of "Macbeth" cigars. I told the guard Andy wanted me to have them, left them to me in his will. Actually, I never smoked them all. Maybe it was the idea of Andy, but somehow they gave me indigestion.

'Well, what's there to say about capital punishment? I'm not against it. Revenge is all it is, but what's wrong with revenge? It's very important. If I was kin to the Clutters, or any of the parties York and Latham dispensed with, I couldn't rest in peace till the ones responsible had taken that ride on the Big Swing. These people that write letters to the newspapers. There were two in a Topeka paper the other day – one from a minister. Saying, in effect, what is all this legal farce, why haven't those sonsabitches Smith and Hickock got it in the neck, how come those murdering sonsabitches are still eating up the taxpayers' money? Well, I can see their side. They're mad 'cause they're not getting what they want – revenge. And they're not going to get it if I can help it. I believe in hanging. Just so long as I'm not the one being hanged.'

But then he was.

Another three years passed, and during those years two exceptionally skilful Kansas City lawyers, Joseph P. Jenkins and Robert Bingham, replaced Shultz, the latter having resigned from the case. Appointed by a Federal judge, and working without compensation (but motivated by a hard-held opinion that the defendants had been the victims of a 'nightmarishly unfair trial'), Jenkins and Bingham filed numerous appeals within the framework of the Federal court system, thereby avoiding three execution dates: 25 October 1962, 8 August 1963, and 18 February 1965. The attorneys contended that their clients had been unjustly convicted because legal counsel had not been appointed them until after they had confessed and had waived preliminary hearings; and because they were not competently represented at their trial, were convicted with the help of evidence seized without a search warrant (the shotgun and knife taken from the Hickock home), were not granted a change of venue even though the environs of the trial had been 'saturated' with publicity prejudicial to the accused.

With these arguments, Jenkins and Bingham succeeded in carrying the case three times to the United States Supreme Court – the Big Boy, as many litigating prisoners refer to it – but on each occasion the Court, which never comments on its decisions in such instances, denied the appeals by refusing to grant the writs of *certiorari* that would have entitled the appellants to a full hearing before the Court. In March 1965, after Smith and Hickock had been confined in their Death Row cells almost two thousand days the Kansas Supreme Court decreed that their lives must end between midnight and 2 a.m., Wednesday, 14 April 1965. Subsequently, a clemency appeal was presented to the newly elected Governor of Kansas, William Avery; but Avery, a rich farmer sensitive to public opinion, refused to intervene – a decision he felt to be in the 'best interest of the people of Kansas'. (Two months later, Avery also denied the clemency appeals of York and Latham, who were hanged on 22 June, 1965.)

And so it happened that in the daylight hours of that Wednesday morning, Alvin Dewey, breakfasting in the coffee shop of a Topeka hotel, read on the first page of the Kansas City *Star*, a headline he had long awaited: DIE ON ROPE FOR BLOODY CRIME. The story, written by an Associated Press reporter, began: 'Richard Eugene Hickock and Perry Edward Smith, partners in crime, died on the gallows at the state prison early today for one of the bloodiest murders in Kansas criminal annals. Hickock, 33 years old, died first, at 12.41 a.m.; Smith, 36, died at 1.19 ...'

Dewey had watched them die, for he had been among the twenty-odd witnesses invited to the ceremony. He had never attended an execution, and when on the midnight past he entered the cold warehouse, the scenery had surprised him: he had anticipated a setting of suitable dignity, not this bleakly lighted cavern cluttered with lumber and other debris. But the gallows itself, with its two pale nooses attached to a crossbeam, was imposing enough; and so, in an unexpected style, was the hangman, who cast a long shadow from his perch on the platform at the top of the wooden instrument's thirteen steps. The hangman, an anonymous leathery gentleman who had been imported from Missouri for the event, for which he was paid six hundred dollars, was attired in an aged double-breasted pin-striped suit overly commodious for the narrow figure inside it – the coat came nearly to his knees; and on his head he wore a cowboy hat which, when first bought, had perhaps been bright green, but was now a weathered, sweat-stained oddity.

Also, Dewey found the self-consciously casual conversation of his fellow witnesses, as they stood awaiting the start of what one witness termed 'the festivities', disconcerting.

'What I heard was, they was gonna let them draw straws to see who dropped first. Or flip a coin. But Smith says why not do it alphabetically. Guess 'cause S comes after H. Ha!'

'Read in the paper, afternoon paper, what they ordered for their last meal? Ordered the same menu. Shrimp. French fries. Garlic bread. Ice-cream and strawberries and whipped cream. Understand Smith didn't touch his much.'

'That Hickock's got a sense of humour. They was telling me how, about an hour ago, one of the guards says to him, "This must be the longest night of your life." And Hickock, he laughs and says, "No. The shortest." '

'Did you hear about Hickock's eyes? He left them to an eye doctor. Soon as they cut him down, this doctor's gonna yank out his eyes and stick them in somebody else's head. Can't say I'd say I'd want to be that somebody. I'd feel peculiar with them eyes in my head.'

'Christ! Is that *rain*? All the windows down! My new Chevy. Christ!'

The sudden rain rapped the high warehouse roof. The sound, not unlike the rat-a-tat-tat of parade drums, heralded Hickock's arrival. Accompanied by six guards and a prayer-murmuring chaplain, he entered the death place handcuffed and wearing an ugly harness of leather straps that bound his arms to his torso. At the foot of the gallows the warden read to him the official order of execution, a two-page document; and as the warden read, Hickock's eyes, enfeebled by half a decade of cell shadows, roamed the little audience until, not seeing what he sought, he asked the nearest guard, in a whisper, if any member of the Clutter family was present. When he was told no, the prisoner seemed disappointed, as though he thought the protocol surrounding this ritual of vengeance was not being properly observed.

As is customary, the warden, having finished his recitation, asked the condemned man whether he had any last statement to make. Hickock nodded. 'I just want to say I hold no hard feelings. You people are sending me to a better world than this ever was'; then, as if to emphasize the point, he shook hands with the four men mainly responsible for his capture and conviction, all of whom had requested permission to attend the executions: K.B.I. Agents Roy Church, Clarence Duntz, Harold Nye, and Dewey himself. 'Nice to see you,' Hickock said with his most charming smile; it was as if he were greeting guests at his own funeral.

The hangman coughed – impatiently lifted his cowboy hat and settled it again, a gesture somehow reminiscent of a turkey buzzard huffing, then smoothing its neck feathers – and Hickock, nudged by an attendant, mounted the scaffold steps. 'The Lord giveth, the Lord taketh away. Blessed is the name of the Lord,' the chaplain intoned, as the rain sound accelerated, as the noose was fitted, and as a delicate black mask was tied round the prisoner's eyes. 'May the Lord have mercy on your soul.' The trap-door opened, and Hickock hung for all to see a full twenty minutes before the prison doctor at last said, 'I pronounce this man dead.' A hearse, its blazing headlights beaded with rain, drove into the warehouse, and the body, placed on a litter and shrouded under a blanket, was carried to the hearse and out into the night.

Staring after it, Roy Church shook his head: 'I never would have believed he had the guts. To take it like he did. I had him tagged a coward.'

The man to whom he spoke, another detective, said, 'Aw, Roy, the guy was a punk. A mean bastard. He deserved it.'

Church, with thoughtful eyes, continued to shake his head.

While waiting for the second execution, a reporter and a guard conversed. The reporter said, 'This your first hanging?'

'I seen Lee Andrews.'

'This here's my first.'

'Yeah. How'd you like it?'

The reporter pursed his lips. 'Nobody in our office wanted the assignment. Me either. But it wasn't as bad as I thought it would be. Just like jumping off a diving board. Only with a rope around your neck.'

'They don't feel nothing. Drop, snap, and that's it. They don't feel nothing.'

'Are you sure? I was standing right close. I could hear him gasping for breath.'

'Uh-huh, but he don't feel nothing. Wouldn't be humane if he did.'

'Well. And I suppose they feed them a lot of pills. Sedatives.'

'Hell, no. Against the rules. Here comes Smith.'

'Gosh, I didn't know he was such a shrimp.'

'Yeah, he's little. But so is a tarantula.'

As he was brought into the warehouse, Smith recognized his old foe, Dewey; he stopped chewing a hunk of Doublemint gum he had in his mouth, and grinned and winked at Dewey, jaunty and mischievous. But after the warden asked if he had anything to say, his expression was sober. His sensitive eyes gazed gravely at the surrounding faces, swerved up to the shadowy hangman, then downward to his own manacled hands. He looked at his fingers, which were stained with ink and paint, for he'd spent his final three years on Death Row painting self-portraits and pictures of children, usually the children of inmates who supplied him with photographs of their seldom-seen progeny. 'I think,' he said, 'it's a helluva thing to take a life in this manner. I don't believe in capital punishment, morally or legally. Maybe I had something to contribute, something – ' His assurance faltered; shyness blurred his voice, lowered it to a just audible level. 'It would be meaningless to apologize for what I did. Even inappropriate. But I do. I apologize.'

Steps, noose, mask; but before the mask was adjusted, the prisoner spat his chewing-gum into the chaplain's outstretched palm. Dewey shut his eyes; he kept them shut until he heard the thud-snap that announces a rope-broken neck. Like the majority of American law-enforcement officials, Dewey was certain that capital punishment is a deterrent to violent crime, and he felt that if ever the penalty had been earned, the present instance was it. The preceding execution had not disturbed him, he had never had much use for Hickock, who seemed to him 'a small-time chiseller who got out of his depth, empty and worthless'. But Smith, though he was the true murderer, aroused another response, for Perry possessed a quality, the aura of an exiled animal, a creature walking wounded, that the detective could not disregard. He remembered his first meeting with Perry in the interrogation room at Police Headquarters in Las Vegas – the dwarfish boy-man seated in the metal chair, his small booted feet not quite brushing the floor. And when Dewey now opened his eyes, that is what he saw: the same childish feet, tilted, dangling.

Dewey had imagined that with the deaths of Smith and Hickock he would experience a sense of climax, release, of a design justly completed. Instead, he discovered himself recalling an incident of almost a year ago, a casual encounter in Valley View Cemetery, which, in retrospect, had somehow for him more or less ended the Clutter case.

The pioneers who founded Garden City were necessarily a Spartan people, but when the time came to establish a formal cemetery, they were determined, despite arid soil and the troubles of transporting water, to create a rich contrast to the dusty streets, the austere plains. The result, which they named Valley View, is situated above the town on a plateau of modest altitude. Seen today, it is a dark island lapped by the undulating surf of surrounding wheat fields – a good refuge from a hot day, for there are many cool paths unbrokenly shaded by trees planted generations ago.

One afternoon the previous May, a month when the fields blaze with the green-gold fire of half-grown wheat, Dewey had spent several hours at Valley View weeding his father's grave, an obligation he had too long neglected. Dewey was fifty-one, four years older than when he had supervised the Clutter investigation; but he was still lean and agile, and still the K.B.I.'s principal agent in western Kansas; only a week earlier he had caught a pair of cattle rustlers. The dream of settling on his farm had not come true, for his wife's fear of living in that sort of isolation had never lessened. Instead the Deweys had built a new house in town; they were proud of it, and proud, too, of both their sons, who were deep-voiced now and as tall as their father. The older boy was headed for college in the autumn.

When he had finished weeding, Dewey strolled along the quiet paths. He stopped at a tombstone marked with a recently carved name: Tate. Judge Tate had died of pneumonia the past November; wreaths, brown roses, and rain-faded ribbons still lay upon the raw earth. Close by, fresher petals spilled across a newer mound – the grave of Bonnie Jean Ashida, the Ashidas' elder daughter, who while visiting Garden City had been killed in a car collision. Deaths, births, marriages – why, just the other day he'd heard that Nancy Clutter's boy friend, young Bobby Rupp, had gone and got married.

The graves of the Clutter family, four graves gathered under a single grey stone, lie in a far corner of the cemetery – beyond the trees, out in the sun, almost at the wheat field's bright edge. As Dewey approached them, he saw that another visitor was already there: a willowy girl with white-gloved hands, a smooth cap of dark-honey hair, and long, elegant legs. She smiled at him, and he wondered who she was.

'Have you forgotten me, Mr Dewey? Susan Kidwell.'

He laughed; she joined him. 'Sue Kidwell. I'll be darned.' He hadn't seen her since the trial; she had been a child then. 'How are you? How's your mother?'

'Fine, thank you. She's still teaching music at the Holcomb School.'

'Haven't been that way lately. Any changes?'

'Oh, there's some talk about paving the streets. But you know Holcomb. Actually, I don't spend much time there. This is my junior year at K.U.,' she said, meaning the University of Kansas. 'I'm just home for a few days.'

'That's wonderful, Sue. What are you studying?'

'Everything. Art, mostly. I love it. I'm really happy.' She glanced across the prairie. 'Nancy and I planned to go to college together. We were going to be room-mates. I think about it sometimes. Suddenly, when I'm very happy, I think of all the plans we made.'

Dewey looked at the grey stone inscribed with four names, and the date of their death: 15 November 1959. 'Do you come here often?'

'Once in a while. Gosh, the sun's strong.' She covered her eyes with tinted glasses. 'Remember Bobby Rupp? He married a beautiful girl.'

'So I heard.'

'Colleen Whitehurst. She's really beautiful. And very nice, too.'

'Good for Bobby.' And to tease her, Dewey added, 'But how about you? You must have a lot of beaux.'

'Well. Nothing serious. But that reminds me. Do you have the time? Oh,' she cried, when he told her it was past four, 'I've got to run! But it was nice to have seen you, Mr Dewey.'

'And nice to have seen you, Sue. Good luck,' he called after her as she disappeared down the path, a pretty girl in a hurry, her smooth hair swinging, shining – just such a young woman as Nancy might have been. Then, starting home, he walked towards the trees, and under them, leaving behind him the big sky, the whisper of wind voices in the wind-bent wheat.

refresh yourself at penguin.co.uk

Visit penguin.co.uk for exclusive information and interviews with
bestselling authors, fantastic give-aways and the
inside track on all our books, from the Penguin Classics
to the latest bestsellers.

BE FIRST

first chapters, first editions, first novels

EXCLUSIVES

author chats, video interviews, biographies, special
features

EVERYONE'S A WINNER

give-aways, competitions, quizzes, ecards

READERS GROUPS

exciting features to support existing groups and
create new ones

NEWS

author events, bestsellers, awards, what's new

EBOOKS

books that click – download an ePenguin today

BROWSE AND BUY

thousands of books to investigate – search, try
and buy the perfect gift online – or treat yourself!

ABOUT US

job vacancies, advice for writers and company
history

Get Closer To Penguin . . . www.penguin.co.uk

essential · penguin

Brighton Rock Graham Greene

A gang war is raging through the dark, seedy underworld of Brighton. Pinkie is only seventeen, yet he has already proved his ruthlessness in the brutal killing of Hale, a journalist. But Pinkie is unprepared for the courageous, life-embracing Ida Arnold, who is determined to avenge Hale's death. 'I read *Brighton Rock* when I was about thirteen. One of the first lessons I took from [Greene's books] was that a serious novel could be an exciting novel – that the novel of adventure could also be the novel of ideas' Ian McEwan, *Guardian*

Animal Farm George Orwell

Having got rid of their human master, the animals of Manor Farm look forward to a life of freedom and plenty. But as a clever, ruthless élite among them takes control, they find themselves hopelessly ensnared in the old ways. 'One of the greatest political fables of all time ... It is the book for everyone and Everyman, its brightness undimmed after fifty years' Ruth Rendell, *Daily Telegraph*

Lucky Jim Kingsley Amis

Jim Dixon has a lousy job at a second rate university. His life is full of things he could happily do without: a tedious and ridiculous Professor, a neurotic semi-detached girlfriend, medieval recorder music and over-enthusiastic students. The solution is straightforward: pull faces behind people's backs, copy others' work and make sure the pretty girls choose his course. But without luck life is never simple. 'It has always made me laugh out loud ... a flawless comic novel' Helen Dunmore, *The Times*

essential · penguin

Breakfast at Tiffany's Truman Capote

Meet Holly Golightly – a free-spirited, lop-sided romantic who owns a fiery red cat as wild and restless as she is. With her tousled blond hair, dark glasses and chic black dresses, she is top notch in the style department and a sensation wherever she goes. Her brownstone apartment vibrates with martini-soaked parties as she plays hostess to millionaires and gangsters alike. Yet Holly never loses sight of her ultimate goal – to find a real life place like Tiffany's that makes her feel at home.

The Prime of Miss Jean Brodie Muriel Spark

Passionate, free-thinking and unconventional, Miss Brodie is a teacher who exerts a powerful influence over her 'special girls' at Marcia Blaine School. They are the Brodie Set, the crème de la crème, each famous for something – Monica for mathematics, Eunice for swimming, Rose for sex – who are initiated into a world of adult games and extra-curricular activities that they will never forget. 'One of the giants of post-war fiction' *Independent*

The Great Gatsby F. Scott Fitzgerald

Everybody who is anybody is seen at the glittering parties held in Jay Gatsby's mansion in West Egg, east of New York. The riotous throng congregates in his sumptuous garden, coolly debating Gatsby's origins and mysterious past – among various rumours is the conviction that 'he killed a man'. A detached onlooker, Gatsby is oblivious to the speculation he creates, but seems always to be watching and waiting, though no one knows what for.

essential · penguin

On the Road   Jack Kerouac

'With its unfastidious relish for life, *On the Road* was pop writing at
its best. It changed the way I saw the world, making me yearn for
fresh experience' Hanif Kureishi, *Independent on Sunday*. '*On the
Road* sold a trillion Levis and a million espresso machines, and also
sent countless kids on the road ... The alienation, the
restlessness, the dissatisfaction were already there waiting when
Kerouac pointed out the road' William Burroughs

A Clockwork Orange   Anthony Burgess

In Anthony Burgess's infamous nightmare vision of youth culture
in revolt, fifteen-year-old Alex and his friends set out on an orgy of
robbery, rape, torture and murder. Alex is jailed for his
delinquency and the State tries to reform him – but at what cost?
'[*A Clockwork Orange* is] not only ... about man's violent nature
and his capacity to choose between good and evil. It is about the
excitements and intoxicating effects of language ... a cleverly
sustained solo of virtuoso phrase-making and jazzy riffs' *Daily
Telegraph*

Wide Sargasso Sea   Jean Rhys

Set against the lush backdrop of 1830s Jamaica, Jean Rhys's
powerful, haunting story was inspired by her fascination with the
first Mrs Rochester, the mad wife in Charlotte Brontë's *Jane Eyre*.
'A tale of dislocation and dispossession, which Rhys writes with a
kind of romantic cynicism, desperate and pungent' *The Times*